ORDER INTO ACTION

CURSOR MUNDI

CURSOR MUNDI IS PRODUCED UNDER THE AUSPICES OF
THE CENTER FOR MEDIEVAL AND RENAISSANCE STUDIES,
UNIVERSITY OF CALIFORNIA, LOS ANGELES.

VOLUME 40

General Director

Chris Chism *(English, UCLA)*

Managing Editor

Allison McCann *(CMRS, UCLA)*

Editorial Board

Matthew Fisher *(English, UCLA)*
Javier Patiño Loira *(Spanish & Portuguese, UCLA)*
Peter Stacey *(History, UCLA)*
Erica Weaver *(English, UCLA)*
Bronwen Wilson *(Art History, UCLA)*
Luke Yarbrough *(Near Eastern Languages & Cultures, UCLA)*

Previously published volumes in this
series are listed at the back of the book.

Order Into Action

How Large-Scale Concepts of World Order Determine Practices in the Premodern World

Edited by
KLAUS OSCHEMA *and*
CHRISTOPH MAUNTEL

BREPOLS

British Library Cataloguing in Publication Data
A catalogue record for this book is available from the British Library

ISBN: 978-2-503-59046-2
e-ISBN: 978-2-503-59047-9
DOI: 10.1484/M.CURSOR-EB.5.120782
ISSN: 2034-1660
e-ISSN: 2565-943X

Printed in the EU on acid-free paper.

D/2022/0095/99

Table of Contents

List of Illustrations 7

Acknowledgements 11

Introduction: Creating Order and Causing Action
Klaus OSCHEMA and Christoph MAUNTEL 13

***Dār al-ḥarb* vs *terra paganorum*:**
On the Practical Implications of
Circumscribing the Sphere of the 'Infidels'
Daniel G. KÖNIG 37

The Concept of Christendom:
***Christianitas* as a Call to Action**
Nora BEREND 71

A 'Medieval Islamist' Versus an 'Arab Machiavelli'?
The Legacy of the Mamluk Scholars Ibn Taymīya
(1263–1328) and Ibn Nubāta (1287–1366)
Albrecht FUESS 97

The Mongol World Order:
From Universalism to Glocalization
Michal BIRAN 127

Between Universal Empire and the Plurality of
Kingdoms: On the Practical Influence of Political
Concepts in Late Medieval Latin Europe
Christoph MAUNTEL and Klaus OSCHEMA 151

Imperial Geography and Fatherly Benevolence:
The Chinese World Order and the Construction
of its Margins
Donatella GUIDA 185

The Advent of the Black Magus:
Moving towards a Continental Hierarchy
Michael WINTLE 209

Beyond Eurasia — The African Contribution to the Premodern World: Examining the Global and the Local in the Kilwa Sultanate, East Africa
Mark HORTON 237

Seeing Through the Rainbow: Aboriginal Australian Concepts of an Ordered Universe
Veronica STRANG 263

Translating Otherworlds: The Encounter of Mesoamerican and European Cosmologies in Colonial Missionary and Indigenous Texts from Highland Guatemala
Frauke SACHSE 291

Index
Michael Aljoscha SENGSTMANN 319

List of Illustrations

Christoph Mauntel and Klaus Oschema

Figure 6.1. Thomas III of Saluzzo, *Le Livre du Chevalier Errant*: Encampment of the princes of the Occident, convened by Fortune, Paris, Bibliothèque nationale de France, MS fr. 12559, fol. 161v. Circa 1404. © Bibliothèque nationale de France. 168

Figure 6.2. Thomas III of Saluzzo, *Le Livre du Chevalier Errant*: Encampment of the princes of the Orient, convened by Fortune, Paris, Bibliothèque nationale de France, MS fr. 12559, fol. 162r. Circa 1404. © Bibliothèque nationale de France. 169

Donatella Guida

Figure 7.1. The concentric structure of the world as described by *The Tribute of Yu*. Drawing by the author. 190

Figure 7.2. *Sihai HuaYi Zongtu* 四海華夷總圖 (*General Map of Chinese and Barbarian Lands within the Four Seas*), undated, from Zhang Huang 章潢, *Tushu bian* 圖書編 (1613), *juan* 29, in *Siku Quanshu*. 192

Figure 7.3. *Yudi Shanhai quantu* 輿地山海全圖 (*Complete Map of Mountains and Seas*), from Zhang Huang 章潢, *Tushu bian* 圖書編 (1613), *juan* 29, in *Siku Quanshu*. 193

Figure 7.4. *Siyi zongtu* 四夷總圖 (*General Map of the Four Barbarians*), from Zhang Huang 章潢, *Tushu bian* 圖書編 (1613), *juan* 50, in *Siku Quanshu*. 194

Michael Wintle

Figure 8.1. 'The Adoration of the Magi', detail (bottom left-hand panel) of Triptych with depiction of the Salvation Story, Cologne, 1340–50. Collection of Ferdinand Franz Wallraf, Wallraf Richartz Museum Cologne, inv. no. WRM 0001. Photo: © Rheinisches Bildarchiv / Sabrina Walz, rba_d032478_01. By kind permission. 213

Figure 8.2. 'The Adoration of the Magi', The Polling altarpiece (*Marienaltar*), 1444. Munich, Alte Pinothek, inv. no. 1360. © bpk 50009563 | Bayerische Staatsgemäldesammlungen. By kind permission. 213

Figure 8.3. 'Coats of arms attributed to the Magi', Brussels, *c.* 1360; adapted and recorded in Köllmann and Wirth, 'Erdteile' (1967), col. 1116. 216

Figure 8.4. Stone sealing the loculus (niche tomb) of Severa, marble, with the Magi. From the cemetery of Priscilla on the Via Salaria, Rome, *c.* 250–325 CE. Vatican City, Musei Vaticani, cat. 28594. © 2020, Photo Scala, Florence. 222

Figure 8.5. Mosaic of the three Magi, Basilica of Sant' Apollinare Nuovo, in Ravenna. *c.* 620 CE. <https://commons.wikimedia.org/wiki/File:RavennaMosaico.jpg> public domain. 223

Figure 8.6. Meister Bertram von Minden, 'The Adoration of the Kings'. Panel of a double-winged altarpiece from the Petrikirche in Buxtehude, inside left wing of the altar, *c.* 1390/1415. Hamburg, Kunsthalle, inv. no. HK-501a–4; collection: Alte Meister. © bpk image 00032686. By kind permission. 224

Figure 8.7. Miguel Perrin (sculptor), 'The Adoration of the Magi', in the tympanum above the Puerta de los Palos, Cathedral of Seville, 1520–23. Author's photograph. 227

Figure 8.8. Master of the Prado, 'Adoration of the Magi', free copy of the central panel of the *Columba Triptych* by Rogier van der Weyden in Munich (Alte Pinakothek), in the style of Hans Memling, 1460s. © Madrid, Museo Nacional del Prado, inv. P01558. By kind permission. 230

Veronica Strang

Figure 10.1. Alma Wason at a long-term campsite on the Mitchell River, Cape York, Queensland. Photo: Veronica Strang. 264

Figure 10.2. Rock art depicting ancestral figures, Cape York, Queensland. Photo: Veronica Strang. 265

Figure 10.3. King plate, Kowanyama, Cape York. Photo: Veronica Strang. 270

Figure 10.4. Carved 'passport' sticks, with clan designs. Photo: Veronica Strang. 272

Figure 10.5. Traditional humpy, wooden frame with cabbage palm leaves, Cape York, Australia. Photo: Veronica Strang. 273

Figure 10.6. Elder cooking wallaby in *cup mari* [sand oven]. Photo: Veronica Strang. 279

Figure 10.7. Contemporary crop irrigation in Queensland. Photo: Veronica Strang. 282

Acknowledgements

The contributions to this volume were first presented and discussed at the conference 'Order into Action. How Large-Scale Concepts of World-Order Determine Practices in the Premodern World' at Heidelberg on 10–12 November 2016. We would like to express our gratitude to the Heidelberg University's Cluster of Excellence 'Asia and Europe in a Global Context' for making this conference possible through its generous funding. We equally want to thank the Heidelberg University Library and its staff (particularly Veit Probst, Maria Effinger, and Karin Zimmermann) for the permission to use the rooms of its Department of Manuscripts, which provided a particularly welcoming and inspiring environment. Special thanks are also due to Laura Kilgus, Paula Simon, and Sara Tot (all Heidelberg), who not only cared for the material well-being of the participants, but who oversaw the entire practical arrangements and took it upon them to produce a conference report. We also thank Michael Aljoscha Sengstmann (Bochum) for his precious help in preparing the manuscripts. We would also like to thank the members of the Editorial Board of 'Cursor Mundi' for accepting our volume, as well as the two anonymous reviewers for their extremely helpful comments. Special thanks go to Guy Carney at Brepols, who patiently accompanied the production of this volume from the very outset, and to Katharine Bartlett for her excellent work on our manuscript.

KLAUS OSCHEMA AND
CHRISTOPH MAUNTEL

Introduction

Creating Order and Causing Action

The central idea and the topic of the present volume constitute nothing less than an experiment. Inspired by the work and the insights generated in a research project on 'World Orders in Transcultural Perspective' at Heidelberg University's Cluster of Excellence 'Asia and Europe in a Global Context',[1] we asked ourselves a seemingly simple question that had hitherto not been discussed in detail in Medieval Studies: how did ideas about the appropriate 'order' of the world influence the actions of collectives or individuals?

To be more precise, we were not so much thinking about normative ideas that present an ideal image of how the world and its elements were supposed to be, thereby explicitly seeking to influence specific ways of acting (e.g. through laws or explicit religious prescriptions). Our interest rather concerned models of 'order' that present themselves as being 'descriptive' and thus merely seem to provide a stable framework in which concrete phenomena could be arranged and interpreted. A pertinent example to illustrate our focus of interest could be furnished by an idea that was widely held by authors in medieval Latin Christianity, namely that the Earth consisted of three known parts, Asia, Europe, and Africa, in which individual regions and their populations could be situated.[2] Although much work has been done on the reconstruction of such

1 The project ran from 2013 to 2016 and was co-directed by Bernd Schneidmüller and Klaus Oschema. Publications from our work include Mauntel, Oschema, Ducène, and Hofmann, 'Mapping Continents'; Jones, Mauntel, and Oschema ed., *A World of Empires*; Mauntel, 'Linking Seas and Lands'; Mauntel, 'Fra Mauro's View'; Mauntel and Oesterle, 'Wasserwelten'; Oschema, 'Trouver l'Europe en Asie?'; Oschema, 'An Irish Making of Europe'; Oschema, 'De l'universalisme périmé au refuge de la chrétienté'. See also the project-website: <https://www.asia-europe.uni-heidelberg.de/en/research/a-governance-administration/a27-world-orders.html> [accessed 21 June 2021].

2 See Oschema, *Bilder von Europa*, pp. 88–91 and 206–18; Christoph Mauntel is currently

Klaus Oschema (klaus.oschema@rub.de), Ruhr-Universität Bochum, Germany

Christoph Mauntel (christoph.mauntel@uni-tuebingen.de), Eberhard Karls Universität Tübingen, Germany

Order into Action: How Large-Scale Concepts of World-Order determine Practices in the Premodern World, ed. by Klaus Oschema and Christoph Mauntel, CURSOR 40 (Turnhout: Brepols, 2022), pp. 13–35
BREPOLS PUBLISHERS 10.1484/M.CURSOR-EB.5.123842

premodern perceptions of the world and its peoples,[3] the ensuing effects of these 'ordered' images of the world (*Weltbilder*)[4] on individual and collective actions have received considerably less attention.

Our question was at once simple and difficult to answer: we wanted to know, whether and how these models of 'world order' that have been reconstructed in an impressive number of detailed studies, had identifiable effects on the actions and behaviour of the individuals and groups that had constructed them and believed in them. Answering this question, we feel, is important for several reasons, only two of which we want to point out at this point: firstly, the answers might provide better insights into the effects of what has been called the 'social construction of reality' for the premodern period; secondly, these insights might help us to better understand how societies interacted with each other on a larger scale and in a longer chronological perspective.

Perspectives on Ordering the World

In 1966, Peter Berger and Thomas Luckmann argued in their seminal study on *The Social Construction of Reality* that social institutions are to a large extent, if not exclusively, constructed.[5] This perspective has, of course, become so widely acknowledged that an explicit confirmation might seem to constitute nothing less than a truism. At the same time, some of its implications have been considered rather less consistently, since many contributions gladly content themselves with the mere identification of certain phenomena as being, in fact, socially constructed. What has often been neglected, however, at least in the study of premodern societies, are the effects that result from the constructed entities, once they become reified and accepted as a natural given by the members of the cultures in question.[6]

The contributions to the present volume seek to build on this perspective in a transcultural dimension by focusing on a specific domain of socially constructed entities, namely the seemingly inactive (since merely receptive) models and ideas of order. Ordering 'things' in the broadest possible sense can obviously be understood as a theoretical exercise and a process of passive reception: the world that we perceive around us furnishes an enormous

---

preparing a monograph on the concept of continents in the Middle Ages to be published in 2022: *Asien – Europa – Afrika. Die Erdteile in der Weltordnung des Mittelalters*.

3 See e.g. Edson and Savage-Smith, *Medieval Views of the Cosmos*; Kline, *Maps of Medieval Thought*; Lilley ed., *Mapping Medieval Geographies*; Reichert, *Das Bild der Welt*; Campbell, *The Witness*; Markschies and others ed., *Atlas der Weltbilder*.

4 Bachorski and Röcke ed., *Weltbildwandel*; Billion and Bronner ed., *Weltbilder im Mittelalter*; Edson and Savage-Smith, *Medieval Views of the Cosmos*.

5 Berger and Luckmann, *The Social Construction of Reality*.

6 See for an analogous attempt in medieval studies Schneidmüller and Weinfurter, 'Ordnungskonfigurationen', here p. 8.

amount of data that might sometimes appear to be chaotic. Ordering this data means to establish criteria for their organization and to build groups of information that we arrange according to certain categories, which are themselves constructed.[7]

This idea might be considered to be self-evident by many of our fellow researchers in the vast field of cultural studies, but its implications are still not often fully taken into account. One aspect that has been rarely considered, at least in historical studies, concerns the effects that the constructions we are interested in had on individuals and collectives: numerous studies focus on the processes that pertain to the work of 'constructing' and on its result (the 'construction'); however, they rarely ask how the latter becomes in turn effective and influences further action. This blind spot might be a result of the fact that many studies actually start with observations concerning these very effects and then try to analyse the underlying structures — a movement that makes it easy to lose sight of the original point of departure.

We believe, on the other hand, that the very moment when theoretical or abstract ideas and 'orders' (in the sense of mental structures and representations)[8] become effective is particularly interesting: in contrast to a widespread misunderstanding (especially outside of the strictly academic discourse), the fact that social institutions — like family, laws, economy, schools and universities, church and religion, to name but a few — are socially constructed, does in no way imply that they were not 'real'. Quite on the contrary, Berger and Luckmann have convincingly argued that these constructions become 'reified' through processes of social interaction and that societies establish mechanisms to create and uphold their force in a process that can be described as 'social institutionalization'. As a result of this complex and incessant process, any given society's members tend to behave towards these institutions as if they were natural entities rather than human inventions.

While the concrete categories that were used in premodern societies for 'ordering' the world — 'realms', 'empires', but also 'continents' — do not immediately qualify as 'social institutions' *per se*, it is important to acknowledge that they are equally socially constructed, if we want to interpret their effects adequately. And even if they belong to the field of the epistemological rather than the ethical and social, it seems reasonable to assume that they did (and do) influence human actions and behaviour on an individual as well as on a collective level. This assumption is certainly not unheard of, since it lies at the very heart of numerous works on modern science;[9] it has, however, not yet been adequately considered in the context of (general) premodern history:

---

7 Kleinschmidt, *Perception*; Foucault, *The Order of Things*; see also Anter, *Macht der Ordnung*.

8 For a short critical overview on the semantics of 'order' and its relation with notions like 'system' and 'structure' see Anter, *Macht der Ordnung*, pp. 11–42.

9 The identification of the fundamental categories, concepts, and models used in modern science as 'constructed' underlies the work of authors like Fleck, in his *Denkstile und Tatsachen*, and Fleck, *Genesis and Development*; Kuhn, *Structure of Scientific Revolutions*,

While many contributions have asked (and reconstructed) how premodern societies mentally ordered the world around them, we want to know how this artificial order in turn affected the way they acted.

To give a simple example: one might ask if it makes a difference to cross the river Don, as the Franciscan missionary and envoy William of Rubruck did on his way to the Mongol Khan in 1254, if the individual who does so believes it to mark the border between the continents of Europe and Asia — or if she or he considers it to be just another river?[10] Did premodern travellers behave differently towards foreign people that they considered to belong either to Europe or to Asia? As Michael Wintle shows in his contribution to this volume, 'Europeans' might have defended their place in an imagined hierarchy of continents increasingly fervently towards the end of the Middle Ages. While his observations clearly invite us not to over-generalize the effects we can observe, they also attest to the fertility of the outlook we propose. Asking the kind of questions that we have in mind can open up new and innovative perspectives on texts and sources that seem to be only too familiar, but that still have new insights to offer. It also directs our attention to the practical and creative processes that are connected with the activity of ordering, since this practice inevitably entails, amongst others, the construction of borders that uphold the distinction between different categories and units, which form the building blocks of order.[11]

Insights into a Globally Connected World

A viable answer to the kind of relatively abstract interrogations we want to focus on, can obviously only be given on the basis of the work of our predecessors and in cooperation with colleagues who contribute the perspective of their specialization. Once we venture to address the question, however, it can considerably improve our understanding of premodern cultures and of the way their members acted. In addition, our subject strongly invites us to develop comparative and transcultural perspectives:[12] For obvious reasons, there was not one unified premodern *Weltbild* that would have been shared by the different cultures of the premodern ecumene. If we want to understand how the different *Weltbilder* influenced individual or collective actions, comparisons become inevitable. Only they enable us to see those differences which might

---

or Latour and Woolgar, *Laboratory Life*. For potential approaches from the perspective of premodern cultural studies see Friedrich, 'Ältere deutsche Literatur'.

10 While crossing the river, William indeed pointed out its function as a border, see Guglielmo di Rubruk, *Viaggio in Mongolia*, ed. by Chiesa, XIII.7, p. 64.

11 Even though the abstract phenomenon of 'order' itself can best be described as a 'relation', see Anter, *Macht der Ordnung*, pp. 37–40.

12 On the concept of transculturality, see for example Herren, Rüesch, and Sibille ed., *Transcultural History*; cf. Christ and others, *Transkulturelle Verflechtungen*.

be better explained by referring to the respective systems of order. This book is intended to be a tentative first step on this path.

This brings us to the second important reason for our experiment: if we accept that the *Weltbilder* of premodern societies varied to a considerable degree, and if we assume that they had important effects on the actions of individuals, groups, and societies that subscribed to them, their analysis can help us to better understand a series of further phenomena on a larger scale and in a longer chronological perspective. One helpful side-effect of our endeavour might thus be a contribution to the ongoing debates about 'Little' or 'Great Divergences' between different regions of the world and the cultures that inhabit them.[13] Considering *Weltbilder* as an important factor might in fact help to overcome the rift between interpretations that are largely based on the less clear-cut notion of 'mentality', on the one hand, and more 'materialistic' approaches[14] (which often have a deterministic outlook), on the other.

Michal Biran's contribution to this volume shows, for example, that the Mongols' idea of expansion became deeply entangled with the traditional Chinese notion of a 'Mandate of Heaven'. After the fall of the Mongol Yuan dynasty (1368), the Ming continued to build on these traditions and developed a diplomatic system based on tributes that mirrored their sense of superiority, as Donatella Guida demonstrates. Gifts and presents constituted a central element of these exchanges, but the Ming rulers interpreted them as tributes that established the sought-after relation of formal superiority. This furnished the basis on which further relations could develop. A seemingly analogous practice of gift-exchange appears in premodern Europe — where it was often meant to convey an entirely different message, as Christoph Mauntel and Klaus Oschema argue: towards the end of the Middle Ages, the political landscape of the Latin-Christian was characterized by a multitude of kingdoms that interacted as basically sovereign and (ideally) equal partners. In this context, the exchange of gifts often accompanied diplomatic contacts, and mostly served as a means to ensure communication and mutual engagement in peaceful exchange, but also to display the giver's material potency while honouring the receiver. As such, gift-giving became an instrument that helped

---

13 The expression 'Great Divergence' has been introduced by Pomeranz, *The Great Divergence*; cf. e.g. Grinin and Korotayev, *Great Divergence and Great Convergence*. For the 'Little Divergence' that saw an increasing separation in economic potency between the north of Europe and its south and centre in the pre-industrial era, see, e.g., de Pleijt and van Zanden, 'Accounting for the "Little Divergence"'. For an intercultural perspective see Davids, *Religion, Technology, and the Great and Little Divergences*.

14 This is not meant to oversimplify the ongoing debate and the complex and elaborate explanations that often combine a broad range of criteria. Older contributions often sought to explain Europe's rise to global domination in the modern era through a relatively small set of factors they considered to be decisive, see, e.g., Jones, *The European Miracle*, while more recent studies have become increasingly complex. Parts of the older discussion are summed up in Mitterauer, *Warum Europa?* For an elaborate attempt based on quantifiable units see Morris, *Why the West Rules*.

to organize a pluralistic political order — which characterized much of late medieval political thinking and practices in the Latin-Christian world.

The examples united in this volume also point to a further vital observation that still needs to be explicitly underlined, in spite of the wealth of recent publications: premodern societies interacted with each other over large distances and across so-called 'cultural borders'.[15] Recent contributions on the 'Global Middle Ages' have made it increasingly clear that the inter-connectivity between those regions and cultures that were part of the premodern ecumene had already reached a very high level long before the sixteenth century.[16] Adding to our knowledge about these phenomena, the contributions to the present volume highlight how concepts and ideas of order became particularly relevant in contexts of transcultural contact and exchange.

On a relatively abstract level, the Muslim idea of *dār al-ḥarb* ('the abode of war') that Daniel König focuses on in his contribution, seems to establish a clear-cut difference between Muslim and non-Muslim realms. In this respect, it exemplifies the problems a monotheistic belief system could encounter when dealing with non-believers and it can thus be interpreted as a category that served to 'order' the empirically perceptible world. However, the concept itself was by far less evident than one might think at first glance and it needed interpretation: as König demonstrates, referring to the 'abode of war' could be an act of (political) propaganda that sought to motivate for war (and thus use a concept of 'order' to induce action), as well as a means to advertise pragmatic political solutions. The notion of *christianitas*, as analysed by Nora Berend, shares this ambivalence in a certain respect: while less geographically grounded than the notion of *dār al-ḥarb*, *christianitas* equally represented a category that could pretend to simply 'order' a given reality (by designating the community of the Christian believers). In practice, however, it was mainly used in ambivalent or conflictive situations, in which questions of identity and belonging were at stake (when 'true Christians' were distinguished from heretics), and in which the notion's use ultimately sought to motivate to fight against religiously identified adversaries.

These insights — and many more — are part of the answers our contributors furnished to our initial questions as outlined above. In our common endeavour, we invited colleagues from different backgrounds and fields of

15 On the fertility of borders in the premodern period, see e.g. Herbers and Jaspert ed., *Grenzräume und Grenzüberschreitungen*; Merisalo ed., *Frontiers in the Middle Ages*.

16 The notion of 'Global Middle Ages' has been vividly discussed; while it seems to be well established for studies that focus on transcultural processes of exchange in the 'medieval' period (i.e. before CE 1500), the controversial debate on the question of whether the term 'Middle Ages' constitutes a viable and useful category for the analysis of non-European cultures or global phenomena in the period between the tenth and fifteenth centuries has not yet been settled. With a focus on the first aspect, see e.g. the contributions in Holmes and Standen ed., *The Global Middle Ages*; Frankopan, 'Why We Need to Think'; for the ongoing discussion, see e.g. Davis and Altschul, 'Introduction'; McClure, 'A New Politics'.

expertise concerning premodern societies around the globe, and asked them to reply to the same question:[17] does the material you are familiar with indicate that specific ideas or concepts led to actions or practices, and if so, how? We were very happy to receive numerous positive and enthusiastic reactions to the challenge that our invitation doubtlessly posed. This enthusiasm enabled us to assemble a group of scholars that included experts in Chinese-Mongol history or in East African archaeology as well as specialists of the Mesoamerican Maya and Australian Aboriginal culture. Focusing on a choice of categories from the fields of politics, religion, and geography that we considered to be particularly fertile and promising, we sought to understand if, and how, they influenced specific types of behaviour and actions in their respective context.

Approaches and Examples

In the course of our exchanges, we realized that our central question is indeed hard, if not impossible to answer with any certainty. One particular problem that has become increasingly clear during our discussions arises from the fact that our question analytically singles out one particular moment (or facet) of what is, in reality, a constant and ongoing process. While we posit that *Weltbilder* do have a strong effect on the ways individuals and collectives act, they are in turn themselves established and modified on the basis of experiences and ideas that result from actions and their effects. In this regard, the approaches of cultural studies (often focusing on the impact of ideas and concepts on social life) and of practice theory (highlighting the importance of the material and bodily dimension of the cultures under observation)[18] can be fruitfully combined. This can conveniently be demonstrated by two well-known examples.

In a series of studies, Johannes Fried has convincingly argued that late medieval thinkers increasingly appreciated the use of empirical data. This relatively new approach became stronger from the thirteenth century onwards, and it seems reasonable to assume that it was decisively influenced by the experience of the Mongol incursions into Eastern Europe. Even though it was at first an involuntary, confusing, and violent contact, the experience led to a series of travels of Latin missionaries and envoys into the hitherto unknown realms of Asia.[19] Leaving aside the additional factors that contributed to making

17 The proceedings collected in this volume are the results of a conference held 10–12 November 2016 in Heidelberg, which marked the end of our research project on 'World Orders in a Transcultural Perspective'. For a conference report, see Kilgus, Simon, and Tot, 'Conference Report "Order into Action"'.

18 See e.g. the recent remarks by de Boer, 'Praktiken, Praxen und Praxisformen' with further references.

19 For a synthesis of Fried's ideas see Fried, *Das Mittelalter*, here esp. pp. 301–06 (Mongols) and 349–93 ('reason' in the Middle Ages); Fried, 'Wissen als soziales System', pp. 24–26,

the conflictive situation a fertile moment for intellectual advancement,[20] this case exemplifies how real-world experience could have a profound influence on the modification of an existing *Weltbild*.[21] On the other hand, the reaction to the experience of the Mongol incursions might well have been different, had not the shared *Weltbild* of Latin Christians motivated them to react the way they did in the first place.

A famous second example is, of course, Christopher Columbus's travels that led to the establishment of permanent contacts between the populations of Europe and the Americas (including all their catastrophic effects). When Columbus set sail in order to explore a sea-route to India, his endeavour amounted to nothing less than going west in order to arrive in the East.[22] This action would hardly have been conceivable without a long series of intellectual forerunners who had convincingly argued for the spherical form of the Earth as well as for the fact that this sphere was small enough to be successfully circumnavigated.[23] In fact, the cover picture of this volume expresses this very same idea: the miniature illustrates a fourteenth-century copy of Gossuin de Metz's *Image du monde*,[24] taking up the author's explanation that the Earth was of spherical shape and could thus be perambulated (at least in theory).[25] Gossuin was, of course, not the first author who described the Earth's form as spherical, but could draw on a long tradition that ultimately had its roots in Antiquity.[26]

However, the theoretical (and thinkable) possibility of travelling around the entire globe did not lead to concrete action for a very long time. One of

---

and Fried, 'Auf der Suche nach der Wirklichkeit'. See also Schmieder, 'L'evoluzione del questionario'.

20 There was, amongst others, a confluence of millenaristic ideas that increased the motivation to get a clearer idea of who the hitherto unknown adversaries were: according to widespread beliefs, the migration of certain tribes would be a precursor to the apocalypse, see Ruotsala, *Europeans and Mongols*; Klopprogge, *Ursprung und Ausprägung des abendländischen Mongolenbildes*.

21 It should be noted, however, that the complete integration of the newly available empirical data took a considerable amount of time, see Oschema, 'Trouver l'Europe en Asie?', pp. 249–50.

22 This approach could indeed lead to confusion, as is explained in a letter of the Florentine mathematician and cartographer Paolo dal Pozzo Toscanelli to the confessor of the Portuguese king Alfonso V, Fernam Martins de Roriz (25 June 1474): 'Et non miremini si voco occidentales partes vbi sunt aromata cum communiter dicantur orientales quia nauigantibus ad occidentem semper ille partes inueniuntur per subterraneas nauigaciones. Si enim per terram et per superiora itinera ad orientem senper [*sic*] reperirentur'. See Vignaud, *Toscanelli*, p. 296.

23 The most important influence on Columbus was Pierre d'Ailly, *Ymago mundi*; see Mauntel, 'Linking Seas and Lands', pp. 121–26. Cf. also Russel, *Inventing the Flat Earth*.

24 Paris, Bibliothèque nationale de France, MS fr. 574, fol. 42^r.

25 *L'Image du monde de maître Gossouin*, pp. 95–99.

26 See Simek, *Heaven and Earth*, pp. 24–38. On the spherical form of the Earth in the seventh-century encyclopaedia of Isidore of Seville, see Stevens, 'Figure'.

the main obstacles was, in fact, another essential motif in the theories on geographical order, namely climate theory: for centuries, authors who reflected on the geographical structure of the Earth were convinced that the sphere was divided into a series of different climates. In their eyes, the polar regions and the regions around the equator were in fact not habitable, which made travelling across these regions impossible. The Ocean that surrounded the continents was also imagined as being impossible to cross. It took an individual person, material support, and an environment which allowed risk-taking in order to act on the idea that the Earth's sphere could indeed be circumnavigated — a powerful reminder of the importance of political, cultural, economic, and social circumstances. Columbus's so-called 'discovery' of a hitherto unknown part of the world (unknown to the inhabitants of the old ecumene of Asia, Africa, and Europe, that is) was to have profound consequences for the ideas European Christians had about the nature of the human race, but also about their approach to the question of the accessibility of all the parts of the globe.[27] But if it was, at least amongst other elements, his *Weltbild* that made Columbus's endeavour thinkable and feasible, his experience in turn led to further empirical knowledge and new information about the shape and disposition of the world — and thus to the *Weltbild*'s modification.

For this volume, we were, however, not only thinking along the lines of such obvious and spectacular connections between order — in the sense of a theoretical model — and action. The phenomena we are interested in reach far deeper and are more intricate. A closer look rapidly reveals that every act of 'ordering' the perceptible world entails consequences that potentially or actually inform human actions, because ordering relies on the creation of categories — and constructing categories inevitably means to erect boundaries which include and exclude.[28] Far from being a neutral and innocuous practice, the very phenomenon of ordering thus has immediate effects on our outlook on the world and, by extension, our behaviour and actions.

This can be demonstrated by examples dealt with in this volume: the Muslim notion of *dār al-ḥarb* circumscribed a world inhabited by 'outsiders' and the territories they ruled over (Daniel König). When it was used in contexts in which it sought to motivate the believers to reduce this 'outside', it can be compared in its effects to the sense of unity that kept the Mongols'

27 Since the ensuing debates developed mostly after the period we want to focus on in this volume, we exclude the details from this introduction. See, however, for a first overview, Headley, *The Europeanization of the World*, esp. pp. 9–62 (Chap. 1: 'The Renaissance Defining and Engagement of the Global Arena of Humanity'); Herzog, 'Identities and Processes of Identification'; Muldoon, 'Papal Responsibility for the Infidel'. For the contemporary discussions about Columbus's ideas see Randles, 'The Evaluation of Columbus' "India" Project'; concerning the question of practical accessibility, see, e.g., Hiatt, *Terra incognita*, and Randles, 'La Navigabilité de l'Atlantique'.

28 On the relation of 'order' and 'power' see briefly Anter, *Macht der Ordnung*, pp. 97–103, who mostly focuses on the ensuing effects of hierarchy; cf. also, with a focus on education, Peters and Besley, 'Social Exclusion/Inclusion'.

expansionist drive alive, even when their empire was dissolving into a plurality of realms (Michal Biran). An analogous dynamic can be identified in the case of *christianitas*, that was equally used to evoke solidarity and to draw boundaries in conflicts, even though it was mostly applied in inner-Christian conflicts (Nora Berend). The dangerous potential of these seemingly 'descriptive' categories becomes all too clear when a concept like 'race' is applied in the construction of, or the distinction between, in-groups and out-groups (Michael Wintle).

Despite the fundamental differences that we obviously have to keep in mind when discussing these examples together, they all have one aspect in common: each and every one of them reminds us that many actions do not arise spontaneously, but are driven by underlying ideas that need not be explicitly normative or appellative in themselves. At the same time, they make clear that only individuals and/or groups can turn ideas into actions.

The ambivalence of the individual's role becomes particularly clear in Albrecht Fuess's comparison of two Muslim thinkers, who, at the turn of the thirteenth century, developed quite different ideas to legitimize the Mamluk rule over Egypt. In the end, Ibn Nubāta's pragmatic approach prevailed over the more dogmatic ideas of his rival Ibn Taymīya — perhaps not least due to the latter's quarrelsome character. This latter observation reminds us of the importance of seemingly unimportant circumstances. Even though this might not come as a surprise, we should certainly keep in mind that practical conditions may of course in fact prevent the success of certain actions, in spite of the individual's efforts to put his or her ideas into practice: the fourteenth-century Sultan of Kilwa (East Africa) for example, Hasan ibn Sulaiman, fervently tried to use imperial architecture and coinage in order to further his aspiration to the title of Caliph — but nothing came of it in the long run (Mark Horton).

While this example effectively reminds us of the importance to keep in mind the limits of our approach, the latter still has much to offer, as we want to underline with a final example that constitutes a conscious anachronism: The potential consequences of categories that pretend to merely represent a descriptive 'order', at least at first glance, become particularly evident through a closer look at the concept of the 'nation state' that profoundly structures the realities and ideas about political order in the modern world.[29] While there exists an impressive number of stateless individuals,[30] the quasi-normal situation for the overwhelming majority of people is to be a citizen of at least one nation state — but this attribution entails much more than the sheer fact of affiliation and basic rights of participation. Citizenship in a nation state

29 For the historical development in a broad chronological perspective, see, e.g., Hirschi, *The Origins of Nationalism*; cf. White, 'Globalization and the Mythology of the Nation State'.

30 The UNHCR estimates that several million people are currently stateless for a number of reasons, see <https://www.unhcr.org/statelessness-around-the-world.html> [accessed 21 June 2021]. For a statistical overview see the *UNHCR Statistical Yearbook 2016*, pp. 6–17 (Tables 1 and 2).

determines a broad set of rights of access to material support, education facilities, medical assistance, etc. While some of this might seem relatively unproblematic at first glance, recent phenomena of large-scale migration have led to renewed debates about the adherence to individual nation states that demonstrate how fluid and precarious the seemingly well-established categories of the nation state and citizenship actually are. In quite a number of these discussions, the concept of 'nation' became mixed up with other categories that are far more problematic. The most prominent of these are probably 'religion' and 'race', and both of these are prone to furnish the basis on which individuals and groups can be either included in or excluded from certain categories on a cultural or even (pseudo-)biological level. While it is already more than problematic to try and render 'objective' the category of 'race' by means of DNA-tests, the ensuing temptation to define nations as biologically grounded units is only too obvious.[31]

In other words: what may begin as a seemingly innocuous endeavour that proposes to gather and order data about the outside world 'as it is', can easily become an instrument for the organization of future action. What is even more: once objects, phenomena, or people are singled out and categorized in a certain way, there is only a small step from this process of ordering to using its results in potentially harmful ways on the basis of arguments and conclusions that draw on characteristics that might have appeared to be relatively 'objective' on the outset and charge them with additional values. While the medieval or premodern material and cultures might not furnish examples that are so wide-reaching as the DNA-tests we just mentioned, structurally analogous processes abound in our sources. Focusing on them can doubtlessly help us to shed further light on phenomena that are currently vividly debated and that concern, amongst other topics, the question of the presence and development of the category of 'race' and the ensuing phenomenon of racism.[32]

While we discussed the presentations on which the contributions to this volume are based, one aspect became particularly clear: it is not always easy to determine whether certain actions were motivated and set off by pre-existing ideas and categories of 'order', or if the latter were rather influenced by specific actions and the ensuing experiences.[33] Processes of experience, perception,

31 UK Immigration services currently only seem to use DNA-testing in order to establish family relations between siblings; see, however, the recent *Internal Review of the Government's Policy on Requirements to Provide DNA in Visa and Asylum Cases*. The Canadian border agency recently acknowledged to use DNA-tests as an indicator for nationality, see Kassam, 'Canada Uses DNA and Ancestry Sites'. Cf. Benjamin, 'The Emperor's New Genes', esp. pp. 134–36; on a recent debate in Germany see Lipphardt, 'Vertane Chancen?' For a broader range of contexts and effects of DNA-testing see also Quinn, de Paor, and Blanck ed., *Genetic Discrimination*.

32 See Heng, *The Invention of Race*, and several of the contributions to Albin, Erler, O'Donnell, Paul, and Rowe ed., *Whose Middle Ages?*

33 Recently, the historian Philippe Buc pointed out that 'Premodern sources [...] seldom allow the historian to determine whether an event was interpreted after the fact according to a

model-building, and ensuing action are, of course, intimately connected. If we want to understand them in their entirety, though, we have to get a better idea of the individual steps and elements that are part of the whole. In the present volume we choose to focus on the relation between theoretical models and practical outcomes, in order to enrich our understanding of the dynamics of premodern societies in a transcultural perspective.

If this endeavour can indeed contribute to further debates, including the 'Great Divergence', as we believe it does, our focus might also help to demonstrate the relevance of research on premodern societies, since it allows us to analyse the relation between ideas and practices in a context that is less prone to be accused of political partisanship than the analysis of contemporary phenomena. The 'distant mirror'[34] of premodern cultures might thus provide insights that we would be less willing to accept, if the mirror was nearer.

In terms of chronology, the contributions to this volume focus on premodern phenomena, or more precisely on the period between the thirteenth and sixteenth centuries. This time-frame has been consciously chosen, since the ecumene of Asia, Europe, and Africa had once again developed relatively intensive contacts in this period.[35] At the same time, the ensuing exchanges that can be witnessed did not yet lead to what has been described as the 'globalization of Europe' (or rather the 'Europeanization of the World'), which dominated large parts of modern history.[36] This means that a certain amount of mutual knowledge existed, as far as different systems of belief or approaches to order the world in geographical, political, or religious categories are concerned. But while the presence of this knowledge (that sometimes went hand in hand with vivid polemics and conflicts) did in many cases influence specific *Weltbilder*, these were not yet fused together in complete hybridization, nor have some of them been replaced by imported, seemingly more successful rival systems.[37]

The Contributions — a Brief Outline

The contributions to the present volume are organized in four sections, following a combination of thematic and geographic orientations. In the first three sections, our authors discuss and analyse phenomena that pertain

---

given framework, or whether this framework led people to act in the way they did'. See Buc, *Holy War*, p. 9.

34 See Tuchman, *A Distant Mirror*.

35 For recent overviews in a 'global' perspective, see, e.g., Fried and Hehl ed., *Weltdeutungen und Weltreligionen*, and Reinhard ed., *Empires and Encounters*.

36 See, e.g., Gruzinski, *The Eagle and the Dragon*; Headley, *The Europeanization of the World*; Jones, *The European Miracle*.

37 On the reception of Western geography and cartography in sixteenth-century China, see briefly Mauntel, Oschema, Ducène, and Hofmann, 'Mapping Continents', p. 328.

to the fields of 'Religion', 'Politics', and 'Geography' by comparing examples and contributions from Latin Europe, the Arabic-Islamic world and China. These foci are by no means meant to be exhaustive, especially in geographic and cultural terms, but they can provide us with paradigmatic insights into different parts of the premodern ecumene. In order to broaden our perspective and to allow for more fundamental comparison, we included a fourth section that consciously oversteps the boundaries of the 'old ecumene' by focusing on cultures that are often somewhat neglected or even ignored in the recent development of premodern history in a globalized perspective, i.e. sub-Saharan Africa, Australia, and Mesoamerica.

Rather than combining syntheses on the individual cultures and societies that try to systematically cover the (vast) field circumscribed by our rather general question, the contributions seek to provide case studies that build on the authors' individual expertise: They furnish paradigmatic insights that can be read in a comparative and/or contrasting perspective and thus invite our readers to further reflection and discussion. At this point, and this brings us back to the experimental character of our volume, an exhaustive discussion of our exciting topic simply does not appear to be feasible. In addition, our approach does not seek to replace established perspectives by initiating yet another 'turn': quite the contrary, we are convinced that it can become most fertile if it is included as an additional layer in future research. While our aim at the initial conference was to establish a first exchange, this volume wants to broaden the audience, in order to present our ideas and findings and invite further discussion.

Our collection opens with two contributions that focus on explicitly 'religious' concepts that entail consequences in a number of further contexts. As already mentioned above, Daniel König analyses the Arab notion of *dār al-ḥarb* ('the abode of war') in comparison with the Latin expression *terra paganorum* ('land of the infidels'). Both terms are characterized by their spatial orientation and describe regions under the paradigm of religious alterity. In contrast to the rather rare formula *terra paganorum*, however, the notion of *dār al-ḥarb* conveyed a far more elaborate idea: it acquired clear normative and juridical implications and defined the aims and rules of Muslim foreign policy towards the non-Muslim sphere. Its effects were, however, not uniform: while there certainly were expansionist tendencies in Islamic realms, where the concept of the 'abode of war' may have motivated or justified military action against neighbouring non-Muslim territories, König demonstrates that foreign relations were often also dominated by more pragmatic considerations.

If the notion of the 'land of the infidels' apparently did not incite considerable missionary or expansive movements, the Latin term *christianitas* ('Christianity'/'Christendom'), on the other hand, could in fact be used to motivate such actions. Nora Berend highlights the polyvalent meanings of *christianitas*: even though most authors used the term in a descriptive rather than in a prescriptive manner, a series of examples shows that the concept could also be employed in order to call for the help and defence of 'Christendom', thereby trying to motivate actions. Quite surprisingly, however, these calls to action were mostly used in internal, intra-Christian discourses and confrontations rather than in conflicts with other religious groups, as for example the Muslims. Aiming at local or inner-Christian conflicts, the alleged loyalty based on the Christian faith was to surpass any other ties and bonds, although, as Berend points out, this idea only rarely had the intended effects.

Our second section unites three case studies that focus on primarily 'Political' concepts: Albrecht Fuess demonstrates how two Mamluk scholars who lived at the turn of the thirteenth century tried to find strategies to stabilize the emerging Mamluk rule that was still threatened by non-Muslim enemies. Ibn Nubāta and Ibn Taymīya proposed two quite distinct ways in which, as they believed, the Mamluk rulers should try to cope with this situation. Offering different paths, both scholars sought to implement their ideas of a good, orderly society by influencing their rulers. Ibn Taymīya called for the absolute rule of God that he perceived to be prescribed in the Koran, the Sunna, and the Hadith (i.e. the sayings and deeds of the Prophet). Ibn Nubāta, on the other hand, advocated a more pragmatic approach, prioritizing the practical interests of the ruler and his government. As Fuess argues, Ibn Nubāta's strategy seems to have been more successful in his own time. Ibn Taymīya, on the other hand, ended up in prison because of his dogmatic and uncompromising teachings but also his rather difficult personal character — a striking example of the importance of the social and political circumstances as well as individual characteristics with regard to the possibility of putting ideas of order into action.

In the following contribution, Michal Biran moves our focus to the Mongol Empire that covered large parts of Eurasia during the thirteenth and fourteenth centuries. One specific means in Chinggis Khan's quest to unify the different Mongol tribes was his claim to dispose of the 'Mandate of Heaven' — which meant in turn that he had to seek further expansion and prove his legitimacy by victories on the battlefield. At least in theory the Khans' 'Mandate' to conquer and rule encompassed the entire world. As a consequence, at the height of their power the Mongols accepted peaceful submission but no foreign relations on an equal footing. The developments after the Mongol Empire's disintegration into four different polities after 1260 furnish a most telling example for our central question: in spite of (sometimes violent) conflicts that arose between the Mongol leaders, they continued to hold on to the ideal of a Chinggisid unity. This orientation led to an enormous increase in interest and knowledge about the world, especially at the Chinese-Mongol court, as Biran argues.

Focusing mainly on the thirteenth to fifteenth centuries, Christoph Mauntel and Klaus Oschema then present a kind of European 'counter-model' to the Mongol political idea of world domination. Although the (Holy) Roman Empire was frequently still perceived to be at least ideally the highest-ranking polity in medieval Latin Europe, it was in fact impossible for the emperors to implement this idea in terms of concrete political action. Several of the other European kingdoms were equally (or even more) powerful; in addition, they explicitly challenged any idea of the Empire's practical political predominance. The ensuing idea that the kingdoms were to operate on what might be described as a level playing field entailed quite specific political consequences: the kings or their representatives and envoys increasingly relied on diplomatic means to discuss important political matters and to form alliances in order to solve individual problems. Thus, even in times of danger (for example during the Ottoman expansion), there were rarely calls for one supreme leader, but rather for a unified coalition of all Christian princes. As Mauntel and Oschema argue, the resulting establishment of the idea of a pluralistic world order might be considered an important element for the successful expansion of European powers in the early modern period.

Donatella Guida's analysis of the basic cosmological ideas of Ming China (1368–1644), which opens our third section on 'geographic' concepts, chronologically and geographically connects up to Biran's study. Like their Mongol predecessors, the Ming rulers (as 'Sons of Heaven') claimed the right (and at the same time the duty) to universal rule. In their perception, China constituted the geographical as well as the cultural centre of the world, while other peoples and states were assigned specific places in an appropriate distance to this centre. As a means to visualize their power and enforce its acceptance, the Chinese bureaucracy implemented and exalted a tributary system: collecting tribute became a standard method for administering the relations with other political entities. Thus, the diplomatic ritual was shaped and construed according to the basic geographic and ideological assumptions of the Ming elite, to communicate their sense of cosmological order.

Scrutinizing the visual tradition of the 'three Magi', who, according to the Gospel of St Matthew, came to adore the new-born Jesus Christ, Michael Wintle pursues the inquiry into theoretical models of global order and the ensuing effects. From the fifteenth century onwards (mainly in the German-speaking sphere), one of the Magi was frequently depicted with dark skin. Wintle interprets this 'black Magus' as a representation of Africa, one of the three continents of the known ecumene, implying that the other Magi represented Asia and Europe. This model enabled artists to project ideas of their own part of the world and relate them to the other two. Wintle argues that the typical visualization of the three Magi became an expression of a hierarchy of the continents: Asia, being the largest and most distinguished part of the Earth, as an aged man; Europe, the part with which the authors and painters in question identified, as an elegant and dynamic man; and Africa, a continent that evoked ideas of wildness, but also of wealth and commodities, as a younger coloured man. This model can be read as an expression of growing European self-consciousness, including a clear sense of superiority. Wintle's interpretation provides an excellent example for the intricacy of this volume's topic. While the three Magi might have become a symbol for the idea of European superiority, thus becoming one possible expression of a collective sentiment or political idea, it is hardly the reason or a motive for the contemporary process of European expansion. In this case we can observe how 'order' and 'action' co-evolve, merge, and mutually influence each other, making it impossible to decide definitively which comes first.

Our fourth section provides an additional perspective on political, religious, and geographical concepts, with case studies on societies and cultures that are only infrequently compared to their European and Asian counterparts. Focusing on sub-Saharan Africa, Australia, and Mesoamerica, these contributions provide, of course, only a small selection of the wealth and breadth of possible examples.

Delivering a fervent plea for the inclusion of Africa into the study of premodern global history, Mark Horton deals with the East African Sultanate of Kilwa. Between the thirteenth and fifteenth centuries, Kilwa became an important port city as an entrepôt for the supply of gold and ivory from southern Africa. The ruling Mahdali dynasty, particularly Sultan Hasan ibn Sulaiman (*c.* 1310–33), used this new importance and mercantile power to stage an impressive building programme. Horton interprets an ensemble of three newly erected stone buildings as an expression of aspirations to claim the title of Caliph: the Mahdali were well aware of the end of the Caliphate in Baghdad in 1258, and the Sultans of Kilwa deliberately sought out an architectural style they deemed 'Islamic' in order to further their prestige and to underline Islamic antecedents. The creation of such an Islamic landscape, which followed the ideas of a particularly 'Caliphal' architecture, had the specific commercial function of enriching the ruling dynasty at the cost of the other Kilwa merchants. In the long run, however, the Mahdali failed to establish themselves as a regional power: buildings collapsed and merchants went to other trading centres. Nevertheless, their example provides an instructive case study for the way in which a political programme was acted out (in this case through the erection of a series of buildings), and how it could be influenced by underlying political ideas of sovereignty. It seems particularly revealing that this set of ideas was derived from one of the monotheistic religions.

In a staggering counter-example to these 'universalistic' approaches, Veronica Strang offers insights into the ways in which the concept of an ordered universe influenced the Australian Aboriginal way of living. According to Strang, this represents one of the world's most long-lasting ways of life, with a tradition that might be as old as 40,000 years. The Aboriginal imaginary is based on the idea of a cosmos that had been created in a distant past: the 'Dreamtime' (or 'Story Time'). All life is believed to have emerged from the water, which led to the creation of a hydro-theological cycle that carries life from the invisible, non-material ancestral domain into material being, and then back again. Analysing the material, social, and spatial order, Strang highlights that the most fundamental tenets of Aboriginal Law determined that it was the responsibility of Aboriginal societies to care for the land they inhabited and to ensure the sustainability of their resources as well as to keep up the link with their ancestors. This led, for example, to a rigidly organized agricultural system as well as to limited travelling — in short, a society with rules that aimed to conserve their traditional sense of order. What seems most remarkable, in addition, is that ideas of political superiority or the urge to expand political rule, appear to be entirely absent.

In our final contribution, Frauke Sachse explores the mid-sixteenth century *Theologia Indorum* ('Theology for the Indians'), which was written to teach the Christian world-view and doctrine to the K'iche', a native people and major political power during the conquest of the American continent by the Spanish. The author, a Dominican friar, deliberately used the native language, K'iche', to communicate concepts of Heaven and Hell by appropriating terminology from indigenous ritual discourse that was meaningful within the framework of the Highland Maya world-view. While missionaries often appropriated K'iche' terminology, indigenous authors embedded doctrinal discourse into their texts, thus helping to preserve concepts of K'iche' cosmology within the framework of Christian order. Analysing this hybridization, Sachse argues that it is an indicator of the K'iche' elites' active cooperation in the process of Christianization, while trying to maintain political influence in different times.

In the end, we neither can nor want to claim that the contributions collected in this volume provide a definitive answer to our initial questions. However, we strongly believe that they demonstrate the potential as well as the specific difficulties of our approach. Having worked together with our authors during the conference and the ensuing process of the preparation of their texts for the published volume, we feel that our collection outlines a field of research that has so far remained rather underexplored. While we might not be able to give definitive and conclusive answers, the aim of this volume remains similar to that of our conference: to open up new perspectives, to provoke innovative thoughts and to stimulate further discussion.

Works Cited

Manuscripts

Paris, Bibliothèque nationale de France, MS fr. 574 (Gossuin de Metz, *Image du monde*)

Primary Sources

Guglielmo di Rubruk, *Viaggio in Mongolia (Itinerarium)*, ed. by Paolo Chiesa, Scrittori greci e latini (Rome: Fondazione Lorenzo Valla/Mondadori, 2011)

L'Image du monde de maître Gossouin. Rédaction en prose, ed. by Olivier H. Prior (Paris: Payot, 1913)

Pierre d'Ailly, *Ymago mundi. Texte latin et traduction française des quatre traités cosmographiques de d'Ailly et des notes marginales de Christophe Colomb. Étude sur les sources de l'auteur*, 3 vols, ed. by Edmond Buron (Paris: Maisonneuve frères, 1930)

Secondary Studies

Albin, Andrew, Mary C. Erler, Thomas O'Donnell, Nicholas L. Paul, and Nina Rowe, ed., *Whose Middle Ages? Teachable Moments for an Ill-Used Past* (New York: Fordham University Press, 2019)

Anter, Andreas, *Die Macht der Ordnung. Aspekte einer Grundkategorie des Politischen*, 2nd rev. edn (Tübingen: Mohr Siebeck, 2007)

Bachorski, Hans-Jürgen, and Werner Röcke, ed., *Weltbildwandel: Selbstdeutung und Fremderfahrung im Epochenübergang vom Spätmittelalter zur Frühen Neuzeit*, Literatur, Imagination, Realität, 10 (Trier: WVT, 1995)

Benjamin, Ruha, 'The Emperor's New Genes: Science, Public Policy, and the Allure of Objectivity', *Annals of the American Academy of Political and Social Science*, 661 (2015), 130–42

Berger, Peter L., and Thomas Luckmann, *The Social Construction of Reality: A Treatise in the Sociology of Knowledge* (Garden City, NY: Anchor Books, 1966)

Billion, Philipp, and Dagmer Bronner, ed., *Weltbilder im Mittelalter: Perceptions of the World in the Middle Ages* (Bonn: Bernstein, 2009)

Buc, Philippe, *Holy War, Martyrdom, and Terror: Christianity, Violence, and the West* (Philadelphia: University of Pennsylvania Press, 2015)

Campbell, Mary B., *The Witness and the Other World: Exotic European Travel Writing 400–1600* (Ithaca: Cornell University Press, 1988)

Christ, Georg, Saskia Dönitz, Daniel König, Şevket Küçükhüseyin, Margit Mersch, Britta Müller-Schauenburg, Ulrike Ritzerfeld, Christian Vogel, and Julia Zimmermann, *Transkulturelle Verflechtungen. Mediävistische Perspektiven* (Göttingen: Universitätsverlag Göttingen, 2016), <https://doi.org/10.17875/gup2016-981> [accessed 21 June 2021]

Davids, Karel, *Religion, Technology, and the Great and Little Divergences: China and Europe Compared, c. 700–1800*, History of Science and Medicine Library, 32 / Knowledge Infrastructure and Knowledge Economy, 2 (Leiden: Brill, 2013)

Davis, Kathleen and Nadia Altschul, 'Introduction: The Idea of "the Middle Ages" Outside Europe', in *Medievalisms in the Postcolonial World: The Idea of 'the Middle Ages' Outside Europe*, ed. by Kathleen Davis and Nadia Altschul (Baltimore: Johns Hopkins University Press, 2009), pp. 1–24

De Boer, Jan-Hendryk, 'Praktiken, Praxen und Praxisformen, oder: Von Serienkillern, verrückten Wänden und der ungewissen Zukunft', in *Praxisformen. Zur kulturellen Logik von Zukunftshandeln*, ed. by Jan-Hendryk de Boer, Kontingenzgeschichten, 6 (Frankfurt: Campus, 2019), pp. 21–43

De Pleijt, Alexandra M., and Jan Luiten van Zanden, 'Accounting for the "Little Divergence": What Drove Economic Growth in Pre-industrial Europe, 1300–1800?', *European Review of Economic History*, 20,4 (2016), 387–409

Edson, Evelyn, and Emilie Savage-Smith, *Medieval Views of the Cosmos* (Oxford: Bodleian Library, 2004)

Fleck, Ludwik, *The Genesis and Development of a Scientific Fact*, ed. by Thaddeus J. Trenn and Robert K. Merton, with a foreword by Thomas Kuhn (Chicago: University of Chicago Press, 1979 [German orig. 1935])

——, *Denkstile und Tatsachen. Gesammelte Schriften und Zeugnisse*, ed. by Sylwia Werner and Claus Zitte (Berlin: Suhrkamp, 2011)

Foucault, Michel, *The Order of Things: An Archaeology of the Human Sciences* (New York: Pantheon, 1970)

Frankopan, Peter, 'Why We Need to Think About the Global Middle Ages', *Journal of Medieval Worlds*, 1 (2019), 5–10

Fried, Johannes, 'Auf der Suche nach der Wirklichkeit. Die Mongolen und die europäische Erfahrungswissenschaft im 13. Jahrhundert', *Historische Zeitschrift*, 243 (1986), 287–332

——, *Das Mittelalter. Geschichte und Kultur*, 2nd edn (Munich: C. H. Beck, 2011)

——, 'Wissen als soziales System: Wissenskultur im Mittelalter', in *Wissenskulturen. Über die Erzeugung und Weitergabe von Wissen*, ed. by Johannes Fried and Michael Stolleis (Frankfurt: Campus, 2009), pp. 12–42

Fried, Johannes, and Ernst-Dieter Hehl, ed., *Weltdeutungen und Weltreligionen, 600 bis 1500*, WBG Weltgeschichte, 3 (Darmstadt: Wissenschaftliche Buchgesellschaft, 2010)

Friedrich, Udo, 'Ältere deutsche Literatur', in *Germanistik als Kulturwissenschaft. Eine Einführung in neue Theoriekonzepte*, ed. by Claudia Benthien and Hans Rudolf Velten (Reinbek bei Hamburg: Rowohlt, 2002), pp. 83–102

Grinin, Leonid, and Andrey Korotayev, *Great Divergence and Great Convergence: A Global Perspective* (Cham: Springer, 2015)

Gruzinski, Serge, *The Eagle and the Dragon: Globalization and European Dreams of Conquest in China and America in the Sixteenth Century* (London: Polity, 2014)

Headley, John M., *The Europeanization of the World: On the Origins of Human Rights and Democracy* (Princeton: Princeton University Press, 2008)

Heng, Geraldine, *The Invention of Race in the European Middle Ages* (Cambridge: Cambridge University Press, 2018)

Herbers, Klaus, and Nikolas Jaspert, ed., *Grenzräume und Grenzüberschreitungen im Vergleich. Der Osten und der Westen des mittelalterlichen Lateineuropa*, Europa im Mittelalter, 7 (Berlin: Akademie, 2007)

Herren, Madeleine, Martin Rüesch, and Christiane Sibille, ed., *Transcultural History: Theories, Methods, Sources*, Transcultural Research — Heidelberg Studies on Asia and Europe in a Global Context (Heidelberg: Springer, 2012)

Herzog, Tamar, 'Identities and Processes of Identification in the Atlantic World', in *The Oxford Handbook of the Atlantic World, c. 1450–1850*, ed. by Nicholas Canny and Philip Morgan (Oxford: Oxford University Press, 2011), pp. 480–95

Hiatt, Alfred, *Terra incognita: Mapping the Antipodes Before 1600* (London: British Library, 2008)

Hirschi, Caspar, *The Origins of Nationalism: An Alternative History from Ancient Rome to Early Modern Germany* (Cambridge: Cambridge University Press, 2011)

Holmes, Catherine, and Naomi Standen, ed., *The Global Middle Ages*, Past & Present Supplement, 13 (Oxford: Oxford University Press, 2018)

Internal Review of the Government's Policy on Requirements to Provide DNA in Visa and Asylum Cases, <https://assets.publishing.service.gov.uk/government/uploads/system/uploads/attachment_data/file/751546/DNA-REVIEW.pdf> [accessed 21 June 2021]

Jones, Chris, Christoph Mauntel, and Klaus Oschema, ed., *A World of Empires: Claiming and Assigning Imperial Authority in the Middle Ages* (Los Angeles: Sage, 2017 [*The Medieval History Journal*, 20,2])

Jones, Eric, *The European Miracle: Environments, Economies and Geopolitics in the History of Europe and Asia*, 3rd edn (Cambridge: Cambridge University Press, 2003)

Kassam, Ashifa, 'Canada Uses DNA and Ancestry Sites to Check Migrants' Identity', *The Guardian*, 30 July 2018, <https://www.theguardian.com/world/2018/jul/30/canada-uses-dna-and-ancestry-sites-to-check-migrants-identity> [accessed 21 June 2021]

Kilgus, Laura, Paula Simon, and Sara Tot, 'Conference Report "Order into Action: How Large-Scale Concepts of World-Order determine Practices in the Premodern World", 10.11.2016–12.11.2016 Heidelberg', *H-Soz-Kult*, 24 February 2017, <https://www.hsozkult.de/conferencereport/id/tagungsberichte-7019> [accessed 21 June 2021]

Kleinschmidt, Harald, *Perception and Action in Medieval Europe* (Woodbridge: Boydell, 2005)

Kline, Naomi Reed, *Maps of Medieval Thought: The Hereford Paradigm* (Woodbridge: Boydell, 2001)

Klopprogge, Axel, *Ursprung und Ausprägung des abendländischen Mongolenbildes im 13. Jahrhundert. Ein Versuch zur Ideengeschichte des Mittelalters*, Asiatische Forschungen, 122 (Wiesbaden: Harrassowitz, 1993)

Kuhn, Thomas S., *The Structure of Scientific Revolutions*, 4th edn (Chicago: University of Chicago Press, 2012)

Latour, Bruno, and Steve Woolgar, *Laboratory Life: The Social Construction of Scientific Facts* (Beverly Hills: Sage, 1979)

Lilley, Keith D., ed., *Mapping Medieval Geographies: Geographical Encounters in the Latin West and Beyond, 300–1600* (Cambridge: Cambridge University Press, 2013)

Lipphardt, Veronika, 'Vertane Chancen? Die aktuelle politische Debatte um Erweiterte DNA-Analysen in Ermittlungsverfahren', *Berichte zur Wissenschaftsgeschichte*, 41 (2018), 279–301

Markschies, Christoph and others, ed., *Atlas der Weltbilder*, Interdisziplinäre Arbeitsgruppen: Forschungsberichte, 25 (Berlin: Akademie, 2011)

Mauntel, Christoph, 'Fra Mauro's View on the Boring Question of Continents', *Peregrinations: Journal of Medieval Art and Architecture* 673 (2018), 54–77, <https://digital.kenyon.edu/perejournal/vol6/iss3/4> [accessed 21 June 2021]

——, 'Linking Seas and Lands in Medieval Geographic Thinking during the Crusades and the Discovery of the Atlantic World', in *Entre mers — outre mer: Spaces, Modes and Agents of Indo-Mediterranean Connectivity*, ed. by Nikolas Jaspert and Sebastian Kolditz (Heidelberg: Heidelberg University Publishing, 2018), pp. 107–28, <https://heiup.uni-heidelberg.de/heiup/catalog/book/355> [accessed 21 June 2021]

Mauntel, Christoph, and Jenny Rahel Oesterle, 'Wasserwelten. Ozeane und Meere in der mittelalterlichen christlichen und arabischen Kosmographie', in *Wasser in der mittelalterlichen Kultur / Water in Medieval Culture: Gebrauch — Wahrnehmung — Symbolik / Uses, Perceptions, and Symbolism*, ed. by Gerlinde Huber-Rebenich, Christian Rohr, and Michael Stolz, Das Mittelalter. Beihefte 4 (Berlin/Boston: de Gruyter, 2017), pp. 59–77

Mauntel, Christoph, Klaus Oschema, Jean-Charles Ducène, and Martin Hofmann, 'Mapping Continents, Inhabited Quarters, and The Four Seas: Divisions of the World and the Ordering of Spaces in Latin-Christian, Arabic-Islamic, and Chinese Cartography, 12th–16th Centuries — a Critical Survey and Analysis', *Journal of Transcultural Medieval Studies*, 5,2 (2018), 295–376

McClure, Julia, 'A New Politics of the Middle Ages: A Global Middle Ages for a Global Modernity', *History Compass*, 13,11 (2015), 610–19

Merisalo, Outi, ed., *Frontiers in the Middle Ages*, Textes et études du Moyen Âge, 25 (Louvain-la-Neuve: Fédération Internationale des Instituts d'Études Médiévales, 2006)

Mitterauer, Michael, *Warum Europa? Mittelalterliche Grundlagen eines Sonderwegs* (Munich: C. H. Beck, 2003)

Morris, Ian, *Why the West Rules — For Now: The Patterns of History and What They Reveal About the Future* (London: Profile, 2011)

Muldoon, James, 'Papal Responsibility for the Infidel: Another Look at Alexander VI's "Inter Caetera"', *Catholic Historical Review*, 64,2 (1978), 168–84

Oschema, Klaus, *Bilder von Europa im Mittelalter*, Mittelalter-Forschungen, 43 (Ostfildern: Jan Thorbecke, 2013)

——, 'An Irish Making of Europe (Early and High Middle Ages)', in *'A Fantastic and Abstruse Latinity?' Hiberno-Continental Cultural and Literary Interactions in the Middle Ages*, ed. by Wolfram R. Keller and Dagmar Schlüter, Studien und Texte zur Keltologie, 12 (Münster: Nodus, 2017), pp. 12–30

——, 'De l'universalisme périmé au refuge de la chrétienté: l'Europe de Philippe de Mézières', in *Philippe de Mézières et l'Europe: Nouvelle histoire, nouveaux espaces, nouveaux langages*, ed. by Joël Blanchard and Renate Blumenfeld-Kosinski (Geneva: Droz, 2017), pp. 27–50

——, 'Trouver l'Europe en Asie? Expériences et réactions des auteurs latins aux contacts avec le monde extra-européen (XIIIe siècle)', in *Histoire monde, jeux d'échelles et espaces connectés*, ed. by Société des Historiens Médiévistes dans l'Enseignement Supérieur Public (Paris: Éditions de la Sorbonne, 2017), pp. 237–50

Peters, Michael A., and Tina A. C. Besley, 'Social Exclusion/Inclusion: Foucault's Analytics of Exclusion, the Political Ecology of Social Inclusion and the Legitimation of Inclusive Education', *Open Review of Educational Research*, 1,1 (2014), 99–115

Pomeranz, Kenneth, *The Great Divergence: China, Europe, and the Making of the Modern World Economy* (Princeton: Princeton University Press, 2000)

Quinn, Gerard, Aisling de Paor, and Peter Blanck, ed., *Genetic Discrimination: Transatlantic Perspectives on the Case for a European-Level Legal Response* (London: Routledge, 2014)

Randles, William G. L., 'La Navigabilité de l'Atlantique au Moyen Âge selon les universitaires et selon les marins', in *L'Europe et l'océan au Moyen Âge. Contribution à l'histoire de la navigation*, ed. by Société des Historiens Médiévistes de l'Enseignement Supérieur (Nantes: CID, 1988), pp. 211–16

——, 'The Evaluation of Columbus' "India" Project by Portuguese and Spanish Cosmographers in the Light of the Geographical Science of the Period', *Imago Mundi*, 42 (1990), 50–64

Reichert, Folker, *Das Bild der Welt im Mittelalter* (Darmstadt: WBG, 2013)

Reinhard, Wolfgang, ed., *Empires and Encounters, 1350–1750*, Harvard History of the World (Cambridge, MA: Harvard University Press, 2015)

Ruotsala, Antti, *Europeans and Mongols in the Middle of the Thirteenth Century, Encountering the Other*, Suomalaisen Tiedeakatemian Toimituksia, Humaniora, 314 (Helsinki: Finnish Academy of Science and Letters, 2001)

Russel, Jeffrey B., *Inventing the Flat Earth: Columbus and Modern Historians* (Westport: Praeger, 1991)

Schmieder, Felicitas, 'L'evoluzione del questionario per l'osservazione empirica e il suo impiego', in *Religiosità e civiltà. Conoscenze, confronti, influssi reciproci tra le religioni (secoli X–XIV)*, ed. by Giancarlo Andenna (Milan: Vita e pensiero, 2013), pp. 227–38

Schneidmüller, Bernd, and Stefan Weinfurter, 'Ordnungskonfigurationen. Die Erprobung eines Forschungsdesigns', in *Ordnungskonfigurationen im hohen Mittelalter*, ed. by Bernd Schneidmüller and Stefan Weinfurter, Vorträge und Forschungen, 64 (Ostfildern: Jan Thorbecke, 2006), pp. 7–18

Simek, Rudolf, *Heaven and Earth in the Middle Ages: The Physical World Before Columbus* (Woodbridge: Boydell, 1996)

Stevens, Wesley M., 'The Figure of the Earth in Isidore's "De natura rerum"', *Isis*, 71 (1980), 268–77

Tuchman, Barbara, *A 'Distant Mirror': The Calamitous 14th Century* (New York: Alfred Knopf, 1978)

UNHCR Statistical Yearbook 2016, <http://www.unhcr.org/statistics/country/5a8ee0387/unhcr-statistical-yearbook-2016-16th-edition.html> [accessed 21 June 2021]

Vignaud, Henry, *Toscanelli and Columbus. The Letter and Chart of Toscanelli. A Critical Study* (London: Sands & Co., 1902)

White, Philip L., 'Globalization and the Mythology of the Nation State', in *Global History: Interactions Between the Universal and the Local*, ed. by A. G. Hopkins (Basingstoke: Palgrave, 2006), pp. 257–84

DANIEL G. KÖNIG

Dār al-ḥarb vs *terra paganorum*

On the Practical Implications of Circumscribing the Sphere of the 'Infidels'

This chapter analyses how two large-scale concepts of premodern world order were translated into concrete action. It compares the medieval use of two monotheistic concepts that define spaces characterized by their adherence to a different religious world-view — the Arabic-Islamic concept of *dār al-ḥarb* and the Latin-Christian concept of *terra paganorum*. Before delving into the intricacies of comparison, it is necessary to discuss if and to which degree such a comparison is legitimate by taking into account both terms' composite structure, semantic content, potential alternatives, research history, and overall historical significance.

The Arabic term *dār al-ḥarb* is often translated literally as 'the abode of war', whereas the Latin term *terra paganorum* translates roughly as 'the land of the infidels/heathens'. Both compound terms are neither conterminous nor congruent: *dār* denominates an enclosed space, *terra* can refer to the earth, vast expanses of land, or landed property; *ḥarb* describes the human action of waging war, *pagani* a group characterized by a non-monotheistic world-view and the practice of idolatry.[1] A comparison of both terms only seems legitimate, if they are understood with reference to their respective antonyms — 'the abode of Islam' (*dār al-islām*) in the case of *dār al-ḥarb*, 'the land of the Christians' (*terra Christianorum*) in the case of *terra paganorum*.

1 The Latin term *paganus* originally meant 'rural' and had a clear tinge of backwardness and lack of sophistication. In its Christianized form, it retained these derogative aspects, but, of course, acquired a strong religious connotation. The equation of rurality with non-monotheism probably came up when ancient and Late Antique Christianity, a decidedly urban religion since the proselytism of the apostles, began to spread into a countryside marked by a wide range of cults associated — from a Christian perspective — with idolatrous practices and the lack of a sophisticated theoretical framework, cf. Chuvin, 'Sur l'origine', pp. 7–16; Wirth, 'Paganus', col. 1624; Harmening, *Superstitio*.

Daniel G. König (daniel.g.koenig@uni-konstanz.de), Chair of the History of Religions, University of Konstanz, Germany

Order into Action: How Large-Scale Concepts of World-Order determine Practices in the Premodern World, ed. by Klaus Oschema and Christoph Mauntel, CURSOR 40 (Turnhout: Brepols, 2022), pp. 37–69
BREPOLS PUBLISHERS 10.1484/M.CURSOR-EB.5.123843

It becomes clear that both terms are made up of a similar set of binary elements: a spatial term followed by what the antonym allows us to define as an indicator of religious alterity. The particular combination of spatial and ideological components in *dār al-ḥarb* and *terra paganorum* exhibits parallel characteristics: both terms push religious alterity to a certain extreme by connoting it with warfare in the case of *dār al-ḥarb*, and with religious error in the case of *terra paganorum*. Moreover, they do not refer to a particular manifestation of religious thought and practice, e.g. Christianity or Islam, but cover a range of religious alterities.

Medieval Arabic and Latin both feature alternative compound terms that equally combine a spatial term with an indicator of religious alterity. In the case of Arabic, the expression 'lands of the Christians' (*bilād al-naṣārā*) focuses on one particular form of religious alterity, whereas 'land of the enemy' (*arḍ al-ʿadūw*) lacks a religious component if divorced from its context. The terms 'lands of the unbelievers' (*bilād al-kafara*), 'abode of unbelief' (*dār al-kufr*), and 'abode of polytheism' (*dār al-širk*) are generally treated as synonyms of *dār al-ḥarb* in medieval Arabic-Islamic sources, but — in my admittedly rather impressionistic assessment — appear more often in narrative sources, have less legal connotations, and, consequently, seem to be of minor conceptual value. Especially with regard to their research history, treated further below, they are of less relevance for the reconstruction of premodern concepts of world order, whereas *dār al-ḥarb* undoubtedly constitutes the most encompassing and historically most influential concept of spatialized religious alterity produced within the Muslim orbit.

In the case of Latin, there seems to exist no alternative term to *terra paganorum* that could be fully equated with *dār al-ḥarb*. Apart from the fact that they lack a compound structure, the terms *paganitas* and *gentilitas* do not always feature a clear-cut spatial dimension (e.g. if translated as 'pagandom'/'heathendom'), since they can also apply to groups of people and entire religious systems (if translated as 'pagans'/'heathens' or 'paganism'/'heathenism'). The alternative 'land of the Saracens' (*terra Saracenorum*) focuses on one particular form of alterity, that has both ethnic and religious connotations.[2] The compound terms *terra infidelium* and *partes infidelium*, which fulfil exactly the same requirements as *terra paganorum*, did not procure the same number of results during preparatory research in the most pertinent databases and thus seem to be less important.[3]

---

2 The Latin term *Saraceni* is generally used for Muslims in medieval Latin-Christian sources. Although often associated with Abraham's wife Sara, the term is much more ambiguous than its frequent terminological alternatives in medieval Latin sources, i.e. *Mauri* (from the African region Mauretania), *Ismaelitae* (from Abraham's son Ishmael) and *Agareni* (from Ishmael's mother Hagar). On alternative explanations for the etymology of the term *Saraceni*, see Graf, 'Saracens', pp. 14–15; Shahîd and Bosworth, 'Saracens', p. 27; Hoyland, *Arabia*, p. 235; Tolan, *Saracens*, pp. 10–11.

3 Even the phrase *in partibus infidelium* could only be located in one medieval source, i.e. by

In sum, *dār al-ḥarb* and *terra paganorum* seem to represent the best alternatives for comparison because they outdo terminological alternatives in terms of their composite structure, semantic and conceptual content, and relevance. We must acknowledge, however, that their respective research history and overall historical significance differs considerably. *Dār al-ḥarb* had already reached a much higher degree of conceptualization than *terra paganorum* in the medieval period. The concept is often depicted as representing the Muslim world-view *par excellence* and it is well known among those who are interested in the question how the Islamic sphere conceptualized its relations to the non-Muslim sphere. As a consequence, it has elicited scholarly and non-scholarly comment from various sides, and even boasts an entry in the highly respected *Encyclopaedia of Islam*.[4] It also continues to play a role in contemporary reflections on the relations between Muslim and non-Muslim spheres: Islamophobic polemics, in particular, regard it as the epitome of an expansionist world-view allegedly characteristic of Islam.[5] Modern Muslim scholarship has considered it to be influential enough to deserve elaborate treatment in the debate around issues related to the status of Muslims in contemporary Europe.[6]

Research on the concept of *terra paganorum*, on the other hand, is decidedly poorer. The factors that account for this discrepancy are manifold and the notion itself seems to have played an important role only for a limited time, namely the twelfth and thirteenth centuries, i.e. a period that was marked by different forms of Latin-Christian expansionism. Then it ceased to be of relevance in a Latin-Christian tradition and was increasingly side-lined by processes of secularization and vernacularization that involved both a general loss of appeal of medieval Latin-Christian concepts and the replacement of Latin by national vernaculars in all fields of intellectual endeavour. As

---

Pope Hormisdas I (sed. 514–23), *ep.* LXX *ad possessorem episcopum*. Regular use of this phrase seems to postdate the Tridentine Council (1545–63). It pertains to the title of titular bishops expelled from former Christian territories by non-Christian rulers, e.g. Muslims or Mongols, and is associated with the activities of the *Congregatio de propaganda fidei*, cf. *De episcopo titulari*, ed. by Andreucci, pp. 1–4.

4 Abel, 'Dār al-Ḥarb', p. 126. See the most recent and differentiated treatment in Calasso, 'Constructing and Deconstructing', which forms part of the first entire volume by various specialists on the subject: Calasso and Lancioni, ed., *Dār al-islām / dār al-ḥarb*.

5 Compare the exemplary literature cited in König, 'Wie eine Religion', p. 12.

6 See the discussion of the term in Ramadan, *To Be a European Muslim*, pp. 99, 123, 126, and throughout. Ramadan argues that the conceptual dichotomy of *dār al-islām* and *dār al-ḥarb*, which he regards as a typical feature of medieval Muslim legal thought, cannot be upheld in view of the fact that, apart from minor restrictions, contemporary Western societies grant Muslims the possibility of freely exercising their religion. This, Ramadan argues, forbids classifying these societies as *dār al-ḥarb*. However, since Western societies do not function according to Islamic law, they cannot be regarded as *dār al-islām* either. Ramadan proposes the new category *dār al-šahāda*, i.e. 'the abode of testimony', which can be used to classify societies in which Muslims can freely bear testimony to their faith. Also see Albrecht, *Dār al-Islām Revisited*.

opposed to *dār al-ḥarb*, the term *terra paganorum* is poorly documented and, in consequence, has hardly received any scholarly recognition. To my knowledge, not a single encyclopaedia entry or article has been dedicated to this compound term so far. Confined to the dustbin of medieval history, it has never elicited any extra-academic debate. This blatant discrepancy raises two important questions: why did one religious sphere develop a much stronger and historically much more influential concept of spatialized religious alterity than the other? And: does this discrepancy imply that the sphere boasting the more developed and more influential concept also excelled in terms of putting this concept into practice?

Based on these preliminary terminological and methodological reflections and keeping these two questions in mind, I will first describe each concept separately, focusing on its emergence, documentation, and use, including the question if and how each concept elicited concrete action. In a second step, I will then compare these findings. Due to the extent of the endeavour, this chapter can only proffer initial results. A complete analysis of the use of *dār al-ḥarb* would demand considering several centuries of juridical reflections and elaborations documented in hundreds of volumes. To provide an insight into its conceptual qualities as well as its potential field of application, I chose to focus on how the concept was used and implemented in one particular region and time-frame, i.e. Muslim al-Andalus of the eleventh century. Since research on *terra paganorum* is largely lacking, I collected and contextualized as many references as possible, which I found in digitalized text collections, including *Patrologia Latina, Documenta catholica omnia, Monumenta Germaniae Historica*, digitalized volumes of the *Rolls Series*, as well as a number of legal texts produced in the border zones of Latin Christianity. Since this somewhat asymmetrical procedure can only procure tentative results, the concluding part of the chapter, dedicated to the comparison of the analysed concepts, can only formulate hypotheses, which more extensive research will have to confirm or invalidate.

Dār al-ḥarb

Emergence and Documentation

The term *dār al-ḥarb* is not mentioned in the Qur'ān.[7] Thus, from a dogmatic point of view, it cannot count as a concept invested with divine authority. To my knowledge, its use is first attested in al-Buḫārī's (d. 256/870) collection of the sayings and deeds of the prophet Muḥammad. Since it only forms part of a chapter heading, the term is only used to structure the sayings and deeds attributed to Muḥammad, but not put into the latter's mouth.[8]

7 However, see Villano, 'Qur'ānic Foundations'.

8 Al-Buḫārī, *Ǧāmi' al-ṣaḥīḥ*, ed. by al-Ḫaṭīb and 'Abd al-Bāqī, vol. II, book 56 'kitāb al-ǧihād

The term probably first appeared in Islamic normative literature of the eighth and ninth centuries. In juridical works, *dār al-ḥarb* forms part of a larger group of legal concepts that denote different kinds of relations between the Muslim and the non-Muslim sphere. Whereas *dār al-ṣulḥ* is used to define a territory appropriated by the Muslims following a surrender agreement (*ṣulḥ*), the terms *dār al-hudna* and *dār al-ʿahd* generally refer to territories under non-Muslim rule that possess a peace treaty (*hudna, ʿahd*) with a Muslim polity.[9] Finally, *dār al-islām* constitutes an antonym of *dār al-ḥarb,* since it circumscribes the socio-political sphere subject to Islamic norms.

Intra-Textual Use

Since it is impossible to provide a full overview of the term's use over the centuries, the following paragraphs will focus on a single work of Islamic jurisdiction written in the frontier and contact zone between the Arabic-Islamic and the Latin-Christian sphere on the Iberian Peninsula during the eleventh century.[10] I will discuss later whether we can regard this work as representative of the Muslim juridical tradition, and if we can use it as historical evidence for Christian-Muslim relations on the Iberian Peninsula.

The *Kitāb al-Muḥallā fī šarḥ al-maǧallā bi-l-ḥuǧǧaǧ wa-l-āṯār* ('The Adorned Book that Explains What Has Been Revealed With the Help of Arguments and Evidence') was written around 440/1048 by Ibn Ḥazm of Córdoba (d. 456/1064). It is made up of eleven volumes, each consisting of around 300 to 600 pages. All in all, it deals with 2308 juridical issues or questions, called *masāʾil* in Arabic.[11]

Dār al-ḥarb (or its equivalents *arḍ al-ḥarb, dār al-kufr*) is only mentioned in fifty-three *masāʾil.* Its distribution within the work indicates, however, that the issue of how to deal with the *dār al-ḥarb* touches upon a large range of topics that are relevant to Islamic law. It is associated with the normative frameworks of praying (*al-ṣalāh*), inhumation (*al-ǧanāʾiz*), alms (*al-zakāh*), fasting (*al-ṣiyām*), jihād (*al-ǧihād*), debts and insolvency (*al-mudāyināt wa-l-taflīs*), recovery of abandoned land and distribution of land (*iḥyāʾ al-mawāt wa-l-iqṭāʿ*), selling (*al-buyūʿ*), manumission of slaves (*al-ʿitq*), heritage (*al-mawarīṯ*), testaments (*al-waṣāyā*), condemnations (*al-aqḍiyya*), marriage (*al-nikāḥ*) and divorce (*al-ṭalāq*), capital crimes and

---

wa-l-siyar', chapter heading 180, ḥadīth 3058, p. 375: 'bāb iḏā aslama qawm fī dār al-ḥarb wa-lahum māl wa-arḍūn fa-hiya lahum' [subchapter: If people in the *dār al-ḥarb* embrace Islam, and possess money or land, it belongs to them [i.e. remains in their keeping]].

9 Abel, 'Dār al-Ḥarb', p. 126; İnalcik, 'Dār al-ʿAhd', p. 116; Macdonald and Abel, 'Dār al-Ṣulḥ', p. 131; Khadduri, 'Hudna', p. 547.

10 See Fierro and Molina, 'Some Notes', for an overview on the role of the concept of *dār al-ḥarb* on the early medieval Iberian Peninsula.

11 The edition was produced over a period of several years by several editors: Ibn Ḥazm, *Kitāb al-Muḥallā* I–VI, ed. by Šākir; VII, ed. by al-Ǧazīrī; VIII–XI, ed. by al-Dimašqī. On the work see Ljamai, *Ibn Ḥazm et la polémique*, pp. 75–78.

their compensation (*al-dimā' wa-l-qaṣṣāṣ wa-l-diyāt*), as well as Qur'ānic punishments (*al-ḥudūd*). While it is not possible to deal with all these topics in detail, a survey of the different *masā'il* allows us to distil three major forms of understanding the term.

First, the term *dār al-ḥarb* is understood as a sphere to be conquered. This becomes clear from its use in *masā'il* that describe different forms or even methods of expansion. In Ibn Ḥazm's interpretation, Islamic law prescribes that children who have been captured in the *dār al-ḥarb*, or who are the offspring of illicit concubinage (including rape) with women from the *dār al-ḥarb*, should be taken care of and educated as Muslims.[12] He asserts that Muslims have a right to claim abandoned land in the *dār al-ḥarb*.[13] He maintains that Islamic law grants amnesty to all persons coming from the *dār al-ḥarb* who submit to the framework of Islamic society either as Jews and Christians or by converting to Islam, and legally acknowledges all their possessions in the *dār al-ḥarb*.[14] There can be no doubt that all these norms serve, in one way or another, to enlarge the Muslim sphere either in terms of human resources or in terms of geographic extension.

Ibn Ḥazm even claims that every kind of violence against inhabitants of the *dār al-ḥarb* and their possessions is licit.[15] Other Muslim jurists did not necessarily share this rather extreme view. In *mas'ala* 928, for example, Ibn Ḥazm explicitly argues against Muslim jurists who condemn every form of violence against civilians in the *dār al-ḥarb* and only regard violence against combatants as licit. He asserts:

> Concerning their [i.e. the other jurists'] statement that we [only] kill those who fight us: this is wrong. For we fight everyone until death who is called to Islam until he believes or pays the poll tax (*ǧizya*) if he belongs to the people of the book, as God most High has decreed in the Qur'ān.[16]

Addressing the question as to what may be received from inhabitants of the non-Muslim sphere (*ahl al-ḥarb*), *mas'ala* 936 then shows that Ibn Ḥazm regards the *dār al-ḥarb* as a kind of self-service pillaging ground created by God for the Muslims:

---

12 Ibn Ḥazm, *Kitāb al-Muḥallā*, VII, ed. by al-Ǧazīrī, mas'ala 935, p. 309.

13 Ibn Ḥazm, *Kitāb al-Muḥallā*, VIII, ed. by al-Dimašqī, mas'ala 1348, p. 233.

14 Ibn Ḥazm, *Kitāb al-Muḥallā*, XI, ed. by al-Dimašqī, mas'ala 2170, p. 136; VII, ed. by al-Ǧazīrī, mas'ala 937, pp. 309–11.

15 Ibn Ḥazm, *Kitāb al-Muḥallā*, VII, ed. by al-Ǧazīrī, mas'ala 924, p. 294.

16 Ibn Ḥazm, *Kitāb al-Muḥallā*, VII, ed. by al-Ǧazīrī, mas'ala 928, p. 298: 'ammā qawluhum: innamā naqtul [*sic*] man qātala fa-bāṭil bal naqtul [*sic*] kull man yud'ā ilā l-islām minhum ḥattā yu'min aw yu'addī l-ǧizya in kāna kitābiyan kamā amara Allāh ta'ālā fī l-Qur'ān [...]'. Ibn Ḥazm alludes to the exhortation to kill in Qur'ān 9:5 without contextualizing this verse and without considering that this particular verse is framed by various verses, which call for a different and much more differentiated treatment of non-Muslims.

> According to the word of God: 'He has made you heirs to their lands, their houses and their riches' [*Qur'ān* 33:27], God has created them so that we may inherit from them. The transfer of this heritage does not take place except by seizure and appropriation, for if not, nothing would have been inherited that our hands have not been able to seize. For God most High has created their riches for the pillager, not for those who do not pillage them.[17]

Engaging with other passages that are less aggressive, we are confronted with a second way of understanding the term *dār al-ḥarb*. The relevant *masā'il* show that, even in a juridical work encouraging aggression against the non-Muslim sphere, the latter was actually regarded as highly entangled with neighbouring Muslim societies.

Thus, Ibn Ḥazm accepts that diplomatic and commercial relations exist with the *dār al-ḥarb*, that security is to be granted to all envoys and merchants, and that Muslim envoys may even receive presents from the population of the *dār al-ḥarb*. In his opinion, problems only arise in particular situations. This is the case when foreign envoys arrive with slaves that were previously subjects of Islamic society; if presents brought by foreign envoys previously belonged to Muslims or non-Muslims subject to Islamic law; if Muslim merchants are mistreated; or if they dare to export strategically relevant products such as arms and horses to the *dār al-ḥarb*.[18]

Apart from diplomacy and commerce, the *Kitāb al-Muḥallā* mentions other forms of relations between Muslims and members of the *dār al-ḥarb* that call for juridical regulation. Thus, Ibn Ḥazm addresses the issue of what happens if a person from the *dār al-ḥarb*, i.e. *al-kāfir al-ḥarbī*, dies during his or her stay in a Muslim-ruled society.[19] Discussing what is to be done, if a Muslim kills a person from the *dār al-ḥarb* who possesses a security guarantee (i.e. *al-musta'man*) within the *dār al-islām*, he decrees that the Muslim should be punished, but not sentenced to death, as not to give a Muslim life for the life of a non-Muslim.[20] He asserts that non-Muslim slaves visiting the *dār al-ḥarb* will be granted instant freedom if they convert to Islam before their master does.[21] He considers marriages of non-Muslim captives from the *dār al-ḥarb* legally valid, regardless of the fact if their spouse has remained behind

17 Ibn Ḥazm, *Kitāb al-Muḥallā*, VII, ed. by al-Ğazīrī, mas'ala 936, p. 309: 'bi-qawl Allāh: "awraṯakum arḍahum wa-diyārahum wa-amwālahum" [cf. Qur'ān 33:27]. fa-ğa'ala Allāh ta'ālā lahum ilā an awraṯanā iyyāhā. wa-l-tawrīṯ lā yakūn illā bi-l-aḫḏ wa-l-tamalluk wa-illā fa-lam yūraṯ ba'd mā lā taqdir aydaynā 'alayhi, innamā ğa'ala Allāh ta'ālā amwālahum li-l-ġānim lahā lā li-kull man lam yaġnimuhā'.

18 Ibn Ḥazm, *Kitāb al-Muḥallā*, VII, ed. by al-Ğazīrī, mas'ala 932, p. 306; VII, mas'ala 936, p. 309; VII, mas'ala 962, p. 349; IX, ed. by al-Dimašqī, mas'ala 1568, p. 65.

19 Ibn Ḥazm, *Kitāb al-Muḥallā*, V, ed. by Šākir, mas'ala 564, p. 117.

20 Ibn Ḥazm, *Kitāb al-Muḥallā*, X, ed. by al-Dimašqī, mas'ala 2011, p. 348; X, mas'ala 2012, p. 355.

21 Ibn Ḥazm, *Kitāb al-Muḥallā*, VII, ed. by al-Ğazīrī, mas'ala 943, p. 318.

in the *dār al-ḥarb* or not.[22] Finally, he also accepts the possibility of freeing a non-Muslim slave who resides in the *dār al-ḥarb*.[23]

One could regard the regulations put down in the *Kitāb al-Muḥallā* as a very basic form of premodern, unilaterally proclaimed 'international' law. In spite of Ibn Ḥazm's aggressive stance, he clearly regarded the existence of a non-Muslim sphere as a reality that had to be dealt with in legal terms. Consequently, the work addresses a broad range of legal issues arising from the interaction of two different systems of society functioning according to different norms.

However, relations between these two societal systems were certainly deemed problematic. Thus, turning to the third way of understanding the *dār al-ḥarb*, we repeatedly find passages describing the latter as a sphere that poses a threat to Muslim norms. Here, interaction with the *dār al-ḥarb* is subjected to certain restrictions that have the aim of protecting the Muslim sphere: it is forbidden to take a Qur'ān to the *dār al-ḥarb* in order to avoid its appropriation by non-Muslims;[24] even more important is the prohibition against exporting strategically relevant merchandise to the *dār al-ḥarb*.[25] In addition, many *masā'il* deal with problems resulting from hostile relations with the *dār al-ḥarb*. The presence of Muslim captives[26] and stolen Muslim possessions[27] in the *dār al-ḥarb* raises problematic questions, for example whether it is licit to buy back Muslim possessions that have been stolen by an inhabitant of the *dār al-ḥarb*.[28] In spite of these problems, Ibn Ḥazm believes that Muslims are allowed to live in the *dār al-ḥarb*, under the condition that they abstain from aggression against Muslim societies.[29]

Although Ibn Ḥazm does not forbid Muslim residence in the *dār al-ḥarb*, the *Kitāb al-Muḥallā* emphasizes that, from a Muslim legal point of view, the latter is deficient. Because its system and societal rhythm are not geared towards Muslim norms, Muslims — especially captives — have difficulties upholding their ritual obligations, e.g. of fasting or praying.[30] In view of these difficulties, he discusses whether travelling in the *dār al-ḥarb* justifies reducing the number of obligatory prayers.[31]

---

22 Ibn Ḥazm, *Kitāb al-Muḥallā*, x, ed. by al-Dimašqī, mas'ala 1940, pp. 132–33.

23 Ibn Ḥazm, *Kitāb al-Muḥallā*, ix, ed. by al-Dimašqī, mas'ala 1672, p. 208.

24 Ibn Ḥazm, *Kitāb al-Muḥallā*, i, ed. by Šākir, mas'ala 116, p. 83.

25 Ibn Ḥazm, *Kitāb al-Muḥallā*, vii, ed. by al-Ǧazīrī, mas'ala 962, p. 349; ix, ed. by al-Dimašqī, mas'ala 1568, p. 65.

26 Ibn Ḥazm, *Kitāb al-Muḥallā*, vi, ed. by Šākir, mas'ala 769, p. 261; vii, ed. by al-Ǧazīrī, mas'ala 932, p. 306; vii, mas'ala 935, p. 309.

27 Ibn Ḥazm, *Kitāb al-Muḥallā*, vii, ed. by al-Ǧazīrī, mas'ala 931, pp. 300–02; vii, mas'ala 932, p. 306.

28 Ibn Ḥazm, *Kitāb al-Muḥallā*, viii, ed. by al-Dimašqī, mas'ala 1283, p. 178.

29 Ibn Ḥazm, *Kitāb al-Muḥallā*, xi, ed. by al-Dimašqī, mas'ala 2198, pp. 199–200. On the discussion of this question in Islamic jurisprudence see Abou El Fadl, 'Islamic Law', pp. 141–87.

30 Ibn Ḥazm, *Kitāb al-Muḥallā*, vi, ed. by Šākir, mas'ala 769, pp. 261–62.

31 Ibn Ḥazm, *Kitāb al-Muḥallā*, v, ed. by Šākir, mas'ala 515, pp. 26–27.

Extra-Textual Implementation?

Having established the role played by the concept of *dār al-ḥarb* within a single work of Islamic jurisdiction produced in eleventh-century al-Andalus, we can now turn to the issue of representativity. We must thus ask ourselves whether the concept played a noticeable role in the intellectual scene and the foreign politics of Muslim al-Andalus in the eleventh century, and if this concept was actually translated into action.

According to essentialist interpretations of Islam, the concept of *dār al-ḥarb* stands at the basis of all Muslim dealings with the non-Muslim sphere, regardless of time and space. The highly influential Orientalist, Bernard Lewis, for example, claimed the following:

> In the Muslim world view the basic division of mankind is into the House of Islam (*Dār al-Islām*) and the House of War (*Dār al-Ḥarb*) [...]. The logic of Islamic law, however, does not recognize the permanent existence of any other polity outside Islam. In time, in the Muslim view, all mankind will accept Islam or submit to Islamic rule. In the meantime, it is a religious duty of Muslims to struggle until this end is accomplished.[32]

It remains doubtful whether the term *dār al-ḥarb* can really be reduced to expansionist ambitions. The analysis of Ibn Ḥazm's work suggested that its theoretical scope is much wider. Moreover, a closer look at the environment in which the *Kitāb al-Muḥallā* was produced, i.e. the Iberian Peninsula of the eleventh century, suggests that the concept never played the dominant role that Lewis attributes to it.

Ibn Ḥazm admittedly held some rather extreme opinions supporting aggressive Muslim expansion into the non-Muslim sphere. However, he also felt compelled to justify his stance vis-à-vis other Muslim jurists who did not share his extreme views. In fact, detailed studies have shown that many contemporary Mālikī jurists actively refuted and even attacked Ibn Ḥazm's interpretation of Islamic law.[33] Maria Rosa Menocal even postulated that, because of these conflicts, Ibn Ḥazm 'died an angry old man, alienated from almost everyone around him, having written terribly vitriolic attacks on dozens of his contemporaries'.[34]

Moreover, Ibn Ḥazm wrote the *Kitāb al-Muḥallā* in a political context that was no longer characterized by uncontested Muslim hegemony on the Iberian Peninsula. In his lifetime, he witnessed and was personally affected by the breakdown of Umayyad rule and the fragmentation of the Umayyad caliphate into a plethora of petty kingdoms, which were soon exposed to the

---

32 Lewis, *Muslim Discovery*, pp. 60–61.

33 Arnaldez, *Grammaire et théologie*, p. 218; Kaddouri, 'Identificación de un manuscrito andalusí', pp. 299–320; Kaddouri, 'Kitāb al-Tanbīh', pp. 95–108; Kaddouri, 'Refutations of Ibn Ḥazm', pp. 539–99.

34 Menocal, *The Ornament of the World*, p. 117.

increasing pressure of northern Iberian Christians.[35] Thus, the *Kitāb al-Muḥallā* was not written from a position of Muslim strength, but rather by someone who 'died believing that the culture he had loved and defended was dead'.[36] Against this backdrop, Ibn Ḥazm's aggressive stance vis-à-vis the non-Muslim sphere acquires a rather exhortative quality and cannot simply be read as a description of contemporary realities.

Contemporary historiography, however, might create the impression that Ibn Ḥazm was not the only Muslim of eleventh-century al-Andalus who mourned a great past and endorsed violence against the *dār al-ḥarb* as a means to recover former greatness.[37] Ibn Ḥayyān's (d. 469/1076) multi-volume history of al-Andalus clearly glorifies past military victories against neighbouring Christian realms and repeatedly highlights infidel enmity vis-à-vis Muslim al-Andalus through its choice of terminology. Depicting events from the eighth to the tenth century, it regularly recounts instances in the history of al-Andalus in which Muslims fought with non-Muslims. In these passages, the latter inhabit an area defined alternatively or simultaneously as 'the abode of war' (*dār al-ḥarb*), 'the territory of the unbelievers' (*arḍ al-kafara*), 'the lands of the enemy' (*bilād* or *arḍ al-ʿadūw*),[38] or countries that 'God may destroy' (*dammarahā Allāh*).[39] Raids against these areas are classified as *ǧihād*,[40] rulers undertaking such campaigns described as 'striving in the path of God' (*muǧāhidan fī sabīl Allāh*).[41] In such instances, Muslims are confronted by 'the Frankish enemy — may God divide them' (*al-ʿadūw min al-Firanǧa — qaṣamahum Allāh*),[42] and battle 'the hosts of polytheism' (*ǧumūʿ al-širk*),[43]

---

35 On this political situation see Wasserstein, *Rise and Fall*; Scales, *Fall of the Caliphate*.

36 Menocal, *The Ornament of the World*, p. 117.

37 Clément, *Pouvoir et légitimité*, p. 14, suggests that Ibn Ḥayyān also regarded the transition from Umayyad al-Andalus to the taifa-principalities as a decline; Martínez Enamorado, 'Ibn Hayyan, el abanderado', p. 33.

38 Ibn Ḥayyān, *al-Muqtabis* II-1 / *Crónica*, ed. by Makkī and trans. by Corriente, AH 180, fol. 91v, p. 103 (AR), p. 24 (ES), on a raid against Calahorra in 80/796; AH 185, fol. 95v, p. 117 (AR), p. 37 (ES), on a raid against Álava de los Castillos in 185/801; AH 208, fol. 176v, p. 418 (AR), p. 282 (ES); Ibn Ḥayyān, *al-Muqtabis* II-2, ed. by Makkī, AH 249, fol. 265r, p. 318; AH 253, fol. 268r, p. 320, on raids against Álava de los Castillos in 208/823, 249/863 and 253/867.

39 Ibn Ḥayyān, *al-Muqtabas* V, ed. by Chalmeta and Corriente, AH 305, fol. 88r, p. 135, on a raid against Castile in 305/917; AH 312, fol. 121r, p. 189, on a raid against the Basques in 312/924.

40 Ibn Ḥayyān, *al-Muqtabis* III, ed. by al-ʿArabī, AH 280, p. 35, on a raid against Álava de los Castillos and Pamplona in 280/893.

41 Ibn Ḥayyān, *al-Muqtabis* V, ed. by Chalmeta and Corriente, AH 308, fols 103–04, pp. 159–61, on a raid of ʿAbd al-Raḥmān III against León and Pamplona in 308/920.

42 Ibn Ḥayyān, *al-Muqtabis* II-1, ed. by Makkī and trans. by Corriente, AH 185, fol. 95v, p. 116 (AR), p. 37 (ES), on the Frankish conquest of Barcelona in 185/801.

43 Ibn Ḥayyān, *al-Muqtabis* II-1 / *Crónica*, ed. by Makkī and trans. by Corriente, AH 186, fols 96r–v, pp. 118–19 (AR), pp. 38–39 (ES), on hostilities with Pamplona and Álava de los Castillos in 186/802.

'the unbelievers of Galicia' (*kafarat Ǧillīqiyya*),[44] or the 'infidel enemies of God' (*a'dā' Allāh al-kafara*).[45]

Such passages seem to confirm that, in spite of Ibn Ḥazm's abovementioned conflicts with the mainstream juridical establishment, his views of the *dār al-ḥarb* were not only widely shared, but actually constituted a principle that guided Muslim foreign policy on the Iberian Peninsula since its beginnings. Bettina Münzel has already shown, however, that Arabic-Islamic historiography from al-Andalus only uses aggressive terminology in passages dealing with concrete tensions.[46] In fact, Ibn Ḥayyān's history of al-Andalus never employs the term *dār al-ḥarb* in descriptions of peaceful relations with the non-Muslim sphere. The term does not appear, for example, when the Umayyad dissident 'Abd Allāh seeks refuge at the court of Charlemagne in 181/797,[47] when al-Ḥakam I and Charlemagne conclude a peace treaty in 191/806,[48] when Charles the Bald and Muḥammad I exchange several embassies,[49] when Borrell II of Barcelona sends envoys to al-Ḥakam II in 360/971,[50] or even when al-Ḥakam II sends spies to Galicia one year later.[51] Although Ibn Ḥayyān qualifies each Iberian-Christian or Frankish ruler as 'tyrant' (*al-ṭāġiya*) in his descriptions of peaceful relations, these passages lack the violent terminology used in connection with military hostilities. Ramiro II of León, who is regularly defined as 'enemy of God', constitutes the only exception, probably because he broke several peace treaties concluded between 321/933 and 328/940.[52]

What is also striking in connection with Ibn Ḥayyān's use of the term *dār al-ḥarb* and other aggressive terminology is that he solely applies it to the neighbouring Christian sphere on the Iberian Peninsula. To my knowledge, neither he nor any other contemporary Arabic-Islamic author from al-Andalus ever classifies the Frankish realm beyond the Pyrenees as *dār al-ḥarb*; instead, he always refers to it by using compounds of geo- and ethnographic terminology, e.g. *bilād al-Ifranǧ*, i.e. 'lands of the Franks'.[53] Can we conclude

---

44 Ibn Ḥayyān, *al-Muqtabis* II-1 / *Crónica*, ed. by Makkī and trans. by Corriente AH 191, fol. 100r, p. 131 (AR), p. 48 (ES), on a raid against Galicia in 192/807.

45 Ibn Ḥayyān, *al-Muqtabis* V, ed. by Chalmeta and Corriente, AH 312, fol. 121r, p. 189, on a raid against the Basques in 312/924.

46 Münzel, *Feinde, Nachbarn, Bündnispartner*.

47 Ibn Ḥayyān, *al-Muqtabis* II-1 / *Crónica*, ed. by Makkī and trans. by Corriente, AH 181, fol. 90r, p. 97 (AR), p. 20 (ES).

48 Ibn Ḥayyān, *al-Muqtabis* II-1 / *Crónica*, ed. by Makkī and trans. by Corriente, AH 191, fol. 100r, p. 130 (AR), p. 47 (ES).

49 Ibn Ḥayyān, *al-Muqtabis* II-2, ed. by Makkī, pp. 130–31.

50 Ibn Ḥayyān, *al-Muqtabis* VII, ed. by al-Ḥaǧǧī, AH 360, pp. 20–21.

51 Ibn Ḥayyān, *al-Muqtabis* VII, ed. by al-Ḥaǧǧī, AH 361, p. 76.

52 Ibn Ḥayyān, *al-Muqtabas* V, ed. by Chalmeta and Corriente, AH 323, p. 365; AH 324, p. 379; AH 328, pp. 450–51, 467; AH 330, pp. 483–84.

53 See König, *Arabic-Islamic Views*, pp. 192–99. Among the works analysed in the indicated passages, only Ibn Ḥabīb (d. 238/853) defines the Frankish sphere as 'land of the enemy' (*arḍ al-'adūw*) in connection with the earliest Muslim raids beyond the Pyrenees, whereas al-Iṣṭaḫrī (4th/10th cent.) classifies the Franks as the largest group among the 'kinds of

that, after the initial confrontations between the expanding Muslims and the Frankish realm in the eighth century, Iberian Muslims of the eleventh century did not strive to possess territories beyond the Pyrenees, and only perceived those territories as *dār al-ḥarb* that constituted a potential menace to their own society?

Moreover, we must also consider that Muslims from eleventh-century al-Andalus did not only describe the non-Muslim sphere in terms of friends or foes. Ṣāʿid al-Andalusī's (d. 462/1070) treatise on the history of science, for example, opens up a completely different perspective: he classifies the peoples of the earth according to their intellectual achievements and distinguishes between those who cultivated the sciences and those who did not.[54] Ṣāʿid al-Andalusī was certainly not disposed favourably towards the Christians of Europe: he describes the Galicians, i.e. the northern Iberian Christians, as intellectually inert, as subjected to tyranny and ignorance, in spite of the fact that they lived in a temperate climate zone.[55] In line with ancient Greek thinkers such as Hippocrates,[56] Ṣāʿid al-Andalusī regarded peoples living further north as lacking intellectual capacities because of the harsh climate they lived in.[57] He asserts, however, that — as opposed to nomads (*ahl al-bādiyya*) and a few other peoples — they also lived in cities, were governed by rulers, and guided by divine norms (*nāmūs ilāhī*).[58] Although this description is neither accurate nor favourable, Ṣāʿid al-Andalusī — after all a *qāḍī* of Toledo and thus a Muslim jurist — does not have recourse to the category *dār al-ḥarb* in his entire work, in spite of the fact that large parts of it are dedicated to non-Muslim peoples past and present.[59]

In al-Bakrī's (d. 487/1094) contemporary ethno- and geographic treatise, categorizations of the non-Muslim sphere also follow a different taxonomy. Generally, he describes the Latin-Christian sphere in terms of ethnonyms, toponyms, anthroponyms, and titles, thus contradicting Bernard Lewis's assertion that 'the division of the world into countries and nations [...] is of comparatively minor importance in the world of Islam'.[60] Al-Bakrī only uses a terminology reminiscent of the term *dār al-ḥarb* in two cases, namely when he describes hostilities with the Christian realms of al-Andalus.[61] He never

unbelief' (*min aṣnāf al-kufr*) and points to 'lands of polytheism' (*bilād al-širk*) that lie between Muslim al-Andalus and the Franks (*al-Ifranǧa*). See König, *Arabic-Islamic Views*, p. 191, n. 10, and p. 199, n. 53, for references.

54 Ṣāʿid al-Andalusī, *Kitāb Ṭabaqāt al-umam*, ed. by Šayḫū, pp. 5–8.

55 Ṣāʿid al-Andalusī, *Kitāb Ṭabaqāt al-umam*, ed. by Šayḫū, p. 9.

56 Ancient Greek climate theories were also reproduced by other Arabic-Islamic authors, e.g. al-Masʿūdī, *Kitāb al-Tanbīh wa-l-išrāf*, ed. by de Goeje, pp. 23–24.

57 Ṣāʿid al-Andalusī, *Kitāb Ṭabaqāt al-umam*, ed. by Šayḫū, p. 9: 'lam yastaʿmilū afkārahum fī l-ḥikma wa-lā rāḍū anfusahum bi-taʿallum al-falsafa'.

58 Ṣāʿid al-Andalusī, *Kitāb Ṭabaqāt al-umam*, ed. by Šayḫū, p. 9.

59 On the work see Martinez-Gros, 'La Première histoire', pp. 200–17.

60 Lewis, *Muslim Discovery*, p. 60.

61 Al-Bakrī, *Kitāb al-Masālik*, ed. by van Leeuwen and Ferré, II, § 1504, p. 898; § 1523, p. 908.

defines the rest of the Latin-Christian sphere beyond the Pyrenees by way of using these or comparable terms.[62]

This short overview shows that Andalusian Muslims of the eleventh century used various categories to define and describe the non-Muslim sphere. While the term *dār al-ḥarb* could play a role in episodes of foreign policy characterized by aggressive or defensive measures vis-à-vis neighbouring non-Muslim realms, this concept neither dominated Muslim thought nor the entire range of Christian-Muslim foreign relations.

Due to the lack of contemporary letters or treaties documented independently of historiographical works, it is unfortunately not possible to verify whether the concept *dār al-ḥarb* played a role in official relations between Christian Europe and the Arabic-Islamic sphere in the eleventh century. Only from the twelfth century onwards can we rely on a large range of bilingual Latin-Arabic treaties, mainly concluded between North African rulers and the maritime powers of Christian Europe.[63] Apart from the fact that the accompanying Christian-Muslim correspondence often addresses the respective other in the most polite and obliging terms,[64] these treaties do not adhere to juridical Muslim norms believed to be true by scholars upholding the conviction that an aggressive understanding of *dār al-ḥarb* stood at the basis of Muslim foreign policy throughout the ages. According to Majid Khadduri 'most [Muslim] jurists concur that the maximum period of peace with the enemy should not exceed ten years […]'.[65] However, of a total of thirty-three Muslim-Christian peace treaties documented by Louis de Mas Latrie for the period between the late twelfth and the fifteenth century, nineteen are concluded for longer periods, ranging from fifteen to forty years.[66] In one case, a treaty dating from 1421, the parties even concluded 'an eternal peace', documented both in the Latin and Arabic version.[67]

---

62 See the many references to al-Bakrī in König, *Arabic-Islamic Views*.

63 Mas Latrie, *Traités*; Wansbrough, 'Documents'; Wansbrough, 'Mamluk Commercial Treaty', pp. 39–79; Wansbrough, 'Venice', pp. 483–523; Holt, 'Treaties', pp. 67–76; Köhler, *Allianzen*; Burns and Chevedden, *Negotiating Cultures*; Holt, *Early Mamluk Diplomacy*.

64 See the highly polite forms of address in Latin and Arabic, documented in Amari, *Diplomi Arabi*.

65 Khadduri, 'Hudna', p. 546.

66 Mas Latrie, *Traités*, I, p. 28 (15 November 1186, Pisa-Almohads — 25 years), p. 31 (August 1229 or 1234, Pisa-Hafsids — 30 years), p. 43 (11 August 1264, Pisa-Hafsids — 20 years), p. 93 (21 November 1270, France-Hafsids — 15 years), p. 108 (1160, Genoa-Almohads — 15 years), p. 113 (August 1188, Genoa-Mallorca — 20 years), p. 134 (19 October 1433, Genoa-Hafsids — 20 years), p. 142 (29 December 1445, Genoa-Hafsids — 12 years), p. 151 (15 March 1465, Genoa-Hafsids — 30 years), p. 188 (January 1313, Aragonese Mallorca-Hafsids — 12 years), p. 116 (05 October 1231, Venice-Hafsids — 40 years), p. 199 (01 April 1251, Venice-Hafsids — 40 years), p. 203 (June 1271, Venice-Hafsids — 40 years), p. 216 (12 May 1317, Venice-Hafsids — 15 years), pp. 250–51 (Venice-Hafsids, 30 May 1438–20 years), pp. 255–56 (Venice-Hafsids, 09 October 1456–30 years), pp. 286–87 (Aragon-Hafsids, 02 June 1285–15 years), pp. 355–56 (Florence-Hafsids, 23 April 1445–30 years).

67 Mas Latrie, *Traités*, I, p. 353 (Florence/Pisa-Hafsids, 05 October 1421): 'Et hoc est

With regard to the conceptualization and implementation of the term *dār al-ḥarb,* we can conclude the following: in view of the many polemical and non-polemical terminological alternatives used to define and describe the non-Muslim sphere in Arabic-Islamic texts, the concept of *dār al-ḥarb* can definitely not be regarded as 'the embodiment' of Muslims' world-views regardless of time and space. Even one single region, in this case al-Andalus, produced such a large number of variegated Muslim perceptions of the non-Muslim sphere in the course of only one century, that we must classify the aggressive-expansionist stance usually associated with the term *dār al-ḥarb* as only one among various alternative forms of Muslim perceptions. As Khaled Abou el Fadl has already underscored, the conceptual dominance of *dār al-ḥarb* should not mislead us into believing that Muslims of all places and ages, including legal specialists, adhered to and acted upon a clear-cut binary world-view:

> Although scholars often have claimed that Islamic law divides the world into two basic categories, *dār al-Islām* and *dār al-ḥarb* (alternatively, *dār al-kufr* or *dār al-shirk*), these two categories do not reflect the complexity of Islamic thought on the issue. Muslim jurists did attempt to find a way to distinguish between the jurisdiction of Muslims and non-Muslims, but they could not agree on a definition of *dār al-Islām* or on the number of categories into which the world was divided. Consequently, the classification of territories in Islamic law is laden with ambiguity.[68]

This may also explain why Muslim foreign policy, although occasionally defensive, hostile, and even aggressive, does not seem to have adhered to the aggressive-expansionist stance usually associated with the term *dār al-ḥarb*. The latter plays no role in the bilingual Latin-Arabic documentation of economic and diplomatic relations between Muslim North Africa and European-Christian maritime powers. Against this backdrop, we must ask ourselves whether the modern scholarly and extra-academic (mainly Islamophobic and Islamist) reception of the term *dār al-ḥarb* has been doing justice to its historical and legal complexity. The analysis of one of the most aggressive interpretations of this concept in Ibn Ḥazm's *Kitāb al-Muḥallā* has revealed that the concept of *dār al-ḥarb* represents far more than a terminological expression for expansionist ambitions. Rather, it constitutes a central legal concept that addresses all issues relevant to the Muslim sphere's relations to neighbouring societies ruled by non-Muslims. Considering this, we can regard the corpus of legal norms surrounding the term *dār al-ḥarb* as a basic form of premodern 'international' law in Islamic garb. In its effort to safeguard and define the rights of the Muslim faithful according to the precepts of Islamic law, this corpus constitutes a rather

---

instrumentum pacis perpetue secundum voluntatem prefati domini regis Tunisii'; cf. the Arabic original in Amari, *Diplomi arabi*, doc. XXXVI, p. 163: 'wa-ḏālik ṣulḥ mustamirr ʿalā l-dawām bi-dawām'.

68 Abou El Fadl, 'Islamic Law', p. 161.

impressive achievement in the history of legal thought that, to my knowledge, had no equivalent in contemporary medieval legal systems. This becomes clear as soon as we turn to the concept of *terra paganorum*.

Terra paganorum

Emergence and Documentation

Although Christian forms of Latin literature have existed since the second century CE, the term *terra paganorum* is not attested before the ninth century CE. In view of the fact that Christian writings have dealt with spheres characterized by a religious world-view perceived as erroneous from early times onwards, this calls for an explanation. It seems as if ancient, Late Antique, and early medieval Christian writings did not perceive extra-Christian spheres in spatial terms. Envisioning the conversion of the Jewish and gentile population within the Roman Empire, the apostle Paul did not regard himself as a missionary entering 'the land of the unbelievers' (*terra paganorum*), but as a 'teacher of the peoples' (1 Timothy 2. 7: *διδάσκαλος ἐθνῶν*). Early Roman-Christian legislation as documented in the *Theodosian Code* was firmly bound to the Roman sphere of influence. Although it contains masses of norms regulating the religious sphere of pagans, Jews, and heretics, e.g. in Book XVI, it never does so in spatial terms.[69]

This characteristic of Christian conceptual terminology for non-Christian spheres remained unchanged, even when Christianity began to venture into areas lying outside the Roman Empire. When the Late Antique historiographer Orosius (d. *c.* 417) dealt with the spread of Christianity beyond the borders of the Roman Empire, he wrote about the conversion of peoples, not of territories.[70] Missionary hagiography of the sixth to ninth century also fails to envision conversion in spatial terms, but proffers masses of ethnonyms and references to 'pagans' (*pagani*). In the eighth-century *Vita Willibrordi*, for example, the proselytizing saint does not go to Friesland, but to the 'pagan Frisian king Radbod with his people'.[71] Even in the context of the Carolingian conversion of the Saxons, which entailed the simultaneous conquest of Saxony, terminology focuses on people, not on spaces. In Eigil's *Vita Sturmi*, produced around the turn of the eighth to the ninth century, Charlemagne arrives in Saxony, 'converts the greatest part of the Saxons to the faith of Christ', and then divides the province into various parishes.[72] Although the

---

69 *Theodosiani libri*, ed. by Mommsen and Meyer.

70 Paulus Orosius, *Historiae adversus paganos*, ed. and trans. by Arnaud-Lindet, vol. III, book VII, chap. 41,8, p. 122.

71 Alcuinus, *Vita Willibrordi*, ed. by Levison, chap. 9, p. 123: 'regem Fresonum Rabbodum cum sua gente paganum'.

72 Eigil, *Vita Sturmi*, ed. by Pertz, chap. 22, p. 376: 'maxima ex parte gentem illam ad fidem

text clearly regards Saxony as a territory, its former 'infidelity' is not defined in spatial terms. Even in this context, we find no Latin-Christian equivalent of *dār al-ḥarb*.

When the compound term *terra paganorum* first appears in Benedict of Aniane's ninth-century concordance of monastic rules, it does not apply to contemporary medieval realities, but to the biblical prophet Job who is described as living 'in the land of the pagans' (*in terra paganorum*).[73] The next appearance dates two centuries later and relates to the Islamic sphere of the pre-crusade era. In their description of the so-called Great German pilgrimage of 1064–1065, the *Annales Altahenses* describe the way to Jerusalem as having led 'through the land of the pagans' (*per terram paganorum*), an area presented as hostile.[74] From this period onward, the term is employed much more frequently. If the preliminary results of this research can be trusted, it appears nearly exclusively in texts from the twelfth and thirteenth centuries that deal with some form of Latin-Christian expansion into non-Christian territories.[75]

Intra-Textual Use

We can classify the texts that use either *terra paganorum* or a similar term (*terra infidelium, terrae paganae*, etc.) in terms of geography and genre. The greater part of references is found in historiography dealing with forms of Latin-Christian expansionism into the Mediterranean, predominantly Crusader campaigns, but also expansionist activities related to the *Reconquista* and to Mediterranean trade. In a few cases, the term also appears in historiography dealing with areas of north-eastern Europe that were being subject to Christianization. The term also features, albeit rarely, in legal documents produced in the same two geographical areas.

In medieval historiography dealing with the Mediterranean, the term *terra paganorum* primarily serves to distinguish territories under Muslim authority from territories under Christian rule. In this role, however, it fulfils various functions. In some cases, the term is used as a means of spatial orientation in a textual context characterized by a lower or higher degree of religious othering. Roger of Hoveden (d. after 1201), who defines north-western Africa and parts of the Iberian Peninsula as *terra paganorum*,[76] recounts that, setting out from Marseille to Acre, one sees the *terra paganorum* on

---

Christi convertit; et post non longum tempus totam provinciam illam in parochias episcopales divisit'.

73 Benedictus Anianensis, *Concordia regularum*, ed. by Migne, chap. LVXIII, col. 1318 A: De monachis peregrinis, qualiter suscipiantur, § 1: ex regula sancti Benedicti.

74 *Annales Altahenses maiores*, ed. by von Oefele, a. 1065, p. 67.

75 One should consider in this context, that editions of medieval texts such as the *Patrologia Latina* or the *Monumenta Germaniae Historica* largely focus on texts produced before the fourteenth and fifteenth century.

76 Rogerius de Hovedene, *Chronica Magistri*, ed. by Stubbs, pars posterior, a. 1190, pp. 47,

the right, the *terra Christianorum* on the left.[77] Richer of Senones (d. *c.* 1266) clearly situates Mecca and the tomb of Muḥammad in the *terra paganorum*, alternatively defined as *terra Sarracenorum citra mare in partibus orientis.*[78] In a book on miracles, written around 1178, a reference to the *terra paganorum* underscores the moral improvement achieved by monastic conversion. The author, Herbert of Clairvaux, later archbishop of Porto Torres in Sardinia, mentions a monk from Fontenay who had traded with the *terra paganorum* before choosing a monastic life.[79]

The term also features regularly in passages dealing with Christian-Muslim confrontation. In depictions of combat, it highlights the superior numbers of the enemy and the crusaders' valour, e.g. when Petrus Tudebodus, a monk from Poitou and eye-witness of the First Crusade, describes how Crusader Jerusalem defended itself against Muslim attacks shortly after the conquest of the city in 1099. According to Petrus, ships 'from the entire land of the heathens' (*de omni terra paganorum*) retreated when they saw that a Muslim commander had been put to flight by the crusaders.[80] In another context, it stands as a placeholder for territories to be conquered, thus expressing military ambitions: notes added to the *Annales Pisani*, written in their Latin version until 1175, report that, during the second crusade, the German king Conrad III intended to conquer Damascus, Aleppo, and 'the entire pagan sphere' (*tota terra paganorum*). Here, the *terra paganorum* is contrasted with 'the entire territory of the Christians in the Orient' (*tota terra christianorum in oriente*).[81] The *Chronicon Montis Sereni*, written between 1225 and 1230 near Halle, depicts how crusaders from England, Cologne, and Flanders helped to conquer Muslim Lisbon in 1147, defined here as *terra paganorum.*[82] Two sources describing the crusade against Damietta between 1217 and 1221 — the thirteenth-century *Gesta obsidionis Damiatae* and the *Liber duelli Christiani in obsidione Damiata exacti* — even mention predictions according to which the crusaders would gain control over 'the entire pagan sphere' (*tota[m] terra[m] paganorum*).[83]

In the few cases in which historiographical texts apply the term *terra paganorum* to non-Christian spheres in north-eastern Europe, they usually deal with territories that had gone or were going through a process of Christianization. A rather dubious document, the *Epistola inedita Mathildis*

52; copied with slight variations in Walterius de Coventria, *Memoriale*, ed. by Stubbs, pp. 406–07; *Gesta regis Henrici et Ricardi*, ed. by Stubbs, p. 122.

77 Rogerius de Hovedene, *Chronica Magistri*, ed. by Stubbs, pars posterior, a. 1190, p. 51.

78 Richerus monachus Senoniensis, *Gesta ecclesiae Senoniensis*, ed. by Waitz, book 4, chap. 40, p. 325.

79 Herbertus Turrium, *De miraculis libri tres*, ed. by Migne, III, chap. 35, col. 1381B.

80 Petrus Tudebodus, *Historia de Hierosolymitano itinere*, ed. by Hill and Hill, p. 148.

81 *Annales Pisani*, ed. by Pertz, notae pisanae, a. 1148, p. 266.

82 *Chronicon Montis Sereni*, ed. by Ehrenfeuchter, a. 1147, p. 147.

83 Iohannes de Tulbia, *Gesta obsidionis Damiatae*, ed. by Holder-Egger, chap. 16, p. 696; *Liber duelli Christiani*, ed. by Holder-Egger, chap. 7, p. 687; chap. 16, p. 697.

Sueviae sororis Gislae imperatricis refers to Charlemagne's introduction of the Christian religion *in terras paganas* in a letter allegedly sent to the Polish ruler Mieszko II and parts of his entourage.[84] In terms of content, the letter would have to be dated to 1025, the year in which Mieszko II acceded to the throne and Mathilda died. The fact that this letter contains the term *Muhamedani* (as opposed to *Mahometani* or *Saraceni*), a term, which, to my knowledge, never appears in medieval sources, suggests that we are dealing with a document written much later.[85] Other references to Eastern European areas as *terra paganorum* are linked to the Teutonic Order's forced appropriation and Christianization of the Baltic area in the thirteenth century, e.g. in a reference to Livonia as *terra paganorum* found in a chronicle written by the Cistercian monk Alberic of Trois-Fontaines (d. *c.* 1252).[86]

We can thus conclude with some certainty that the term *terra paganorum* generally designates either the Mediterranean Muslim sphere or an Eastern European area still awaiting Christianization. In historiography, the term provides spatial and religious orientation or defines the territory of a religious 'Other' subjected to conquest and conversion. Lacking any further connotations, its conceptual content is rather limited.

The few extant legal documents that use *terra paganorum* (or a terminological equivalent) arrive at a higher degree of conceptualization. The term is entirely absent from the twelfth-century *Decretum Gratiani*, after all a collection of papal and synodal decrees that spans several centuries of ecclesiastical legislation. It only seems to appear in legal texts from the thirteenth century whose geographical horizon is restricted to the Mediterranean and north-eastern European areas subject to processes of Christianization.

In a Mediterranean context, legislation or rulings produced in the orbit of the papacy do not use the term *terra paganorum*, but contain the comparable spatial concept *terra Sarracenorum* that has already been addressed in the introduction to this chapter. The *Liber extra* (*c.* 1234), for example, uses this term when threatening Christian merchants venturing to the 'land of the Saracens' (*in terram Saracenorum*) with excommunication. Its imposition of dress codes on Jews and Muslims 'in the lands of the Christians' (*in terris Christianorum*) shows that it clearly distinguishes between different spheres, each characterized by adherence to a specific religious system.[87] This is also valid for Ramon de Penyaforte's *Responsiones ad dubitabilia circa communicationem christianorum cum sarracenis*. This document contains the

---

84 *Epistola inedita*, ed. by Migne, chap. 41 (*A Misegone II. paganos jam, aliosque, Ecclesiae Latinae Regique renitentes, defecisse*), col. 1389D.

85 The entire collection of the Monumenta Germaniae Historica, searchable under www.dmgh.de, does not contain another instance of this term, except in one footnote written by an editor.

86 Albericus monachus Triumfontium, *Chronica a monacho Novi monasterii Hoiensis interpolata*, ed. by Scheffer-Boichorst, a. 1232, p. 930.

87 *Corpus Iuris Canonici, Pars Secunda: Decretalium Collectiones Decretales Gregorii papae IX*, ed. by Richter and Friedberg, book V, title VI, chap. 11, p. 775; book V, title VI, chap. 15, p. 777.

ratified responses to questions addressed to the papal curia by Franciscans and Dominicans situated in Tunis. It is dated 19 January 1235, i.e. to the pontificate of Gregory IX. Using compound terms made up of a spatial element and the ethnonym 'Saracens' (*terra* or *partes Sarracenorum*), this work addresses various problems arising from the sojourn of Christians in Muslim territory and resulting Christian-Muslim entanglement.[88]

One could expect that comparable juridical problems would be dealt with in Christian works of legislation produced in the border zones between societies led by Christian or Muslim elites respectively. The *Siete partidas,* a thirteenth-century legal compilation from Castile, repeatedly dedicates attention to issues of Christian-Muslim entanglement — e.g. by prohibiting sexual relations between Muslim men and Christian women[89] or by regulating linguistic aspects of Christian-Muslim trade.[90] In these cases, however, a spatial concept is not called for since the legal rulings address forms of intra-societal entanglement between Christians and Muslims within the Castilian realm. Accordingly, the *Siete partidas* only employ a spatial concept comparable to *terra paganorum* or *terra Saracenorum* in one paragraph guaranteeing security to envoys arriving at the Castilian court from 'the land of the Moors or other parts' (*de tierra de Moros o otras partes*).[91]

In a Mediterranean context, the only work of legislation that uses a spatial concept associated with the notion of 'paganism' is the compilation of the so-called *Assises de Jérusalem,* commonly dated to the late thirteenth century.[92] Here the legislator deals with the theoretical case of a person from the kingdom of Jerusalem (*la terre dou reaume de Jerusalem*) whose possession has been taken — by any means including force — to what the text defines either as 'land of the Saracens' (*terre de Sarasins*) or what one could translate as 'Pagandom' (*païnime* or *paienime*). Legal problems arise if this possession is returned to the 'land of the Christians' (*la terre des Crestiens*) by someone who is not the former owner, but who claims to have acquired the possession in a legal manner.[93] This resonates strongly with similar discussions in Ibn Ḥazm's *Kitāb al-Muḥallā,* concerning, for example, Muslim possessions taken by force into the *dār al-ḥarb*.[94] In both cases, legal experts confronted a legal issue that resulted from the direct neighbourhood of two spheres adhering to different and mutually exclusive theological tenets as well as derived legal norms.

---

88 Tolan, *Ramon de Penyaforte's Responses* §§ 4, 5, 7, 15, 23, 40, pp. 11, 13, 15, 17.

89 *Siete Partidas,* ed. by Real Academia de la Historia, III, Partida septima, titulo 25, ley 10, p. 681.

90 *Siete Partidas,* ed. by Real Academia de la Historia, III, Partida quinta, titulo 11, ley 1, p. 255.

91 *Siete Partidas,* ed. by Real Academia de la Historia, III, Partida septima, titulo 25, ley 9, p. 680.

92 Nielen-Vandervoorde, 'Un livre méconnu', pp. 103–05.

93 *Assises de Jérusalem, II: Livre des Assises de la Cour des Bourgeois,* ed. by Beugnot, chap. 232, p. 161.

94 Ibn Ḥazm, *Kitāb al-Muḥallā,* VII, ed. by al-Ǧazīrī, mas'ala 931, pp. 300–02; mas'ala 932, p. 306; VIII, ed. by al-Dimašqī, mas'ala 1283, p. 178.

Analogous juridical problems are not addressed in legal documents dealing with north-eastern European areas subject to Christianization. The few texts that use the term *terra paganorum* in this context were produced in the early 1230s under the pontificate of Pope Gregory IX and are concerned with the establishment of the Teutonic Order in Chełmno (Germ. 'Kulmerland').[95] In a document dated 12 September 1230, the Pope grants the Order 'whatever your brothers are able to obtain in the land of the pagans'. He confirms these property rights on 'whatever you will be able to acquire with God's help from the land of the pagans in this same province in your effort to defend Christianity', in a document dated 2 August 1234.[96] In this context, the term *terra paganorum* boasts a certain degree of conceptualization in that it is clearly used to legitimize the forced appropriation of a hitherto unsubjected territory, allegedly necessary for what is euphemistically described as the 'defence' of Christianity.

Extra-Textual Implementation?

In comparison to *dār al-ḥarb*, the concept of *terra paganorum* does not display the same degree of conceptual sophistication, not least because it obviously failed to become a juridical concept of any importance. This does not preclude, however, that it could have been translated into action. Even if regarded as a mere 'notion' (rather than a 'concept'), and thus lacking complexity, it clearly divides the known world into a Christian and a non-Christian sphere. Consequently, one would presuppose that it could have served as a fundamental concept that underlay expansionist Christian enterprises which were directed against non-Christian territories.

With regard to the Mediterranean sphere, Arabic-Islamic sources certainly suggest that Christians were actively and consciously going against the Muslim sphere in the same period in which the term *terra paganorum* began to be used more frequently in Latin sources, i.e. the twelfth and thirteenth centuries. Ibn al-Aṯīr's (d. 630/1233) chronicle, for example, contains a condensed narrative of the European Christians' rise to power: according to the chronicler, the so-called 'Franks' (*al-Ifranǧ*) first extended their power into al-Andalus and onto Sicily, then conquered the Syrian Levant, and finally took possession of Constantinople.[97] In view of this, Latin-Christian expansionism and the rise

95 Also see Mažeika and Chollet, 'Familiar Marvels?', p. 58, for the use of *terra infidelium* in this context.

96 *Preußisches Urkundenbuch*, I/1: *Die Bildung des Ordensstaates*, ed. by Philippi, doc. 80 (12 September 1230), p. 61: 'quicquid fratres vestri in terra paganorum poterint obtinere, cedat ordini memorato'; doc. 108 (3 August 1234), p. 84: 'Que vero in futurum, largiente domino, insistendo defensioni christianitatis de terra paganorum in eadem provincia vos contigerit adipisci, firma et illibata vobis vestrisque successoribus sub iure ac proprietate sedis apostolice eodem modo statuimus permanenda'.

97 Ibn al-Aṯīr, *Al-Kāmil fī l-tārīḫ*, ed. by Tornberg, I, pp. 242–43 (Leiden edition), pp. 338–39 (Beirut edition).

of a dichotomizing Christian-pagan conception of world order seem to be congruent. In view of the many texts produced during or in reaction to the crusades and the *Reconquista*, etc., one wonders, however, why the term *terra paganorum* appears so rarely, rather than carving out a belated, but respectable conceptual career comparable to that of *dār al-ḥarb* in Muslim juridical literature. In the specific context of trans-Mediterranean Christian-Muslim relations, several reasons come to mind.

One factor hampering the conceptual career of *terra paganorum* may have been that, in the twelfth century at the latest, many Christians had become aware of the fact that the Muslims, i.e. the so-called Saracens, were actually not pagans, but monotheists who rejected belief in the divine sonship of Jesus. Otto of Freising's (d. 1158) explicit refutation of the story that Bishop Thiemo of Salzburg had been martyred to death by the Saracens because he had refused to venerate the latter's idols, is revealing in this regard. Otto's short but comparatively accurate presentation of Islamic monotheism proves that a twelfth-century intellectual and statesman did not regard Islam as a form of idolatrous paganism, but still deemed it necessary to correct the belief that Muslims were actually pagans.[98] Research has established that the depiction of Islam as paganism in medieval Latin-Christian and vernacular sources first served the purposes of crusading propaganda and ideology during the First Crusade and in its immediate aftermath.[99] This depiction remained rampant in unlearned popular imagination and was colourfully elaborated in vernacular fiction.[100] Since even comparatively well-informed Latin texts attributed idolatrous elements to Muslim practices of worship, such as the veneration of the Ka'ba in Mecca, it is impossible to distinguish clearly between 'popular' and 'learned' attitudes towards Islam.[101] Nevertheless, many ecclesiastically trained intellectuals of the high and late Middle Ages regarded Islam as an erroneous interpretation of monotheism rather than a form of paganism — Pope Gregory VII's letter to the Ḥammādid ruler al-Nāṣir b. 'Alannās, which stresses the common Abrahamic roots of Christianity and Islam in 1076, represents only one among many examples.[102] This may explain why the abovementioned papal rulings employ the term *terra Saracenorum* rather than *terra paganorum*, when they mention the Muslim sphere.

A second factor hampering the conceptual career of *terra paganorum* may have been that Latin-Christian expansionist ventures such as the crusades or the *Reconquista* were not necessarily regarded as campaigns directed against 'pagan' territory. In Robert the Monk's (d. 1122) version of Pope Urban II's

---

98 Otto Frisingensis, *Chronica sive historia*, ed. by Hofmeister, book VII, chap. 7, p. 317; cf. Tolan, 'Muslims as Pagan Idolaters', pp. 97–98.
99 Tolan, 'Muslims as Pagan Idolaters', pp. 97–117.
100 Daniel, 'Learned and Popular Attitudes', pp. 46–47; Hoeppner Moran Cruz, 'Popular Attitudes', pp. 55–81; Tolan, *Saracens*, pp. 126–34.
101 Akbari, *Idols in the East*, pp. 200–47.
102 Gregorius VII, *Registrum*, ed. by Caspar, III, ep. 21, pp. 287–88.

speech in Clermont in 1095, the Pope did not call for a conquest of *terrae paganorum*. Rather, he was calling for the liberation of a land 'given by God into the possession of the children of Israel' (*filiis Israel a Deo in possessionem data fuit*) and 'now held captive by enemies' (*nunc a hospitis captiva tenetur*).[103] From this perspective, the Holy Land was a Christian possession lost to the infidels and could not be defined as *terra paganorum*. The same is valid for the underlying ideology of the *Reconquista*.[104] Even Muslim historiographers such as Ibn ʿIḏārī (d. after 712/1312–13) acknowledged that the Christians of northern Spain did not claim to conquer foreign pagan lands, i.e. *terrae paganorum*, but reclaimed territory that they regarded as their own possession. According to Ibn ʿIḏārī, Fernando I of León and Castile said to the Muslims of Toledo in the middle of the eleventh century: 'we demand back our lands that you have conquered from us in ancient times [...]. So now, go back to your shores and leave our lands to us'.[105] Thus, in the context of the crusades and the *Reconquista*, the European-Christian theological or historical claim to the desired territories made it difficult to classify them as *terrae paganorum*.

Finally, missionary enterprises also contributed little to diffusing or even establishing this territorial concept. Peter the Venerable (d. 1156) justified his verbal combat against Islam by complaining — in very spatial terms — that the Saracens had deprived Christianity of Asia, Africa, and even parts of Europe.[106] However, he did not call for a missionary thrust into a spatially defined *terra paganorum*, but for a theological deconstruction of Islam,[107] and — in his treatise *Contra sectam Saracenorum* — for direct communication with the 'Arab sons of Ishmael, who serve the law of the one called Muḥammad'.[108] Those who followed in the footsteps of the Cluniac abbot and dedicated themselves to missionary enterprises were interested in the conversion of souls, not of territories. This is again reflected in the terminology: Ramon Lull (d. *c.* 1316), for example, wished to effect the 'conversion of infidels' (*conversio infidelium*). His elaborate plan to instruct missionaries in the necessary languages admittedly contains spatial terminology. The monasteries, in which instruction was to take place, were supposed to be constructed 'outside the abodes of the gentiles' (*extra gentium mansiones*). Appropriate language teachers were to be found by sending people 'to those regions' (*ad illas partes*).[109] This distinction between Christian and non-Christian territories, however, was of

103 Robertus monachus, *Historia Iherosolimitana*, ed. by Kempf, I, chaps 3–4, p. 6.

104 See Jaspert, 'Reconquista', pp. 445–65.

105 Ibn ʿIḏārī, *Kitāb al-Bayān*, ed. by Colin and Lévi-Provençal, III, p. 282: 'fa-innamā naṭlub bilādinā allatī ġalabtumūnā ʿalayhā qadīman [...] fa-irḥalū ilā ʿudwatikum wa-utrukū lanā bilādanā [...]'.

106 Petrus Venerabilis, 'Summa totius haeresis Saracenorum', ed. and trans. by Glei, chap. 11, p. 14.

107 Petrus Venerabilis, 'Epistola de translatione sua', ed. and trans. by Glei, § 3, pp. 24–25.

108 Petrus Venerabilis, 'Contra sectam Saracenorum', ed. and trans. by Glei, chaps 23–24, p. 62: 'Arabibus Ismaelis filiis, legem illius qui Mahumeth dicitur servantibus'.

109 Ramon Lull, 'De fine,' ed. by Madre, pp. 280–83.

secondary importance. Of greater relevance were the 'infidel peoples' (*populos infideles*), the human souls to be converted, that are mentioned in the acts of the council of Vienne (1311–12).[110]

In the abovementioned north-eastern European context, the term *terra paganorum* is probably used so sparingly because north-eastern Europe of the thirteenth century only featured few areas that had not yet been Christianized. As Helmhold of Bosau already reminds us in the twelfth century, the Slavonic peoples populating the Baltic and more southern regions — including Russians (*Ruci*), Poles (*Polani*), Bohemians (*Boemos*), Moravians (*Marahi*), Carinthians (*Karinthi*), and Sorbs (*Sorabi*) — had all accepted Christianity: 'Except for the Prussians (*Pruzos*), all these nations have been adorned with the honorific of Christianity'.[111] In this region, there was not enough *terra paganorum* left to facilitate a large-scale employment and documentation of the term.

In sum, the extant documentation of the term *terra paganorum* suggests that its heyday falls into a period in which Latin Christians actively and consciously penetrated non-Christian territories by force. The dearth and complexity of our sources make it impossible to say which came first — the concept or the action. The preceding analysis has shown, however, that the term *terra paganorum* was conceptually inadequate, in that it could only be applied with difficulty to many non-Christian regions penetrated by expanding Latin Christians. In consequence, alternative spatial conceptualizations, generally featuring ethnonyms, were preferred. Eventually, this seems to have sounded the death knell for a conceptual term that would never reach the sophisticated conceptual elaboration of its Arabic-Islamic equivalent *dār al-ḥarb*.

Conclusions: Comparing *dār al-ḥarb* and *terra paganorum*

Although the introduction took great pains to justify the comparison of the two conceptual compound terms *dar al-ḥarb* and *terra paganorum*, the preceding elaborations have shown that we are dealing with two decidedly different concepts of circumscribing a foreign sphere characterized by religious alterity.

Dār al-ḥarb represents a sophisticated geo-religious concept designating areas beyond the sphere of influence of Islamic norms as they were ideally guaranteed by the rule of Muslim elites. Developed by Muslim jurists in the first centuries after the rise of Islam — i.e. in a period of Muslim geopolitical expansion — and commented upon until today, the term *dār al-ḥarb* has clear normative and juridical connotations: it purports to define the aims and rules of Muslim interaction with the non-Muslim sphere in military, diplomatic, economic, and social terms. The norms subsumed under this

110 'Concilium Viennense', ed. and trans. by Alberigo and Wohlmuth, decretum 24, p. 379.

111 Helmholdus Presbyterus Bozoviensis, *Cronica Slavorum*, ed. by Lappenberg and Schmeidler, i, p. 5: 'Omnes hee naciones preter Pruzos Christianitatis titulo decorantur'.

term serve to protect, defend, and even expand a form of social order defined as being in accordance with the divine guidelines of Islam. One interesting result is certainly that geo- and ethnographical treatises employing the term *dār al-ḥarb* or similar terms do not seem to apply it indiscriminately to all known non-Muslim societies, but only to those which constitute a potential or concrete challenge to the Muslim sphere. The literal and generalizing translation 'abode of war' thus falls short of the concept's complexity. A 'translation' of *dār al-ḥarb* that tries to do justice to this complexity could be 'a sphere not bound to Muslim norms that — if in a potential state of hostility vis-à-vis Muslims, their faith, norms, and social order — must be contained, maybe even reduced, among others by military means'.

In comparison, *terra paganorum* represents a rather unelaborate geo-religious concept designating areas dominated by non-Christian, in particular idolatrous forms of religion. Probably due to the fact that early Christian forms of classifying religious alterity were group-bound rather than spatial, the compound term came up rather late, i.e. in the ninth century. Judging from the sources analysed in this chapter, regular use of this term is only attested for the twelfth and the first half of the thirteenth century, i.e. a period in which the Latin-Christian sphere expanded militarily, commercially, and religiously into non-Christian spheres hitherto ruled by Muslim and non-monotheist elites. The term is primarily documented in historiographical texts where it serves as a means of spatial orientation and displays a lower or higher degree of religious othering. In the rare instances in which *terra paganorum* or an analogous term features in legal documents, it is either used — in a Mediterranean crusading context — to explain problems arising from the neighbourhood of two distinct legal spheres, or — in a Baltic crusading context — to justify the conquest of a particular area. Already in the period of its heyday, the term only inadequately characterized regions bordering on Latin-Christian Europe. Regions marked by forms of idolatry had become rare, whereas the Muslim sphere was increasingly considered as following a form of deviant monotheism, rather than a form of idolatrous paganism. Consequently, Latin-Christian authors often preferred conceptual alternatives that linked a spatial term with an ethnonym. As opposed to the compound term *dār al-ḥarb*, the term *terra paganorum* thus failed to acquire a high degree of conceptual sophistication, seems to have been abandoned altogether in later periods, and would thus never stand at the centre of a corpus of norms that could be defined as a premodern variant of unilaterally formulated 'international' law.

In practice, both concepts probably played a less important role than could be assumed at first sight. Admittedly, the term *dār al-ḥarb* was associated with the entire range of military, diplomatic, commercial, and social relations with individuals and groups stemming from societies outside the sphere of Muslim rule. Consequently, one could imagine that various norms based on this concept were actually implemented in practice, e.g. when people from the *dār al-ḥarb* entered the *dār al-islām* and thus became subject to Muslim jurisdiction. Within the framework of bilateral relations, the implementation of such norms seems to have depended on the relative strength of the powers involved. The concept of *dār al-ḥarb* may have motivated or justified military action against neighbouring non-Muslim realms. One would assume, however, that pragmatic considerations regarding the existing balance of powers were more important than the given normative framework. As a part of bilateral negotiations, the concept does not seem to have played an explicit role, e.g. in the diplomatic and/or commercial relations attested between Christian maritime powers and Muslim North Africa in the late medieval period. Since the normative framework associated with the term *dār al-ḥarb* was formulated from a unilateral point of view and had not been developed in direct negotiation with the respective diplomatic or commercial partner, it would have probably been refused by the latter. If at all, the concept could have played an implicit role as a kind of invisible conceptual safeguard against non-Muslim political or commercial encroachment. Modern (mainly Islamophobic and Islamist) interpretations of the concept of *dār al-ḥarb* define the latter as the expression of an aggressive and expansionist attitude allegedly underlying every Muslim world-view. The analysed material should have shown that such an interpretation ignores clearly documented alternative Muslim world-views, the term's complex legal framework, and the practical limitations that obstructed the implementation of related norms.

With regard to the implementation of the concept of *terra paganorum* things stand differently. Medieval Latin texts written between the twelfth and the fifteenth centuries do not only attest to the existence of a conceptualized geo-religious dichotomy of Christian and non-Christian spheres. In this period of Latin-Christian expansionism, this geo-religious dichotomy was also put into practice in various forms, ranging from military confrontation to commercial and missionary activity. But although these activities are reflected in a more frequent, albeit not exactly abundant use of the term *terra paganorum* in texts of the same period, it seems as if the abovementioned conceptual deficiencies of this term were too important as to make it a relevant motor of action.

On a regular basis, *dār al-ḥarb* was used much earlier than *terra paganorum* (at the latest in the ninth century, as opposed to the twelfth). Consequently, one could assume that the former concept inspired the latter. Islam certainly constituted the most formidable and influential representative of religious alterity for medieval Latin Christianity.[112] However, this does not automatically imply that specific Arabic-Islamic concepts such as *ǧihād, dār al-ḥarb, al-ribāt,* etc. had an impact on ideas and concepts in Latin-Christian societies — especially if one lacks concrete evidence for processes of transmission and reception.[113] In spite of intensive Christian-Muslim interaction in the medieval period,

112 Southern, *Western Views*, p. 3.

113 See König, 'Charlemagne's "Jihād"', pp. 32–33; and König, *Islam und die Genese Europas*, with further literature on these processes of transmission and reception as well as the impact of the Arabic-Islamic sphere on medieval Europe.

examples for the direct access of Latin Christians to concepts of Islamic law are hard to come by. The latter played no role in the Arabic-Latin translation movement of the twelfth to the sixteenth century.[114] Even when Islamic dogma and some aspects of its legal thought were transferred into Castilian by Muslims from the late medieval Iberian Peninsula, the concept *dār al-ḥarb* played no role. Written for the benefit of Romance-speaking Muslims living under Christian rule, the Castilian *Leyes de moros* of the fourteenth, or the *Suma de los principales mandamientos y devededamientos de la Ley y Çunna* of the fifteenth century, contain many technical terms of Arabic origin. However, they eschew the concept of *dār al-ḥarb* — obviously because they focus on matters of cult as well as on inner-Muslim organization under Christian rule.[115] Apart from the lack of evidence for direct influence, the geo-religious concepts of *dār al-ḥarb* and *terra paganorum* differ fundamentally in terms of documentary context and conceptual sophistication. An inspiration of the latter by the former thus seems very improbable.

In sum, this essay shows how difficult it is to make a definite statement on the theory and practice of specific premodern notions of world order. One is not only confronted with the anticipated causality dilemma of the so-called 'chicken-and-egg'-problem, in this case the question whether conceptual thought inspired certain actions, or whether certain actions led to conceptualization. The specific examples of *dār al-ḥarb* and *terra paganorum* present us with an additional curiosity. The concept of *dār al-ḥarb* emerged in the wake of the Arabic-Islamic expansion of the seventh and eighth centuries, i.e. after the period in which the imposition of Islamic normative frameworks on non-Muslim societies was most intensive. Given its conceptual breadth, it can be regarded as a roughly systematized manifestation of premodern 'international' law that probably failed to spread beyond the sphere of Muslim rule because it had been formulated unilaterally on the basis of precepts not necessarily accepted by non-Muslims. However, the rather rich documentation and sophistication of this concept does not seem to have been matched by an equally high degree of historical application and implementation in the complex, flexible, and ever-changing relations between the Latin-Christian and the Arabic-Islamic sphere, in particular after the onset of Latin-Christian expansionism in the eleventh century. The much less impressive documentation and conceptual sophistication of *terra paganorum*, in turn, fails to reflect the actual vigour and extent of Latin-Christian expansionism in the period of its most extensive documentation. We can certainly not claim that the spatial dimensions of religious othering were irrelevant to the expanding Latin-Christian orbit. However, to reconstruct these spatial dimensions — e.g. the spatial imaginaries of crusading- and *Reconquista*-ideology — the term *terra paganorum* is of

114 Burnett, 'Translation from Arabic', pp. 1220–31.

115 *Tratados de legislación musulmana*, ed. by Real Academia de Historia; see the glossary, pp. 427–49, for an impression of which legally relevant Arabic terms were given a Castilian form. Also see Catlos, '"Secundum suam Zunam"', pp. 13–26.

no real help. A comparative analysis of these two premodern conceptions of world order thus allows us to measure different degrees of conceptual sophistication and inspires us to reflect upon the underlying causes for this discrepancy. In addition, it also makes clear that two compound terms can only reflect to a limited degree how Muslims and Christians in the medieval period perceived and conceived of their world.

Works Cited

Primary Sources

Albericus monachus Triumfontium, *Chronica a monacho Novi monasterii Hoiensis interpolata*, ed. by Paul Scheffer-Boichorst, in *Monumenta Germaniae Historica: Scriptores in folio*, XXIII (Hannover: Hahn, 1874), pp. 631–950

Alcuinus, *Vita Willibrordi*, ed. by Wilhelm Levison, in *Monumenta Germaniae Historica: Scriptores rerum Merovingicarum*, VII (Hannover: Hahn, 1920), pp. 81–141

Amari, Michele, ed., *I Diplomi Arabi del R. Archivio Fiorentino* (Florence: Le Monnier, 1863)

Annales Altahenses maiores, ed. by Edmund L. B. von Oefele, in *Monumenta Germaniae Historica: Scriptores rerum Germanicarum in usum scholarum*, IV (Hannover: Hahn, 1891)

Annales Pisani, ed. by Karl Pertz, in *Monumenta Germaniae Historica: Scriptores in folio*, XIX (Hannover: Hahn, 1866), pp. 236–66

Assises de Jérusalem, II: *Livre des Assises de la Cour des Bourgeois*, ed. by Arthur-Auguste Beugnot (Paris: Imprimerie Royale, 1843)

al-Bakrī, *Kitāb al-Masālik wa-l-mamālik*, ed. by Aadrian van Leeuwen and André Ferré, 2 vols (Tunis: Dār al-ʿarabiyya li-l-kitāb, 1992)

Benedictus Anianensis, *Concordia regularum*, in *Patrologiae cursus completus: series latina*, ed. by Jacques-Paul Migne, CIII (Paris: Garnier, 1844–64), cols 701–1380

al-Buḫārī, *Ǧāmiʿ al-ṣaḥīḥ*, ed. by Muḥibb al-Dīn al-Ḫaṭīb and Muḥammad Fuʾād ʿAbd al-Bāqī, II (Cairo: al-maṭbaʿa al-salafiyya, 1403/1982)

Chronicon Montis Sereni, ed. by Ernst Ehrenfeuchter, in *Monumenta Germaniae Historica: Scriptores in folio*, XXIII (Hannover: Hahn, 1874), pp. 123–226

'Concilium Viennense (a. 1311–12)', ed. and trans. by Giuseppe Alberigo and Joseph Wohlmuth, in *Konzilien des Mittelalters*, ed. by Joseph Wohlmuth, II: *Vom ersten Laterankonzil (1123) bis zum fünften Laterankonzil (1512–1517)* (Paderborn: Schöningh, 2000), pp. 33–402

Corpus Iuris Canonici, Pars Secunda: Decretalium Collectiones Decretales Gregorii papae IX, ed. by Emil Ludwig Richter and Emil Friedberg (Leipzig: Bernhard Tauchnitz, 1881)

Eigil, *Vita Sturmi*, ed. by Georg Heinrich Pertz, in *Monumenta Germaniae Historica: Scriptores in folio*, II (Hannover: Hahn, 1829), pp. 365–77

De episcopo titulari seu in partibus infidelium: Tractatus canonico-theologicus, ed. by Andrea Hieronymo Andreucci (Rome: De Rubeis, 1732)

Epistola inedita Mathildis Suevae sororis Gislae imperatricis, in *Patrologiae cursus completus: series latina*, ed. by Jacques-Paul Migne, CLI (Paris: Garnier, 1844–64), cols 1327–1400

Gesta regis Henrici et Ricardi, ed. by William Stubbs, Rolls Series, 49, 2 vols (London: Longman, 1867)

Gregorius VII, *Registrum*, ed. by Erich Caspar, Monumenta Germaniae Historica: Epistolae selectae in usum scholarum, II, 1 (Berlin: Weidmann, 1920)

Helmholdus Presbyterus Bozoviensis, *Cronica Slavorum*, ed. by Johann Lappenberg and Bernhard Schmeidler, Monumenta Germaniae Historica: Scriptores rerum Germanicarum in usum scholarum, XXXII (Hannover: Hahn, 1937)

Herbertus Turrium, *De miraculis libri tres*, in *Patrologiae cursus completus: series latina*, ed. by Jacques-Paul Migne, CLXXXV (Paris: Garnier, 1844–64), cols 1273–1384

Hormisdas I, *ep. LXX ad possessorem episcopum*, in *Patrologiae cursus completus: series latina*, ed. by Jacques-Paul Migne, CXIII (Paris: Garnier, 1844–64), col. 490

Ibn al-Aṯīr, *Al-Kāmil fī l-tārīḫ*, ed. by Carolus Tornberg, 14 vols (Leiden: Brill, 1852–76, and Beirut: Dār Ṣādir, 1965–67)

Ibn Ḥayyān, *Al-Sifr al-ṯānī min kitāb al-muqtabis* [al-muqtabis II-1] / *Crónica de los emires Alḥakam I y ʿAbdarraḥmān II*, ed. by Maḥmūd Makkī, trans. by Federico Corriente (Riyad: Markaz al-malik Fayṣal, 2003 / Zaragoza: Instituto de estudios islámicos, 2001)

——, *Al-Muqtabis min anbāʾ ahl al-Andalus* [al-muqtabis II-2], ed. by Maḥmūd Makkī (Beirut: Dār al-kitāb al-ʿarabī, 1973)

——, *Kitāb al-Muqtabis fī tārīḫ al-Andalus* [al-muqtabis III], ed. by Ismāʿīl al-ʿArabī (Beirut: Dār al-āfāq al-ǧadīda, 1990)

——, *Kitāb al-Muqtabas (al-ǧuzʾ al-ḫāmis)* [al-muqtabis V], ed. by Pedro Chalmeta and Federico Corriente (Madrid, Rabat: al-Maʿhad al-isbānī al-ʿarabī li–l-ṯaqāfa, 1979)

——, *Kitāb al-Muqtabis fī aḫbar balad al-Andalus* [al-muqtabis VII], ed. by ʿAbd al-Raḥmān al-Ḥaǧǧī (Beirut: Dār al-ṯaqāfa, 1965)

Ibn Ḥazm, *Kitāb al-Muḥallā fī šarḥ al-maǧallā bi-l-ḥuǧǧaǧ wa-l-āṯār*, I-VI, ed. by Aḥmad Muḥammad Šākir (Cairo: Idārat al-ṭibāʾa al-munīriyya, 1348/1929–1349/1930); VII, ed. by ʿAbd ar-Raḥmān al-Ǧazīrī (Cairo: Idārat al-ṭibāʾa al-munīriyya, 1349/1930); VIII–XI, ed. by Muḥammad Munīr al-Dimašqī (Cairo: Idārat al-ṭibāʾa al-munīriyya, 1350/1931–1352/1933)

Ibn ʿIḏārī, *Kitāb al-Bayān al-muġrib*, ed. by George S. Colin and Évariste Lévi-Provençal, 3 vols (Beirut: Dār al-ṯaqāfa, 1980–83)

Iohannes de Tulbia, *Gesta obsidionis Damiatae (1217–20)*, ed. by Oswald Holder-Egger, in *Monumenta Germaniae Historica: Scriptores in folio*, XXXI (Hannover: Hahn, 1903), pp. 669–704

Liber duelli Christiani in obsidione Damiatae exacti, ed. by Oswald Holder-Egger, in *Monumenta Germaniae Historica: Scriptores in folio*, XXXI (Hannover: Hahn, 1903), pp. 669–705

al-Masʿūdī, *Kitāb al-Tanbīh wa-l-išrāf*, ed. by Michael J. de Goeje (Leiden: Brill, 1893)

Otto Frisingensis, *Chronica sive historia de duabus civitatibus*, ed. by Anton Hofmeister, Monumenta Germaniae Historica: Scriptores rerum Germanicarum in usum scholarum, XLV (Hannover: Hahn, 1912)

Paulus Orosius / Orose, *Historiarum adversum paganos libri VII* / *Histoires contre les païens*, ed. and trans. by Marie-Pierre Arnaud-Lindet, 3 vols (Paris: Les Belles Lettres, 1991)

Petrus Tudebodus, *Historia de Hierosolymitano itinere*, ed. by John Hugh Hill and Laurita L. Hill, Documents relatifs à l'histoire des croisades, XII (Paris: Paul Geuthner, 1977)

Petrus Venerabilis, 'Summa totius haeresis Saracenorum', in *Petrus Venerabilis: Schriften zum Islam*, ed. and trans. by Reinhold Glei, Corpus Islamo-Christianum. Series Latina, 1 (Altenberge: CIS, 1985), pp. 2–22

——, 'Epistola de translatione sua', in *Petrus Venerabilis: Schriften zum Islam*, ed. and trans. by Reinhold Glei, Corpus Islamo-Christianum. Series Latina, 1 (Altenberge: CIS, 1985), pp. 22–28

——, 'Contra sectam Saracenorum', in *Petrus Venerabilis: Schriften zum Islam*, ed. and trans. by Reinhold Glei, Corpus Islamo-Christianum. Series Latina, 1 (Altenberge: CIS, 1985), pp. 30–224

Preußisches Urkundenbuch, Politische Abteilung, 1,1: *Die Bildung des Ordensstaates*, ed. by Rudolf Philippi (Königsberg: Hartung, 1882)

Ramon Lull, 'De fine', in *Raimundi Lulli Opera Latina, Tomus IX, 120–22, in Monte Pessulano anno MCCCV composita*, ed. by Alois Madre, Corpus Christianorum, Continuatio Mediaevalis, XXXV (Turnhout: Brepols, 1981)

Richerus monachus Senoniensis, *Gesta ecclesiae Senoniensis*, ed. by Georg Waitz, in *Monumenta Germaniae Historica: Scriptores in folio*, XXV (Hannover: Hahn, 1880), pp. 249–345

Robertus monachus, *Historia Iherosolimitana*, ed. by Damien Kempf and Marcus Bull (Woodbridge: Boydell, 2013)

Rogerius de Hovedene, *Chronica Magistri Rogeri de Houedene*, ed. by William Stubbs, Rolls Series, 51, 4 vols (London: Longman, 1870)

Ṣāʿid al-Andalusī, *Kitāb Ṭabaqāt al-umam*, ed. by Lūwīs Šayḫū (Beirut: Imprimerie Catholique, 1912)

Siete Partidas, ed. by Real Academia de la Historia, III (Madrid: Imprenta de la Real Academia de Historia, 1807)

Theodosiani libri XVI cum constitutionibus Sirmondianis et leges novellae ad Theodosiam pertinentes, ed. by Theodor Mommsen and Paul M. Meyer (Berlin: Weidmann, 1962 [orig. 1905])

Tratados de legislación musulmana, ed. by Real Academia de Historia (Madrid: Imprenta de la Real Academia de Historia, 1853)

Walterius de Coventria, *Memoriale fratris Walteris de Coventria*, ed. by William Stubbs, Rolls Series, 58, 2 vols (London: Longman, 1872)

Secondary Studies

Abel, Armand, 'Dār al-Ḥarb', in *Encyclopaedia of Islam: Second Edition*, II, ed. by Bernard Lewis, Charles Pellat, and Joseph Schacht (Leiden: Brill, 1965), p. 126

Abou El Fadl, Khaled, 'Islamic Law and Muslim Minorities: The Juristic Discourse on Muslim Minorities from the Second / Eighth to the Eleventh / Seventeenth Centuries', *Islamic Law and Society*, 1,2 (1994), 141–87

Akbari, Suzanne C., *Idols in the East: European Representations of Islam and the Orient, 1100–1450* (Ithaca: Cornell University Press, 2009)

Albrecht, Sarah, *Dār al-Islām Revisited: Territoriality in Contemporary Islamic Legal Discourse on Muslims in the West*, Muslim Minorities, 29 (Leiden: Brill, 2018)

Arnaldez, Roger, *Grammaire et théologie chez Ibn Ḥazm* (Paris: Vrin, 1956)

Burnett, Charles, 'Translation from Arabic to Latin in the Middle Ages', in *Übersetzung: Ein internationales Handbuch zur Übersetzungsforschung*, II, ed. by Harald Kittel (Berlin: de Gruyter, 2007), pp. 1220–31

Burns, Robert I., and Paul E. Chevedden, *Negotiating Cultures: Bilingual Surrender Treaties in Muslim-Crusader Spain under James the Conqueror*, The Medieval Mediterranean, 22 (Leiden: Brill, 1999)

Calasso, Giovanni, 'Constructing and Deconstructing the Classical dār al-islām / dār al-ḥarb Opposition: Between Sources and Studies', in *Dār al-islām / dār al-ḥarb: Peoples, Territories, Identities*, Studies in Islamic Law and Society, 40, ed. by Giovanni Calasso and Giuliano Lancioni (Leiden: Brill, 2017), pp. 19–47

Catlos, Brian M., '"Secundum suam Zunam", Muslims in the Laws of the Aragonese "Reconquista"', *Mediterranean Studies*, 7 (1998), 13–26

Chuvin, Pierre, 'Sur l'origine de l'équation "paganus" — païen', in *Impies et païens entre Antiquité et Moyen Âge*, ed. by Lionel Mary and Michel Sot (Paris: Picard, 2002), pp. 7–16

Clément, François, *Pouvoir et légitimité en Espagne musulmane à l'époque des Taifas (Ve–XIe siècles)* (Paris: Harmattan, 1997)

Daniel, Norman, 'Learned and Popular Attitudes to the Arabs in the Middle Ages', *Journal of the Royal Asiatic Society of Great Britain and Ireland*, 1 (1977), 41–52

Fierro, Maribel, and Luis Molina, 'Some Notes on dār al-ḥarb in Early al-Andalus', in *Dār al-islām / dār al-ḥarb: Peoples, Territories, Identities*, Studies in Islamic Law and Society, 40, ed. by Giovanni Calasso and Giuliano Lancioni (Leiden: Brill, 2017), pp. 203–34

Graf, David F., 'The Saracens and the Defense of the Arabian Frontier', in David F. Graf, *Rome and the Arabian Frontier: From the Nabataeans to the Saracens* (Farnham: Ashgate, 1997), Article 9, pp. 1–26

Harmening, Dieter, *Superstitio: Überlieferungs- und theoriegeschichtliche Untersuchungen zur kirchlich-theologischen Aberglaubensliteratur des Mittelalters* (Berlin: E. Schmidt, 1979)

Hoeppner Moran Cruz, Jo Ann, 'Popular Attitudes Towards Islam in Medieval Europe', in *Western Views of Islam in Medieval and Early Modern Europe: Perception of Other*, ed. by David R. Blanks and Michael Frassetto (New York: Palgrave Macmillan, 1999), pp. 55–81

Holt, Peter Malcolm, 'The Treaties of the Early Mamluk Sultans with the Frankish States', *Bulletin of the School of Oriental and African Studies*, 43 (1980), 67–76

——, *Early Mamluk Diplomacy (1260–1290): Treaties of Baybars and Qalāwūn with Christian Rulers*, Islamic History and Civilization, 12 (Leiden: Brill, 1995)

Hoyland, Robert, *Arabia and the Arabs: From the Bronze Age to the Coming of Islam* (London: Routledge, 2001)

İnalcik, Halil, 'Dār al-ʿAhd', in *Encyclopaedia of Islam: Second Edition*, II, ed. by Bernard Lewis, Charles Pellat, and Joseph Schacht (Leiden: Brill, 1965), p. 116

Jaspert, Nikolas, 'Reconquista. Interdependenzen und Tragfähigkeit eines wertekategorialen Deutungsmusters', in *Christlicher Norden — Muslimischer Süden. Die Iberische Halbinsel im Kontext kultureller, religiöser und politischer Veränderungen zwischen dem 11. und 15. Jahrhundert*, Erudiri Sapientia, 7, ed. by Alexander Fidora and Matthias Tischler (Münster: Aschendorff, 2011), pp. 445–65

Kaddouri, Samir, 'Identificación de un manuscrito andalusí anónimo de una obra contra Ibn Ḥazm al-Qurṭubī', *Al-Qanṭara*, 23 (2001), 299–320

——, 'Kitāb al-Tanbīh ʿalā šuḏūḏ Ibn Ḥazm, taʾlīf al-qāḍī Abī l-Aṣbaġ ʿĪsā b. Sahl al-Ǧayyāni (t. 486 h/1093 m)', *al-Ḏaḫāʾir*, 15–16 (2003), 95–108

——, 'Refutations of Ibn Ḥazm by Mālikī Authors from al-Andalus and North Africa', in *Ibn Ḥazm of Cordoba: The Life and Works of a Controversial Thinker*, Handbook of Oriental Studies, I, 103, ed. by Camilla Adang, Maribel Fierro, and Sabine Schmidtke (Leiden: Brill, 2013), pp. 539–99

Khadduri, Majid, 'Hudna', in *Encyclopaedia of Islam: Second Edition*, III, ed. by Bernard Lewis, Victor Louis Ménage, Charles Pellat, and Joseph Schacht (Leiden: Brill, 1971), p. 547

Köhler, Michael A., *Allianzen und Verträge zwischen fränkischen und islamischen Herrschern im Vorderen Orient: Eine Studie über das zwischenstaatliche Zusammenleben vom 12. bis ins 13. Jahrhundert*, Studien zur Geschichte und Kultur des islamischen Orients, N.F., 12 (Berlin: de Gruyter, 1991)

König, Daniel G., 'Wie eine Religion Staat und Gesellschaft durchdringt', in *Staat und Religion in Frankreich und Deutschland*, ed. by Felix Heidenreich, Jean-Christophe Merle, and Wolfram Vogel (Berlin: LIT, 2008), pp. 12–62

——, *Arabic-Islamic Views of the Latin West: Tracing the Emergence of Medieval Europe* (Oxford: Oxford University Press, 2015)

——, 'Charlemagne's 'Jihād' Revisited: Debating the Islamic Contribution to an Epochal Change in the History of Christianization', *Medieval Worlds*, 3 (2016), 3–40

——, *Der Islam und die Genese Europas. Zwischen Ideologie und Geschichtswissenschaften* (Saarbrücken: Universitätsverlag des Saarlandes, 2018)

Lewis, Bernard, *The Muslim Discovery of Europe* (New York: Norton, 2001)

Ljamai, Abdelilah, *Ibn Ḥazm et la polémique islamo-chrétienne dans l'histoire de l'islam*, The Medieval and Early Modern Iberian World, 17 (Leiden: Brill, 2003)

Macdonald, Duncan B., and Armand Abel, 'Dār al-Ṣulḥ', in *Encyclopaedia of Islam: Second Edition*, II, ed. by Bernard Lewis, Charles Pellat, and Joseph Schacht (Leiden: Brill, 1965), p. 131

Martinez-Gros, Gabriel, 'La Première histoire andalouse des sciences', in *Tolède, XIIe–XIIIe siècles: Musulmans, chrétiens et juifs: Le savoir et la tolerance*, ed. by Louis Cardaillac (Paris: Edition Autrement, 1991), pp. 200–17

Martínez Enamorado, Virgilio, 'Ibn Hayyan, el abanderado de la historia de al-Andalus', *Jábega*, 97 (2008), 30–34

Mas Latrie, Louis de, *Traités de paix et de commerce et documents divers concernant les relations des chrétiens avec les arabes de l'Afrique septentrionale au moyen âge*, 2 vols (Paris: H. Plon, 1866)

Mažeika, Rasa, and Loïc Chollet, 'Familiar Marvels? French and German Crusaders and Chroniclers Confront Baltic Pagan Religions', *Francia*, 43 (2016), 41–62
Menocal, Maria Rosa, *The Ornament of the World: How Muslims, Jews, and Christians Created a Culture of Tolerance in Medieval Spain* (Boston: Little, 2002)
Münzel, Bettina, *Feinde, Nachbarn, Bündnispartner: Themen und Formen der Darstellung christlich-muslimischer Begegnungen in ausgewählten historiographischen Quellen des islamischen Spanien* (Münster: Aschendorff, 1994)
Nielen-Vandervoorde, Marie-Adélaïde, 'Un livre méconnu des Assises de Jérusalem: les *Lignages d'outremer*', *Bibliothèque de l'École des Chartes* 153/1 (1995), 103–30
Ramadan, Tariq, *To Be a European Muslim: A Study of Islamic Sources in the European Context* (Leicester: The Islamic Foundation, 1999)
Scales, Peter C., *The Fall of the Caliphate of Córdoba: Berbers and Andalusis in Conflict* (Leiden: Brill, 1994)
Shahîd, Irfan, and Clifford E. Bosworth, 'Saracens', *Encyclopaedia of Islam: Second Edition*, IX, ed. by Clifford E. Bosworth, Emeri J. van Donzel, and Wolfhart P. Heinrichs (Leiden: Brill, 1997), p. 27
Southern, Richard W., *Western Views of Islam in the Middle Ages* (Cambridge, MA: Harvard University Press, 1962)
Tolan, John, 'Muslims as Pagan Idolaters in Chronicles of the First Crusade', in *Western Views of Islam in Medieval and Early Modern Europe: Perception of Other*, ed. by David R. Blanks and Michael Frassetto (New York: Palgrave Macmillan, 1999), pp. 97–117
——, *Saracens: Islam in the Medieval European Imagination* (New York: Columbia University Press, 2002)
——, *Ramon de Penyaforte's Responses to Questions Concerning Relations Between Christians and Saracens: Critical Edition and Translation*, Relmin Working Paper, <https://hal.archives-ouvertes.fr/hal-00761257> [accessed 21 June 2021]
Villano, Raoul, 'The Qur'ānic Foundations of the dār al-islām / dār al-ḥarb Dichotomy: An Unusual Hypothesis', in *Dār al-islām / dār al-ḥarb: Peoples, Territories, Identities*, Studies in Islamic Law and Society, 40, ed. by Giovanni Calasso and Giuliano Lancioni (Leiden: Brill, 2017), pp. 125–46
Wansbrough, John, 'Documents for the History of Commercial Relations Between Egypt and Venice 1442–1512' (unpublished doctoral thesis, University of London, 1961)
——, 'A Mamluk Commercial Treaty Concluded with the Republic of Florence in 894/1489', in *Documents from Islamic Chanceries*, ed. by Samuel Miklos Stern (Oxford: Cassirer, 1965), pp. 39–79
——, 'Venice and Florence in the Mamluk Commercial Privileges', *Bulletin of the School of Oriental and African Studies*, 28,3 (1965), 483–523
Wasserstein, David J., *The Rise and the Fall of the Party Kings: Politics and Society in Islamic Spain 1002–1086* (Princeton: Princeton University Press, 1985)
Wirth, Gerhard, 'Paganus', in *Lexikon des Mittelalters*, VI (Stuttgart: Metzler, 1993), col. 1624

NORA BEREND

The Concept of Christendom

Christianitas *as a Call to Action**

'Christendom' has become a widely accepted designation in modern scholarship, used to characterize medieval Christian lands, with its corollary 'Latin Christendom' more specifically for Catholic areas. Two separate, although interrelated historical questions pertain to this designation: medieval Christendom's political, socio-cultural, and religious community (or level of uniformity) on the one hand, and its conceptual unity on the other. The socio-cultural and religious unity or diversity of (Latin) Christian lands has been debated; whether one sees key commonalities or multi-centred 'Christianities' (or 'micro-Christendoms') is largely a matter of perspective. For example, the significance one gives to political hostilities or to the effectiveness of papal headship, and whether one emphasizes common institutions or their great variability on the ground will provide different results.[1] Medieval conceptualizations of Christendom, regardless of real unity or diversity, need to be investigated based on medieval usage, and it is to that enterprise I wish to contribute here.

'Christendom' entered modern historiography as a translation of the medieval term *christianitas*, a term that would signal that contemporaries espoused and conceptualized a common identity. 'Christendom' would thus designate a medieval identification, one of the main ways in which medieval people conceptualized (territorial) community, the largest common framework that could unite people in action. This conceptual cohesion, we are told, was in principle strong, and enabled a crucial way of ordering the world in the medieval world-view, superseding political differences, even if in practice

* This work has been carried out in the project "El ejercicio del poder: espacios, agentes y escrituras (siglos XI-XV)" (HAR2017-84718-P), funded by MICINN, AEI, UE-FEDER.

1 See e.g. for perspectives that underline unity: Bartlett, *Making of Europe*, pp. 19–21, 243–50; Smith, *Europe after Rome*, p. 239; Angenendt, *Das Frühmittelalter*. For perspectives that stress diversity: Noble and Smith ed., *Early Medieval Christianities*; Noble, 'Introduction'; Brown, *The Rise of Western Christendom*, pp. 216–32.

Nora Berend (nb213@cam.ac.uk), University of Cambridge, United Kingdom

Order into Action: How Large-Scale Concepts of World-Order determine Practices in the Premodern World, ed. by Klaus Oschema and Christoph Mauntel, CURSOR 40 (Turnhout: Brepols, 2022), pp. 71–95
BREPOLS PUBLISHERS 10.1484/M.CURSOR-EB.5.123844

its evocation was more or less successful depending on local circumstances. A recent work, for example, suggests that the term 'Christendom' was used as a concept of world unity by the Roman Church, and was simultaneously an area with borders in the here and now, as well as a universal idea.[2] Referring to Christendom, therefore, we would be using a notion defined by medieval Christians.[3]

A chronology of how the term *christianitas* gained the meaning 'Christendom' has also been elaborated and is now often repeated, with some contested details. Religious meaning emerged in the fourth century[4] and forerunners of a communal sense appeared in patristic texts.[5] *Christianitas* had a multiplicity of meanings in the early Middle Ages, including the Christian religion, faith, being a Christian, a way of addressing Frankish kings, administering the sacraments, ecclesiastical power and jurisdiction, and ecclesiastical units of varying sizes (parish, monastic community, diocese).[6] The formation of the notion of Christendom has been seen as a shift in the meaning of the term to a community of all believers, that also came to include a territorial aspect.[7] Historians have debated the chronology of *christianitas*'s morphing into Christendom (the Carolingian era, the late ninth, or the eleventh century, or a process entailing two turning points), as well as its cause: papal aspirations for headship, external threat in general or more specifically a new collective identity in the face of Islam (already during the ninth century, or only during the crusades), or a combination of the two.[8] Depending on which modern author one turns to, this identity became significant in the early Middle Ages, from the mid- or late-eleventh or the twelfth century.[9] The papacy of Innocent III

2 Whalen, *Dominion of God*, pp. 3, 6, 12, 71.

3 Bartlett, *Making of Europe*, pp. 250–54; Mastnak, *Crusading Peace*, pp. 91–152; Whalen, *Dominion of God*, pp. 2–6; Tolan, 'Constructing Christendom', pp. 277–86.

4 Field, 'Christendom before Europe?'.

5 Daly, 'Caesarius of Arles'; cf. Field, 'Christendom before Europe?', pp. 142–43; Geelhaar, *Christianitas*, pp. 37–133.

6 For a detailed study now see Geelhaar, *Christianitas*.

7 Rupp, *L'Idée de la chrétienté*; Ladner, 'The Concepts of "Ecclesia" and "Christianitas"'; Laarhoven, '"Christianitas"'; Iogna-Prat, *La Maison Dieu*, pp. 196–203; Iogna-Prat, '"Ecclesia/Christianitas"'; Rousset, 'La Notion de chrétienté'.

8 For the use in confrontations with barbarians and Muslims during the seventh to ninth centuries see Manselli, '"Christianitas"'; Carolingian elite: Baschet, 'Chrétienté'; reform papacy: Ladner, 'The Concepts of "Ecclesia" and "Christianitas"'; Laarhoven, '"Christianitas"', esp. pp. 8, 25–31; papal supremacy: Pécout, 'Chrétienté'; Whalen, *Dominion of God*, pp. 9–41; papal power and crusading: Kempf, 'Das Problem der Christianitas', pp. 116–17; crusades: Rousset, 'La Notion de chrétienté'; Katzir, 'The Second Crusade', p. 4; Buc, *Holy War, Martyrdom*, p. 56. Rupp, *L'Idée de la chrétienté*, p. 117, contests the role of Muslim attacks. Iogna-Prat, *La Maison Dieu*, p. 201, claims there were two turning points, i.e. the papacy of Pope John VIII and mid-eleventh century papal reform. For the eleventh to twelfth centuries, see Rousset, 'La Notion de chrétienté'; on Christendom defining itself against what it was not, see Tolan, 'Constructing Christendom', p. 285.

9 See e.g. Rupp, *L'Idée de la chrétienté*, p. 47 (from pontificate of John VIII); Bartlett, *Making*

(1198–1216) is frequently designated as the period when Christendom became a fully fledged notion and identity.[10]

It has more or less been taken for granted that if one pinpoints the emergence of the new meaning, from then on, we can speak of the existence of 'Christendom' as a communal identity. It can even be seen as a more precise designation than the term 'Europe' for most or part of the Middle Ages, a way to avoid suggesting a 'European identity' *avant la lettre*. It is understood that self-designation eventually changed from 'Christendom' to 'Europe'; although when (in the early modern period or already in the thirteenth century for example) and why this happened is debated.[11] The unity of Christendom (or at least of Latin Christendom) is often understood to have been broken apart in the late Middle Ages, in the fourteenth or fifteenth century.[12] The start of the fragmentation of Christendom, and reconceptualization of identity has been tied to the pretensions of Philip IV of France (r. 1285–1314),[13] and the impossibility of mounting a common defence against the Ottomans is seen as the final proof of disintegration.[14]

The assumption that *christianitas* is an unproblematic expression of medieval communal identity has been challenged. Part of such criticism is against modern, romanticizing or politically motivated appropriations, pointing out that medieval Christendom never existed in the way that modern imagination depicts it.[15] Such criticism is very important in contexts where modern political players use distorted versions of the past as legitimation; it is, however, not my concern in this chapter. The other type of criticism started from a keener focus on medieval understandings of *christianitas*. From an initial lone voice here and there concerning some specific aspect of medieval usage, to a more sustained monographic treatment of early medieval word use, the evidence by now is in favour of re-examining the concept.[16] Here I hope to develop further this critical approach to the concept of 'Christendom'.

---

of Europe, pp. 252–54 (from later 11th c.); Laarhoven, '"Christianitas"', pp. 94–95 (first reality then conceptualized by Innocent III); Nirenberg, 'Christendom and Islam', p. 155 (11th–12th c.); Paravicini Bagliani, *Il trono di Pietro*, pp. 225–26 (12th–13th c.).

10 Rupp, *L'Idée de la chrétienté*, pp. 99–123; Hay, *Europe: Emergence*, p. 35; Mastnak, *Crusading Peace*, p. 92; Iogna-Prat, *La Maison Dieu*, p. 201.

11 See e.g. Hay, *Europe: Emergence*, pp. 56–95; Schmieder, 'Von der "Christianitas"', p. 236; Oschema, *Bilder von Europa*, pp. 75–76; Greengrass, *Christendom*.

12 Hay, *Europe in the Fourteenth and Fifteenth Centuries*, pp. 81–83, 426–27; Laarhoven, '"Christianitas"', p. 6; Geelhaar, 'Talking About Christianitas', p. 8; Guenée, *L'Occident*, pp. 57–59.

13 Mastnak, *Crusading Peace*, pp. 252–53.

14 Examples: Keen, *Pelican History of Medieval Europe*, pp. 11–14; Housley, *Religious Warfare*, pp. 62–85; Chaunu, *Le temps des Réformes*. Arguing, however, for the continued existence of unity: Mayeur ed., *De la réforme à la réformation*, pp. 211–13.

15 Étienne Gilson, cited in Laarhoven, 'Chrétienté et croisade', p. 28.

16 See e.g. Laarhoven, '"Christianitas"', p. 87; Laarhoven, 'Chrétienté et croisade'; Geelhaar, *Christianitas*, pp. 20–23, and Geelhaar, 'Talking About Christianitas', pp. 8–9, on earlier critics.

I suggest that the medieval use of *christianitas* was more prescriptive than descriptive, more a call to action, an appeal, than a shared collective identity. Tim Geelhaar's observation that it almost never occurs in the nominative, and was used mostly as 'an attributive complement' indicating 'a non-existent autonomy on a semantic level', may be understood in that framework.[17] *Christianitas*, instead of denoting a matter-of-fact self-understanding and identification, was a term that was used in constructs trying to mobilize support for particularistic local enterprises through an appeal to a constructed, universalizing ideal bond of loyalty.[18] Such a call insinuated that there should be an overarching 'order' of Christian loyalty that should supersede other considerations and mobilize people to action. *Christianitas*, rather than a term for regular everyday use, was attached to appeals and claims exploiting a heightened emotional tone. Even during the alleged heyday of Christendom's unity, the term had to do with vulnerability and contestation.

Further, in this usage there was no radical divide between earlier and later medieval periods, no breakdown in an earlier existing conceptual unity of Christendom due to a fragmentation along national lines: the same type of appeal was made in the name of *christianitas* in the ninth century as in the thirteenth or fifteenth century. The success of such calls did not depend on the conceptual cohesion of Christendom, but on the conjuncture of the self-interest inherent in particularistic aims. I shall not investigate other possible self-conceptualizations during the medieval period, nor do I try to assess how frequently (or rarely) other communal terms, such as *christiani*, or *terra christianorum* were used.[19] My aim is to clarify the medieval uses of the term *christianitas* and its relationship to our concept of 'Christendom', through reconsidering the implications of previous studies and analysing a sample of exemplary cases where authors appealed to *christianitas* as a call to action.

One must be mindful of a few problems when discussing *christianitas* as a motivating factor for action. First, the term's multivalence continued beyond the early Middle Ages. In particular, deciding on the presence of a socio-political and territorial component — whether we translate *christianitas*

---

17 Based on the analysis of the 'Patrologia Latina' corpus: Geelhaar, 'Talking About Christianitas', pp. 12–13. On the low number of nominative uses in Late Antiquity and the Carolingian period, see Geelhaar, *Christianitas*, p. 256.

18 The beginning of more self-reflexive ideas of Europe may be contemporary to the height of appeals to *christianitas*, cf. Schmieder, 'Von der "Christianitas"', p. 214, and Oschema, *Bilder von Europa*, pp. 335–90.

19 See e.g. the terms listed in Laarhoven, 'Chrétienté et croisade', pp. 32, 36. *Terra christianorum* as opposed to *terra paganorum* was used, for example, for the Iberian Peninsula, by Roger of Hoveden in the late twelfth century (Roger of Hoveden, *Chronica*, ed. by Stubbs, vol. III, pp. 43, 49, 175, 178); by Walter of Coventry in the late thirteenth century (Walter of Coventry, *The Historical Collections*, ed. by Stubbs, vol. I, p. 407); in a twelfth-century maritime travel narrative to describe whether jurisdiction over the coastal land was held by Christians or Muslims (Hiatt, 'From Hulle to Cartage', p. 148), and in an Italian Renaissance crusade text (Hankins, 'Renaissance crusaders', p. 362).

as Christendom or Christianity — is often a question of interpretation, rather than of an unambiguous clarity in the sources. Sometimes the distinction is not operative at all, as both are meant, or rather, the distinction is ours.[20] In all cases discussed here, however, *christianitas* appears as a notion appealing to unity — be it territorial or a collectivity sharing the Christian faith — that is deployed to motivate action.

Second, as Philippe Buc pointed out: 'Premodern sources [...] seldom allow the historian to determine whether an event was interpreted after the fact according to a given framework, or whether this framework led people to act in the way they did'.[21] However, while it would be a hazardous enterprise to try to determine whether people *were* motivated to act for *christianitas,* since medieval authors may well have ascribed such a motivation retrospectively, it is quite clear that the authors of several texts thought that an appeal to *christianitas* had the power to stir people into action.

Communal and territorial connotations of *christianitas* emerged in the Carolingian period, yet a concept of Christendom did not, as Tim Geelhaar's excellent monograph demonstrated. Occasionally in statutes and at the court *christianitas* appeared in a socio-political communal sense, and the Carolingian period saw an increased use and diversification of the meaning of *christianitas.*[22] Sporadically politicized in a specific context (for example already in Late Antiquity, in the Donatist debate), the term was not shaped by active conceptualization.[23] Alcuin linked *regnum* and *imperium* to *christianitas* in a metaphysical sense, emphasizing the subordination of the polity to God and Christian lordship (rather than 'Christendom'), and Angilbert around 800 first used a spatial, territorial *christianitas,* gathering relics 'de diversis partibus totius christianitatis' (from different parts of all the Christian lands). Such usages, however, were exceptional, and neither represents the birth of a political concept.[24] A personal sense of Christian virtue and conduct, and pastoral-theological meanings dominated when the term was used.

Further, one cannot speak of a unified elite use of the term *christianitas;* the Carolingian world was characterized by diversified, regionalized word use, accompanied by the expansion and transformation of meaning (which remained diffuse and woolly) from the second half of the ninth century.[25] Short-lived, failed word-use experiments[26] and patchy usage, mostly referring to the faith, and not resulting in a clear territorial-communal concept (despite politicization in the context of the Saxon wars) in a missionary

---

20 On intentional ambiguity, Geelhaar, 'Talking About Christianitas', p. 17. Translations in some languages retained multivalence, like German *Christenheit* or French *chrétienté.*

21 Buc, *Holy War, Martyrdom*, p. 9.

22 Geelhaar, *Christianitas*, pp. 346, 349, 353.

23 Geelhaar, *Christianitas*, pp. 112–15, 341–42.

24 Geelhaar, *Christianitas*, pp. 309–13, 335–36.

25 Geelhaar, *Christianitas*, pp. 336–37, 340–41, 347–50.

26 Ruler's title: Geelhaar, *Christianitas*, pp. 200–09, 261–69, 343–44.

context[27] demonstrate that there was no linear development of a Carolingian 'Christendom'. The collective and territorial meaning of *christianitas* was available from the Carolingian period, but did not become a fixed, stable concept.

John VIII and *Christianitas*

Pope John VIII (872–82) figures prominently in much of the scholarship, credited with the first or real turning point in the fortunes of *christianitas*, creating the concept of Christendom.[28] The combination of the survival of large parts of his registers that provide a rich source base for such an investigation, his use of *christianitas* in several letters, and the historical context, a time of destructive Arab raids and the real threat of further Arab expansion, explains such an approach. Already Jean Rupp saw him as the originator of a papal concept of Christendom, a socially and spatially defined unity of Christians, Christian temporal society (as distinct from the Church), of which Rome was the head.[29] According to this argument, the fact that the pope used the terminology of *defensio christianitatis* demonstrates that *christianitas* became a social reality separate from Church and Empire.[30] The concept was then also linked to facing an external enemy, Islam; the pope used the term in the context of defence, and condemned Christian alliances with non-Christians.[31] At the most extreme, the invention of *christianitas* as Christendom is described as a dramatic moment.[32]

It is easy to see Arab expansion as a natural backdrop to a new, socio-political and territorial-communal identity, the invention of Christendom. The Arabs established themselves in North Africa (*Ifrīqiyyah*) and conducted raids against Sicily already in the seventh century. From 827, they started to conquer cities in Sicily, and the rivalry of the various Christian powers in Italy prompted some to turn to the Arabs for help. Thus in 837 Naples formed an alliance with them against the Lombard Prince Sicard of Benevento. Yet this was to be no mere temporary aid: it facilitated the start of Arab raids on the mainland, in Southern Italy, and paved the way for future alliances between Italian Christians and Muslims. Conquests in Sicily continued despite Byzantine resistance. Arab naval power was superior to Byzantine and Venetian ones; in

27 Geelhaar, *Christianitas*, pp. 275–304.

28 I am drawing on my unpublished paper 'The Concept of Christendom: A Product of Crisis?', in which I analysed the texts of Pope John VIII in detail, at the conference 'Crisis, What Crisis? The Long Ninth Century' (The Mellon Foundation's Sawyer Seminar Series, McDonald Institute for Archaeological Research, University of Cambridge, 8–9 March 2010).

29 Rupp, *L'Idée de la chrétienté*, pp. 35, 47.

30 Rupp, *L'Idée de la chrétienté*, p. 47; Laarhoven, '"Christianitas"', p. 11.

31 Manselli, '"Christianitas"', col. 1916; Hageneder, 'Kirche und Christenheit', pp. 221–22.

32 Iogna-Prat, '"Ecclesia/Christianitas"', pp. 201–02.

840, the Arabs established a permanent base at Taranto, and in 841 took Bari and Brindisi (again in alliance with one Lombard prince against another). In 846 they attacked Rome, and pillaged the Vatican. During the 870s, Louis II and the Byzantines started to wage war effectively against the Arabs, who were expelled from Bari (871) and Taranto (880), but in the same period established a permanent raiding base on the west coast of Italy, which they held until the early tenth century. It was only then that they were defeated completely on mainland Italy.[33]

Dominique Iogna-Prat developed a detailed case for the birth of the concept of Christendom during John's pontificate.[34] The building of walls, the construction of a navy, and repeated calls for help testify to the dire situation in which the pope had to defend Rome and the papal state against Saracen pirates. Thus, although the pope used *christianitas* in traditional ways as well (to address Michael, king of the Bulgarians,[35] or to describe a community from which one can be separated as punishment[36]), above all, he had recourse to the term to argue that all Christians must defend the community of the disciples of Christ against Islam, and highlighted especially royal duty[37] and papal ministry[38] for this defence. The pope developed a new vocabulary of a territorial Christendom: the 'defence of the whole of Christendom' (*defensio totius christianitatis*). It was a dramatic moment, mirrored in the modern shift from *chrétienté* (Christianity) to capitalized *Chrétienté* that signals the invention of Christendom.[39]

As already noted by Iogna-Prat, a *glissement intéressant*, an interesting slippage or synecdoche is noticeable in the papal letters: the defence of the whole of Christendom in fact stands in for the defence of 'our land', the 'land of St Peter'.[40] In a letter to Lambert, count of Spoleto (878), the pope wrote about fighting for the defence of the territory and of the people of the Lord, designating it as a fight concerning all the land of the Prince of the Apostles, to preserve the city of Rome.[41] So Rome and the papal state represent the territorial aspect of Christendom.

The evidence of these papal letters has been understood in very different ways. While Iogna-Prat detects the birth of Christendom, one author even denied that the papal arguments and policies concerning the Arabs had any

33 Kennedy, 'Muslims in Europe'; Engreen, 'Pope John the Eighth'; Gilchrist, 'The Papacy and War'.
34 Iogna-Prat, *La Maison Dieu*, p. 196; Iogna-Prat, '"Ecclesia/Christianitas"', pp. 201–02.
35 *Registrum Iohanis VIII papae*, p. 146 (Ep. 182).
36 *Registrum Iohanis VIII papae*, p. 140 (Ep. 173): *consortium christianitatis*.
37 *Registrum Iohanis VIII papae*, p. 233 (Ep. 263).
38 *Registrum Iohanis VIII papae*, p. 70 (Ep. 74).
39 Iogna-Prat, *La Maison Dieu*, p. 196; Iogna-Prat, '"Ecclesia/Christianitas"', pp. 201–02.
40 Iogna-Prat, *La Maison Dieu*, p. 202; *Registrum Iohanis VIII papae*, p. 194 (Ep. 217): 'our land'; p. 74 (Ep. 78): 'St Peter's land'. Geelhaar, 'L'Autorité du pape', p. 232, instead suggests that only the lands of St Peter are defined in spatially concrete terms.
41 *Registrum Iohanis VIII papae*, p. 74 (Ep. 78). Other letters on the defence of the Roman Church and Rome, e.g. pp. 7 (Ep. 8), 51 (Ep. 56), 126–27 (Ep. 150).

religious aspect, instead writing of a frontier situation which made both cooperation and military clashes between various parties inevitable.[42] Tim Geelhaar's work went a long way towards providing a more nuanced analysis of John VIII's contribution to the concept of *christianitas*. First of all, John VIII was not the first to use such terminology. Carolingian bishops preceded him; around 800 some diocesan statutes already spoke of *pro totius christianitatis salute* (for the salvation of the whole Christian community), and they in turn drew on Late Antique usage.[43] Even the idea of Saracens as enemies of *christianitas* (although not as enemies of a territory, but of the faith) goes back to the early ninth century.[44] Second, John VIII made very limited use of the term *christianitas*. Moreover, in two-thirds of the cases, *christianitas* meant the totality of all Christians, mostly as a spiritual community; and, finally, the idea may in fact have come from John's Chancellor.[45] Geelhaar concluded that no definite concept of *christianitas* emerged in John VIII's letters, and we should not assume that papal authority is the key to understanding the concept of *christianitas*.[46]

I would go further in analysing the peculiar use of *christianitas* here. The Arabs were not the only and sometimes not even the main threat to the pope: local Christian powers were. As Tom Noble has argued, factions emerged out of rivalry for patronage, and John VIII needed protection from the Romans and from Christian powers of Italy just as much as, if not more than he needed it from the Arabs.[47] Pope John's life and death themselves are evidence of the danger from Christians: in 878 he was driven out of Rome by factionalism, and several years later he died murdered (according to the 'Annals of Fulda') by members of his own entourage. While the pope sometimes used *christianitas* to call on Frankish rulers to lend military aid,[48] in fact, several of the letters are not only or not at all about Muslims, but about Christian enemies of the pope, such as Count Lambert of Spoleto and Amalfi.[49] The papal letters often pair the danger from Saracens and iniquitous Christians in one sentence, for example, complaining about the frequent incursions of pagans and ambushes by Christians,[50] or saying explicitly that what the Saracens do not take, the wicked Christians do.[51]

42 Engreen, 'Pope John the Eighth'.

43 Geelhaar, *Christianitas*, pp. 333–34, 352.

44 Geelhaar, *Christianitas*, p. 332 n. 84 (815). Cf. Leo III's letter to Charlemagne about Saracens, writing that *a christianorum finibus eos abiciamus* (let us cast them out from the borders of Christians), clearly referring to the community of Christians: *Leonis III. papae epistolae*, pp. 97–99 (Ep. 7), see p. 98 (11 November 813).

45 On the possible role of Anastasius, Chancellor of Pope Nicholas I and John VIII, see Geelhaar, *Christianitas*, p. 178 note 93.

46 Geelhaar, 'L'Autorité du pape'; Geelhaar, *Christianitas*, pp. 346–47.

47 Noble, 'The Papacy', pp. 572–73.

48 *Registrum Iohanis VIII papae*, pp. 22 (Ep. 19), 29 (Ep. 31), 31 (Ep. 32), 233 (Ep. 263).

49 *Registrum Iohanis VIII papae*, pp. 69–71 (Ep. 74), 194 (Ep. 217).

50 *Registrum Iohanis VIII papae*, p. 69 (Ep. 74, dated 878). Engreen, 'Pope John the Eighth', p. 319 n. 1, counted fourteen allusions to 'pagans and wicked Christians'.

51 *Registrum Iohanis VIII papae*, pp. 225–26 (Ep. 257). Geelhaar, 'L'autorité du pape', p. 232 n. 24;

Often, John used *christianitas* exactly in such contexts: for example, he reproached Count Lambert of Spoleto for invading the lands of St Peter that he should have protected, recalling that the ministry of the pope was for the salvation of the whole of *christianitas*.[52] Similarly, another letter addressed to Lambert admonished the Count not to oppress the Roman Church and its lands, but instead, on pain of excommunication, to work for the defence of the lands of St Peter and the whole of *christianitas*.[53] The Pope reiterated in a complaint to the Frankish ruler Carloman II that the counts Lambert and Adalbert, and not just pagans, oppress the Church, to the 'dishonour' (*dehonestatione*) of the Roman Church.[54] He asked Charles III to defend the Roman Church and *christianitas* against bad Christians and Saracens.[55]

The focus on Pope John VIII's measures of protection against the Arabs — constructing a fleet, building a wall, paying them off and trying to negotiate alliances against them — has been counterproductive in explaining his use of *christianitas*. Instead, I suggest, we should focus on his strategies against Christian enemies. While he had recourse to traditional means (excommunication, admonition, promise of bribes, and alliances), he also started to use a rhetorical device, *christianitas*.

Noble has highlighted the discrepancy between the rhetoric and reality of papal power in the ninth century. Ninth-century popes started to advance claims inherited from Late Antiquity, particularly fifth-century ones on the nature of papal power: the primacy of Peter and his successors, and the Gelasian doctrine implying the superiority of spiritual (hence papal) power. Yet they did not possess real power to put such ideas into practice: historical reality constantly showed up the weakness of the papacy. The slippage into talking about *christianitas* when calling for the defence of the Roman Church, papal lands, and the city of Rome, was to compensate for and rhetorically hide the real weakness of the papal position.

Pope John did not invent a well-defined concept, but used an existing terminology of *christianitas* in an emotionally charged way. This was an element of his strategy of protection, primarily aimed at Christian protagonists, meant to put moral pressure on the recipient so they would correct their behaviour. Linking the term *christianitas* to a call for the protection of papal lands, demanding that bad Christians cease to persecute these lands, the pope tried to shame some of his local enemies into acting in ways seen as honourable for Christians, or at least desisting from dishonourable actions. It was traditional factionalism rather than a unification in the face of the Muslim

---

Geelhaar, *Christianitas*, p. 271 n. 49, and pp. 347, 351.

52 *Registrum Iohanis VIII papae*, p. 69 (Ep. 74): 'pro totius Christianitatis salute'.

53 *Registrum Iohanis VIII papae*, p. 74 (Ep. 78): 'pro salute [...] ac defensione terre sancti Petri et totius Christianitatis'.

54 *Registrum Iohanis VIII papae*, p. 85 (Ep. 89). Various other letters castigate iniquitous Christians, e.g. *Registrum Iohanis VIII papae*, pp. 35 (Ep. 36), 214 (Ep. 246), 219–20 (Ep. 251).

55 *Registrum Iohanis VIII papae*, p. 226 (Ep. 257).

threat that served as the impulse for this use of *christianitas*, and the term, far from expressing an existing unity and a common identity, demanded loyalty to the true faith in the service of a local goal.

Although 'Christendom' has been identified as the means providing continuity after the disintegration of the Carolingian Empire,[56] a thorough analysis of a sermon from 920 shows that *christianitas* was nowhere nearer becoming a firm concept, let alone 'Christendom', in the post-Carolingian world. *Christianitas* did carry an emotional charge, denoting an eschatological city of God and the Spouse of Christ. It was used in the context of attack and defence, to motivate resistance to depredations of ecclesiastical property, and console those suffering depredations with reference to a spiritual realm.[57]

Change in the Eleventh Century?

Pope Gregory VII (1073–1085) has also been assigned a key role in the development and propagation of the concept of Christendom in the service of papal power.[58] Yet, as Laarhoven already pointed out, Gregory in fact seldom used the notion.[59] On the contrary, he associated papal power to the Christian faith, Christian religion, Christian people, and the church.[60] In contexts that from a modern perspective would be ideally suited to an emphasis on 'Christendom', the pope referred to the Christian religion.[61] Bishops who take the pope's side against Henry IV defend the Christian religion and Christian faith.[62] Those, however, who take Henry IV's part destroy 'Christian religion'.[63] Even Saracens pose a danger to 'Christian people' rather than to Christendom.[64]

---

56 The classic formulation can be found in Fossier, *Cambridge Illustrated History*, p. 525; see also Nagy, 'La Notion de *Christianitas*', pp. 132, 138.

57 Nagy, 'La Notion de *Christianitas*'.

58 Rupp, *L'Idée de la chrétienté*, pp. 53–71; Laarhoven, '"Christianitas"'; Whalen, *Dominion of God*, pp. 31–41; Ladner, 'The Concepts of "Ecclesia" and "Christianitas"'. Cf. Paravicini Bagliani, *Il trono di Pietro*, pp. 226–29; Alphandéry, *La Chrétienté*, vol. 1, p. 30. Despite the title, Magdalino, 'Church, Empire and Christendom', does not analyse the concept of Christendom in Gregory's register.

59 Laarhoven, '"Christianitas"', p. 80.

60 Examples: *Register Gregors VII*, ed. by Caspar, pp. 253 (III 6*), 263–67 (III 10). On equivalent terms to Christendom, see Rupp *L'Idée de la chrétienté*, pp. 25–33; Laarhoven, '"Christianitas"', pp. 89–93.

61 Some cases are open to interpretation, see e.g. Magdalino, 'Church, Empire and Christendom', p. 26, who renders II 51 as 'defender of "Christianity"', while *Epistolae vagantes*, ed. and trans. by Cowdrey, p. 143, translates it as 'Christendom'. Cf. Cowdrey, *Pope Gregory VII*, p. 566.

62 *Register Gregors VII*, ed. by Caspar, pp. 293–97 (IV 2), 297–300 (IV 3) at 299; *Epistolae vagantes*, ed. and trans. by Cowdrey, n° 54; Cowdrey, *Pope Gregory VII*, pp. 232–33, 236.

63 *Register Gregors VII*, ed. by Caspar, pp. 389–91 (VI 1) at 390: 'christianam religionem destruere'.

64 *Register Gregors VII*, ed. by Caspar, pp. 421–23 (VI 16) at 421: 'super christianam gentem [...] grave sentio periculum imminere'.

Gregory VII used *christianitas* for example in the context of the Roman Church's primacy and the need to respect its judgement concerning the excommunication of a simoniac bishop.[65] Arguing that papal legates needed to scrutinize the election of an archbishop, the pope maintained that the canonical election of bishops was necessary for the salvation of the whole of *christianitas*.[66] The prayers of the 'faithful of all *christianitas*' (*totius christianitatis fidelium*) were required to support the pope.[67] Gregory VII used *christianitas* in relation to his struggle against Henry IV in one case, when he warned that the danger and harm caused by the upheavals in the 'Teutonic kingdom' affected not just the kingdom itself, but all as far as the borders (*fines*) of *christianitas*.[68] Gregory also asked for one of the Danish king's sons to take an area, which may be Dalmatia, from heretics, as the defender of *christianitas*.[69] The term also occurs to emphasize the importance of a place: hence Monte Cassino is famous *per totam [...] christianitatem* (throughout all of Christendom).[70] A handful of cases only, and they confirm Laarhoven's judgement that Gregory was more concerned with trying to create a socio-political reality rather than a concept of Christendom, and that no such concept was neatly defined during Gregory's pontificate.[71] That the initiator of an ambitious papal programme showed so little interest in the term demonstrates that the medieval practice of creating papal headship did not proceed through the conceptualization of *christianitas*.[72] Additionally, Laarhoven showed that in the *Libelli de lite*, the polemical works of the Investiture Controversy, the term is almost never used.[73] Strikingly, however, several of these instances where Gregory has recourse to the term are calls to action, where the pope uses *christianitas* to add emotional weight to his demands.

Similarly to Gregory VII, the First Crusade is also often privileged as either creating the concept of Christendom, or at least helping spread its use through an intensified identification with the Christian community in confronting Islam.[74] While crusading triggered evocations of a socio-political

---

65 *Register Gregors VII*, ed. by Caspar, pp. 23–25 (I 15) at 24: 'sancta Romana ecclesia, mater [...] totius christianitatis'. Laarhoven, '"Christianitas"', p. 81, renders it as 'totality of Christians'.

66 *Register Gregors VII*, ed. by Caspar, pp. 352–54 (V 5).

67 *Register Gregors VII*, ed. by Caspar, pp. 80–81 (I 53); Laarhoven, '"Christianitas"', p. 82.

68 *Register Gregors VII*, ed. by Caspar, pp. 356–58 (V 7) at 358. Laarhoven, '"Christianitas"', p. 83: 'territorial Christendom'.

69 *Register Gregors VII*, ed. by Caspar, pp. 192–94 (II 51); Cowdrey, *Pope Gregory VII*, pp. 440–41, 456.

70 *Epistolae Vagantes*, ed. and trans. by Cowdrey, p. 74 (n° 28).

71 Laarhoven, '"Christianitas"', pp. 79–80, 87–89, 94–95.

72 Cf. Geelhaar, *Christianitas*, p. 352.

73 Laarhoven, 'Chrétienté et croisade', pp. 29–30.

74 Rousset, 'La Notion de chrétienté'; Mastnak, *Crusading Peace*, pp. 130–32; Nirenberg, 'Christendom and Islam', pp. 155–60; Laarhoven, 'Chrétienté et croisade'; Dupront, *Du sacré*, pp. 264–87; Whalen, *Dominion of God*, p. 70.

and territorial *christianitas* in crusade chronicles (with its traditional meanings, however, remaining preponderant[75]), this by no means became a standard designation.[76] For example, when Fulcher of Chartres reported his version of Urban II's speech at the Council of Clermont, he designated Christians and Turks as 'gens', and advanced territorial arguments about the land of the Christians and the need to drive the Turks out from 'our' lands. He did not attribute to Urban any use of the term *christianitas*, but used it himself in his initial summing up of the speech.[77]

Innocent III, usually credited with the development of full papal headship of Christendom in practice, in fact did not innovate in creating a concept and seldom used the term *christianitas*.[78] At this stage of research, it seems that it was not the papacy, but perhaps clerics at rulers' courts who contributed most to its use. Especially from the thirteenth century onwards, *christianitas* was appropriated as a reference point at these courts, in order to pressure the pope to accept the validity of their own local causes and interests.[79]

Evidence from the Late Middle Ages

The Venetian doge Enrico Dandolo in 1204 wrote to Innocent III, and justified the siege and conquest of Constantinople, which had been condemned by the pope, by portraying the Greeks as traitors to *christianitas*, and the enterprise as benefiting *christianitas*. Presenting actions that served Venetian interests as being to the advantage of *christianitas* was clearly seen as compelling justification by the author.[80] Arguments about acting in the interests of *christianitas* were used to criticize the papacy, for example in connection with the Albigensian crusade or the crusades against Christian powers, as harmful to the cause of the Holy Land.[81] The same type of argument was used in order to persuade the pope to end hostilities with Emperor Frederick II, or to arrange peace between secular powers.[82] Apocalyptic references to the fate of *christianitas*

75 Laarhoven, 'Chrétienté et croisade', p. 33.

76 Laarhoven, 'Chrétienté et croisade', pp. 31–43.

77 Fulcher of Chartres, *Fulcheri Carnotensis Historia*, ed. by Hagenmeyer, pp. 119–38. Fulcher's summary: 'non minus tribulationis iam dictae, sed et maius aut pessimum ex altero mundi climate Christianitati obesse adiecit' (p. 132); pope as exhorting Christians to fight: 'ad id genus nequam de regionibus nostrorum exterminandum' (p. 135).

78 Geelhaar, 'Talking About Christianitas', pp. 12–18; Rupp, *L'Idée de la chrétienté*, pp. 118–19; Hageneder, 'Kirche und Christenheit', p. 222.

79 Geelhaar, 'Talking About Christianitas', p. 11, attributes this to geographical position: '*christianitas* was understood differently in different parts of the Christian world'.

80 *Register Innocenz' III*, ed. by Hageneder and others, pp. 351–54 (n° 202), see p. 353: 'Christianitatis proditores', 'civitatum Constantinopolitanam ad honorem Dei et sancte Romane ecclesie et Christianitatis subventionem decrevimus debellandam'.

81 Throop, *Criticism of the Crusade*, pp. 26–37, 52–53, 61–62 (by Templars in Holy Land); Weiler, '"Negotium Terrae Sanctae"', pp. 32–35.

82 Weiler, '"Negotium Terrae Sanctae"', p. 19.

were used against the papacy.[83] I have discussed such claims in Hungary and the Iberian Peninsula during the thirteenth century, where kings used the argument of defending Christendom in their correspondence with the papacy to gain various benefits.[84] The term seemed so valuable in calls to action that it was even used by King Henry III of England, who asked for higher taxes from his barons and clergy by arguing that King Alfonso X of Castile (1252–1284) wished to invade England with an army of Saracens, enemies of Christendom.[85]

Even outside Latin Europe, *christianitas* started to be used in correspondence with the papacy in order to solicit or extort papal help. Byzantine emperors referred to the common cause of Christians and the community of all Christians in their diplomacy with the West.[86] King Leo (Levon) II (1187–1219) of Cilician Armenia tied his own cause to that of *christianitas*. In a letter to Pope Innocent III, which is incorporated into the papal response, he wrote that the Hospitallers who provided aid to the king against the pagans who wanted to attack his kingdom rendered that service to the whole of *christianitas*.[87] He also underlined that the Armenians would fight for the honour of all of *christianitas*, which is why they can ask Pope Innocent III for help against the barbarians.[88] According to the 'Gesta' of Pope Innocent III, King Leo also presented the war with the Count of Tripoli as pernicious to Christendom, and threatened Innocent that without papal help, he would be incapable of serving Christendom, but offered an army of 20,000 warriors *ad servitium christianitatis* if he were to receive a favourable response in his dispute with the Count of Tripoli.[89]

The instrumental use of the term was on the rise, and spread into the vernacular as well. The *Estoria de España* (or *La Primera Crónica General* as its editor called it) uses the liberation of *cristiandad* (the vernacular equivalent of *christianitas* and equally multivalent) as a motive for action. It attributes to don Pelayo after the Arab-Berber conquest of the peninsula the desire to liberate Christendom (*librar la cristiandad*).[90]

In the *Estoria*, the battle of Las Navas de Tolosa is described as one of the most important events since the creation of the world; people arrived

83 Whalen, *Dominion of God*, pp. 149–227.
84 Berend, 'Défense de la chrétienté'.
85 Weiler, '"Negotium Terrae Sanctae"', p. 20.
86 Chrissis, 'Byzantine Crusaders', pp. 267, 269, 271.
87 Innocent III, *Regesta*, ed. by Migne, book 13, col. 306: 'non solum nobis, verum etiam universae Christianitati magnum et necessarium contulisse succursum contra infinitam paganorum barbariem super nos et regnum nostrum aggregatam, quam Deus disperdat'. (The new edition of the 'Regesta', as quoted in note 79, has not reached year 13 yet.).
88 Innocent III, *Regesta*, ed. by Migne, book 2, col. 776 (nº 217), cols 811–12 (nº 252; cf. cols 813–14, nº 253), book 5, cols 1004–06 (nº 43) (letters between the King of Armenia and Innocent III). See also Geelhaar, 'Talking About Christianitas', pp. 22–25, on other occurrences of *christianitas* in the correspondence between the Armenians and the pope.
89 *Gesta Innocentii*, ed. by Migne, col. 155; *The Deeds of Pope Innocent III*, trans. by Powell (not all the letters in Powell's translation are included in *Gesta Innocentii*), pp. 210–11, 222, 226.
90 *Primera Crónica General*, ed. by Menéndez Pidal, p. 319 (chap. 565).

from everywhere for the deed (*el fecho*) of the faith and law of Christ.[91] The *Estoria* puts in King Alfonso's mouth two speeches just before the day of the battle, expounding two slightly different views of motivation, which refer to *cristiandad* as a motive for action. Alfonso speaks to those who come from various parts of the Iberian Peninsula first; then he talks to those coming from other areas of Europe separately. He addresses the first group, Iberians, as friends, and emphasizes that what unites them is that 'we are all españoles'. He speaks of a territorial war: the Moors (*moros*) entered the land and occupied it by force, so Christians must take revenge and expel them. Towards the end of his speech, the king recalls the defeat of Alarcos, and tells those present that they came to help him take vengeance and repair the ill that has befallen him and *cristiandad*.

When Alfonso addresses those people who arrived from other parts of Europe, he insists on the unifying force of the Church and *cristiandad*: 'en la cristiandad et en la eglesia todos eramos unos' (in Christendom/the Christian faith and in the Church, we were all united). The harm done to *cristiandad* by the Moorish victory touches all; vengeance for these wrongs will honour all of *cristiandad* and the Church.[92] The *Estoria* also describes the victory of Las Navas de Tolosa as the defeat of the enemies of the cross, and the exaltation of Christians faithful to Christ, that honours God and *cristiandad*.[93] Thus Alfonso evokes *cristiandad* in a minor function when giving his motivating speech to the inhabitants of the Iberian Peninsula — and puts it in first place as the unifying element and motivation in his speech to those from outside the peninsula. *Cristiandad* as motivation for action is deployed particularly towards those who do not have an immediate, territorial interest themselves. Whether Alfonso actually employed these arguments — and if he did, whether his audience was motivated by them — or whether the author of the *Estoria* invested *cristiandad* with such a force after the fact is a moot point.

Not much later at the opposite end of Catholic Europe, a regional debate erupted about who has the better claim to demand action appealing to *christianitas* and place blame for inaction. Around 1250, a cleric at the royal chancery, writing in the name of King Béla IV of Hungary reproached the pope, the emperor, and the French king — the three principle courts of *christianitas* — for failing to help him against the Mongol invasion of 1241–42.[94] The manuscript of the royal letter, that developed the image of Hungary as

---

91 *Primera Crónica General*, ed. by Menéndez Pidal, pp. 689–92 (chaps 1011–13), 694–704 (chaps 1014–20). For further analysis of this episode, see Berend, 'Défense de la chrétienté', pp. 1021–26; Oschema, *Bilder von Europa*, pp. 258–59.

92 *Primera Crónica General*, ed. by Menéndez Pidal, p. 693 (chap. 1013). On a similar distinction in Rodrigo Jiménez de Rada's *Historia de Rebus Hispanie*, see Oschema, *Bilder von Europa*, p. 236.

93 *Primera Crónica General*, ed. by Menéndez Pidal, pp. 702 (chap. 1019), 704 (chap. 1020).

94 Città del Vaticano, Archivio Segreto Vaticano (ASV), AA Arm. I–XVIII-605; see *Vetera Monumenta*, ed. by Theiner, pp. 230–32 (nº 440): 'super condicto negocio tres tocius christianitatis principaliores Curias [...] requiri fecimus: de quibus omnibus nichil consolacionis vel subsidii recepimus, nisi verba'. For a description of the document, see

the gate of Christendom survives in the Vatican Archives, under a golden bull. The king emphasized that a fresh imminent Mongol attack targets not just Hungary, but the whole of *christianitas*, used here in a clearly territorial sense, interchangeable with Europe.[95] The letter also evoked Attila the Hun, who used to have his capital on the Danube; this reference to dangers past (the negative image of Attila was prevalent) reinforced the seriousness of the present menace.[96] The way Attila's name is rendered as Totila also provides an indication of the Italian formation of the author, who was trying to gauge what arguments may move the papacy to grant help to King Béla. The letter writer exploited the historical precedent to blackmail the papacy, called on to act in the interest of *christianitas*, and also reproached for not having acted earlier. Without help, in a future attack, Hungary would collapse and leave the gate open towards Europe.

Bishop Bruno of Olomouc a generation later in a report to the pope in preparation for the Second Council of Lyons (1274), saw the danger to *christianitas* coming from Hungary, whose very queen-regent, Elisabeth, was Cuman, with close relatives who were pagans. Bruno's report was linked to the political aspirations of Otakar II Přemysl of Bohemia, eventually to die in the battle of Dürnkrut (1278), against the combined forces of Elisabeth's son Ladislas the Cuman, king of Hungary, and Rudolf of Habsburg. Thus Bruno was not a neutral narrator of events, but rather formulated arguments to convince the pope of the Hungarian danger; in order to gain leverage, he pointed to the maintenance of Cumans, heretics and schismatics in the kingdom, and to marriage ties to the enemies of the Church. He also evoked *christianitas*, rather than Bohemia, as the entity that was endangered by developments in Hungary.[97]

It is often thought that 'Christendom' ceased to provide a unifying force in the late medieval period; yet *christianitas* was used in the same way at the end of the fifteenth century as it had been in the thirteenth to pressure the pope. In 1480, King Matthias of Hungary was asking Cardinal Gabriel, bishop of Eger, to intercede with the pope in preparing a peace treaty with the German Emperor.[98] For Gabriel's (and the pope's) benefit, the author,

---

Martini, *I sigilli d'oro dell'Archivio Segreto Vaticano*, 9E; for further analysis, see Berend, *At the Gate of Christendom*, pp. 163–70; Berend, 'Défense de la chrétienté', pp. 1010–16.

95 *Vetera Monumenta*, ed. by Theiner, p. 231 (n° 440): 'Rumores enim de Tharthari de die in diem nobis adveniunt, quod non solum contra nos [...] ymmo eciam contra totam christianitatem condixerunt, et prout a quam pluribus fide dignis pro certo dicitur, firmiter in brevi proposuerint contra totam Europam suum innumerabilem exercitum destinare'. Europe is used several times in the letter (pp. 231–32), see Berend, *At the Gate of Christendom*, p. 166, Berend, 'Défense de la chrétienté', p. 1011. Also see Oschema, *Bilder von Europa*, pp. 293–94.

96 Bozóky, *Attila*, pp. 71–145; Oschema, *Bilder von Europa*, pp. 119–20.

97 *Vetera Monumenta*, ed. by Theiner, pp. 307–08: 'Hec sunt pericula a Regno Ungarie christianitati imminentia'. See Baldwin, *Pope Gregory X*, pp. 57–58, 137–38.

98 For the background, see Housley, *Later Crusades*, pp. 80–150; for the letter, *Mathiae Corvini Hungariae regis epistolae*, ed. by Fraknói, pp. 604–07.

probably a humanist at the royal chancery, although the king dictated some of the letters and corrected many others, described Matthias's fight 'against the Turks' (*contra Turcos*). He emphasized that the Turks (the standard term for the Ottomans) not only did not attack the lands of Hungary, but had even explicitly informed the king that they meant no harm to his lands while marching through them, and even returned some captives to prove their good-will. Despite this, Matthias decided to confront them, because the Turks' raids are 'to the detriment of *christianitas*' (*in detrimentum totius christianitatis*). Matthias thus gathered his army to fight the Turks, who had entered imperial territory and started raiding and had taken 70,000 people captive just from imperial lands. According to his letter, the Hungarian king could not stand by to see such great damage to *christianitas* because of the emperor's 'negligence and idleness'.[99] Matthias claims that he, rather than the emperor, acts in the interest of *christianitas*: 'We march against them not because of our own injuries and damages, but those of others, we go to battle for *christianitas*'.[100] The king also expresses his certainty that divine mercy for *christianitas* will grant him victory.[101]

Matthias states that he wanted the emperor to cease hostilities against him, and conclude peace, so he could concentrate on fighting the Turks, he who was never lazy to serve the good of *christianitas*, who is much more willing to sacrifice for the defence of *christianitas* than for anything else.[102] Matthias is presented as a champion of *christianitas*, to gain papal support in his political struggles with the emperor. In fact, Matthias, despite his promises, was quite uninterested in fighting against the Ottomans and prioritized his ambitions against Christian neighbours.

Matthias was writing from the position of a Christian king who was the neighbour of the Ottomans; but quite soon, the boundaries became much more blurry. After the 1526 battle of Mohács, and the Ottoman conquest of Buda in 1541, the Kingdom was partitioned into three: Habsburg Hungary,

---

99 *Mathiae Corvini Hungariae regis epistolae*, ed. by Fraknói, p. 606: 'et christianitas, negligentia et desidia imperatoris, tale detrimentum patiatur'.

100 *Mathiae Corvini Hungariae regis epistolae*, ed. by Fraknói, p. 606: 'ibimus contra illos, non pro nostris [...] sed pro alienis iniuriis et dampnis, intuitu christianitatis pugnati, et ibimus eo animo eoque proposito firmo et constanti, ut ubicumque Turcos illos pervenire poterimus, omnino cum illis confligamus'.

101 *Mathiae Corvini Hungariae regis epistolae*, ed. by Fraknói, p. 606: 'Scimus quippe et certi sumus divinam pietatem victoriam hanc miseratione christianitatis nobis favere'.

102 *Mathiae Corvini Hungariae regis epistolae*, ed. by Fraknói, p. 607: 'Sed hec ideo significare voluimus, ut intelligeret nos ad ea que christianitatis commoda et utilitatem concernunt, nunquam fuisse vel esse desides vel negligentes, nec placere nobis, derelicto fidei negotio, privatis et intestinis vacare discordiis, nisi hominum perversitate cogeremur, longeque libentius defensioni christianitatis incumbere, que omnibus aliis, si viderimus eos quorum interest, prout rei necessitas exigeret, debitum suum facere et uos in tam sancto et necessario negotio fidei opportune adiuvare'. For other examples, see Tafiłowski, 'Anti-Turkish Correspondence.'

Ottoman Hungary, and the Principality of Transylvania, a vassal of the Ottoman Empire, until 1699, the year of the final Habsburg victory over the Ottomans. Hungary was a contact zone, experiencing periodic raids, sometimes war, and constant border skirmishes that entailed looting and taking captives.[103] This world also fostered people with multiple or shady loyalties, moving between the opposing camps.

The Ottomans used many local people not only as soldiers, but also as scribes, who could, as such, hold significant importance. Arslan (in vernacular Hungarian rendered as Oroszlán) pasha of Buda, in a letter written in the vernacular Hungarian, asked the Habsburg Emperor Maximilian in 1565 to send him correspondence in Hungarian, because there were few who knew Latin (*deák*), and he had trouble getting someone to explain what letters written in Latin meant.[104] Such reliance on local talent could have a steep price. A scribe in the service of the same Arslan pasha, called János (John) Yahya Yazichi, wrote to János Pethő, captain of the fort of Komárom, in vernacular Hungarian in 1565 to offer his services as a spy, invoking the good of Christendom:

> I am letting you know that I am a Christian by birth. As a child, I fell captive together with my father, and my father converted and I was also made a Turk, and a slave of Mahmud bey of Székesfehérvár. I was sent to a Turkish school, and so I learned Turkish and now am serving Oroszlán pasha. When a letter from His highness the [Habsburg] king is sent, I write [translate] it into Turkish, and therefore my lord, among these Turks, I am very wise about all sorts of things and all sorts of perfidy, both about matters concerning the emperor, and about the beys and viziers; never can news come so secretly that I quickly won't learn about it, and therefore I want the good of poor Christendom, as I want my own; I don't dare to write more about it to You because I fear you may announce it to others, but rather I sent a few words to you through Matthias Belay. Believe me and send me a secret answer. God keep you. 27 Oct 1565. Yahya Yazichi, in Hungarian János, your servant. Either here at the pasha's or in Fehérvár, but only for you, I can find a secure person so that I can always send you the recent news and serve His Highness the king loyally.[105]

---

103 For background see Fodor and Dávid ed., *Ottomans, Habsburgs*; Almási and others ed., *A Divided Hungary*.

104 *A budai basák*, ed. by Takáts, Eckhart and Szekfű, p. 17: 'kerem te felsd mint kegielmes vramat hog mikor te felsd ennekem leuelet jr tehat magyar nieluen jrasa felsd mert deak jrast az ky jol twd jt nalonk jgen szwk es neha neha nag nehezen magaraztatom meg az felsd leuelet'.

105 *A budai basák*, ed. by Takáts, Eckhart, and Szekfű, pp. 17–18: 'en az zegeni kereszttensegnek oly jawat akarom mint zinthe en magamnak' (p. 18, on Christendom; for lack of space I cannot quote the entire text in the Hungarian original).

In this case, Christendom was invoked as a motivation for action by a Hungarian turned 'Turk', who acted for his own advantage in playing both sides. The evocation of such a noble motive presumably served to persuade the recipient to accept his services.

Conclusion

Christianitas may seem to be a descriptive way of ordering the world into Christians and others, conveniently translated as Christendom: a passive perception of religious divides. Medieval authors, however, unlike modern ones, were prone to using *christianitas* as a prescriptive rather than a descriptive term, an appellative notion with an emotional charge. Seemingly a concept expressing a universal self-identification, it was often invoked in the service of particularistic aims; it conflated local interests with the interest of all Christians. There was no real break in this usage in the later Middle Ages.

It is important to note that if we collate the results of earlier studies, we must draw the conclusion that there was no linear chronological development in the meaning of the term *christianitas*. It is untenable to claim a foundational invention that changed the way the word was used ever after. Thus, for example, demonstrating that Pope John VIII used *christianitas* in a social-geographical sense does not mean that he invented the concept of Christendom that would constitute a turning point in the use of the term. Debates on the chronological evolution of the term's meaning can continue because there was no uniform, unidirectional change. John VIII in the late ninth century used it, but the reform papacy in the second half of the eleventh century and Innocent III in the early thirteenth century barely did.[106] The crusade chronicles used the communal sense, but Thomas Aquinas reverted to an ecclesiological meaning.[107] The term's multivalence continued beyond the early Middle Ages, after the 'invention' of Christendom as a socio-political, territorial unit. There was no transformation of meaning once and for all; meaning was determined in the local context of each iteration of the term.

Referring to the good or defence of *christianitas* was used to try to compel others to action, and was claimed by some as the motivating force that spurred them into action. Instead of a clearly defined concept (in many cases, in fact, the Latin term could be translated as either Christendom or Christianity) used for communal identification, *christianitas* was a term in political discourse serving local interests. It was not the favoured expression of a strong papacy, or an expression of the commonality and connectedness of people, but rather an appeal to 'groupness' in the terminology developed by social theorists.[108] In

---

106 Geelhaar, 'L'Autorité du pape'; Laarhoven, '"Christianitas"', pp. 80, 87–89, 94; Laarhoven, 'Chrétienté et croisade', pp. 29–30; Geelhaar, 'Talking About Christianitas'.

107 Laarhoven, 'Chrétienté et croisade'; Melloni, *Innocenzo IV*.

108 Brubaker and Cooper, 'Beyond "Identity"', p. 20.

other words, it was a way to create and claim community, rather than a sign of an existing unity and identification. It was an effort to mobilize people in the name of a loyalty deemed superior to others, because of its connection to the faith. *Christianitas* could be used in a political way without being a political concept.[109] It had more to do with contestation than with unity in the early and high medieval periods, and continued to be used as a political tool for particularistic aims in the later medieval period. Tensions and appropriations were central to the use of *christianitas* throughout the medieval centuries, rather than being the result of crisis in the later Middle Ages.

In spite of the prevalent view that the socio-political, communal meaning of 'Christendom' was developed by the papacy in search for power and/or developed as a self-understanding in the face of confrontation with external (Muslim) danger,[110] we find appeals to *christianitas* in internal, intra-Christian discourse, as a device to shame the Christian recipient into action. *Christianitas* as a term of appeal continued to be used in the late medieval period in the same way as in the central Middle Ages.

A revision of our concept of Christendom as a mere translation of the medieval concept of *christianitas* is in order. Christendom can be used, just like any other term, in modern historiography, but we should be aware of and clarify the distinction between medieval and modern usage.[111] Let us acknowledge this is our term, and not invest it with a medieval pedigree of *christianitas* it does not possess. *Christianitas* was not a crystallized, defined concept that was potent until a later disintegration of Christian unity. Some already intuited that the birth of the concept of Christendom may be found in Catholic historiography of the first half of the twentieth century,[112] and the modern uses of the narrative of Christian Europe in identity politics have been analysed.[113] A detailed study of the concept's modern origins is a book waiting to be written. It is perhaps unsurprising that so many of our basic concepts can be so flawed; after all, the very name of our discipline ('medieval' history) is borrowed from a Renaissance invention.

It is time to move away from a view of medieval *christianitas* in its 'Christendom' sense as the fruit of papal aspirations, or a concept, a self-understanding that gained definition in confrontation with Islam. *Christianitas* as Christendom may be better viewed as a term that was intended to mobilize support within Christian lands (the extent of which could be defined more narrowly as areas under the Catholic Church, or more broadly as those encompassing all Christians), by calling on a supposed (idealized) loyalty

109 Geelhaar, *Christianitas*, p. 349.

110 Although internal enemies and contestation are sometimes acknowledged in these paradigms, see Whalen, *Dominion of God*, p. 41; Tolan, 'Constructing Christendom', pp. 283, 285.

111 Geelhaar, *Christianitas*, pp. 353–54.

112 Laarhoven, 'Chrétienté et croisade', p. 28.

113 Perkins, *Christendom and European Identity*.

that should bind Christians together. This self-conception did not develop along a linear timescale; it was used in contexts where such a call to action was seen as advantageous. It was often used in internal disputes between Christians, including against the pope. The supposed loyalty based on faith (conceived of as the truth) was to surpass any other ties. This was never the case in reality (just as in other eras, particular interests always exert a centrifugal force), but it was a reprimand seen to carry moral force because of its referent ultimately being based on religious truth. In practice, whether such an admonition worked on the intended recipient depended on the particular conjuncture of circumstances.

Works Cited

Manuscripts

Città del Vaticano, Archivio Segreto Vaticano (ASV), AA Arm. I–XVIII-605

Primary Sources

A budai basák magyar nyelvű levelezése, ed. by Sándor Takáts, Ferencz Eckhart, and Gyula Szekfű, I: *1553–1589* (Budapest: Históriaantik Könyvkiadó, repr. 2011)

The Deeds of Pope Innocent III by an Anonymous Author, trans. by James M. Powell (Washington, DC: The Catholic University of America Press, 2004)

The Epistolae Vagantes of Pope Gregory VII, ed. and trans. by Herbert Edward John Cowdrey (Oxford: Clarendon Press, 1972)

Fulcher of Chartres, *Fulcheri Carnotensis Historia Hierosolymitana (1095–1127)*, ed. by Heinrich Hagenmeyer (Heidelberg: Carl Winters Universitätsbuchhandlung, 1913)

Gesta Innocentii PP. III ab auctore anonymo sed coaetaneo scripta in *Patrologiae cursus completus: series latina*, ed. by Jacques-Paul Migne, CCXIV (Paris: Garnier, 1844–64), cols 16–228

Innocent III, *Regesta*, in *Patrologiae cursus completus: series latina*, ed. by Jacques-Paul Migne, Books 2 and 5, CCXIV, and Book 13, CCXVI (Paris: Garnier, 1844–64)

Leonis III. papae epistolae, ed. by Karl Hampe, in *Monumenta Germaniae Historica Epistolarum*, V / *Epistolae Karolini Aevi*, III (Berlin: Weidmann, 1899), pp. 85–104

Mathiae Corvini Hungariae regis epistolae exterae. Mátyás király levelei: Külügyi osztály 1458–1490, ed. by Vilmos Fraknói, reprint (Budapest: Nap Kiadó, 2008)

Primera Crónica General de España, ed. by Ramón Menéndez Pidal, 2 vols (Madrid: Editorial Gredos, 1955)

Das Register Gregors VII, ed. by Erich Caspar, in *Monumenta Germaniae Historica Epistolae Selectae* II, fasc. 1 (Berlin: Weidmannsche Buchhandlung, 1920)

Die Register Innocenz' III, VII: *7. Pontifikatsjahr, 1204/1205*, ed. by Othmar Hageneder and others, Publikationen des Historischen Instituts beim Österreichischen Kulturinstitut in Rom, II. Abteilung, I. Reihe, 7 (Vienna: Österreichische Akademie der Wissenschaften, 1997)

Registrum Iohannis VIII papae, ed. by Erich Caspar, in *Monumenta Germaniae Historica Epistolarum*, VII / *Epistolae Karolini Aevi*, V (Berlin: Weidmann, 1928), pp. 1–333

Roger of Hoveden, *Chronica Magistri Rogeri de Houedene*, III, ed. by William Stubbs (Cambridge: Macmillan, 1870)

Vetera Monumenta Historica Hungariam Sacram Illustrantia, I: *1216–1352*, ed. by Augustinus Theiner (Rome: Vatican, 1859)

Walter of Coventry, *The Historical Collections of Walter of Coventry*, I, ed. by William Stubbs (Cambridge: Cambridge University Press, 2012)

Secondary Studies

Almási, Gábor, and others, ed., *A Divided Hungary in Europe: Exchanges, Networks and Representations, 1541–1699*, 3 vols (Newcastle upon Tyne: Cambridge Scholars Publishing, 2014)

Alphandéry, Paul, *La Chrétienté et l'idée de croisade*, 2 vols (Paris: Albin Michel, 1954–1959)

Angenendt, Arnold, *Das Frühmittelalter. Die abendländische Christenheit von 400 bis 900* (Stuttgart: W. Kohlhammer, 1990)

Baldwin, Philip B., *Pope Gregory X and the Crusades*, Studies in the History of Medieval Religion, 41 (Woodbridge: Boydell, 2014)

Bartlett, Robert, *The Making of Europe: Conquest, Colonization and Cultural Change 950–1350* (Princeton: Princeton University Press, 1993)

Baschet, Jérôme, 'Chrétienté', in *Dictionnaire des faits religieux*, ed. by Danièle Hervieu-Léger and Régine Azria (Paris: Presses universitaires de France, 2010), p. 132

Berend, Nora, *At the Gate of Christendom: Jews, Muslims and 'Pagans' in Medieval Hungary, c. 1000–c. 1300* (Cambridge: Cambridge University Press, 2001)

——, 'Défense de la Chrétienté et naissance d'une identité: Hongrie, Pologne et péninsule ibérique au Moyen Âge', *Annales HSS*, 58,5 (2003), 1009–27

Bozóky, Edina, *Attila et les Huns: vérités et légendes* (Paris: Perrin, 2012)

Brown, Peter, *The Rise of Western Christendom: Triumph and Diversity, A.D. 200–1000* (Oxford: Blackwell, 1997)

Brubaker, Roger, and Frederick Cooper, 'Beyond "Identity"', *Theory and Society*, 29 (2000), 1–47

Buc, Philippe, *Holy War, Martyrdom and Terror: Christianity, Violence and the West* (Philadelphia: University of Pennsylvania Press, 2015)

Chaunu, Pierre, *Le Temps des Réformes. Histoire religieuse et système de civilisation. La crise de la chrétienté, l'éclatement (1250–1550)* (Paris: Fayard, 1996)

Chrissis, Nikolaos G., 'Byzantine Crusaders: Holy War and Crusade Rhetoric in Byzantine Contacts with the West (1095–1341)', in *The Crusader World*, ed. by Adrian Boas (London: Routledge, 2016), pp. 259–77

Cowdrey, Herbert Edward John, *Pope Gregory VII, 1073–1085* (Oxford: Clarendon Press, 1998)

Daly, William M., 'Caesarius of Arles, a Precursor of Medieval Christendom', *Traditio*, 26 (1970), 1–28

Dupront, Alphonse, *Du sacré: Croisades et pèlerinages, images et langages* (Paris: Gallimard, 1987)

Engreen, Fred E., 'Pope John the Eighth and the Arabs', *Speculum* 20,3 (1945), 318–30

Field, Lester L. Jr, 'Christendom before Europe? A Historiographical Analysis of "Political Theology" in Late Antiquity', in *Plenitude of Power: The Doctrines and Exercise of Authority in the Middle Ages: Essays in Memory of Robert Louis Benson*, ed. by Robert C. Figueira (Aldershot: Ashgate, 2006), pp. 141–70

Fodor, Pál, and Géza Dávid, ed., *Ottomans, Habsburgs and Hungarians in Central Europe: The Military Confines in the Era of Ottoman Conquest* (Leiden: Brill, 2000)

Fossier, Robert, ed., *The Cambridge Illustrated History of the Middle Ages*, I: 350–950 (Cambridge: Cambridge University Press, 1989)

Geelhaar, Tim, 'L'Autorité du pape sur la chrétienté, développement d'une idée au IXe siècle? Auctoritas et christianitas dans les lettres de Jean VIII (872–82)', *Hypothèses: Travaux de l'École doctorale d'Histoire, publications de la Sorbonne* (2011), 225–37

——, *Christianitas: Eine Wortgeschichte von der Spätantike bis zum Mittelalter*, Historische Semantik, 24 (Göttingen: Vandenhoeck & Ruprecht, 2015)

——, 'Talking About Christianitas at the Time of Innocent III (1198–1216): What does Word Use Contribute to the History of Concepts?', *Contributions to the History of Concepts*, 10,2 (2015), 7–28

Gilchrist, John, 'The Papacy and War Against the Saracens 795–1216', *The International History Review*, 10,2 (May 1988), 174–97

Greengrass, Mark, *Christendom Destroyed: Europe 1517–1648* (London: Penguin, 2015)

Guenée, Bernard, *L'Occident aux XIVe et XVe siècles: Les États*, 6th edn (Paris: Presses universitaires de France, 1998)

Hageneder, Othmar, 'Kirche und Christenheit in der neuen Ekklesiologie des Papsttums', in *Pensiero e sperimentazioni istituzionali nella 'Societas Christiana' (1046–1250). Atti della sedicesima Settimana internazionale di studio, Mendola, 26–31 agosto 2004*, ed. by Giancarlo Andenna (Milan: Vita e Pensiero, Largo A. Gemelli, 2007), pp. 215–36

Hankins, James, 'Renaissance Crusaders, Humanist Crusade Literature in the Age of Mehmed II', in *Humanism and Platonism in the Italian Renaissance*, I, Storia e Letteratura Raccolti di Studi e testi, 215 (Rome: Edizioni di Storia e Letteratura, 2003, 2nd repr. 2005), pp. 293–424 (Chap. 11)

Hay, Denys, *Europe: The Emergence of an Idea*, rev. edn (Edinburgh: Edinburgh University Press, 1968)

——, *Europe in the Fourteenth and Fifteenth Centuries*, 2nd edn (London: Longman, 1989)

Hiatt, Alfred, '"From Hulle to Cartage": Maps, England, and the Sea', in *The Sea and Englishness in the Middle Ages: Maritime Narratives, Identity and Culture*, ed. by Sebastian I. Sobecki (Cambridge: Brewer, 2011), pp. 133–57

Housley, Norman, *The Later Crusades: From Lyons to Alcazar 1274–1580* (Oxford: Oxford University Press, 1992)

——, *Religious Warfare in Europe 1400–1536* (Oxford: Oxford University Press, 2002)

Iogna-Prat, Dominique, *La Maison Dieu: une histoire monumentale de l'Église au Moyen Âge* (Paris: Seuil, 2006)

——, '"Ecclesia/Christianitas": identité universelle et identité religieuse', in *Religiosità e civiltà. Identità delle forme religiose (secoli X–XIV), Atti del Convegno Internazionale, Brescia, 9–11 settembre 2009*, ed. by Giancarlo Andenna, 'Le Settimane internazionali della Mendola', Nuove Serie 2007–2011 (Milan: Vita e Pensiero, 2011), pp. 193–206

Katzir, Yael, 'The Second Crusade and the Redefinition of Ecclesia, Christianitas and Papal Coercive Power', in *The Second Crusade and the Cistercians*, ed. by Michael Gervers (New York: Saint Martin's Press, 1992), pp. 3–11

Keen, Maurice, *The Pelican History of Medieval Europe* (Harmondsworth: Penguin, repr. 1981)

Kempf, Friedrich, 'Das Problem der Christianitas im 12. und 13. Jahrhundert', *Historisches Jahrbuch*, 79 (1959), 104–23

Kennedy, Hugh N., 'The Muslims in Europe', in *The New Cambridge Medieval History, II: c. 700–c. 900*, ed. by Rosamond McKitterick (Cambridge: Cambridge University Press, 1995), pp. 249–71

Laarhoven, Jan van, '"Christianitas" et réforme Grégorienne', *Studi gregoriani per la storia di Gregorio VII e della riforma gregoriana*, 6 (1959–61), 1–98

——, 'Chrétienté et croisade. Une tentative terminologique', *Cristianesimo nella storia*, 6 (1985), 27–43

Ladner, Gerhart B., 'The Concepts of "Ecclesia" and "Christianitas" and their Relation to the Idea of Papal "Plenitudo Potestatis" from Gregory VII to Boniface VIII', in *Sacerdozio e regno da Gregorio VII a Bonifacio VIII*, ed. by Friedrich Kempf, Miscellanea historiae pontificiae, 18 (Rome: Pontificia Università Gregoriana, 1954), pp. 49–77

Magdalino, Paul, 'Church, Empire and Christendom in c. 600 and c. 1075: The View from the Registers of Popes Gregory I and Gregory VII', in *Cristianità d'Occidente e Cristianità d'Oriente (secoli VI–XI)*, Settimane di Studio della Fondazione Centro Italiano di Studi sull'Alto Medioevo, LI (Spoleto: Presso La Sede della Fondazione, 2004), pp. 1–30

Manselli, Raoul, '"Christianitas"', in *Lexikon des Mittelalters*, II (Munich: Artemis, 1983), cols 1915–16

Martini, Aldo, ed., *I sigilli d'oro dell'Archivio Segreto Vaticano* (Milan: Franco Maria Ricci, 1986)

Mastnak, Tomaž, *Crusading Peace: Christendom, the Muslim World and Western Political Order* (Berkeley: University of California Press, 2002)

Mayeur, Jean-Marie, ed., *De la réforme à la réformation, 1450–1530*, Histoire du christianisme, 7 (Paris: Desclée, 1995)

Melloni, Alberto, *Innocenzo IV. La concezione e l'esperienza della cristianità come regimen unius personae*, Testi e ricerche di scienze religiose, nuova serie, 4 (Genova: Marietti, 1990)

Nagy, Piroska, 'La Notion de Christianitas et la spatialisation du sacré au Xe siècle: un sermon d'Abbon de Saint-Germain', *Médiévales*, 49 (2005), 121–40

Nirenberg, David, 'Christendom and Islam', in *Christianity in Western Europe c. 1100–c. 1500*, ed. by Miri Rubin and Walter Simons, The Cambridge History of Christianity, 4 (Cambridge: Cambridge University Press, 2009), pp. 149–69

Noble, Thomas F. X., 'The Papacy in the Eighth and Ninth Centuries', in *New Cambridge Medieval History, II: c. 700–c. 900*, ed. by Rosamond McKitterick (Cambridge: Cambridge University Press, 1995), pp. 563–86

——, 'Introduction', in *European Transformations: The Long Twelfth Century*, ed. by Thomas F. X. Noble and John van Engen (Notre Dame, IN: University of Notre Dame Press, 2012), pp. 1–16

Noble, Thomas F. X., and Julia M. H. Smith, ed., *Early Medieval Christianities c. 600–c. 1100*, The Cambridge History of Christianity, 3 (Cambridge: Cambridge University Press, 2008)

Oschema, Klaus, *Bilder von Europa im Mittelalter*, Mittelalter-Forschungen, 43 (Ostfildern: Jan Thorbecke, 2013)
Paravicini Bagliani, Agostino, *Il trono di Pietro: L'universalità del papato da Alessandro III a Bonifacio VIII* (Rome: Carocci, 1996)
Pécout, Thierry, 'Chrétienté', in *Dictionnaire encyclopédique du Moyen Âge*, I (Paris: Cerf, 1997), p. 319
Perkins, Mary Ann, *Christendom and European Identity: The Legacy of a Grand Narrative since 1789*, Religion and Society, 40 (Berlin: Walter de Gruyter, 2004)
Rousset, Paul, 'La Notion de chrétienté aux XIe et XIIe siècles', *Le Moyen Âge*, 69 (1963), 191–203
Rupp, Jean, *L'Idée de la chrétienté dans la pensée pontificale des origines à Innocent III* (Paris: Les Presses Modernes, 1939)
Schmieder, Felicitas, 'Von der "Christianitas" nach "Europa"', in *Die Welt 1000–1250*, ed. by Angela Schottenhammer and Peter Feldbauer (Vienna: Mandelbaum, 2011), pp. 213–38
Smith, Julia M. H., *Europe after Rome: A New Cultural History 500–1000* (Oxford: Oxford University Press, 2005)
Tafiłowski, Piotr, 'Anti-Turkish Correspondence between Matthias Corvinus and Pope Sixtus IV: A Contribution to the History of Propaganda in the International Relations in the Late Middle Ages,' *Rocznik Orientalistyczny*, 66,2 (2013), 14–31
Throop, Palmer Allan, *Criticism of the Crusade* (Amsterdam: Swets and Zeitlinger, 1940)
Tolan, John, 'Constructing Christendom', in *'The Making of Europe': Essays in Honour of Robert Bartlett*, ed. by John Hudson and Sally Crumplin (Leiden: Brill, 2016), pp. 277–98
Weiler, Björn, 'The "Negotium Terrae Sanctae" in the Political Discourse of Latin Christendom, 1215–1311', *International History Review*, 25,1 (2003), 1–36
Whalen, Brett Edward, *Dominion of God: Christendom and Apocalypse in the Middle Ages* (Cambridge, MA: Harvard University Press, 2009)

ALBRECHT FUESS

A 'Medieval Islamist' Versus an 'Arab Machiavelli'?

The Legacy of the Mamluk Scholars Ibn Taymīya (1263–1328) and Ibn Nubāta (1287–1366)

Introduction

Living at the end of the thirteenth century, the Mamluk scholars Ibn Nubāta und Ibn Taymīya witnessed a challenging period for the newly emerging Mamluk Empire. Many of their contemporaries perceived their own time as being decisive not only for the future of the realm but for the religion of Islam as a whole.

There were several reasons for this assessment. Not only had the Mongols sacked Baghdad in 1258 and killed the last Abbasid Caliph al-Mustanṣir; they had also continued their advance towards the west and even conquered Damascus in March 1260, at a time when the Crusader kingdoms were still very much present on the Syro-Palestinian coast. The Mamluk rulers of Cairo feared that the Christian crusaders might conclude an alliance with the Mongol infidels against them. Indeed, several letters had been exchanged between European leaders and the Mongols in an attempt to forge an anti-Mamluk alliance.[1] The Mamluks perceived these diplomatic initiatives as a very real threat, despite the fact that such a Franco-Mongol alliance never came into being, as we know today. The moment thus seemed to be a critical period for the eastern Muslim realms, when — only two years after the fall of Baghdad, the capital of the Islamic Caliphate — the Mamluks defeated Mongol forces under the command of General Kitbuqa at the battle of ʿAyn Jālūt in Palestine in September 1260 and drove them out of Syria.[2] Thanks to this important

1 For an overview on the general situation see, e.g., Jackson, *The Mongols and the West*, and Amitai-Preiss, *Mongols and Mamluks*.

2 Smith, 'Ayn Jālūt'.

Albrecht Fuess (albrecht.fuess@staff.uni-marburg.de), Department of Islamic Studies, Center for Near and Middle Eastern Studies, Philipps-Universität Marburg (University of Marburg), Germany

Order into Action: How Large-Scale Concepts of World-Order determine Practices in the Premodern World, ed. by Klaus Oschema and Christoph Mauntel, CURSOR 40 (Turnhout: Brepols, 2022), pp. 97–125
BREPOLS PUBLISHERS 10.1484/M.CURSOR-EB.5.123845

military achievement, the victors quickly became the heroes of the Muslim world who had won against the 'pagans'. The success of the Mamluks, who were mostly of Turkish descent, against their Central Asian Mongol 'cousins', inspired the legal scholar and historian Abū Shāma (d. 1268) to conclude that 'against every (evil) thing there is a cure from its own kind' (*wa-li-kulli shay'in āfatun min jinsihi*).[3]

Soon after their victory, the Mamluks installed a descendant of the Abbasid dynasty, who had fled the Mongols, as their own 'puppet Caliph' in Cairo, thereby reinforcing their own legitimacy.[4] After all, they were still perceived by some of their fellow Muslims to be unfit to rule themselves, because of their modest origins as military slaves.

However, when they finally prevailed against the Mongols in the first half of the fourteenth century and ousted the crusaders definitively after the fall of Acre in 1291, the Mamluk sultans became the most powerful Muslim rulers in the eyes of many contemporaries, and the people rallied behind them in order to encounter the next external attack. Rumours of troops coming from the east or of ships landing at the coast remained quite common — and in fact, some larger attacks, like the sack of Alexandria by the Cypriot King Peter of Lusignan in 1365, did take place.[5] As a consequence, all members of society remained vigilant in fear of renewed military initiatives by either the Mongols or the crusaders.

At this very moment, when the Mamluk realm was in constant internal disorder and encountered external threats, the two scholars on whom this chapter focuses started to become influential through their personalities and their writings. Both of them tried to bring order into their world by way of guiding rulers and officials through their advice, and they called for specific actions rulers should take in their own interest and in the interest of Islamic society as a whole. However, even though they lived in the same difficult circumstances, their approach to answering the question as to how order should be transformed into action and who was responsible for the execution of orders differed considerably. As will be shown in the following pages, Ibn Taymīya called for the absolute rule of God, and he considered the Qur'ān and Sunna (i.e. the sayings and deeds of the Prophet) to be the concrete guidelines for achieving this reality. He was the first to define a new form of governmental order, which should always be in accordance with the *sharia*. But the *sharia* represents an ambiguous term that was (and is) much disputed by Muslim scholars of the past and the present. Nevertheless, according to modern scholars, Ibn Taymīya was the first Muslim thinker to merge *sharia* and 'politics' (*siyāsa*) to represent a new holistic order.[6] Or as Anjum puts it:

3 Fuess, 'Mamluk Politics', p. 96.

4 Haarmann, 'Der arabische Osten', pp. 229–30.

5 See Fuess, 'Why Venice, not Genoa?'.

6 Bosworth and others, 'Siyāsa'.

'the phrase al-siyāsa al-shar'iyya, despite its stunning simplicity, was unheard of, if not oxymoronic, during the classical age'.[7]

Every action of a ruler had to be justified on this basis of its fitting into the *al-siyāsa al-sharia* — and Ibn Taymīya was never open to compromise: in his eyes, God was always on his side, so why should he change his position? However, his resolution (which some of his contemporaries perceived as stubbornness) never to falter or to doubt his own approach made it difficult even for the Mamluk rulers to support the popular (and populist) but controversial preacher in all aspects of his teachings. It is thus not very surprising that Ibn Taymīya finally ended up in prison, not least because the order he wanted to have put into action led to constant disorder and uproar around him.

Ibn Nubāta, on the other hand, was very much appreciated by his colleagues and well versed in public administration. His ideas and propositions were of a more pragmatic nature and oriented towards practice, including advice that he certainly applied himself when he worked in the administration. Even more important: although he doubtlessly was a pious man, he did not overburden his orders with a divine charge. He rather seems to have assumed that everything that was in the interest of the ruler and his government would obviously and automatically benefit Muslim society. This more 'realistic' approach and his personal willingness to compromise seemed to be more successful in terms of his own personal fate and the stability of Mamluk society generally. Ibn Nubāta would probably never have felt the urge to verify that measures of the government were in accordance with an *al-siyāsa al-sharia* ('*sharia* politics'): I would rather assume that for him both spheres constituted two different entities and that God should be above the daily dealings of the government. Ibn Nubāta and many other scholars of his time, who shared his perspective, were thus highly critical about the new order that Ibn Taymīya tried to impose on society. Seen from this point of view, the present chapter will deal with a new world-view in Islamic political thought, describing how its actual implementation was not successful during the lifetime of its initiator, but had long-lasting effects on Islamic ideas of order up until today. At the same time, it will become clear that the more pragmatic Islamic order as represented by Ibn Nubāta has fallen into oblivion — as has the author himself, when compared to the leading role that Ibn Taymīya and his writings have played in the Muslim public sphere up to the present day.

Ibn Taymīya and Ibn Nubāta — Scholars of the Fourteenth Century

Ibn Taymīya, the elder of our two protagonists, was born in 1263 in Ḥarrān (northern Syria) into a family of important legal scholars from the Ḥanbalī

7 Anjum, *Politics, Law, and Community in Islamic Thought*, p. 30.

school of law.[8] When he was approximately six years old, he had to flee from his hometown, together with his father and his three brothers, in order to escape a Mongol advance. They found refuge in Damascus, but the episode arguably left a deep impression on Ibn Taymīya and his later writings. In the following years, he received an education as a Ḥanbalī scholar in Damascus and went on pilgrimage to Mecca (1292). In 1296 he taught at the Ḥanbalīya madrasa in Damascus. When the Mongols invaded Syria again in 1300, he was described as a leader of the local resistance;[9] he even went to Cairo in order to ask the Sultan an-Nāṣir Muḥammad ibn Qalāwūn (r. 1293–94 / 1299–1309 / 1310–1341) for help against the attack. To all appearances, this initiative was crowned by success: the young sultan took an army to Syria and the Mongols retreated.[10]

During the early years of his career in Damascus, Ibn Taymīya was repeatedly accused by rival scholars of harbouring and expressing 'heterodox' ideas about the attributes of God and their description in the Qur'ān; they particularly criticized his position on qur'ānic expressions like the 'throne of God', 'hand of God', etc. Several of his fellow religious scholars accused him of teaching forbidden anthropomorphism, since he allegedly presented God in terms that made him look like a human.[11] Subsequently, Ibn Taymīya was carefully examined on these questions, but in the end, he was cleared of all accusations. More problematic, however, was his preaching against popular Islam as practised by the Sufis, especially the veneration of saints, which he rejected completely. At one point, he even went so far as to destroy a footprint that the prophet had allegedly left on a rock near Damascus, which some had venerated as sacred.[12] Ibn Taymīya also preached heavily against Muslim sects in the region of Mount Lebanon, and he even took part in military expeditions against them, claiming that internal Muslim enemies were worse than external foes.[13]

While these jihad-inspired activities were perceived as very positive by the authorities (like the Mamluk governor of Damascus or the Mamluk sultan in Cairo), Ibn Taymīya's theological quarrels with his colleagues repeatedly stirred up public order in Damascus. In January 1306, two meetings were held at the residence of the governor al-Afram in Damascus. In the end, the assemblies concluded (not least due to the governor's direct intervention) that Ibn Taymīya's preaching was in fact in accordance with the Qur'ān and

---

8 For a biographical overview see Laoust, 'Ibn Taymiyya'; for a complete scholarly biography in a Western language see Bori, *Ibn Taymiyya*. Current scholarship on various questions regarding Ibn Taymīya can be found in Rapoport and Ahmed ed., *Ibn Taymiyya and His Times*.

9 Laoust, 'Ibn Taymiyya'.

10 Laoust, 'Ibn Taymiyya'.

11 See Holzmann, 'Accused of Anthropomorphism'; Hoover, 'God Acts by His Will and Power'.

12 Laoust, 'Ibn Taymiyya'; see also Olesen, *Culte des Saints et Pèlerinages*.

13 Laoust, 'Remarques sur les expéditions du Kasrawan'; Bārūt, *Ḥamalāt Kisrawān*, pp. 122–56; Winter, *The Shiites of Lebanon*, pp. 62–63.

the Sunna. Nevertheless, the conflicts continued and the noise they created finally reached Cairo, the Mamluk capital. Ibn Taymīya had to present himself in person and in 1307 he was imprisoned, under the accusation of anthropomorphism.[14] Even though he was released after a short time, he had to stay in Cairo. When Sultan Baybars al-Jāshnikīr (r. 1309–10) came to power, he placed the difficult scholar under heavily guarded house arrest in Alexandria. In 1310, Sultan an-Nāṣir Muḥammad ibn Qalāwūn, who returned to the throne for a third time, finally seized power more firmly, thus becoming the effective ruler. He released Ibn Taymīya and was, as will be shown, open to his advice: after 1310, our protagonist remained in regular contact with the Mamluk sultan an-Nāṣir Muḥammad and continued to teach in Egypt. During this period, he also wrote large parts of his work on *sharia* politics. In 1313, Ibn Taymīya was finally allowed to return to Damascus, and he immediately renewed his conflicts with other theologians. This time he quarrelled with them about the correct legal procedure for divorce and, once again, about the veneration of saints.[15] From shortly after 1320, Ibn Taymīya was constantly in and out of prison; he finally died in 1328, after two years of incarceration. According to hagiographical elements related to his biography, he had been deprived of pen and paper and consequently lost the desire to live.[16]

Quite unusually for a scholar in this period, Ibn Taymīya never married nor fathered children — an observation that resonates, of course, with his puritan lifestyle. However, until today there is no scholarly discussion about the actual causes of this. In quite striking contrast to the lack of academic research on this biographical aspect, contemporary Salafi followers of Ibn Taymīya still feel the need to justify his lifestyle and would maintain during internet discussions that he had no time for a family and that even the Prophet had admired followers who practised an ascetic life. In his own time, though, this ostentatiously ascetic lifestyle in combination with his refusal to marry only added to his being perceived as being odd and arrogant.

Unlike Ibn Taymīya, Ibn Nubāta was on good terms with most of his colleagues, as can be illustrated with what his contemporary Ibn Ḥabīb,[17] the important historian and scribe of the chancery of Aleppo, had to say about him: 'On the whole, he was the wonder of the era, the prodigy of this time, the solitaire of the age'.[18] Ibn Nubāta's fame as a poet resonated far into the nineteenth century. But how was he perceived and how did he act in his lifetime? What we know about his personal life comes mostly from his own writings. However, it seems safe to assume that his personality was certainly less controversial than Ibn Taymīya's, who had clearly polarized public opinion.

14 Laoust, 'Ibn Taymiyya'.
15 Laoust, 'Ibn Taymiyya'.
16 Laoust, 'Ibn Taymiyya'.
17 On this Mamluk author see Brinner, 'Ibn Ḥabīb'.
18 Ibn Ḥabīb, *Tadhkirat al-nabīh*, vol. III, p. 305.

In fact, Ibn Nubāta might even be described as a very likeable fellow, as he was very much appreciated by many of his fellow scholars.[19]

Born in Cairo in 1287, Ibn Nubāta belonged to a family of scholars, poets, and administrators, who could trace their illustrious line back to the tenth century.[20] He studied theology and sciences, but he particularly excelled in poetry. At the age of nineteen, in 1306, Ibn Nubāta went to Damascus and witnessed one of the many trials against Ibn Taymīya. In fact, he even became acquainted with two of the judges who were responsible for the case.[21]

Later on, Ibn Nubāta was part of a 'mobile' scholarly family and spent his time between Cairo and Damascus, where his father had moved as a hadith scholar, and he probably earned his living as a poet in the following years. With his poems, he started visiting the residences of regional princes, especially the prince of Ḥamā, in the first Syrian period of his life, and the wealthy local rulers provided him with stipends in exchange for his panegyrics.

His private life was less fortunate, though, as he apparently had to bury sixteen sons who passed away in their early years, between five and seven; he consequently composed many poems for the deceased. In 1342, his patron al-Afḍal, the prince of Ḥamā, was deposed and died immediately afterwards — Ibn Nubāta lost his influence in public life and his financial resources. Therefore, he applied and entered the chancellery (*dīwān al-inshā'*) in Damascus at the rather advanced age of fifty-seven: his reputation as a splendid writer opened many doors for him and he composed and published selections of official documents.[22] In 1349, many of Ibn Nubāta's friends died of the Black Death, as did his father one year later at the age of eighty-four.

At this point, his life was apparently not very prosperous; he even complained of living in poverty. In 1354, however, Sultan an-Nāṣir Ḥasan (r. 1347–51 / 1354–61), son of the above-mentioned an-Nāṣir Muḥammad and an admirer of Ibn Nubāta's poetry, invited him to Cairo. Ibn Nubāta welcomed this invitation but was at first reluctant to go. Finally, in 1360, he returned to Cairo after forty-four years of absence. Unfortunately, he no longer had strong ties with the younger generation of scholars or administrators in Egypt; however, he became part of the chancellery in Cairo. Even though he did not work very often, because of his failing health, he still received a permanent salary. One year later, in 1361, when Sultan an-Nāṣir Ḥasan was killed, Ibn Nubāta apparently was among the few who mourned.[23] Thereafter, he lived a quiet life of writing and continued to be a much-respected scholar until he died in 1366 in the hospital of Sultan al-Manṣūr Qalāwūn at the age of eighty-two.[24]

---

19 Bauer, 'Ibn Nubātah al-Misrī (I)', pp. 1–2.
20 On Ibn Nubāta see Rikabi, 'Ibn Nubāta'.
21 Bauer, 'Ibn Nubātah al-Misrī (I)', p. 13.
22 Bauer, 'Ibn Nubātah al-Misrī (I)', p. 27.
23 Bauer, 'Ibn Nubātah al-Misrī (I)', p. 33.
24 Bauer, 'Ibn Nubātah al-Misrī (I)', p. 35.

Their Works and Teaching

Ibn Taymīya came to be known in his early career as a preacher against the Mongols and the Crusaders, the most eminent foes of Islam. Through this popular preaching in mosques and other public spaces, he gained the favour of Mamluk officials. He called upon them to fight these enemies, and his appeals were heeded, as he mobilized the support of the population towards these goals. While he repeatedly demanded action by the Syrian governor and the Mamluk sultan, he also provided them with the backing of society and with arguments that legitimized interior military operations against local deviant Islamic sects. These practices were not always undisputed, not least because it was not easy to make a clear distinction between different religious groups, especially in the heterodox Syro-Palestinian region.[25] However, the black and white picture Ibn Taymīya painted proved to be useful to the authorities and was also supported by the majority-Sunni society.

Ibn Taymīya thus praised the Mamluks for their victories against the Mongols and the defence of the community of believers, the *umma*:

> In respect to the group which governs Egypt and Syria at the moment, one has to acknowledge that it is they who fight for the religion of Islam and they are the people who deserve to be described by the authentic saying of the prophet — God shall pray for him and grant him peace — when he said: 'A group of my community will not cease to fight for the triumph of the almighty. Nothing can harm them, not the one who fights them nor the one who betrays them, until the hour comes [...]. Their power is the power of Islam and their degradation is the degradation of Islam. If the Tatars [Mongols] would become their masters, there would be no more power in Islam'.[26]

In later decades, Ibn Taymīya's anti-Mongol propaganda had to be adjusted due to the Ilkhanid rulers' conversion: the most prominent Ilkhan, Ghazan Khan (r. 1295–1304), started his rule by converting to Islam, and his Mongol military more or less followed his example. The reasons for this conversion are still unclear, but it has been argued that Ghazan Khan wanted to ease the tensions between the Mongol military elite and the mainly Muslim, Turkish, and Persian inhabitants of the Ilkhanid realm. While the conversion distinguished the Mongol Ilkhanate from its equally Mongol rival in the north, the Golden Horde, it did not end hostilities with the Mamluks. Ghazan continued to seek alliances with the West and his military advances in Syria were hailed by European courts.[27] To the Muslims, Ghazan Khan presented himself as the one who would revive Islam at the beginning of the eighth Islamic century — a rhetoric that responded to the prophet's foretelling in a

---

25 See Fuess, *Verbrannters Ufer*, pp. 328–61; Beydoun, *Identité confessionnelle*.
26 Michot, 'Textes spirituels d'Ibn Taymiyya, XIII', p. 26.
27 Morgan, *Medieval Persia*, pp. 72–74.

hadith that every one hundred years a 'renewer of faith' (*mujaddid al-zamān*) would appear.[28] Using this rationale, Ghazan then declared that he wanted to end the unjust and tyrannical rule of the Mamluk rulers and initiated several military campaigns.

With his conversion, anti-Mongol propaganda had to be modified, because many contemporary Muslims were opposed to fighting a fellow Muslim, who was apparently also a great ruler. In their eyes, when two Muslim rulers fought each other, ordinary people should stay out of the quarrel.

In 1299 (699 *hijrī*) Mongol forces crossed the border to Syria, inflicted defeats on the Mamluk army, and occupied Damascus, but they then had to retreat in February of 1300, because of a lack of provisions. It seems that Ibn Taymīya was chosen to be a member of a delegation of Damascene citizens who went to meet the Ilkhan in order to beg him to spare the life of the Damascenes.[29] We cannot be sure about the proceedings of this meeting — or if it really happened. Even if it did, however, it did not succeed in turning Ibn Taymīya into a friend of the Mongols. He continued his preaching against the Ilkhanids and commented negatively on their 'Muslimness'. In a legal fatwa he explained why the Mongols should continue to be fought: he presented them as one of the groups against which Islam needed to fight, despite their — in his view disingenuous — conversion:[30] according to him, there were still infidels (*al-kuffār*), polytheists (*al-mushrikūn*), and Christians amongst their ranks. How could this mixed Mongol army pretend to be Muslim? For Ibn Taymīya, the Ilkhanids had to be fought continuously, especially in the wake of attempts to create alliances between Frankish crusaders and the Ilkhanid Mongols.[31] To Ibn Taymīya, fighting the Mongols in the East was as essential for the protection of the realm as the fight against the Frankish Christians in the West.

In addition to these activities, Ibn Taymīya also wrote many lines of anti-Crusader propaganda. At the beginning of the fourteenth century, in a treatise carrying the title *al-Murābaṭa bi-l-thughur afḍal am al-mujāwara bi-Makka sharafahā allah taʿālā* ('Is it better to guard the coast than to live in the vicinity of God Blessed Mecca?'), he underlined the merits of coastal war and guardianship against the Christian crusaders.[32] In order to gain a more complete picture of Ibn Taymīya's *jihād* concept, which aimed at guarding the empire against exterior enemies like the crusaders and Mongols, one also has to examine its second component that was directed against alleged interior foes, like Christians, Shiites, and smaller sects like the Nusayris.[33] Ibn Taymīya regarded these groups as a kind of 'fifth column' of the exterior enemies:

28 For the *tajdīd*-discourse in Muslim societies see Corrado, *Mit Tradition in die Zukunft*, pp. 8–17.

29 Aigle, 'The Mongol Invasions of Bilād al-Shām', p. 102.

30 Aigle, 'The Mongol Invasions of Bilād al-Shām', p. 98.

31 Morgan, 'The Mongols and the Eastern Mediterranean'.

32 Ibn Taymīya, *al-Murābaṭa bi-l-thughur*.

33 The Nusayris constitute a Shiite splinter group that dates back to the ninth-century Iraqi

> The doctrine of the Rāfidites [Shiites] is worse than that of the Khārijite renegades. The Rāfidites have the concept of helping the unbelievers against the Muslims, something which the Khārijites would never do. It means that the Rāfidites love the Tatars and their empire.[34]

He continues: 'They [i.e. the Rāfidites] are auxiliaries [of the enemy] like Jews and Nazarenes in their fight against Muslims'.[35]

In order to fight these sects, Ibn Taymīya personally participated in military expeditions against the Shiite Muslim sect of the Nusayris in Kisrawān on the Lebanese coast in 1300, after the Mongol withdrawal from Syria.[36] Putting his own rhetoric into action, these activities and writings, one can imagine, increased his popularity among Mamluk officials and the general public. With his anti-Mongol preaching, Ibn Taymīya sometimes also followed the orders of a sultan: al-Malik al-Manṣūr Lājīn (r. 1297–1299), for example, officially asked him to preach the *jihād*.[37] In the following years, Ibn Taymīya's authority apparently was strong enough to enable him to exhort the sultans in Cairo to intervene against the Mongol incursions in 1300 and 1303.[38] Around this time, *c.* 1300, he had become one of the leading scholars and was highly popular.

So how and why did he fall out with his colleagues, becoming a 'regular' in the Mamluk state prisons? At least in part, his demise can certainly be explained by his personality. Even a century later, the Mamluk author al-Maqrīzī (d. 1441) wrote that 'people are divided into two factions over the question of Ibn Taymīya, for until the present, the latter has retained admirers and disciples in Egypt and Syria'.[39]

One of the main problems Ibn Taymīya caused his contemporary scholars was that he attacked them with charges that they had left the real path of God. By his definition, every action had to be backed by God and had therefore to be grounded in the Qur'ān and the Sunna; any action that could not be demonstrated to be in line with the Qur'ān and the Sunna was to be avoided or reprehended. In cases where there was doubt regarding God's will, as presented in the Qur'ān and the Sunna, however, a knowledgeable scholar

---

scholar Ibn Nuṣayr, who declared himself to be the gate (*bāb*) to the hidden Imām. In the eleventh century, the Nusayris settled in remote areas of the Syrian-Palestinian coast. Even Twelver Shiism perceives them as deviant, since the Nusayris believe in the wandering of souls and the divine character of Ali, the cousin and son-in-law of the Prophet. Since the late nineteenth century, they have depicted themselves as being near to mainstream Islam; they underline this by calling themselves 'Alawites', and by refraining from openly extreme practices and beliefs, see Winter, *A History of the 'Alawis*.

34 Michot, 'Textes spirituels d'Ibn Taymiyya XII', p. 30.
35 Michot, 'Textes spirituels d'Ibn Taymiyya XIII', p. 25.
36 Laoust, 'Ibn Taymiyya'.
37 Laoust, 'Ibn Taymiyya'.
38 Laoust, 'Ibn Taymiyya'.
39 Al-Maqrizī, *Kitāb al-Mawā'iẓ wa-al-I'tibār*, vol. IV, ed. by Wiet, p. 185 (cited after Laoust, 'Ibn Taymiyya').

should be asked for advice — to be precise, Ibn Taymīya obviously meant that he himself should be consulted. Based on these observations, I would hold that the accusations against Ibn Taymīya concerning anthropomorphism of the image of God should actually be understood as charges that he presented himself either as God the almighty, or at least his deputy on Earth. This issue will be illustrated further in due course.

While Ibn Taymīya was not opposed to Sufism in its entirety, he declared many Sufi practices, like the highly popular visitation of shrines and the festivities around them, to be unlawful innovations.[40] This argumentation was directed towards various popular practices and the contemporary scholars who allowed them; these scholars represented all the law schools, except the Ḥanbalīya. But Ibn Taymīya lost even the latter's support — even though he belonged to the Ḥanbalīya himself — when he argued that the practice of uttering triple repudiation in a single instance was un-Islamic. In this case, 'triple repudiation' refers to the act of a husband saying 'I divorce you' three times in the same evening, resulting in his indeed becoming divorced. Other law schools argue that the husband must say the phrase three times in front of witnesses over a three-month period; thus, the divorce is made valid not instantaneously but only after three months. In contrast to the other schools, Ibn Taymīya's own school of law, the Ḥanbalīya, argued that uttering the phrase three times in the same instance was sufficient. Ibn Taymīya disagreed, as already mentioned: according to him, the triple repudiation should happen twice — and the second time only after a waiting period.[41] As he was never married himself, one can easily imagine the polemics his married colleagues levelled against him on that matter.

However, Ibn Taymīya's most important original conceptualization of Islam was the so-called *wasaṭīya* (the happy mean) based on the qur'ānic verse (2:143): 'Thus, we have appointed you as a median nation, to be witnesses for mankind, and the Prophet to be witness for you'.[42] According to the idea of *wasaṭīya*, one should always maintain a middle position and not exaggerate or tend towards extremes.[43] Ibn Taymīya used the *wasaṭīya* argument, for example, in the context of a particularly virulent question about what to understand exactly by the term 'attributes of God' (*ṣifāt*). What was meant, for example, when the Qur'ān spoke of the 'hand' of God? Some rational scholars argued for a purely metaphorical interpretation, others for a strictly literal reading, saying that God had a hand.[44] In this case, Ibn Taymīya argues on the basis of the idea of *wasaṭīya*, that it was necessary to rely on a combination of two contradictory arguments and to find a middle

40 Meri, *The Cult of Saints among Muslims and Jews*, pp. 132–34.

41 Rapoport, 'Ibn Taymiyya on Divorce Oaths'.

42 *The Qur'an*, trans. by Khalidi, p. 19.

43 This is not unlike the Aristotelian 'mesótēs'-concept, see Meier, 'Mesotes'.

44 Talmon and Gimaret, 'Ṣifa'.

ground — in this case between an affirmative and a negative position: affirming without denying would lead to a forbidden anthropomorphic view; denial without affirmation would lead to atheism.[45]

In contrast to many other scholars of his time, Ibn Taymīya held that the Qur'ān and the Sunna of the Prophet were the only sources of knowledge, and that all knowledge was divine. Therefore, every order and action had to be grounded in this divine knowledge. Everything else, on the other hand, even if it was accepted by his contemporaries, he considered to be more or less unlawful innovations that had led Islam in the wrong direction.[46]

When the famous Maghrebinian traveller Ibn Baṭṭūṭa visited Damascus in 1326, he acknowledged that Ibn Taymīya was a well-known scholar, but also mentioned that he had created so many problems that he clearly must have been mentally deranged ('there was something strange in his head' / *fī ʿaqlihi shay'ān*). In fact, Ibn Baṭṭūṭa entitled his passage about Ibn Taymīya as 'the story of the mentally deranged jurist' (*ḥikāyat 'l-faqīh dhī 'l-lūṯa*).[47] Ibn Baṭṭūṭa himself claimed to have seen Ibn Taymīya pretending that the way he descended the pulpit (*minbar*) was the same way in which God would descend to earth.[48] This anecdote clearly reflects that some of his contemporaries accused Ibn Taymīya of thinking of himself as God.

Taking this all together, it would seem that Ibn Taymīya was a real trouble-maker,[49] one who had been very useful for rulers at certain points, but who also caused too many problems towards the end of his life, so that the sultan felt obliged to keep him in prison for maintaining public order. It is strikingly ironic, though, that Ibn Taymīya, who was so keen on ordaining 'divine' order on earth and following it himself while pushing society to do the same, was also one of the main causes of disorder in the Mamluk Empire following the end of the Mongol and Crusader threats after 1310.

Ibn Nubāta, on the other hand, did not do anything of the like. Quite the contrary: he cultivated a far more pragmatic approach and was ready to compromise with others. This meant that his orders were more balanced and did not disturb the public order the same way Ibn Taymīya's ideas did.

As mentioned above, Ibn Nubāta earned his living mainly as a poet writing on special occasions, especially panegyric literature, but he was also versed in other fields. Moreover, it seems that he was unanimously admired by other scholars. Tāj al-Dīn al-Subkī for example, a sworn enemy of Ibn Taymīya, said about Ibn Nubāta:

> He surpassed everyone in his excellence of penmanship, so that no one who tried to vie with him succeeded in matching him in his script or

45 Swartz, 'A Seventh-Century (A.H.) Sunni Creed', p. 96.
46 Swartz, 'A Seventh-Century (A.H.) Sunni Creed', p. 95.
47 Ibn Baṭṭūṭa, *Riḥlat Ibn Baṭṭūṭa*, p. 95.
48 Little, 'Did Ibn Taymiyya Have a Screw Loose?', p. 96.
49 For additional examples see Bori, 'Ibn Taymiyya wa-Jamaʿatuhu'.

> keeping pace with him in the fundamentals of the art of writing or its harmony and fluency.[50]

Although a devout Muslim, Ibn Nubāta usually did not argue on a religious basis in his writings and poems, but preferred to tell practical stories and anecdotes in which he used examples of successful rulers — or, as Thomas Bauer puts it:

> Historical examples from the time of the Prophet and the companions of the prophet are not used — and this is certainly on purpose as it is possible to deduct religious norms out of the actions of the Prophet, but no empirical data about the success rate of his actions are available.[51]

For Ibn Nubāta, it was hard to draw analogies with the outcome of certain prophetic actions, as the time of the Prophet oscillated between real history on the one hand, and 'sacred "a-historical" times' on the other.[52] As the Prophet was helped by God, Ibn Nubāta argued that it was more practical to compare one's own actions with contemporary examples of actual rulers in order to get a better idea of their potential success. Ibn Nubāta's priority was thus to estimate the eventual success of an order: according to him, an order that was highly unlikely ever to be put into action, because of difficult circumstances or fear of failure, should never have been uttered.

Ibn Nubāta's rational thinking becomes particularly clear in one of his poems for the prince of Ḥamā, al-Malik al-Afḍal, on the occasion of his accession to the throne in 1332. Ibn Nubāta had been a regular guest in Ḥamāh, when al-Malik's father Abū l-Fidā', himself a prolific historian and descendant of the Ayyubids, had ruled there as Mamluk viceroy. Ibn Nubāta had in fact benefited from a stipend from Abū l-Fidā' to whom he had dedicated over forty poems. When Abū l-Fidā' died, our poet certainly hoped that the son would be as energetic as his father and would also continue with his financial support.[53] In the poem he wrote for the young al-Malik al-Afḍal, he already offered advice, after having praised him and his father for their noble origin and their deeds: 'Therefore live for the people and stay happy as the happiness of the people consists in you being alive and happy'.[54] According to Ibn Nubāta, he should thus relentlessly use his pen in times of peace — and his bloodthirsty sword in war. This would be the right way to govern — friendly and accessible most of the time, but brutal and determined in times of crisis: 'Favour is to be distributed the way clouds move: limitless. Violence is to be used like the strike of fate: inevitably'.[55]

---

50 Al-Subkī, *Al-Ṭabaqat al-Shāfiʿīya al-kubrā*, ed. by al-Ṭanaḥī, vol. v, p. 253; the translation follows Bauer, 'Ibn Nubātah al-Miṣrī (II)', p. 25.

51 Bauer, *Die Kultur der Ambiguität*, p. 333 (English translation by A. Fuess).

52 Bauer, *Die Kultur der Ambiguität*, p. 333 (English translation by A. Fuess).

53 Bauer, *Die Kultur der Ambiguität*, pp. 326–27.

54 Bauer, 'Der Fürst ist tot, es lebe der Fürst!', pp. 290 (Arabic Text), 294 (German Translation).

55 Bauer, 'Der Fürst ist tot, es lebe der Fürst!', pp. 290 (Arabic Text), 294 (German Translation).

The prince should therefore be generous in order to motivate people to follow him — and force others, who do not obey, to follow nevertheless. Thus, it was not important whether the ruler was really generous: it was only important that he appeared to be in the eyes of his subjects. Moreover, rather than mentioning God as the main keeper of public order, Ibn Nubāta instead places the focus on the prince and his behaviour. Based on this method of argumentation, Thomas Bauer concluded that Ibn Nubāta and his writings could be compared to Machiavelli and his *Il Principe*, which was published roughly two hundred years later — even though Ibn Nubāta caused much less scandal than the Florentine.[56]

Given the lack of uproar or pushback against Ibn Nubāta, it was apparently not a problem for the Mamluk audience to receive advice without explicit reference to the supremacy of Islam or a reliance on religious scholars.[57] We have to keep in mind, though, that he might have been particularly acceptable due to his status as an outstanding member of the *literati*. In any case, Ibn Nubāta was far less controversial, among his peers and in society in general, than his colleague Ibn Taymīya.

The Order they Gave and to Whom

Ibn Taymīya gave quite a lot of advice in his writings. In the following, I will mainly focus on his *Kitāb al-siyāsa al-sharia fī iṣlāḥ al-rā'ī wa 'l-ra'yya* ('The book of Sharia politics for the guidance of the shepherd towards his flock').[58] The book was apparently written between 1309 and 1314, when Ibn Taymīya was still in Egypt because of the public outrage he had caused in Damascus with his teachings of the *wasaṭīya*, which was seen by his adversaries as leading the image of God towards anthropomorphism.[59]

When Ibn Taymīya arrived in Egypt in 1306, the country witnessed an internal power struggle that lasted until the twenty-five-year-old sultan al-Nāṣir Muḥammad ibn Qalāwūn, son of the former sultan Qalāwūn (r. 1279–1290), finally managed to defeat all his rivals in 1310, after which he stayed in power for thirty more years.[60] The sultan apparently held Ibn Taymīya in high esteem and met with the famous scholar from Damascus, who had been so active in the anti-Mongol propaganda between 1310 and the end of 1312, when Ibn Taymīya returned to Syria after a new, but unsuccessful, Mongol advance.[61] In the following years, the sultan and his entourage were keen to stabilize the

56 Bauer, *Die Kultur der Ambiguität*, pp. 337–39.

57 Bauer, *Die Kultur der Ambiguität*, pp. 327, 339.

58 Ibn Taymiyya, *Kitāb al-siyāsa al-sharia*, ed. by Lajna Iḥyā al-Turāth al-'Arabī; *Le Traité de Droit Public d'ibn Taimīya*, ed. by Laoust.

59 *Le Traité de Droit Public d'ibn Taimīya*, ed. by Laoust, pp. xxiv–xxix.

60 See Levanoni, *A Turning Point in Mamluk History*.

61 Laoust, 'Ibn Taymiyya'.

realm after years of external threat and inner turmoil. In order to revive the Mamluk Sultanate and make its administration more efficient, Sultan al-Nāṣir Muḥammad initiated major reforms and was keen on receiving advice.[62]

In this historical context Ibn Taymīya wrote his *Kitāb al-siyāsa al-sharia* in order to give advice to the sultan in particular, and to Muslim rulers in general. The book consists of two parts with a total of seven chapters that deal with the affairs of the state in the following order:

Part 1: The administration of public functions
  Chapter 1.1: The public administration
  Chapter 1.2: The financial income
  Chapter 1.3: Public spending

Part 2: The limits imposed by God and His rights
  Chapter 2.1: The punishments fixed by God (*ḥadd*)
  Chapter 2.2: The punishment for offences at the discretion of the officials (*taʿzīr*)
  Chapter 2.2.1: Private law
  Chapter 2.2.2: Obedience to and cooperation with the state

With this composition Ibn Taymīya stuck to a classical form of advice literature. However, he was intent on validating most, if not all of his statements with examples from the hadith literature or the Qur'ān. He did not even cite anecdotes from the books of old Persian kings, which were quite popular at the time, following the widespread success of the Islamic version of the Alexander romance (*Iskandername*).[63] All of Ibn Taymīya's advice had to be firmly based on the fundamental sources of Islam, i.e. the Qur'ān and the Sunna; anything else he considered to be a forbidden innovation (*bidʿa*).

Ibn Nubāta, on the other hand, felt no such compulsion to base his advice on examples from the Prophet, as he seems to have been far more oriented towards the practical. According to Thomas Bauer, the Prophet could apparently not be used as a real didactic example in kingship matters as he had been helped by the divine, which was not the case for contemporary rulers.[64] In the eyes of Ibn Nubāta, the principles of good governance of a real prince consisted in his noble descent, merits, and luck. As a poet he rendered the three as *al-jaddu wa 'l-jiddu wa 'l-juddu* in Arabic.[65] Since this concept does not refer to divine support, but rather underlines merit and luck, Thomas Bauer again sees a close link to Machiavelli's idea of *virtue* and *fortuna* that a ruler needs to have a successful career.[66]

62 Tsugitaka, *State and Rural Society in Medieval Islam*, pp. 124–220.

63 Abel, 'Iskandar Nāma'.

64 Bauer, *Die Kultur der Ambiguität*, pp. 331, 333.

65 Bauer, *Die Kultur der Ambiguität*, p. 331.

66 Bauer, *Die Kultur der Ambiguität*, p. 331.

Although a devout Muslim himself, Ibn Nubāta never used any qur'ānic evidence nor hadith in order to bolster his argumentation other than in his work's introduction. In order to present his way of thinking, I will focus in the following on his *Kitāb sulūk duwal al-mulūk* ('The Guidance for Kingdoms'; literally: 'The Book of Good Behaviour in the Regencies [Dynasties] of the Princes').[67] Ibn Nubāta organizes his work in six chapters:

Chapter 1: On the merits of kings
Chapter 2: The way the king should conduct himself
Chapter 3: How to guide one's own family
Chapter 4: How to guide the elite
Chapter 5: How to guide the commoners
Chapter 6: On warfare[68]

Each of these chapters is further divided into subchapters, but a mere glimpse at the chapter headings makes clear the differences between the approaches of both scholars. It is remarkable, for example, that Ibn Taymīya deals mainly with the public functions and the legal sides of politics, i.e. *sharia*, whereas Ibn Nubāta focuses on how a king should deal with real life persons and especially with attention towards society's elite.

The addressee of Ibn Nubāta's text differs as well, as he writes for the young Mamluk governor of Ḥamā, al-Malik al-Afḍal ('the most excellent king'), himself a descendant of the famous house of the Ayyubids who had reigned in Egypt and Syria prior to the Mamluks and whose first king Saladin continued to be perceived as a true Muslim hero.[69] Al-Malik al-Afḍal's father was the famous warrior and historian Abu 'l-Fidā', who had been granted Ḥamā as kingship (governorate) because of his merits and out of respect for his royal ancestry. However, when al-Malik al-Afḍal succeeded his father, there were already some doubts about his abilities, and Ibn Nubāta felt that it was necessary to explain to him in a book the issues about which a king should care.

67 Three manuscripts are conserved in the libraries of Oxford, Vienna, and Istanbul, see Hees, 'The Guidance for Kingdoms', p. 381. For the present chapter, I mainly refer to the Oxford manuscript: Oxford, Bodl. Lib., MS Seld. Superius 29. I am very grateful to Thomas Bauer, who provided me with digital copies of all three manuscripts, including Vienna, Staatsarchiv, Krafft 474, and Istanbul, Topkapı, MS III. Ahmet 1822.

68 Ibn Nubāta, *Kitāb sulūk duwal al-mulūk. Ikhtiyār*, Oxford, Bodl. Lib., MS Seld. Superius 29, fols 2^r^, 3^r^, 13^r^, 14^r^, 78^r^, 98^r–v^.

69 On Saladin see, e.g., Eddé, *Saladin*; on the Ayyubid Dynasty, which ruled Egypt and Syria from *c.* 1170 to 1250, no comprehensive monograph is available as yet. Survey articles in larger works include Chamberlain, 'The Crusader Era and the Ayyūbid Dynasty'.

Their Arguments

The following section will compare a selection of arguments, as developed by Ibn Nubāta and Ibn Taymīya, in order to examine the exact nature of each's specific ideas concerning public order with regard to specific topics.

What is the Aim of Politics?

For Ibn Nubāta, the most important aims of politics consist of maintaining social order and maximizing its profit for the ruler. This means, in practical terms, that the king has to control his family, to be very alert when it comes to the behaviour of his nobles, and to occupy the people with different tasks so that they do not cause disturbance to the ruler. As to the nobles, Ibn Nubāta advises that 'the decisive king respects and helps them so that they love and obey him'.[70] Moreover, a king should provide good opportunities for the common people to occupy themselves: 'The decisive king ensures himself that the *ʿāmma* (common people) remain always under his control by making sure that they are occupied with their daily work and will not interfere in the affairs of the ruler'.[71] As has already been mentioned, Ibn Nubāta does not consider it the aim of politics to ensure God's rule on earth; to him, politics are rather about control (of the population and the subjects) and good living conditions.

Ibn Taymīya, on the other hand, represents a quite different approach with his *sharia* politics, arguing that 'it is therefore an obligation to perceive the exercise of government as an act of religion, as an act which brings the ruler closer to God. And this rapprochement to God and his Prophet is the best practice when acting'.[72] In addition, Ibn Taymīya explicitly considers the 'sultan' to be 'the shadow of God on earth'. Nevertheless, he does reflect on the practical effects of politics, explaining, for example, that anarchy has to be completely avoided. In this regard, he cites the authority of the hadith: 'sixty years with an unjust sultan is better than one day without the rule of a sultan'.[73]

How the King Should Act

For Ibn Nubāta, maintaining justice is a central task of the king, not least because it represents the virtue which serves his interests most: 'The decisive king boosts his popularity among his people and the military through good

---

70 Ibn Nubāta, *Kitāb sulūk*, Oxford, Bodl. Lib., MS Seld. Superius 29, fol. 88r; Hees, 'The Guidance for Kingdoms', p. 377.

71 Ibn Nubāta, *Kitāb sulūk*, Oxford, Bodl. Lib., MS Seld. Superius 29, fol. 90r; Hees, 'The Guidance for Kingdoms', p. 378.

72 Ibn Taymīya, *Kitāb al-siyāsa al-sharia*, ed. by Lajna Iḥyā al-Turāth al-ʿArabī, p. 139; *Le Traité de Droit Public d'ibn Taimīya*, ed. by Laoust, pp. 173–74.

73 Ibn Taymīya, *Kitāb al-siyāsa al-sharia*, ed. by Lajna Iḥyā al-Turāth al-ʿArabī, p. 139; *Le Traité de Droit Public d'ibn Taimīya*, ed. by Laoust, pp. 173–74.

deeds towards them and cares that they are treated justly and keeps them away from injustice'.[74] In order to support this position, he cites the story of the Umayyad caliph ʿAbd al-Malik (r. 685–705), who had given favours to the nobles so that they already acknowledged the succession of his son al-Walīd (r. 705–15) during his own lifetime. The succession, therefore, went very well.[75]

In this context it does not seem relevant that the ruler really cares about his subjects; what is important, however, is that he appears to be just. Therefore, he should care for rich people who had become poor or were treated unfairly by the law[76] – not out of mercy, but because it is in the ruler's own interest, as these recently impoverished people might seek revenge and may remain influential because of their former ties.

Ibn Nubāta does not describe the function of individual offices when he deals with the elite of the realm. Either he thought that they were already known to the prince or that he was not interested in this kind of information. Instead he insists that the prince should personally know the officers who hold the positions and use motivation or intimidation, each in the right measure, as instruments of guidance. In addition, a decisive king has to be aware of the intrigues of his viziers and possible misdeeds and falsifications by his scribes. In sum, he should know of all the possible threats to his rule that may be posed by the human factor.[77]

The same holds true when Ibn Nubāta advises prince al-Afḍal to always put his family first: for him, this means watching his family closely and teaching his relatives all the skills that are necessary to rule. This allows and enables the ruling family to perpetuate and further strengthen its powers.[78]

In addition, Ibn Nubāta provides very practical security advice for the daily life of the king. For example, he stresses that 'the decisive king does not use the same road again when riding and travelling'.[79] What is really striking in all of the examples Ibn Nubāta gives, is that he never uses or cites the Prophet as historic example, but instead prefers to speak about effective rulers like the famous Ayyubid sultan Salāḥ al-Dīn, who was, of course, one of al-Afḍal's ancestors. Ibn Nubāta also provides further anecdotes of other great rulers as well, in order to illustrate why it is very advisable for a prince to read guidance literature. For example, he tells a story about the first Umayyad caliph Muʿāwiya (r. 661–80), who allegedly always spent a

74 Ibn Nubāta, *Kitāb sulūk*, Oxford, Bodl. Lib., MS Seld. Superius 29, fol. 13[r]; Bauer, *Die Kultur der Ambiguität*, p. 327.

75 Ibn Nubāta, *Kitāb sulūk*, Oxford, Bodl. Lib., MS Seld. Superius 29, fol. 13[r–v].

76 Ibn Nubāta, *Kitāb sulūk*, Oxford, Bodl. Lib., MS Seld. Superius 29, fols 91[v]–94[v]; Hees, 'The Guidance for Kingdoms', p. 378.

77 Ibn Nubāta, *Kitāb sulūk*, Oxford, Bodl. Lib., MS Seld. Superius 29, fol. 14[r]; Hees, 'The Guidance for Kingdoms', p. 377.

78 Ibn Nubāta, *Kitāb sulūk*, Oxford, Bodl. Lib., MS Seld. Superius 29, fols 13[r], 16[r], 30[r], 32[v]; Hees, 'The Guidance for Kingdoms', p. 376.

79 Ibn Nubāta, *Kitāb sulūk*, Oxford, Bodl. Lib., MS Seld. Superius 29, fol. 12[v]; Hees, 'The Guidance for Kingdoms', p. 373.

third of the night listening to stories of Arab heroes, then slept a third of the night, and finally indulged during the last third in reading advice literature and stories about past kings.[80] Ibn Nubāta clearly presents this caliph as a model ruler — and we should keep in mind that in the Arabic-Islamic tradition Muʿāwiya was far more renowned for being wise and mild than for his personal piety.

The single anecdote about Muʿāwiya that can be found in Ibn Taymīya's 'Sharia Politics', on the other hand, clearly demonstrates that he perceived this caliph quite differently: in the anecdote he relates, a pious man explains to Muʿāwiya that he (the caliph) was only an employee of God the almighty and that all his actions should show recognition that he must obey his master, i.e. God. The pious man says that Muʿāwiya had only been placed by God as his employee in order to look after the people.[81] For Ibn Taymīya the fate of rulers who chose to rule selfishly and only to gain power is like the fate of Pharaoh. Moreover, for those who seek to enrich themselves, there is the example set by the qur'ānic figure Qārūn (Korah in the Bible), whose greed God punished by making the earth swallow him up.[82]

Therefore, for Ibn Taymīya, it is clear that every ruler must obey God and follow the example of the Prophet in order to become an ideal ruler. Every ruler has to be loyal to God alone and should thus not fear what the people say about his orders, as long as they are in accordance with God and the Prophet. But who would tell the ruler what God's commands truly were? One might assume that this would be the role of a well-versed religious scholar like Ibn Taymīya.

This sort of counsel is, of course, quite contrary to what Ibn Nubāta would say, even though he was a devout Muslim too. Nevertheless, to Ibn Nubāta the most important issue for the ruler was the loyalty of the people — by ignoring them and their needs, the ruler would put his realm in danger.

How to Deal with Religious Leaders?

For Ibn Taymīya, there are two classes of people which supersede the rest of the population: the leaders of power, i.e. the military *amirs*, and the religious scholars (*ʿulamā'*).[83] In Ibn Taymīya's works, both appear to occupy an equal level, which seems to be in contradiction to the real circumstances in his period, since military leaders had more influence at court than scholars.

---

80 Ibn Nubāta, *Kitāb sulūk*, Oxford, Bodl. Lib., MS Seld. Superius 29, fol. 12^r; Hees, 'The Guidance for Kingdoms', p. 374.

81 Ibn Taymīya, *Kitāb al-siyāsa al-sharia*, ed. by Lajna Iḥyā al-Turāth al-ʿArabī, pp. 13–14; *Le Traité de Droit Public d'ibn Taimīya*, ed. by Laoust, pp. 8–9.

82 Ibn Taymīya, *Kitāb al-siyāsa al-sharia*, ed. by Lajna Iḥyā al-Turāth al-ʿArabī, p. 141; *Le Traité de Droit Public d'ibn Taimīya*, ed. by Laoust, p. 174.

83 Ibn Taymīya, *Kitāb al-siyāsa al-sharia*, ed. by Lajna Iḥyā al-Turāth al-ʿArabī, p. 136; *Le Traité de Droit Public d'ibn Taimīya*, ed. by Laoust, p. 169.

But Ibn Taymīya goes even further, based on his conviction that every decision had to be founded in the Qur'ān and the Sunna: when the ruler is not sure what to do, he should thus follow the advice of a religious scholar who knows what God and his Prophet would have done in his place.[84] It is quite clear that by giving this order, Ibn Taymīya challenged the supremacy of the political leadership — at least, he wanted to bind it clearly to an obligatory council of religious and legal scholars.

Ibn Nubāta views the role of religious scholars far more pragmatically: he urges the king to generally respect the decisions of scholars and tribunals in order to avoid unrest; in addition, he should also avoid too much turmoil among the scholars themselves. However, Ibn Nubāta does not argue with the Qur'ān and the Sunna but rather out of the interest of the ruler, who should have a good relationship with the scholars while still being able to control them.[85]

Furthermore, he urges the decisive king not to allow the *qāḍī* to issue the final verdict in juridical cases, as this might lead to confusion. Ibn Nubāta explains this directive with the story of a Christian *dhimmī* who was killed by a Muslim in the times of the Abbasid Caliph Hārūn al-Rashīd (r. 786–809). In this case, the famous *qāḍī* Abū Yūsuf had first decided that the family of the killed would have the right of retaliation (*qiṣāṣ*), i.e. the murderer should be killed. Quite foreseeably, this decision led to problems, and under the pressure of the caliph the verdict was changed to a payment of blood-money (*diya*) if the family of the killed could not prove that the deceased had regularly paid their poll tax (*jizya*).[86]

In a similar way, Ibn Nubāta provides special advice in order to avoid urban conflicts:

> The decisive king never lets two preachers preach in the same city as there will be always misunderstandings and different opinions between them, and both of them will gather people around them who will back up the specific scholar.[87]

This advice may, of course, be meant to avoid turmoil, something which Ibn Nubāta always considered important. But it might also be considered an overt critique of Ibn Taymīya, whose preaching had caused so much distress for the realm, which finally led to his constant imprisonment. Ibn Nubāta, in contrast, was an advocate of 'realpolitik' and placed scholars' interests clearly after the ruler's needs.

---

84 Ibn Taymīya, *Kitāb al-siyāsa al-sharia*, ed. by Lajna Iḥyā al-Turāth al-ʿArabī, pp. 136–37; *Le Traité de Droit Public d'ibn Taimīya*, ed. by Laoust, pp. 169–70.

85 Ibn Nubāta, *Kitāb sulūk*, Oxford, Bodl. Lib., MS Seld. Superius 29, fol. 85ʳ; Bauer, *Die Kultur der Ambiguität*, p. 333.

86 Ibn Nubāta, *Kitāb sulūk*, Oxford, Bodl. Lib., MS Seld. Superius 29, fols 28ʳ–29ʳ.

87 Ibn Nubāta, *Kitāb sulūk*, Oxford, Bodl. Lib., MS Seld. Superius 29, fol. 81ʳ; Bauer, *Die Kultur der Ambiguität*, p. 333.

The Notion of Jihād (Holy War)

On the notion of *jihād* (Holy War) Ibn Nubāta has the same stance. He does not take into much account the *sharia* regulations about how to open a war or the processes involved, and he certainly does not prioritize conversion to Islam over political gain:

> When the decisive king has decided to wage war against his enemy, he shall send out reliable scouts in order to find out, if his troops or the troops of the enemy have more fighting power and a stronger readiness to die.

If the enemy had superior powers, then one should refrain from action. As an historic example, Ibn Nubāta even cites the example of the Christian king Pedro I of Aragón, who conquered Huesca in 1096 because he followed this rule.[88] Accordingly, when it comes to concluding peace with the enemy, Ibn Nubāta does not mention the role of religion at all, but only the interest of the ruler: 'The decisive king concludes peace with his enemy, when it suits him best'.[89]

Ibn Taymīya, in contrast, underlines that religious principles have to be respected first and insists that *jihād* is a major feature in Islam, in fact, he even considers it to be on equal footing with the classical five pillars of Islam: 'The essentials of the religion reside in the prayer and the *jihād*'.[90] Citing examples from the early Islamic period, he also insists that 'the prophet, when he sent an *amir* out to war at the head of an expedition, he nominated him at the same time as imam to lead the prayer'.[91] Ibn Taymīya therefore creates a clear link between religious and political functions — an idea Ibn Nubāta would never have put forward. An analogous disagreement can be found when it comes to the question of who should fight: Ibn Nubāta, as we have seen above, perceives this to be the responsibility of the ruler who acts in the interest of the state. Ibn Taymīya insists, however, quoting qur'ānic evidence, on higher religious goals:

> Whoever has received the call of the Prophet to join the religion of Islam, which God has ordered him to spread and who refuses, has to be fought until there is no schism anymore and that the religion entirely belongs to God.[92]

---

88 Ibn Nubāta, *Kitāb sulūk*, Oxford, Bodl. Lib., MS Seld. Superius 29, fols 98v–99r; Bauer, *Die Kultur der Ambiguität*, p. 334.

89 Ibn Nubāta, *Kitāb sulūk*, Oxford, Bodl. Lib., MS Seld. Superius 29, fol. 100r; Bauer, *Die Kultur der Ambiguität*, p. 334.

90 Ibn Taymīya, *Kitāb al-siyāsa al-sharia*, ed. by Lajna Iḥyā al-Turāth al-ʿArabī, p. 21; *Le Traité de Droit Public d'ibn Taimīya*, ed. by Laoust, p. 19.

91 Ibn Taymīya, *Kitāb al-siyāsa al-sharia*, ed. by Lajna Iḥyā al-Turāth al-ʿArabī, p. 20; *Le Traité de Droit Public d'ibn Taimīya*, ed. by Laoust, p. 18.

92 Ibn Taymīya, *Kitāb al-siyāsa al-sharia*, ed. by Lajna Iḥyā al-Turāth al-ʿArabī, p. 102; *Le Traité de Droit Public d'ibn Taimīya*, ed. by Laoust, p. 122.

Turning Ideas into Practice

As already observed, Ibn Taymīya was very successful in his attempts to motivate the leaders of his time to join the *jihād* against the Mongols, and the Mamluk rulers were very keen to have him preach in this context. After the immediate Mongol threat ceased in the aftermath of Ghazan Khān's death in 1304, Ibn Taymīya turned against his colleagues in a variety of issues (like the legal question of the repudiation of wives, anthropomorphism of God, and the veneration of saints), which angered a lot of his contemporary religious scholars.

Still, when Sultan al-Nāṣir Muḥammad ibn Qalāwūn re-conquered the throne for good in 1310, he apparently sent for Ibn Taymīya, who was living in exile in Alexandria at that time, and had him brought to Cairo to listen to his advice.[93] According to the Damascene scholar and disciple of Ibn Taymīya, Ibn Kathīr (d. 1373), it was in these early years of Sultan al-Nāṣir Muḥammad's third regency that Ibn Taymīya's influence on the new sultan rose to its greatest extent and that he apparently composed the *Kitāb al-siyāsa al-sharia* mainly for him.[94]

Likely evidence for this order of events consists in al-Nāṣir Muḥammad's nomination of emir al-Afram as governor of Tripoli in 1311, after he had received counselling on this matter by Ibn Taymīya. The latter owed the emir a personal favour, as he had helped him in his 1306 trial in Damascus as described above.[95] In the same year, Ibn Taymīya seems to have been the decisive force behind the decision to have the newly installed governor of Karak, emir Karāy, imprisoned, who had installed heavy taxation on the population and was harshly criticized by the civilian elite.[96]

In 1313 Sultan al-Nāṣir Muḥammad sent two letters concerning legal procedures to Damascus, which mirrored stipulations of the *al-siyāsa al-sharia*.[97] In the next year, he decreed in another two orders that prostitution, the consumption of alcohol, and other illicit matters should be severely punished in Damascus, thus picking up another set of ideas that Ibn Taymīya had outlined in his *al-siyāsa al-sharia*.[98]

---

93 Laoust, 'La Biographie d'Ibn Taymiya d'après Ibn Kathir', p. 146; Ibn Kathīr, *al-Bidāya wa-nihāya*, vol. XIV, p. 52.

94 *Le Traité de Droit Public d'ibn Taimīya*, ed. by Laoust, pp. xxviii–xxix.

95 Laoust, 'La Biographie d'Ibn Taymiya d'après Ibn Kathir', p. 147; Ibn Kathīr, *al-Bidāya wa-nihāya*, vol. XIV, p. 63. Unfortunately for Ibn Taymīya, his counsel turned out negatively, as emir al-Afram defected to the Mongols one year later since he was not nominated as viceroy of Damascus — a heavy blow for Ibn Taymīya, who had cultivated an anti-Mongol attitude.

96 Laoust, 'La Biographie d'Ibn Taymiya d'après Ibn Kathir', p. 148; Ibn Kathīr, *al-Bidāya wa-nihāya*, vol. XIV, p. 62.

97 Laoust, 'La Biographie d'Ibn Taymiya d'après Ibn Kathir', p. 148; Ibn Kathīr, *al-Bidāya wa-nihāya*, vol. XIV, p. 67.

98 Laoust, 'La Biographie d'Ibn Taymiya d'après Ibn Kathir', p. 151; Ibn Kathīr, *al-Bidāya wa-nihāya*, vol. XIV, p. 70.

During the first years of his regency, the sultan thus clearly favoured Ibn Taymīya and even implemented some of the scholar's advice, especially in moral matters. After 1317, however, relations seem to have deteriorated: the sultan explicitly ordered Ibn Taymīya to stop writing legal counsels (*fatwa*) on the question of repudiation. In fact, complaints about Ibn Taymīya had already reached Cairo in previous years, but what actually triggered the sultan's special order remains unclear.

In 1319, the sultan finally commanded that Ibn Taymīya be imprisoned for six months, because he refused to listen to his orders.[99] With these measures, sultan al-Nāṣir Muḥammad made clear to the scholar who should be obeyed and by whom. In 1326, he gave the final order to put Ibn Taymīya into jail — where he eventually died — because he would not stop causing uproar with his preaching on the veneration of saints.[100] It should have become clear by now, that Ibn Taymīya's ideas were only partially put into action. Whenever he tried to ignore the sultan's orders, because he thought that he understood God's will better, he did not succeed. Instead, his endeavours led him to imprisonment.

Ibn Nubāta, on the other hand, never caused uproar. He wanted the state to function, therefore he advised that rulers should be careful about conflicts among religious scholars.[101] This advice may have been a result of all the quarrels that arose around Ibn Taymīya only ten years before. Ibn Nubāta's main conception was that the individual had to contain human passions and personal vanities, as these were the main problems in human societies. Thus, every ruler had to control himself in order to use his abilities to stabilize his position and his reign; then he had to control his entourage and flock accordingly: only then would he have the power to fight his enemies and preserve his kingdom for the next generation.[102]

The ideas presented in Ibn Nubāta's book of advice did not lead to immediate effects. One reason might have been that his counsel was not directly addressed to Sultan al-Nāṣir Muḥammad, but to the viceroy of Ḥamā, al-Malik al-Afḍal, on the occasion of his accession to the throne. But al-Afḍal did not have any concrete power in the Mamluk realm, despite his noble Ayyubid descent. Moreover, it seems that he had little interest in ruling from the very beginning; during the ten years of his reign the viceroy's inclinations gradually 'worsened', as he became increasingly pious and ascetic. In 1342 he finally lost his governorship and died shortly after.[103]

---

99 Laoust, 'La Biographie d'Ibn Taymiya d'après Ibn Kathir', pp. 153–54; Ibn Kathīr, *al-Bidāya wa-nihāya*, vol. XIV, pp. 78, 93, 97.

100 Laoust, 'La Biographie d'Ibn Taymiya d'après Ibn Kathir', p. 157; Ibn Kathīr, *al-Bidāya wa-nihāya*, vol. XIV, p. 123.

101 Ibn Nubāta, *Kitāb sulūk*, Oxford, Bodl. Lib., MS Seld. Superius 29, fol. 81^r; Bauer, *Die Kultur der Ambiguität*, p. 333.

102 Bauer, *Die Kultur der Ambiguität*, p. 336.

103 Hees, 'The Guidance for Kingdoms', p. 376.

However, Ibn Nubāta's writings and pragmatic knowledge in stately affairs earned him a steady job in the chancellery, despite his old age of fifty-seven.[104] By working for the public administration he could at least put some of his ideas into action. In addition, his popularity as author and poet certainly helped to shape the intellectual climate of the second half of the fourteenth century, after the essential crises of the Crusader wars, the Mongol invasion, and the Black Death. What the realm needed now was pragmatic advice, and Ibn Nubāta could provide just that.

Without pushing historical analogies too far, it is quite remarkable that a religiously fanatical, leading scholar was followed by someone who preferred to work on the basis of *Realpolitik*: the story of Ibn Taymīya and Ibn Nubāta does have some similarities to what can be observed in late-fifteenth-century Florence, when the pragmatic Niccolò Machiavelli entered the Florentine administration after the ascetic preacher Girolamo Savonarola had been burned as a heretic in May 1498. Savonarola seems to have cultivated an Ibn Taymīya-like approach to moral behaviour and the rule of God on earth — and his death sentence resulted in his disturbing the public order and shaking contemporary society.[105]

The Long-Term Legacy of their Works

If one were to compare the influence of both scholars and their work in the early twenty-first century, Ibn Taymīya would certainly be far ahead of Ibn Nubāta. This can conveniently be illustrated with the number of Google hits: while a search for 'Ibn Taymīya' produces 300,000 results, 'Ibn Nubāta' receives only (a still respectable) 17,000 hits. However, if one would have asked religious scholars of the seventeenth and eighteenth centuries which of the two scholars had been more important, the difference would presumably not have been so dramatic. Ibn Taymīya always stayed popular on the fanatical or overly pious side of Islam.[106] His works and thinking witnessed a huge renaissance after Muḥammad ʿAbd al-Wahhāb (d. 1792), the founder of Saudi Wahhabism, re-discovered him and used his ideas as the main reference for his ascetic and puritan view on Islam. This was especially true of Ibn Taymīya's thoughts about fighting infidels, as the possibility to declare someone a 'fake' Muslim, whether pharaoh or Ilkhan, allows one to wage war on the other.

Islamists of the twentieth century, like Sayyid Qutb (executed 1966), developed their ideas of God's rule on earth on the basis of Ibn Taymīya's model. Muḥammad ʿAbd al-Salām Faraj, who was executed in 1982 in connection with the assassination of Egyptian president Anwar al-Sadat in 1981, wrote

---

104 Bauer, 'Ibn Nubātah al-Misrī (1)', p. 27.

105 See, e.g., Fuhr, *Machiavelli und Savonarola*.

106 Bori, 'Ibn Taymiyya (14th to 17th Century)'.

a book on the 'neglected duty', i.e. the *jihād*, which relied on Ibn Taymīya's ideas. The assassin, who was a military officer, apparently shouted: 'I am Khalid Islambuli. I have killed Pharaoh, and I do not fear death'.[107] No wonder that Ibn Taymīya and his works flourished especially during the colonial and post-colonial era, as these times were also perceived as an existential crisis (between neo-crusaders and neo-Mongols), which had to be countered by taking Ibn Taymīya's message seriously again. In achieving rightness, rule had always to be based on the Qur'ān and the Sunna alone. Furthermore, numerous works were written about Ibn Taymīya in the twentieth century by Islamic and Western scholars alike, presenting him as the 'founding father' of modern Islamism.[108] In the light of these developments, it is not very surprising that the so-called 'Islamic State of Iraq and Syria (or al-Sham)' (ISIS, or Daesh) transformed Ibn Taymīya's *al-siyāsa al-sharia* into a textbook under the title 'Sharia Politics for the First Legal Studies'[109] that was subsequently taught in the schools of Raqqa in order to instruct pupils in the fundamentals of the Islamic state.

Ibn Nubāta's long-term legacy is less impressive. However, he is still well known as a poet, and his administrative examples were used in pre-colonial times by people working in such fields. But when imperialist politics transformed the administrations of the Middle East on the basis of the European model, his practical advice seems to have lost its importance. Still, the fact that three copies of his work have survived until today indicates that it was actually used and read, since medieval advice literature rarely survives in more than one copy.

Conclusion

What can we conclude about the advice given by the two scholars and the actions taken by their superiors? As has been demonstrated, Ibn Taymīya's ideas had immediate and long-term consequences, while Ibn Nubāta's concepts were more effective in the medium-term. The differences can be explained with a series of observations: it certainly helped Ibn Taymīya that he gave his counsel directly to a sultan, whereas Ibn Nubāta had to deal with a governor of a Syrian province who did not even listen. On the other hand, Ibn Taymīya's being such a public nuisance also made him a target for criticism. In the end, his determined behaviour backfired, as his royal mentor was not willing to put up with all his fanatical teachings. As Baber Johansen put it:

> It is obvious that in attributing to the government such a strong position in so many domains, he suggests a policy of conflict with those groups

107 Esposito, *Unholy War*, p. 90.

108 See, e.g., Krawietz, 'Ibn Taymiyya, Vater des islamischen Fundamentalismus?'.

109 'Al-Siyāsa al-Shari ʿa li-l-ṣiff al-awwal al-shar ʿī'.

> that he does not admit into the rank of licit political actors. His doctrine on political decision making is more conflict than consensus oriented: the perspective is more that of the imposition of a perfect law on a very imperfect and often unruly society.[110]

My impression is that in doing so, Ibn Taymīya tried to create a pure Sunni population and to win the intellectual fight about what constituted the real Sunna as defined by his concept of *al-siyāsa al-sharia*. However, by excluding all the minorities and non-conforming Arab scholars, he simply could not succeed. In our own time, his ideas profit from the fact that nationalism has effectively removed many of the opposing ethnic groups, colonialism disposed of superstition and Sufi extravagances, and Islamism does not tolerate divergent Islamic sects. Many of the premodern obstacles that led to Ibn Taymīya's final failure thus no longer exist.

Ibn Nubāta, by contrast, was never controversial; apparently, he was liked by most of his contemporaries, who respected his pragmatic advice. But this advice was clearly based in the world of the fourteenth century and it answered to the practical needs of that specific period — while the quasi timeless, though very puritanical, stance of Ibn Taymīya can be re-used as theoretical concept every now and then, whenever its quest for an ideal Islamic government appeals to puritanical parts of society. However, it seems that every generation of government leaders understands after a while that the perspectives opened up by pragmatic scholars, who are well versed in the here and now, might be the better alternative for the inner cohesion of Muslim societies.

A final conclusion that may be drawn is that the lunatic and fanatical scholar finds his public quite quickly, but that he remains very vulnerable in his own time because of his tendency to make numerous enemies. However, there is some potential for long-term success for his works in the long run, if he remains present in historical studies — especially if his end was a dramatic fall from favour, and if he has been a prolific writer. The pragmatic and consensual scholar, on the other hand, might work less visibly to the public, but he keeps society moving forward. He is usually compensated and appreciated in his own times and the immediate aftermath, but his works may be forgotten when a new period dawns that changes the fundamental parameters of societies, which then (again) turn back to the visionaries.

110 Johansen, 'A Perfect Law in an Imperfect Society', p. 285.

Works Cited

Manuscripts

Ibn Nubāta, *Kitāb sulūk duwal al-mulūk. Ikhtiyār*, Oxford, Bodleian Library, MS Seld. Superius 29

Primary Sources

'Al-Siyāsa al-Shari'a li-l-ṣiff al-awwal al-shar'ī' [Schoolbook of ISIS] (Raqqa [?]: Ṭaba'a i 1437 h [2015]) [pdf no longer available online; the author has a copy]

Ibn Baṭṭūṭa, *Riḥlat Ibn Baṭṭūṭa* (Beirut: Dār Ṣādir, 1960–64)

Ibn Ḥabīb, *Tadhkirat al-nabīh fī ayyām al-Manṣūr wa-banīh*, ed. by Muḥammad Muḥammad Amīn and Sa'id 'Abd al-Fattāḥ 'Āshūr, 3 vols (Cairo: Maṭba'at Dār al-Kutub, 1976–86)

Ibn Kathīr, *al-Bidāya wa-nihāya*, 14 vols (Beirut: Dār al-Fikr, 1987)

Ibn Taymīya, *al-Murābaṭa bi-l-thughur afḍal am al-mujāwara bi-Makka sharafahā allah ta'ālā?*, ed. by Abū Muḥammad Ashraf ibn 'Abd al-Maqsūd (Riad: Aḍwā' al-Salaf, 2002)

——, *Kitāb al-siyāsa al-sharia fī iṣlāḥ al-rā'ī wa 'l-ra'yya*, ed. by Lajna Iḥyā al-Turāth al-'Arabī (Beirut: Dār al-Jīl, 1988)

Al-Maqrīzī, *Kitāb al-Mawā'iẓ wa-'l-I'tibār fī dhikr al-khiṭaṭ wa-l-āthār*, ed. by Gaston Wiet, 4 vols (Cairo: Institut Français d'Archéologie Orientale du Caire, 1911–1927)

The Qur'an: A New Translation, trans. by Tarif Khalidi (London: Penguin, 2008)

Al-Subkī, *Al-Ṭabaqat al-Shāfi'īya al-kubrā*, ed. by Maḥmūd Muḥammad al-Ṭanaḥī, 10 vols (Cairo: Maṭba'at 'Īsā al-Bābī al-Ḥalabī, 1964–76)

Le Traité de droit public d'ibn Taimīya. Traduction annoté de la Siyāsa šar'īya , ed. by Henri Laoust (Beirut: Institut Français de Damas, 1948)

Secondary Studies

Abel, A., 'Iskandar Nāma', in *Encyclopaedia of Islam*, 2nd edn, <http://dx.doi.org/10.1163/1573-3912_islam_COM_0385> [accessed 21 June 2021]

Aigle, Denis, 'The Mongol Invasions of Bilād al-Shām by Ghāzān Khān and Ibn Taymīyah's Three "Anti-Mongol Fatwas"', *Mamluk Studies Review*, 11,2 (2007), 89–120

Amitai-Preiss, Reuven, *Mongols and Mamluks: The Mamluk-Ilkhanid War, 1260–1281* (Cambridge: Cambridge University Press, 1995)

Anjum, Ovamir, *Politics, Law, and Community in Islamic Thought: The Taymiyyan Moment* (New York: Cambridge University Press, 2012)

Bārūt, Muḥammad Jamāal, *Ḥamalāt Kisrawān fī al-tārīkh al-siyāsī li-fatāwa Ibn Taymīya* (Doha: al-Markaz al-'arabī li-l-abḥāth wa-dirāsa al-siyāsāt, 2017)

Bauer, Thomas, 'Ibn Nubātah al-Misrī (686–768/1287–1366). Life and Works. Part 1: The Life of Ibn Nubātah', *Mamlūk Studies Review*, 12,1 (2008), 1–35

——, 'Ibn Nubātah al-Misrī (686–768/1287–1366). Life and Works. Part II: The Dīwān of Ibn Nubātah', *Mamlūk Studies Review*, 12,2 (2008), 25–69

——, *Die Kultur der Ambiguität. Eine andere Geschichte des Islams* (Berlin: Verlag der Weltreligionen, 2011)

——, '"Der Fürst ist tot, es lebe der Fürst!" Ibn Nubātas Gedicht zur Inthronisation al-Afḍals von Ḥamāh (732/1332)', in *Orientalistische Studien zu Sprache und Literatur. Festgabe zum 65. Geburtstag von Werner Diem*, ed. by Ulrich Marzolph (Wiesbaden: Harrassowitz, 2011), pp. 285–315

Beydoun, Ahmed, *Identité confessionnelle et temps social chez les historiens libanais* (Beirut: Université Libanaise, 1984)

Bori, Caterina, *Ibn Taymiyya: una vita esemplare. Analisi delle fonti classiche della sua biografia*, Rivista di Studi Orientali. Supplemento monografico, 1 (Pisa-Rome: Istituti Poligrafici Internazionali, 2003)

——, 'Ibn Taymiyya wa-Jamaʿatuhu: Authority, Conflict and Consensus in Ibn Taymiyya's Circle', in *Ibn Taymiyya and His Times*, ed. by Yossef Rapoport and Shahab Ahmed (Karachi: Oxford University Press, 2010), pp. 23–55

——, 'Ibn Taymiyya (14th to 17th Century): Transregional Spaces of Reading and Reception', *The Muslim World*, 108,1 (2018), 87–123

Bosworth, C. E., I. R. Netton, F. E. Vogel, 'Siyāsa', in *Encyclopaedia of Islam*, 2nd edn, <http://dx.doi.org/10.1163/1573-3912_islam_COM_1096> [accessed 21 June 2021]

Brinner, William M., 'Ibn Ḥabīb', in *Encyclopaedia of Islam*, 2nd edn, <http://dx.doi.org/10.1163/1573-3912_islam_SIM_3176> [accessed 21 June 2021]

Chamberlain, Michael, 'The Crusader Era and the Ayyūbid Dynasty', in *The Cambridge History of Egypt, I: Islamic Egypt, 640–1517*, ed. by Carl F. Petry (Cambridge: Cambridge University Press, 1998), pp. 211–41

Corrado, Monica, *Mit Tradition in die Zukunft: Der taǧdīd-Diskurs in der Azhar und ihrem Umfeld* (Würzburg: Ergon, 2011)

Eddé, Anne-Marie, *Saladin* (Paris: Flammarion, 2008)

Esposito, John L., *Unholy War: Terror in the Name of Islam* (Oxford: Oxford University Press, 2002)

Fuess, Albrecht, *Verbranntes Ufer. Auswirkungen mamlukischer Seepolitik auf Beirut und die syro-palästinensische Küste (1250–1517)*, Islamic History and Civilization, 39 (Leiden: Brill, 2001)

——, 'Mamluk Politics', in *Ubi sumus? Quo vademus? Mamluk Studies — State of the Art*, ed. by Stephan Conermann (Göttingen: Bonn University Press, 2013), pp. 95–117

——, 'Why Venice, not Genoa? How Venice Emerged as the Mamluks' Favourite European Trading Partner after 1365', in *Union in Separation — Diasporic Groups and Identities in the Eastern Mediterranean (1100–1800)*, ed. by Georg Christ and others (Rome: Viella, 2015), pp. 251–66

Fuhr, Andreas, *Machiavelli und Savonarola: Politische Rationalität und politische Prophetie* (Frankfurt: Peter Lang, 1985)

Haarmann, Ulrich, 'Der arabische Osten im späten Mittelalter', in *Geschichte der arabischen Welt*, ed. by Ulrich Haarmann, 4th edition (Munich: C. H. Beck, 2001), pp. 217–63

Hees, Syrinx von, 'The Guidance for Kingdoms: Function of a "Mirror for Princes" at Court and its Representation of a Court', in *Court Cultures in the Muslim World: Seventh to Nineteenth Centuries*, ed. by Albrecht Fuess and Jan-Peter Hartung (London: Routledge, 2011), pp. 370–82

Holzmann, Livnat, 'Accused of Anthropomorphism: Ibn Taymiyya's Miḥanas Reflected in Ibn Qayyim al-Jawziyya's al-Kāfiya al-Shāfiy', *Muslim World*, 106,3 (2016), 561–87

Hoover, Jon, 'God Acts by His Will and Power: Ibn Taymiyya's Theology of a Personal God in his Treatise on the Voluntary Attributes', in *Ibn Taymiyya and His Times*, ed. by Yossef Rapoport and Shahab Ahmed (Karachi: Oxford University Press, 2010), pp. 55–77

Jackson, Peter, *The Mongols and the West, 1221–1410* (London: Longman, 2005)

Johansen, Baber, 'A Perfect Law in an Imperfect Society: Ibn Taymiyya's Concept of "Government in the Name of the Sacred Law"', in *The Law Applied. Contextualizing the Islamic Shari'a. A Volume in Honor of Frank E. Vogel*, ed. by Peri Bearman, Wolfhart Heinrichs, and Bernhard G. Weiss (London: I. B. Tauris, 2008), pp. 259–94

Krawietz, Birgit, 'Ibn Taymiyya, Vater des islamischen Fundamentalismus? Zur westlichen Rezeption eines mittelalterlichen Schariatsgelehrten', in *Theorie des Rechts in der Gesellschaft*, ed. by. Manuel Atienza and others (Berlin: Duncker & Humblot, 2003), pp. 39–62

Laoust, Henri, 'Ibn Taymiyya', in *Encyclopaedia of Islam*, 2nd edn, <http://dx.doi.org/10.1163/1573-3912_islam_SIM_3388> [accessed 21 June 2021]

——, 'Remarques sur les expéditions du Kasrawan sous les premiers Mamluks', *Bulletin du Musée de Beyrouth*, 4 (1940), 103–15

——, 'La Biographie d'Ibn Taymiya d'après Ibn Kathir', *Bulletin d'Etudes Orientales de l'Institut Francais de Damas*, 9 (1942), 146

Levanoni, Amalia, *A Turning Point in Mamluk History: The Third Reign of al-Nāṣir Muḥammad Ibn Qalāwūn (1310–1341)*, Islamic History and Civilization, 10 (Leiden: Brill, 1995)

Little, Donald, 'Did Ibn Taymiyya Have a Screw Loose?', *Studia Islamica*, 41 (1975), 93–111

Meier, Mischa, 'Mesotes', in *Brill's New Pauly*, 2006, <http://dx.doi.org/10.1163/1574-9347_bnp_e800980> [accessed 21 June 2021]

Meri, Josef W., *The Cult of Saints among Muslims and Jews in Medieval Syria* (Oxford: Oxford University Press, 2002)

Michot, Yahya, 'Textes spirituels d'Ibn Taymiyya, XII: Mongols et Mamlûks: l'état du monde musulman vers 709/1310 (suite)', *Le Musulman*, 25 (1995), 25–30

——, 'Textes spirituels d'Ibn Taymiyya, XIII: l'état du monde musulman vers 709/1310 (fin)', *Le Musulman*, 26 (1995), 25–30

Morgan, David O., 'The Mongols and the Eastern Mediterranean', in *Latins and Greeks in the Eastern Mediterranean after 1204*, ed. by Benjamin Arbel, Bernard Hamilton, and David Jacoby (London: Routledge, 1989), pp. 198–211

——, *Medieval Persia 1040–1797*, 5th edn (London: Longman 1997)

Olesen, Nils-Henrik, *Culte des Saints et Pèlerinages chez Ibn Taymiyya: 661 (1263)–728 (1328)* (Paris: Librairie orientaliste Paul Geuthner, 1992)

Rapoport, Yossef, 'Ibn Taymiyya on Divorce Oaths', in *The Mamluks in Egyptian and Syrian Politics and Society*, ed. by Michael Winter and Amalia Levanoni (Leiden: Brill, 2004), pp. 191–217

Rapoport, Yossef, and Shahab Ahmed, ed., *Ibn Taymiyya and His Times* (Karachi: Oxford University Press, 2010)

Rikabi, Jawdat, 'Ibn Nubāta', in *Encyclopaedia of Islam*, 2nd edn, <http://dx.doi.org/10.1163/1573-3912_islam_SIM_3325> [accessed 21 June 2021]

Smith, John Massen Jr., 'Ayn Jālūt: Mamlūk Success or Mongol Failure?', *Harvard Journal of Asiatic Studies*, 44,2 (1984), 307–45

Swartz, Merlin L., 'A Seventh-Century (A.H.) Sunni Creed: The 'Aqīda Wāsiṭīya of Ibn Taymiya', *Humaniora Islamica*, 1 (1973), 91–131

Talmon, Rafael, and Daniel Gimaret, 'Ṣifa', in *Encyclopaedia of Islam*, 2nd edn, <http://dx.doi.org/10.1163/1573-3912_islam_COM_1070> [accessed 21 June 2021]

Tsugitaka, Satō, *State and Rural Society in Medieval Islam: Sultans, Muqta's, and Fallahun*, Islamic History and Civilization, 17 (Leiden: Brill, 1997)

Winter, Stefan, *The Shiites of Lebanon under Ottoman Rule, 1516–1788* (Cambridge: Cambridge University Press, 2010)

——, *A History of the 'Alawis: From Medieval Syria to the Turkish Republic, 947–1938* (Princeton: Princeton University Press, 2016)

MICHAL BIRAN

The Mongol World Order

*From Universalism to Glocalization**

In the thirteenth century, Chinggis Khan and his heirs created the largest contiguous empire the world has ever seen, an empire that at its height stretched from Korea to Hungary and from Vietnam, Burma, and Iraq to Siberia, ruling over two thirds of the Old World. Moreover, as the only 'superpower' of the era, the empire also affected regions beyond its control, such as Japan, Southeast Asia, the Indian subcontinent, the Arab Middle East, and Europe, both eastern and western.

The Empire existed as an ever-expanding unified polity ruled from Mongolia up to 1260 and was later dissolved in a process that eventually resulted in the creation of four regional empires, which centred, in turn, on China, Iran, Central Asia, and the Volga region, each of them ruled by a Chinggisid branch.[1] The Great Khan's (or Qa'an's) state (in Mongolian: *Qa'an ulus*) had its centre in China. Its rulers became known as the Yuan dynasty (1271–1368) and their realm enjoyed a nominal, though not uncontested, primacy over its counterparts. The Ilkhanate, literally 'the empire of the submissive khans' (of the Great Khan in China; 1260–1335, in Mongolian: *Ulus Hülegü*), had its centre in modern Iran and Iraq, while the Golden Horde (1260–1502, *Ulus Jochi*) ruled from the Volga region, and the Chaghadaid Khanate (1260–1678, *Ulus Chaghadai*) held power in Central Asia. Despite the many, and often bloody, disputes between the four polities, they retained a strong sense of Chinggisid unity.

* This chapter is largely based on my essay 'The Mongol Imperial Space'. The research leading to these results has received funding from the European Research Council under the European Union's Seventh Framework Programme (FP/2007–13) / ERC Grant Agreement n. 312397, and from the Humboldt Foundation via my Anneliese Maier Research Award.

1 *Ulus* in Mongolian originally meant the people subject to a certain lord. Later it also became an equivalent of a 'nation' and 'state' (as it still does in modern Mongolian today). The states here are named after the leaders of the various Chinggisid branches, either sons or grandsons of Chinggis Khan, or his heir as the leader of the Empire who bore the title Qa'an ('Great Khan').

Michal Biran (biranm@mail.huji.ac.il), Institute for Asian and African Studies, The Hebrew University of Jerusalem, Israel

Order into Action: How Large-Scale Concepts of World-Order determine Practices in the Premodern World, ed. by Klaus Oschema and Christoph Mauntel, CURSOR 40 (Turnhout: Brepols, 2022), pp. 127–149
BREPOLS PUBLISHERS 10.1484/M.CURSOR-EB.5.123846

In the mid-fourteenth century, all four khanates were embroiled in political crises that led to the collapse of the Ilkhanate as well as of Yuan China, and considerably weakened the two other steppe khanates. The fall of the Qa'an state in 1368 is generally deemed to be the end of the 'Mongol Moment' in world history. For heuristic convenience, I shall differentiate between two main periods: 1) the United Mongol Empire (Mongolian: *Yeke Mongghol Ulus*, 1206–60), 2) the four successor states (1260–1368) — although, as we shall see below, from the Mongols' point of view, the distinction between the two eras was not as clear cut as it is presented here and in various textbooks.[2]

This chapter aims to answer the following questions: How did the Mongols conceive of their world? How did these concepts affect their actual actions? How did both concepts and actions influence the future shaping of the Eurasian world order?

The modern concept of 'glocalization' — a combination of 'global' and 'local' that refers to the simultaneous occurrence of both universalizing and particularizing tendencies in social, political, and economic systems[3] — may seem somewhat anachronistic when applied to the Mongol period. However, I choose to use it, since it captures nicely the need of the Mongols and their local elites to combine the highly universal world order of the Chinggisids with the local concepts of their sedentary subjects, thereby creating a new, more complex world order, which had a tremendous effect on the post-Mongol world.

It is not easy to locate the Mongols' own voice, as most of the sources were penned not by the Mongols themselves but by their subjects and neighbours, each bound by the premises of their own civilization. Yet by using *The Secret History of the Mongols* — the only contemporaneous Mongolian source for the rise of Chinggis Khan — together with the Mongols' letters and inscriptions on seals and coins, as well as by comparing sources from different parts of the Empire, the Mongols' indigenous concepts — both spatial and political — can be traced.

The Mongol World Order: Universalism and World Conquest under the United Empire (1206–60)

As is well known, the Mongols' world order, as designed by Chinggis Khan, was based on an ideology of heaven-ordained mandate that gave the Mongols the right to rule upon earth.[4] The notion of the heavenly mandate originated in earlier steppe empires, notably the Turkic empires of the sixth to eighth centuries, and obviously brings to mind the Chinese 'mandate of Heaven'.

2 For general background on the Mongol Empire see, e.g., Morgan, *The Mongols*; May, *The Mongol Conquest*; Biran, 'The Mongol Empire'.

3 For the relatively recent concept of 'glocalization', which has been developed mainly since the 1990s, see, e.g., Roudometof, *Glocalization*, pp. 1–19; Blatter, 'Glocalization'.

4 See, e.g., Biran, *Chinggis Khan*, pp. 12–14.

However, there were quite a few differences between the steppe mandate, which the Mongols adopted and developed, and its Chinese counterpart. As in the older steppe empires, and unlike the Chinese mandate, in the Mongol case Tengri (Heaven), the supreme sky god, conferred heavenly charisma (*suu*) and the right to rule on earth to a single clan, each of whose members could theoretically be elevated to the supreme rulership, represented by the title Qa'an (Great Khan, Turkic: Khaqan / Kaghan). Among the clan members, however, the main criterion in the choice of a future Qa'an was a demonstration of his charisma (*suu*), encompassing his skills, intelligence, and fortune (on and off the battlefield), which practically means that succession struggles were endemic. The Empire was conceived of as the joint property of the entire royal clan, and the Qa'an was therefore expected to share its wealth and territory with his kin. This redistribution in turn contributed both to the dissolution of the empire into various polities and to the ongoing connections among these successor states.

Moreover, unlike the Chinese case, Tengri did not bestow his mandate on every generation; the steppe world was thus often left without a unifying ruler — sometimes (as in the period that precedes the rise of the Mongols) for centuries. Yet the notion of the mandate remained in reserve as an ideological option even during the periods of disunion, ready to be revived if the creation of a supra-tribal empire was to be attempted again. An aspiring Qa'an therefore had to prove that he had received the mandate by displaying the charisma required to hold it, mainly on the battlefield. The possession of the mandate was also confirmed by shamanic ceremonies and reinforced by the ruler's control of sacred territory (see below).[5]

The most important criterion for demonstrating the possession of both the mandate and the charisma, however, was concrete success on the battlefield. This meant that the Mongols had to wage war not only for practical reasons (e.g. in order to keep the military busy and united or to acquire booty for redistribution), but also for ideological ones — to prove their legitimacy. In turn, the spate of victories of Chinggis Khan in the next decades convinced him — and everybody around — that he was indeed destined to rule over the entire world. In addition, as a by-product of this development, the scope of the Mongols' heavenly mandate became considerably broader: when Chinggis Khan was enthroned in 1206, his mandate was limited to ruling 'the people of the felt walled tents', namely the steppe nomads,[6] just like the mandate of his Turkic predecessors in the steppe and despite their universalistic rhetoric. Following Chinggis Khan's continuous

5 Golden, 'Imperial Ideology'; Golden, 'The Türk Imperial Tradition', pp. 39–50; Biran, 'Introduction: Nomadic Culture', p. 3.

6 *The Secret History*, ed. and trans. by de Rachewiltz, § 202, 1, p. 133; § 244, 1, p. 168. Later sources attribute to Chinggis Khan the mandate to rule the whole world from the moment of his coronation in 1206, but this was probably an anachronism, see Jackson, 'World Conquest'.

military successes, however, especially his Central Asian campaign against the Khwārazm Shāh in 1219–25, the mandate was broadened to include the whole word, both steppe and sown. In other words, not only did the world order affect the Mongols' actions, but their actions also impacted the world order. The broadened mandate is made clear in Chinggis Khan's edict: 'This is the order of the everlasting God: In heaven there is only one eternal God; on earth there is only one lord, Chinggis Khan'.[7]

The same idea permeates the titles, seals, and letters of Chinggis Khan's heirs: Ögödei, Chinggis Khan's son and first heir (r. 1229–41), is called *dalai-i-qan* (the 'Oceanic' or 'universal' khan; glossed in Chinese as 'the emperor of all within the seas' [*hainei huangdi* 海内皇帝] or as 'the emperor of all within the four seas' [*sihai huangdi* 四海皇帝]). The same title also appears on the seal of Ögödei's son and heir, Güyük (r. 1246–48).[8] Thus, either at the end of Chinggis Khan's rule or early in Ögödei's reign, the Mongols saw the conquest of the whole world — not only of the steppe — as their goal. The successes of Chinggis Khan's heirs in the next decades — as they completed the submission of North China under the Jin dynasty (1234), pushed the conquest of the steppe up to the gates of Hungary, wreaking terror across eastern Europe (1237–41), and in the 1240–50s subdued Tibet, Sichuan, and Yunnan in south-west China and conquered the Middle East up to Anatolia and Iraq — further bolstered the Chinggisids' universalistic claims. It also encouraged them to take their world conquest mission rather literally,[9] thereby once more manifesting the tangible impact of ideology on the sphere of actions.

As a major element of their ideology, the Mongols' heavenly mandate appeared at the head of their edicts, letters, seals, and titles, both in its terse Mongolian form (*Möngke Tengri-yin küchün-dür; Qa'an-u su-dur*, literally: 'By the Might of Eternal Heaven, by the Good Fortune of the Qa'an') and in various other languages and phrasing, embellished with Quranic verses, references from the Confucian classics or even biblical quotes, according to their prospective audiences, thereby manifesting their ability to glocalize their universal message.[10] Such repetition also served as propaganda — and quite successfully: even a hostile writer like the historian Jūzjānī, who had escaped from the Mongol hordes to Delhi where he wrote *c.* 1260, had to

---

7 William of Rubruck, *The Mission of Friar William*, ed. by Morgan and trans. by Jackson, p. 248. William of Rubruck (*c.* 1220–93) quotes the letter sent by Möngke Qa'an (r. 1250–59) to the French king Louis IX, which begins by citing Chinggis Khan's edict.

8 *The Secret History*, ed. and trans. by de Rachewiltz, § 280, I, p. 216; de Rachewiltz, 'Qan, Qa'an and the Seal of Güyük'; Mostaert and Cleaves, 'Trois documents', pp. 485–95; Kim, 'Was Da Yuan a Chinese Dynasty?', pp. 285–86.

9 Biran, 'The Mongol Empire', p. 537; for a detailed description of Mongol expansion under the united empire see, e.g., Allsen, 'The Rise of the Mongolian Empire'.

10 See above, n. 7 and 8; cf. also Vogelin, 'Mongol Orders of Submission'; *Yuandai baihua bei jilu*, ed. by Cai Meibiao, pp. 21, 25, 35, 36, 37, 38, 39, 40, etc.; Chavannes, 'Inscriptions', pp. 372, 373, 376, 378, 388, 391, etc.; Poppe, *The Mongolian Monuments*, pp. 47, 49, 52.

admit that the Mongols possessed a 'heavenly mandate' (*qaḍā-i āsmānī*) and that 'by the decrees of Heaven and commands of Divine Destiny the turn of world sovereignty (*jahānbānī*) passed from the Rulers of Iran and Turan to Chinggis Khan and his descendants'.[11]

The letter that Chinggis Khan's grandson Hülegü (d. 1265) sent to King Louis IX of France in 1262 illustrates what the Mongols' full-fledged universal claims sounded like. In this letter, Hülegü quotes the Mongol shaman Teb Tengri, who had allegedly enthroned Chinggis Khan by using the words of the prophet Jeremiah:

> I alone am the Almighty God on high and *I have set thee over the nations and over the kingdoms* to be king of all the world *to root out and to pull down and to destroy and to throw down to build and to plant* [Jeremiah 1. 10; quoted verses in italics]. I tell you to announce my command (mandate) to all the nations, tongues and tribes of the East, the South, the North and the West; to promulgate it in all the regions of the whole world where emperors, kings and sovereigns rule, where lordship operates, where horses can go, ships sail, envoys reach, letters be heard, so that those who have ears can hear; those who hear can understand and those who understand can believe. Those who do not believe will later learn that punishment will be meted on those who did not believe my commands.[12]

This letter represents the world order created by the broadened heavenly mandate: it encompasses everything, including the maritime world, and everybody. Indeed, the Mongols divided the world into two parts: the first part consisted of the lands they already conquered, the second part of those that still needed to be subjugated. This concept has some similarities to the concept of the 'abode of Islam' (*dār al-islām*) and the 'abode of war' (*dār al-ḥarb*) in the Muslim world, where the Muslims are supposed to fight the 'abode of war' until it becomes the 'abode of Islam', or the Chinese concept of 'All Under Heaven' (*tianxia* 天下), where extension was expected to come not through war but through the subordinated peoples' recognition of the Chinese emperor's moral superiority.[13] Yet in the Mongol case the division was defined not in territorial terms but in terms of people — just like the wealth of a nomadic chief is measured not in territory, which is quite abundant in the steppe, but in people: a much rarer resource. The Mongols differentiated between those people who were pacified or submissive (*il irgen*) and rebellious ones (*bulgha irgen*), who would eventually be pacified. The rebellion of the latter was directed not only against Mongol authority but also against Heaven

---

11 Minhāj al-Dīn Jūzjānī, *Ṭabaqāt-i nāṣirī*, ed. by Lees, I, pp. 324, 344, 380, and Jūzjānī, *Ṭabaqāt-i nāṣirī*, trans. by Raverty, II, pp. 869, 1006, 1070 (cited in Allsen, 'Ideology', p. 12).

12 Meyvaert, 'Unknown Letter', pp. 252–53; English translation following *Letters from the East*, ed. by Barber and Bate, pp. 156–57.

13 For the 'abode of Islam' and the 'abode of war' see, e.g., Albrecht, 'Dār al-Islām', and König in the present volume; for 'All Under Heaven' see Pines, *Envisioning Eternal Empire*.

that had enabled this authority. As a consequence, it was considered to be both futile and punishable, as the Mongols clearly explained in the ultimatums they sent to various rulers.[14]

Despite this stress on people, Mongol success also had a spatial dimension. The Mongols' popular phrase for describing the universalistic dimensions of their empire was that they ruled 'from the place where the sun rises to the place where it sets' — in other words: from East to West or the entire world. This concept, first used in the letter Güyük Qa'an (r. 1246–48) sent to Pope Innocent IV in 1246, if not earlier,[15] was repeated in a variety of Mongolian, Muslim, and Chinese sources in order to describe the Empire's realm, both throughout its continuous expansion and after it stopped,[16] when the Empire's sheer size was sufficient proof for its legitimization.

This world order resulted in a foreign policy that saw conquest by military power as its main aim. The Mongols were willing to accept peaceful submission, but they were not ready to forge any foreign relations based on equality or any sustainable alliances with other polities. They also took great pains to eliminate competing rulers with universal claims, such as the Abbasid Caliph and the Jin and Song emperors. In addition, they refuted calls for conversion (to Christianity or Islam exclusively), explaining that Heaven was obviously on their side, as proven by their continuous military success.[17]

Besides this success on the battlefield, the heavenly mandate was supposed to be approved by the shamanic apparatus — and Chinggis Khan was indeed enthroned in 1206 by the shaman Teb Tengri. When the latter intervened in

14 See, e.g., de Rachewiltz's commentary in *The Secret History*, ed. and trans. by de Rachewiltz, I, pp. 550–51; Mostaert and Cleaves, 'Trois documents', pp. 492–93; William of Rubruck, *The Mission of Friar William*, ed. by Morgan and trans. by Jackson, pp. 172–73; Fiaschetti, 'The Borders of Rebellion'; Vogelin, 'Mongol Orders of Submission'.

15 ʿAṭā-Malik al-Juwaynī, *Taʾrīkh-i Jahāngushā*, ed. by Qazwīnī, I, p. 114; Juvaini (Juwaynī), *Genghis Khan: The History of the World Conqueror*, trans. by Boyle, p. 145, mentions a similar phrase, allegedly cited from a copy of an edict (*yarligh*) of Chinggis Khan, which his commanders Jebe and Sübe'edei had given the people of Nīshāpūr in 1220, ordering them to submit. Yet, writing around 1260, Juwaynī might have inserted a later phrasing into the commanders' message. See also Jackson, *The Mongols and the Islamic World*, p. 75.

16 For Güyük's letter to the Pope, originally in Mongolian, see, e.g., de Rachewiltz, *Papal Envoys to the Great Khans*, pp. 213–14; see also Möngke's letter to the King of France as cited by William of Rubruck, *The Mission of Friar William*, ed. by Morgan and trans. by Jackson, p. 249 (Latin). This phrasing appears, e.g., in Waṣṣāf al-Ḥaḍrat, *Ta'rīkh-i Waṣṣāf*, p. 452 (Persian); Ibn al-Fuwaṭī, *Talkhīṣ Majma' al-ādāb*, ed. by Muḥammad al-Kāẓim, vol. III, p. 319 (Arabic); Wang Shidian, *Mishujian zhi*, p. 74 (Chinese). See also n. 15 above.

17 See, e.g., Mostaert and Cleaves, 'Trois documents', pp. 450–51; *Mission to Asia*, ed. and trans. by Dawson, pp. 83–86; Rashīd al-Dīn, *Jāmi' al-Tawārīkh*, ed. by Rawshan and Mūsawī, II, pp. 997–1004; Rashīd al-Dīn, *Rashīduddin Fazlullah's Jamiʿu't-Tawarikh*, trans. by Thackston, III, pp. 488–95. The Mongols' religious pluralism on the one hand and their differentiation between the sphere of their indigenous beliefs and that of world religions on the other, often misled monotheists who understood Mongols' sympathy towards their religion as its adoption. See Jackson, 'The Mongols and the Faith of the Conquered', pp. 253–55.

earthly politics, however, Chinggis Khan orchestrated his execution, thereby attesting that the heaven-ordained connection of the charismatic Khan to the Divine was by far closer than that of any shaman or other religious expert.[18]

The original steppe mandate was also reinforced by the control of sacred territories, which were considered repositories of charisma. Such a territory was the Ottükan mountains near the Orkhon river in central Mongolia, which was praised in the Turkic Orkhon inscriptions of the eighth century and in which the Turks' successors, the Uighurs (744–840), later built their capital. The Mongol capital, Qaraqorum, was also established in this region in the 1230s. Both Chinese and Muslim sources attest that, before choosing its location, the Mongols actually sought the remains of former nomadic empires: excavating steles and checking Chinese history books, the Mongols looked for both historical and archaeological evidence as well as folk memories, making the most of them to enhance the charismatic location of their capital.[19] Qaraqorum, however, was established a few dozen kilometres away from the Turkic and Uighur sites, in a location allegedly chosen by Chinggis Khan himself — which made it possible to enjoy the region's repositories of charisma while stressing the uniqueness of the Chinggisid experience.

In 1260, however, Qubilai Qa'an (r. 1260–94), Chinggis Khan's grandson and the Mongols' new Great Khan, transferred the Mongol capital from Qaraqorum to northern China — eventually to Beijing (then known as Dadu or Khanbaliq). This decision can easily be explained by strategic, political, economic, and now even climatic considerations,[20] but it entailed the renunciation of Qaraqorum's repositories of charisma. At this moment, though, the charisma was already so deeply imbedded in the Chinggisid family, which ruled territories that were much vaster than the steppe, that such a concession did not constitute a major problem — just like the ruler's charisma had previously replaced the shamanic one.[21]

Chinggisid Space versus Former Imperial Space: Post-1260 Concepts

Qubilai's transfer of the capital to northern China in 1260, however, also signalled the dissolution of the Mongol Empire. This process originated in

18 *The Secret History*, ed. and trans. by de Rachewiltz, § 244–46, I, pp. 168–74; Biran, 'The Mongol Empire', p. 546.

19 al-Juwaynī, *Ta'rīkh-i jahān gushā*, ed. by Qazwīnī, I, pp. 39–46, 191–92; al-Juwaynī, *Genghis Khan: The History of World Conqueror*, trans. by Boyle, pp. 54–61, 236; Su Tianjue, *Yuan wenlei*, pp. 1b–2a (chap. 26); Song Lian, *Yuanshi*, p. 2999 (chap. 122), 3464–65 (chap. 146), 4159 (chap. 180); Yelü Zhu, *Shuangxi zuiyin ji*, p. 7a (chap. 2); Allsen, 'Spiritual Geography', esp. p. 126; Atwood 'The Uyghur Stone'.

20 Rossabi, *Khubilai Khan*, pp. 51–75; DiCosmo, 'Why Qara Qorum'.

21 For a detailed discussion of the modifications of charisma, see Allsen, 'A Note on Mongol Imperial Ideology', pp. 1–8.

succession struggles, the empire's sheer size, and the fact that its realm had already reached the steppe's ecological borders. The ensuing dissolution led to the eventual consolidation of four polities that centred in China, Iran, Central Asia, and the Volga region, and that were nominally — though not incontestably — subject to the Great Khan in China. While each of these polities voiced universal claims and appropriated the Chinggisid achievements, they also adopted various local elements from their subjects, trying to carve out their separate identities. The world order created at this stage developed and became more complex, combining universal and local elements — what I propose to call a 'glocal world order'.[22]

The four emerging Mongol polities still saw themselves as brotherly states, parts of a common Chinggisid space, and held on to the ideal of a Chinggisid unity, despite the various — and often bloody — disputes among them. Even at the height of the inter-Mongol conflicts in the last decades of the thirteenth century, the rival khanates continued to exchange gifts and messengers. They regarded each other in kinship terms (*aqa* and *ini*, 'big' and 'little brothers'), and referred to their conflicts as family feuds, which were never intended to eliminate their rivals.[23] Moreover, the polities were still connected not only by the postal system that stretched throughout the Chinggisid realm, but also by the apanages (*qubi*) allocated to various Chinggisids from the newly conquered regions during the United Empire period, which were now often territories that became subject to a rival khanate.[24]

The four states also held on to their universalistic claims and to the world conquest ideology. Yet, after 1260 world conquest became much more complicated — not only because the inter-Mongol conflicts prevented the vast mobilization of imperial resources that had characterized former campaigns. These feuds also often hindered the khanates from concentrating their efforts on expansion, as they had to defend themselves against a rival *ulus*. Moreover, because the Empire had already reached the ecological border of steppe nomadism on all its borders, further expansion demanded organization, warfare techniques, and equipment different from the former light cavalry steppe campaigns. The Mongols managed to break the ecological border in southern China — where the gains in terms of both legitimation and economy were by far the greatest. They were less successful on other fronts.[25] Moreover, even in China further attempts at expansion, which took

---

22 For the concept of glocalization see above, n. 3; for the empire's dissolution see Jackson, 'Dissolution'; Jackson, 'From Ulus to Khanate'; Allsen, 'Sharing Out the Empire'.

23 Kim, 'Unity of the Mongol Empire'.

24 For the *jam*, see Silverstein, *Postal Systems*, pp. 141–64, and Allsen, 'Imperial Posts'; for the apanages, see Allsen, 'Sharing Out the Empire'.

25 For the Mongol conquest of Song China, see, e.g., Rossabi, *Khubilai Khan*, pp. 76–95; Davis, 'The Reign of Tu-tsung', pp. 913–19. This conquest was achieved by mobilizing Chinese and Korean infantry and sailors and with the help of Iranian siege engineers — in other words, the successful transfer of experts continued, although on a scale that was completely different from the well-designed campaigns of the united empire. For the situation on other

place simultaneously with or after the Song conquest (1279), were either not very successful (in Java or Burma) or resulted in complete disaster (in the case of Japan). As a consequence, expansion practically came to an end in the fourteenth century, and the dynamics were not renewed afterwards, even after the four Mongol polities concluded a peace agreement in 1304.[26] Under this new order, however, and as a result of the inter-Mongol conflicts, tactical alliances with non-Mongol polities became a legitimate practice. Thus, the Ilkhanate, the Mongol state centred in Iran, invested considerable diplomatic efforts in attempts to forge an alliance with the European West against their common enemy, the Muslim Mamluk Sultanate (1250–1517) in Egypt and Syria. In fact, Hülegü's letter with the impressive opening that was cited above, ended with an invitation to Louis IX to cooperate against the Mamluks, albeit in obeying the Divine order. At the same time, the Golden Horde, the Mongol polity centred in the Volga region and the Ilkhanate's rival, maintained close commercial and diplomatic relations with the Mamluk Sultanate.[27]

All of this does not mean, however, that the Mongol successor states had given up on their universalist claims: since all four *ulus*es were vast polities and, moreover, the Empire was perceived as a joint patrimony of the Chinggisids, each state could appropriate the achievements of Chinggis Khan and his heirs and proudly present them to its local audience as well as to potential allies, for both propaganda and internal legitimization. In other words, when expansion ceased, the mere size of the empire became evidence for its enduring legitimacy.[28]

The continuing adherence to concepts of universal rule found an expression in the commissioning of historical, geographical, and cartographic works by the Mongols — the production of which flourished after the dissolution of the Empire. One important consequence of the Empire's world conquest ideology (whether understood as a completed mission or as a work in progress) was an enormous increase in knowledge about the world, in terms of its geography and history as well as its visual representation in cartography. At first, such information had been collected in order to facilitate further military campaigns.[29] However, the more ambitious Yuan and Ilkhanid works were

---

fronts, see, e.g., Amitai, *Holy War*, pp. 15–36 (Ilkhanid attempts to expand into the Middle East), and Jackson, *Delhi Sultanate*, pp. 217–37 (Chaghadaid invasions of India).

26 For Mongol attacks on Japan and south-east Asia, see, e.g., Rossabi, *Khubilai Khan*, pp. 99–103, 207–20; for the peace of 1304, see Biran, *Qaidu*, pp. 71–74.

27 For these alliances, see, e.g., Amitai-Preiss, *Mongols and Mamluks*, pp. 78–105.

28 See, e.g., Hülegü's letter cited above (*Letters from the East*, trans. by Barber and Bate, pp. 158–59); Waṣṣāf, *Ta'rīkh-i Waṣṣāf*, pp. 560–61; Langlois, 'Song Lian and Liu Ji', pp. 131–62.

29 Chinggis Khan's conquest of Bukhara is an impressive example of the use of such information: Chinggis Khan's main army advanced on the city not in the usual way, through Samarqand, but via the allegedly impenetrable Kizil Kom desert, appearing in early 1220 before Bukhara's gates, some 650 km behind the enemy's line, which in this case sealed the fate of the Khwārazm Shāh's kingdom. This strategic use of information was continued in the period of the successor states: the Mongols collected and/or prepared maps of border

not so much produced because of practical needs, but rather as a result of the prevailing idea of a universal world order and the Empire's unique dimensions.

In 1286, Jamāl al-Dīn, a Muslim astronomer and geographer at Qubilai's court,[30] asked the Great Khan to sponsor the production of a unified geographic treatise that would cover all the lands that the Mongols had conquered and would be accompanied by a map:

> The entire land of China was very small in the past. The geographic books of the Khitai (Northern Chinese) had only forty to fifty types. *Now all of the land from the place of sunrise to sunset has become our territory. And therefore, do we not need a more detailed map? How can we understand distant places?* The Islamic maps are at our hands. And therefore, could we combine them [with the Chinese maps] to draw a [world?] map?[31]

Qubilai was convinced, and ordered the Palace Library to collect geographic gazetteers and maps from every region of his empire in order to compile this treatise. Completed in 1303, the *Treatise on the Great Unified Realm of the Great Yuan (Dayuan yitong zhi* 大元一統志) contained 1300 chapters accompanied by a map. Although no manuscripts of this treatise survive, except for part of the introduction, it must have included extensive descriptions of foreign countries. This is attested by the surviving Korean map that was based upon Jamāl al-Dīn's map. This *Map of Integrated Regions and Terrains and of Historical Countries and Capitals* (*Honil gangli yeokdae gukdo jido* 混一疆理歷代國都) — produced in Korea in 1402 — included more than a hundred places in Europe (including Marseille and Seville) and thirty-five in Africa![32]

The existing Ilkhanid maps are far less impressive, but the most important universal work in this realm belongs to the field of history, not cartography. This is the renowned *Compendium of Chronicles* (*Jāmiʿ al-tawārīkh*), the first world history, compiled by the Ilkhanid vizier and polymath Rashīd al-Dīn (d. 1318). When Ilkhan Öljeitü (r. 1304–16) commissioned the work from Rashīd al-Dīn, he had famously proclaimed:

> Until now no one at any time has made a history of all inhabitants of the climes of the world and the various classes and groups of humans, there

---

regions such as Java, Burma, Yunnan, Anatolia, and the Mediterranean. See, in general, Park, *Mapping the Chinese and Islamic Worlds*, pp. 91–160; Park, 'Cross-Cultural Exchange and Geographic Knowledge'; Allsen, *Culture and Conquest*, pp. 103–14.

30 For Jamāl al-Dīn, see Yang, 'From the West to the East'.

31 Wang Shidian and Shang Qiweng, *Mishujian zhi*, p. 74 [my emphasis]; cited in Park, *Mapping the Chinese and Islamic Worlds*, pp. 103.

32 Kim Hodong, who analysed the toponyms of this map, recently emphasized that the original place names were written in the Mongolian-Uighur script, suggesting that the map of Jamāl al-Dīn's gazetteer was the basis for this one. See Kim, 'Compilation of the Gazetteer'; see also Kauz, *Chinese and Asian Geographical and Cartographical Views*, which contains several articles related to this map.

> is no book in this realm that informs about *all* countries and regions, and no one has delved into the history of the ancient kings. *In these days, when, thank God, all corners of the earth are under our control and that of Chinggis Khan's illustrious family, and philosophers, astronomers, scholars, and historians of all religions and nations — Cathay, Machin, India, Kashmir, Tibet, Uyghur, and other nations of Turks, Arabs, and Franks — are gathered in droves at our glorious court*, each and every one of them possesses copies of the histories, stories, and beliefs of their own people, and they are well informed of some of them. It is our considered opinion that of those detailed histories and stories a compendium that would be perfect should be made in our royal name.[33]

The resulting world history included, apart from the history of the Mongols, those of the Chinese, the Indians, the Muslims, the Jews, the Turks, and the Franks. In addition, it contained a huge amount of geographical information, especially on Mongolia and East Asia.[34]

In Öljeitü's words, just like in Jamāl al-Dīn's address to Qubilai, it is the universal world order that creates knowledge and action — it is because 'we', the Mongols, now rule the world that we want to know more about it. The fact that knowledge was closely connected to charisma in the Mongols' eyes was certainly another stimulant.[35] Interestingly, both the *Compendium* and the map also included regions and people that were not politically ruled by the Mongols. Indeed, in his commission, Öljeitü did not distinguish between people and territories that had been conquered by the Mongols and those that were not — claiming instead that the whole world was under the rule of Chinggis Khan's family. Apparently, the flocking of non-conquered people — Indians, Franks, Arabs — to the Ilkhanid court was taken as a sign of their recognition of Chinggisid superiority.

In China, too, Qubilai Qa'an, alternating between diplomacy and war, continued to present himself as ruling over 'all within the four seas', but he often was content with nominal acknowledgement of his supremacy and the establishment of commercial relations via tribute from the various kingdoms of south and south-east Asia in a way reminiscent of the traditional Chinese tribute system.[36] In other words, the Mongols no longer used military power

---

33 Rashīd al-Dīn, *Jāmi' al-Tawārīkh*, ed. by Rawshan and Mūsawī, I, pp. 8–9, and Rashīd al-Dīn, *Rashīduddin Fazlullah's Jami'u't-Tawarikh*, trans. by Thackston, I, p. 16 [my emphasis].

34 For Rashīd al-Dīn and his work, see, e.g., Allsen, *Culture and Conquest*, esp. pp. 72–82; Akasoy, Burnett, and Yoeli-Tlalim ed., *Rashid al-Din*. The compendium was supposed to include a geographical volume and a map. However, neither have survived, and may never have been compiled.

35 Baumann, 'By the Power of Eternal Heaven', pp. 253–54; Allsen, 'A Note on Mongol Imperial Ideology', pp. 1–7.

36 See, e.g., Fiaschetti, 'Tradition, Innovation and the Construction', pp. 65–96, where the author analyses the combination of Mongol and Chinese rhetoric in Qubilai's diplomacy.

as their main means for world conquest, but turned to methods of 'soft power', namely by way of promoting their economic and cultural prestige. Indeed, after the conquest of southern China with its lively ports (1279), the Mongols combined the maritime and continental routes into one integrated global system.[37] Participants in this integrated system could be seen as the new *il irgen* or 'submitted people', who were taking part in the extensive cross-cultural contacts across the continent. Thus, the idea of explicit world conquest through means of violence and battles was replaced by the exercise of 'soft power', expressed in competition for attracting traders, experts, and diplomats from 'All Under Heaven' to the Mongol courts.

However, side by side with adopting this new universal approach, the Mongol successor states also adopted more local elements and legitimizing concepts. This might have been the result of the adoption of means of soft power, which had a weaker legitimizing force than that of military expansion. It might also have been caused by the empire's dissolution, which resulted in closer connections between the Mongols and their subjects in each polity, due to both practical considerations — such as gaining legitimacy, co-opting local elites, or ruling more effectively — and assimilation. One result of this process was the embracing of universal world religions — Tibetan Buddhism in China, Islam in all the other Mongol khanates — and earlier imperial concepts where such concepts existed, namely in the better-documented China and Iran. In a typical nomadic amalgamation, however, the various concepts of legitimization — Chinggisid, religious, local — and of world order coexisted and were not mutually exclusive.

The adoption of world religions was in sharp contrast to the Mongols' previous refusal to embrace any world religion side by side with Tengri during the United Empire period. It meant that Mongol China was now also part of the Buddhist world order, but the version it embraced — Tibetan Buddhism with its political connotations, magic, and colours — distinguished the Mongols from their Han-Chinese subjects, while appealing to the Tibetan and Uighur population.[38] The other Mongol khanates became part of the Muslim world order, and at least the Ilkhanate in Iran competed for its leadership, which was open to all after the annihilation of the Caliphate. That the Great Khan's state now belonged to the realm of the 'infidels' was ignored by the Mongol Muslim polities, but not by the rival Mamluks, who questioned the Mongols' Islamic belief altogether.[39]

---

37 See, e.g., Kuroda, 'The Eurasian Silver Century'; Biran, 'The Mongol Empire', pp. 550–53.

38 On the Mongol adoption of Tibetan Buddhism, see, e.g, Franke, *From Tribal Chieftain*, pp. 52–64.

39 There is a vast scholarly literature on Mongol Islamization, see, e.g., DeWeese, 'Islamization', and Jackson, *The Mongols and the Islamic World*, pp. 328–80. For the Mamluk criticism of Ilkhanid Islamization, see, e.g., Aigle, 'The Mongol Invasions of Bilād al-Shām', pp. 89–120; Aigle, *The Mongol Empire*, pp. 283–305.

Simultaneously, local imperial concepts were revived in China and Iran: in China this meant the restoration of the Confucian ideal of 'the Great Unity' (*Dayitong* 大一統), namely the unification of the Sinitic world under one ruler, while in Iran the ideal of *Īrān zamīn* (the 'land of Iran') reappeared, i.e. the notion that Iran was to be a political unit independent of the rest of the Muslim world. This represents a revival of the term *Īrān* as a political concept, as opposed to its place in collective memory and literature, for the first time since the fall of the Sassanid Empire in the seventh century.[40]

These concepts fitted quite nicely with the borders of the respective successor states: the territory directly under the Great Khan's rule included — after 1279 — both northern and southern China, united by the Mongols after more than 350 years of division. That it also included many other regions, such as Mongolia, Manchuria, Tibet, Yunnan, and Korea, could only add to Yuan legitimation. The Ilkhanate ruled over Iran, Iraq, Turkmenistan, the Caucasus, and parts of Anatolia and Afghanistan — a territory reminiscent of the Sassanid realm (224–651 CE). In both cases, embracing the local concept must have been quite easy for the Mongols, as both Chinese and Iranian conceptions included a strong universal component and ideological elements similar to the Mongol ones — the Mandate of Heaven was central to the Chinese understanding of legitimacy, and the charisma (Persian: *farnah/farrah/khwarnah*) to the Iranian. Moreover, as highly practical rulers, the Mongols acknowledged the advantages of reviving such concepts for co-opting local elites. The initiative probably came from the Mongols' local advisors, who strove to accommodate their foreign lords into the local tradition, conceiving their realm mainly in its regional context (namely united China or politically independent Iran) and the Mongols as the 'normal' rulers of China and Iran respectively.[41]

The Mongols themselves, however, while using local rituals, titles, and rhetoric, still regarded themselves as universal rulers according to the Chinggisid mode. This is most apparent in the case of the Yuan, the dynasty that ruled the realm of the Mongols' Great Khan. While Yuan emperors were celebrated by their Chinese subjects as champions of China's newly achieved Great Unity, there was not even a Mongolian word for China: the Mongols continued to refer to north China (*Khitai*/Kitad) and south China (*Manzi*/Nangiyas) as separate realms, as did also the Mongols' officials, such as Marco Polo and Rashīd al-Dīn.[42] Moreover, in two Sino-Mongolian inscriptions of 1328 and 1362, the Mongols made clear that for them *Da Yuan*, as their dynasty was known in China (Mongolian: *Dai On*) equalled the 'Great Mongol Nation',

---

40 For *Dayitong*, see, e.g., Pines, *Envisioning Eternal Empire*; for *Īrān zamīn*, see, e.g., Fragner, 'Iran under Ilkhanid rule'; Fragner, 'Ilkhanid Rule and its Contributions'; Krawulsky, 'The Revival of the Ancient Name Īrān'.

41 For such attempts, see especially Melville, 'From Adam to Abaqa', Parts 1 and 2; Humble, 'Princely Qualities and Unexpected Coherence'.

42 Kim, 'Was Da Yuan a Chinese Dynasty?', pp. 287–88, 300–01.

Yeke Mongghol Ulus, as the United Mongol Empire was called in Mongolian.[43] Apparently, for the Mongols 'the great unification' must have referred to the whole Chinggisid space, from Korea to Hungary, not only to that of China, and the 'Great Mongol Nation' still existed, albeit in the form of a Mongol commonwealth composed of brotherly states.

As for the Ilkhans, the first palace they built on Iranian land was located in a former Sassanian (and perhaps also Achaemenid) site known as *Takht-i Sulaymān*, Solomon's throne, and decorated with quotations from the Persian epic *The Book of Kings* (*Shāhnāmah*), which became the Mongols' favourite.[44] Yet, their letters, coins, and inscriptions hardly mention the name Iran or Iranian titles like 'King of Kings' (*Shāhānshāh*).[45] The Chinggisid ideology of world conquest, however, is very much present in these media (see Hülegü's letter cited above) well into the fourteenth century, and remained valid even after 1295, when Islamic formulas were added.[46] Thus, while adopting a more complex glocal world order, the Mongols still stressed its universal aspects, while their subjects clung more to its local components.

Shaping Post-Mongol Eurasia

It was the 'glocal' world order that had the biggest impact on the shaping of the future Eurasian world order. In geopolitical terms, united China, independent Iran and Russia as a Eurasian superpower are still with us, albeit with different borders. Yet, while China and Iran had a long history as Eurasian empires, since they were mainly revived in the Mongol period, the rise of Russia as a Eurasian power was a new phenomenon that, despite Russian efforts to refute this, owed much to the Golden Horde precedent. Moreover, the rise of Muscovy, which had led the Russian principalities in their relations with the Golden Horde, and its taking over Siberia from the sixteenth century onwards, completely changed the nomad–sedentary balance in Eurasia, as the nomads found themselves squeezed in by sedentary empires from both south and north.[47] Another fundamental change inflicted by the Mongol period on the steppe people of Central Asia consisted in a major ethnic reconfiguration: Mongol population movements led to the disappearance of various established steppe peoples, such as the Khitans, Tanguts, Uighurs, and Qipchaqs, and

---

43 Cleaves, 'The Sino-Mongolian Inscription of 1338', pp. 27, 53, 67; Cleaves, 'The Sino-Mongolian Inscription of 1362', pp. 30, 62, 83. See also Cleaves, 'The Sino-Mongolian Inscription of 1335', pp. 36–50; Cleaves, 'The Sino-Mongolian Inscription of 1346', pp. 32, 71, 82; Kim, 'Was Da Yuan a Chinese Dynasty?', pp. 287–88, 300–01.

44 For *Takht-i Sulaymān*, see Huff, 'The Ilkhanid Palace'; for the *Shāhnāmah*, see, e.g., Melville, 'The "Shahnameh" in Historical Context', pp. 3–15 (with further references).

45 See, e.g., Amitai, *Holy War*, pp. 102–05.

46 Amitai, *Holy War*, pp. 37–62.

47 Allsen, 'Eurasia after the Mongols', pp. 165–67; Ostrowski, *Muscovy and the Mongols*.

the emergence of new collectives, such as the Uzbeks, Qazakhs, and Tatars, who became the modern Central Asian Muslim peoples.[48]

The ideology of the Mongol world order also remained influential long after the collapse of the empire itself: its basic tenet was the Chinggisid principle, according to which only descendants of Chinggis Khan were eligible to become khans or qa'ans. Creative manipulations notwithstanding, this principle remained valid in Central Asia until the eighteenth century, all the while influencing monarchical behaviour and social hierarchies in Qing China, Moghul India, Muscovy, and even the Ottoman Empire.[49] Moreover, in the Muslim world, Ilkhanid experiments in combining Chinggisid and Muslim concepts of kingship created the kind of sacred-messianic Islamic kingship that was characteristic of the early modern Muslim empires.[50]

Other facets of the Mongols' impact were of a more utilitarian nature: the Mongols left to their followers a host of functioning imperial institutions that continued to be used across Eurasia, contributing not only to the Mongols' direct successor states but also to other regional empires and facilitating the emergence — especially from the sixteenth century onwards — of a group of regional empires (Mughals, Ottomans, Safavids, Ming and Qing China, Muscovite Russia) that were vaster and more enduring than most of the pre-Mongol polities.[51] Paradoxically, these developments also led to the disintegration of the nomadic world order that had given rise to Chinggis Khan. This was not only an effect of the rise of Russia that has been described above, but also a result of the division of the steppe between Muslims and Tibetan Buddhists, especially after the Mongols' second adherence to Buddhism in the sixteenth century, that prevented the unification of the entire steppe under the standard of Tengri. Moreover, the 'imperial toolkit' of the Mongols — proudly adhered to by the Manchus and entirely refuted by the Russians — as well as the gunpowder technology that the Mongol Empire had disseminated westwards (and which the Jesuits brought back to China from Europe in the sixteenth century) eventually enabled Qing China (1644–1911) and Imperial Russia (1721–1917) to divide the steppe between them in the eighteenth century, at the expense of the nomads.[52]

More indirectly, it can even be argued that the Mongols' new 'glocal' world order paved the way for the beginning of the early modern period and even

48 Biran, *Chinggis Khan*, pp. 101–02; Golden, 'I Will Give the People unto Thee'.

49 Biran, *Chinggis Khan*, pp. 102–06.

50 Brack, 'Theologies of Auspicious Kingship'.

51 For a general evaluation of the legacy of Mongol statecraft, see Biran, 'The Mongol Transformation', pp. 358–61; Biran, *Chinggis Khan*, pp. 102–07; see also McChesney, *Central Asia*; Ostrowski, *Muscovy and the Mongols*; Crossley, *A Translucent Mirror*; Manz, 'Mongol History Rewritten and Relived'; Robinson ed., *Culture, Courtiers and Competition*; Balabanillar, *Imperial Identity in the Mughal Empire*; Neumann and Wigen, 'Remnants of the Mongol Imperial Tradition'; Robinson, *In the Shadow of the Mongol Empire*.

52 Allsen, 'Eurasia after the Mongols'.

for the rise of Europe. By virtue of the expansion of long-distance commercial and financial exchange, the growing interest in maritime power, the formation of new collectives, the accelerated rates of diffusion or 'connectivity' among different regions, the quantum leap forward in the knowledge of the Old World, which resulted also in religious and cultural relativism, as well as the new model of charismatic leadership with direct connection to the Divine, the Mongols ushered in the early modern period.[53] Moreover, the Mongol legacy was not limited to the continental empires. The Mongols' 'soft power' phase, in particular, closely connected Europe, both Eastern and Western, to Asia in terms of intensive economic and cultural contacts, thereby considerably broadening the European horizons. The lands beyond the Middle East, formerly only vaguely known (if at all) and allegedly inhabited mainly by various monsters, became part of the European knowledge of the world and were often famed for their affluence.[54] Thus, when Columbus set out on his first voyage in 1492, his principal objective was to find the land of the 'Great Khan' as described in the 'Book' of Marco Polo, whom he ardently admired.[55] As a consequence, the world order in both Asia and Europe owes much to the Mongols' imperial enterprise.

In conclusion, the Mongol world order was created by the Empire — and just like it, it was mobile and transformative. It began with a universal, heaven-ordained mandate to rule over earth, which led to the ideal of 'world conquest' and an ensuing, unprecedented territorial expansion by military power that not only proved the reality of the Mandate, but also broadened its scope. In the dissolved post-1260 Mongol world, when expansion was much harder, this universal world order was replaced by a 'glocal' world order that combined universal aspirations with local elements and concepts of legitimization. Under this 'glocal' world order, military power was gradually replaced by 'soft power', namely economic and cultural prestige as the main channels of claiming universal leadership, while world religions and pre-Mongol imperial concepts also played a larger role and affected the actual behaviour of the various Mongol polities, eventually deepening the gaps between the different members of the 'Mongol commonwealth'. It was this composite 'glocal' world order that had a tremendous impact on the shaping of the future world order, both regionally and globally, not least by ushering in the transition from the medieval to the early modern world and facilitating the discovery of the New World.

---

53 Allsen, 'Ever Closer Encounters', pp. 1–21; Subrahmanyam, 'Connected Histories'; Kuroda, 'The Eurasian Silver Century'; Atwood, 'Mongol Empire and Early Modernity'; Brack, 'Theologies of Auspicious Kingship'.

54 See, e.g., Adshead, *Central Asia in World History*, p. 77; Jackson, *The Mongols and the West*, pp. 255–95, 333–61.

55 Biran, 'The Mongol Empire', p. 555.

Works Cited

Primary Sources

Chavannes, Édouard, 'Inscriptions et pièces de chancellerie chinoises de l'époque mongole (2nd series)', *T'oung-pao*, 9 (1908), 297–448

Cleaves, Francis W., 'The Sino-Mongolian Inscription of 1362 in Memory of Prince Hindu', *Harvard Journal of Asiatic Studies*, 12 (1949), 1–133

——, 'The Sino-Mongolian Inscription of 1335 in Memory of Chang Ying-jui', *Harvard Journal of Asiatic Studies*, 13 (1950), 1–131

——, 'The Sino-Mongolian Inscription of 1338 in Memory of Jigüntei', *Harvard Journal of Asiatic Studies*, 14 (1951), 1–104

——, 'The Sino-Mongolian Inscription of 1346', *Harvard Journal of Asiatic Studies*, 15 (1952), 1–123

Ibn al-Fuwaṭī, Kamāl al-Dīn ʿAbd al-Razzāq b. Aḥmad, *Majmaʿ al-ādāb fī muʿjam al-alqāb*, 6 vols, ed. by Muḥammad al-Kāẓim (Tehran: Muʾassasat al-ṭibāʿa wa-l-nashr, 1416/1995)

al-Juwaynī [Juvaini], ʿAṭā-Malik, *Taʾrīkh-i Jahāngushā*, 3 vols, ed. by Mīrzā Muḥammad Qazwīnī (London: Luzac, 1912–37)

——, *Genghis Khan: The History of the World Conqueror*, trans. by John A. Boyle (repr. Manchester: Manchester University Press, 1997)

Jūzjānī, Minhāj al-Dīn, *Ṭabaqāt-i nāṣirī*, ed. by W. Nassau Lees, Bibliotheca Indica, XLIV (Calcutta: College Press, 1864)

——, *Ṭabaqāt-i nāṣirī*, II, trans. by H. G. Raverty (repr. New Delhi: Oriental Book Reprint, 1970)

Letters from the East: Crusaders, Pilgrims and Settlers in the 12th–13th Centuries, trans. by Malcolm Barber and Keith Bate, Crusader Texts in Translation, 18 (Fordham: Ashgate, 2010)

Meyvaert, Paul, 'An Unknown Letter of Hulagu, Il-Khan of Persia, to King Louis IX of France', *Viator*, 11 (1980), 245–59

Mission to Asia, ed. and trans. by Christopher Dawson (Toronto: University of Toronto Press in association with the Medieval Academy of America, 1980)

Mostaert, Antoine, and Francis W. Cleaves, 'Trois documents mongols des archives secrètes vaticanes', *Harvard Journal of Asiatic Studies* 15 (1952), 419–506

Poppe, Nicholas, *The Mongolian Monuments in hP'ags-pa Script* (Wiesbaden: Harrassowitz, 1957)

Rashīd al-Dīn, *Jāmiʿ al-Tawārīkh*, ed. by Muḥammad Rawshan and Muṣṭafā Mūsawī (Tehran: Nashr-i Alburz, 1994)

——, *Rashīduddin Fazlullah's Jamiʿu't-Tawarikh: A History of the Mongols*, 3 vols, trans. by Wheeler Thackston (Cambridge, MA: Harvard University, Dept. of Near Eastern Languages and Civilizations, 1998–99)

The Secret History of the Mongols: A Mongolian Epic Chronicle of the Thirteenth Century, 3 vols, ed. and trans. by Igor de Rachewiltz (Leiden: Brill, 2004–13)

Song Lian 宋濂, *Yuan shi* 元史 [Yuan Official History], 15 vols (Beijing: Zhongua shuji, 1976)

Su Tianjue 蘇天爵, ed., *Yuan wenlei* 元文類 [Categorized Literature from the Yuan Period] (Taipei: Shijie shuju, 1967)

Wang, Shidian 王士點, and Shang, Qiweng 商企翁, *Mishujian zhi* 秘書監志 (Accounts of the Palace Library), ed. by Gao Rongsheng 高榮盛 (Hangzhou: Zhejiang guji chubanshe, 1992)

Waṣṣāf al-Ḥaḍrat, Sharaf al-Dīn ʿAbd-Allāh b. Faḍl-Allāh al-Shīrāzī, *Tajziyat al-Amṣār wa Tazjiyat al-A'ṣār* (*Tārīkh-i Waṣṣāf*), lithograph (Bombay: Muḥammad Mahdī Iṣfahānī, 1853)

William of Rubruck, *The Mission of Friar William of Rubruck*, ed. by David Morgan and trans. by Peter Jackson (London: The Hakluyt Society, 1990)

Yelü, Zhu 耶律鑄, *Shuangxi zuiyin ji* 雙溪醉隱集 [Yelü Zhu's Literary Collection] ([n.p.]: Siku quanshu ed., [n.d.])

Yuandai baihua bei jilu 元代白话碑集录, ed. by Cai Meibiao 蔡美彪 (Beijing: Kexue chubanshe, 1955)

Secondary Studies

Adshead, Samuel A. M., *Central Asia in World History* (New York: St Martin's Press, 1993)

Aigle, Denise, 'The Mongol Invasions of Bilād al-Shām by Ghāzān Khān and Ibn Taymīyah's Three "Anti-Mongol" Fatwas', *Mamluk Studies Review*, 11 (2007), 89–120

——, *The Mongol Empire between Myth and Reality: Studies in Anthropological History*, Iran Studies, 11 (Leiden: Brill, 2014)

Akasoy, Anna, Charles Burnett, and Ronit Yoeli-Tlalim, ed., *Rashīd al-Dīn: Agent and Mediator of Cultural Exchanges in Ilkhanid Iran*, Warburg Institute Colloquia, 24 (London: The Warburg Institute, 2013)

Albrecht, Sarah, 'Dār al-Islām and dār al-ḥarb', in *Encyclopaedia of Islam THREE*, ed. by Kate Fleet, Gudrun Krämer, Denis Matringe, John Nawas, and Everett Rowson, <http://dx.doi.org/10.1163/1573-3912_ei3_COM_25867> [accessed 21 June 2021]

Allsen, Thomas T., 'The Rise of the Mongolian Empire and Mongol Rule in North China', in *The Cambridge History of China, VI: Alien Regimes and Border States, 907–1368*, ed. by Herbert Franke and Dennis Twitchett (Cambridge: Cambridge University Press, 1994), pp. 321–413

——, 'Spiritual Geography and Political Legitimacy in the Eastern Steppe', in *Ideology and the Formation of the Early State*, ed. by Henri J. M. Claessen and Jarich G. Oosten (Leiden: Brill, 1996), pp. 116–35

——, *Commodity and Exchange in the Mongol Empire: A Cultural History of Islamic Textiles* (Cambridge: Cambridge University Press, 1997)

——, 'Ever Closer Encounters: The Appropriation of Culture and the Apportionment of Peoples in the Mongol Empire', *Journal of Early Modern History*, 1 (1997), 2–23

——, *Culture and Conquest in Mongol Eurasia* (Cambridge: Cambridge University Press, 2001)

——, 'Sharing Out the Empire: Apportioned Lands under the Mongols', in *Nomads in the Sedentary World*, ed. by Anatoly Khazanov and André Wink (London: Curzon, 2001), pp. 172–90
——, 'A Note on Mongol Imperial Ideology', in *The Early Mongols: Studies in Honor of Igor de Rachewiltz on the Occasion of his 80th Birthday*, ed. by Volker Rybatzki and others, Uralic and Altaic Series, 173 (Bloomington: Indiana University, 2009), pp. 1–9
——, 'Imperial Posts, West, East and North: A Review Article: Adam J. Silverstein, *Postal Systems in the Pre-Modern Islamic World*', *Archivum Eurasiae Medii Aevi*, 17 (2011), 237–76
——, 'Eurasia after the Mongols', in *The Cambridge World History, VI: The Construction of a Global World, 1400–1800*, Part 1: *Foundations*, ed. by Jerry H. Bentley, Sanjay Subrahmanyam, and Merry Wiesner-Hanks (Cambridge: Cambridge University Press, 2015), pp. 159–81
——, 'Ideology', in *The Cambridge History of the Mongols*, ed. by Michal Biran and Kim Hodong (Cambridge: Cambridge University Press, forthcoming)
Amitai, Reuven, *Holy War and Rapprochement: Studies in the Relations between the Mamluk Sultanate and the Mongol Ilkhanate (1260–1335)*, Miroir de l'Orient Musulman, 4 (Turnhout: Brepols, 2013)
Amitai-Preiss, Reuven, *Mongols and Mamluks: The Mamluk-Īlkhānid War, 1260–1281* (Cambridge: Cambridge University Press, 1995)
Atwood, Christopher P., 'The Uyghur Stone: Archaeological Revelations in the Mongol Empire', in *The Steppe Lands and the World Beyond Them: Studies in Honor of Victor Spinei on his 70th Birthday*, ed. by Florin Curta and Bogdan-Petru Maleon (Iaşi: Editura Universităţii 'Alexandru Ioan Cuza', 2013), pp. 315–43
——, 'Mongol Empire and Early Modernity', in *Asia and the Early Modern*, ed. by I. Kaya Şahin and Hendrik Spruyt (forthcoming)
Balabanillar, Lisa, *Imperial Identity in the Mughal Empire: Memory and Dynastic Politics in Early Modern South and Central Asia* (London: Tauris, 2012)
Baumann, Brian, 'By the Power of Eternal Heaven: The Meaning of Tenggeri to the Government of the Pre-Buddhist Mongols', *Extrême-Orient Extrême-Occident*, 35 (2013), 233–84
Biran, Michal, *Qaidu and the Rise of the Independent Mongol State in Central Asia* (Richmond: Curzon, 1997)
——, 'The Mongol Transformation: From the Steppe to Eurasian Empire', *Medieval Encounters*, 10 (2004), 339–61
——, *Chinggis Khan* (Oxford: OneWorld Publications, 2007)
——, 'The Mongol Empire and the Inter-Civilizational Exchange', in *The Cambridge World History, V: Expanding Webs of Exchange and Conflict, 500 CE–1500 CE*, ed. by Benjamin Kedar and Merry Wiesner-Hanks (Cambridge: Cambridge University Press, 2015), pp. 534–58
——, 'Introduction: Nomadic Culture', in *Nomads as Agents of Cultural Change: The Mongols and their Eurasian Predecessors*, ed. by Reuven Amitai and Michal Biran (Honolulu: University of Hawai'i Press, 2015), pp. 1–9

——, 'The Mongol Imperial Space: From Universalism to Glocalization', in *The Limits of Universal Rule: Eurasian Empires Compared*, ed. by Yuri Pines, Michal Biran, and Jörg Rüpke (Cambridge: Cambridge University Press, 2021), pp. 220–256

Blatter, Joachim, 'Glocalization', *Encyclopaedia Britannica Online*, <https://www.britannica.com/topic/glocalization> [accessed 21 June 2021]

Brack, Jonathan Z., 'Theologies of Auspicious Kingship: The Islamization of Chinggisid Sacral Kingship in the Islamic World', *Comparative Studies in Society and History*, 60 (2018), 1143–71

Crossley, Pamela K., *A Translucent Mirror: History and Identity in Qing Imperial Ideology* (Berkeley: University of California Press, 1999)

Davis, Richard L., 'The Reign of Tu-tsung (1264–1274) and His Successors to 1279', in *The Cambridge History of China*, vol. V/1: *The Sung Dynasty and Its Precursors*, ed. by Denis Twitchett and Paul Jakov Smith (Cambridge: Cambridge University Press, 2009), pp. 913–62

DeWeese, Devin, 'Islamization in the Mongol Empire', in *The Cambridge History of Inner Asia: The Chinggisid Age*, ed. by Nicola Di Cosmo, Allen J. Frank, and Peter B. Golden (Cambridge: Cambridge University Press, 2009), pp. 120–34

DiCosmo, Nicola, 'Why Qara Qorum? Climate and Geography in the Early Mongol Empire', *Archivum Eurasiae Medii Aevi*, 21 (2014–15), 67–78

Fiaschetti, Francesca, 'The Borders of Rebellion: The Yuan Dynasty and the Rhetoric of Empire', in *Political Strategies of Identity Building in non-Han Empires in China*, ed. by Francesca Fiaschetti and Julia Schneider (Wiesbaden: Harrassowitz, 2014), pp. 127–45

——, 'Tradition, Innovation and the Construction of Qubilai's Diplomacy', *Mingqing yanjiu*, 18 (2014), 65–96

Fragner, Bert G., 'Iran under Ilkhanid Rule in a World History Perspective', in *L'Iran face à la domination mongole*, ed. by Denis Aigle (Tehran: Institut français de recherche en Iran/Louvain: Peeters, 1997), pp. 121–31

——, 'Ilkhanid Rule and its Contributions to Iranian Political Culture', in *Beyond the Legacy of Genghis Khan*, ed. by Linda Komaroff (Leiden: Brill, 2006), pp. 68–80

Franke, Herbert, *From Tribal Chieftain to Universal Emperor and God: The Legitimation of the Yüan Dynasty*, Bayerische Akademie der Wissenschaften. Phil.-hist. Klasse, Sitzungsberichte, 1978,2 (Munich: Bayerische Akademie der Wissenschaften, 1978) [repr. in Herbert Franke, *China under Mongol Rule* (Aldershot: Ashgate/Variorum, 1994), article IV]

Golden, Peter B., 'Imperial Ideology and the Sources of Political Unity amongst the Pre-Činggisid Nomads of Western Eurasia', *Archivum Eurasiae Medii Aevi*, 2 (1982), 37–76

——, '"I Will Give the People unto Thee": The Chinggisid Conquests and their Aftermath in the Turkic World', *Journal of the Royal Asiatic Society*, 10/1 (2000), 21–41

——, 'The Türk Imperial Tradition in the Pre-Chinggisid Era', in *Imperial Statecraft*, ed. by David Sneath (Bellingham: Western Washington University

Press, 2006), pp. 23–61 [repr. in Peter B. Golden, *Turks and Khazars: Origins, Institutions, and Interactions in Pre-Mongol Eurasia* (Farnham: Ashgate/ Variorum, 2010)]

Huff, Dietrich, 'The Ilkhanid Palace at Takht-i Sulayman: Excavation Results', in *Beyond the Legacy of Genghis Khan*, ed. by Linda Komaroff (Leiden: Brill, 2006), pp. 94–110

Humble, Geoffrey, 'Princely Qualities and Unexpected Coherence: Rhetoric and Representation in "Juan" 117 of the "Yuanshi"', *Journal of Song-Yuan Studies*, 45 (2015), 307–37

Jackson, Peter, 'The Dissolution of the Mongol Empire', *Central Asiatic Journal*, 32 (1978), 186–244

——, *The Delhi Sultanate: A Political and Military History* (Cambridge: Cambridge University Press, 1999)

——, 'From Ulus to Khanate: The Making of the Mongol States, c. 1220–c. 1290', in *The Mongol Empire and its Legacy*, ed. by Reuven Amitai-Preiss and David O. Morgan (Leiden: Brill, 1999), pp. 12–38

——, 'The Mongols and the Faith of the Conquered', in *Mongols, Turks and Others: Eurasian Nomads and the Sedentary World*, ed. by Reuven Amitai and Michal Biran (Leiden: Brill, 2005), pp. 245–90

——, 'World-Conquest and Local Accommodation: Threat and Blandishment in Mongol Diplomacy', in *History and Historiography of Post-Mongol Central Asia and the Middle East: Studies in Honour of John E. Woods*, ed. by Judith Pfeiffer and Sheila A. Quinn, in collab. with Ernest Tucker (Wiesbaden: Harrassowitz, 2006), pp. 3–22

——, *The Mongols and the Islamic World: From Conquest to Conversion* (New Haven: Yale University Press, 2017)

——, *The Mongols and the West 1221–1410*, 2nd edn (London: Routledge, 2018)

Kauz, Ralph, ed., *Chinese and Asian Geographical and Cartographical Views on Central Asia and Its Adjacent Regions*, Special Issue: *Journal of Asian History*, 49 (2015), 1–266

Kim, Hodong. 'The Unity of the Mongol Empire and Continental Exchanges over Eurasia', *Journal of Central Eurasian Studies*, 1 (2009), 15–42

——, 'The Compilation of the Gazetteer of the Grand Unification (Dayitong zhi) and the Origin of the Mongol World Map' (unpublished paper read at the conference *Chinese and Asian Geographical and Cartographical Views on Central Asia and its Adjacent Region*, Bonn, January 10–11, 2014)

——, 'Was Da Yuan a Chinese Dynasty?', *Journal of Song-Yuan Studies* 45 (2015), 279–305

Krawulsky, Dorothea, 'The Revival of the Ancient Name Īrān under the Mongol Īlkhāns (r. 656–736/1258–1336)', in Dorothea Krawulsky, *The Mongol Īlkhāns and their Vizier Rashīd al-Dīn* (Frankfurt: Peter Lang, 2011), pp. 43–52

Kuroda, Akinobu, 'The Eurasian Silver Century, 1276–1359: Commensurability and Multiplicity', *Journal of Global History*, 4 (2009), 245–69

Langlois, John M., 'Song Lian and Liu Ji in 1358 on the Eve of Joining Zhu Yuanzhang', *Asia Major*, 22 (2009), 131–62

Manz, Beatrice F., 'Mongol History Rewritten and Relived', *Revue des mondes musulmans et de la Méditerranée*, 89–90 (2000), 129–49

May, Timothy, *The Mongol Conquest in World History* (London: Reaction-Globalities, 2012)

McChesney, R. D., *Central Asia: Foundations of Change* (Princeton: Princeton University Press, 1996)

Melville, Charles, 'From Adam to Abaqa: Qāḍī Baiḍāwī's Rearrangement of History', *Studia Iranica*, 30 (2001), 67–86

——, 'From *Adam to Abaqa*: Qādī Baidāwī's Rearrangement of History (Part 2)', *Studia Iranica*, 36 (2007), 7–64

——, 'The "Shahnameh" in Historical Context', in *Epic of the Persian Kings: The Art of Ferdowsi's Shahnameh*, ed. by Barbara Brend and Charles Melville (London: Tauris, 2010), pp. 3–15

Morgan, David O., *The Mongols*, 2nd edn (Oxford: Blackwell, 2007)

Neumann, Iver B., and Einar Wigen, 'Remnants of the Mongol Imperial Tradition', in *Legacies of Empire: Imperial Roots of the Contemporary Global Order*, ed. by Sandra Halperin and Ronen Palan (Cambridge: Cambridge University Press, 2015), pp. 1–42, <http://eprints.lse.ac.uk/66009/> [accessed 21 June 2021]

Ostrowski, Donald G., *Muscovy and the Mongols: Cross-Cultural Influences on the Steppe Frontier, 1304–1589* (Cambridge: Cambridge University Press, 1998)

Park, Hyunhee, *Mapping the Chinese and Islamic Worlds: Cross-Cultural Exchange in Pre-Modern Asia* (Cambridge: Cambridge University Press, 2012)

——, 'Cross-Cultural Exchange and Geographic Knowledge of the World in Yuan China', in *Eurasian Influences on Yuan China*, ed. by Morris Rossabi (Singapore: Institute of Southeast Asia Studies, 2013), pp. 125–58

Pines, Yuri, *Envisioning Eternal Empire: Chinese Political Thought of the Warring States Era* (Honolulu: University of Hawai'i Press, 2009)

Pines, Yuri, Michal Biran, and Jörg Rüpke, ed., *The Limits of Universal Rule: Eurasian Empires Compared* (Cambridge: Cambridge University Press, 2021)

Rachewiltz, Igor de, *Papal Envoys to the Great Khans* (Stanford: Stanford University Press, 1971)

——, 'Qan, Qa'an and the Seal of Güyük', in *Documenta Barbarorum: Festschrift für Walter Heissig zum 70. Geburtstag*, ed. by Klaus Sagaster and Michael Weiers (Wiesbaden: Harrassowitz, 1983), pp. 272–81

Robinson, David M., ed., *Culture, Courtiers and Competition: The Ming Court (1368–1644)* (Cambridge, MA: Harvard University Asia Center, 2008)

——, *In the Shadow of the Mongol Empire: Ming China and Eurasia* (Cambridge: Cambridge University Press, 2019)

Rossabi, Morris, *Khubilai Khan: His Life and Times* (Berkeley: University of California Press, 1988)

Roudometof, Victor, *Glocalization: A Critical Introduction* (Abingdon: Routledge, 2016)

Silverstein, Adam J., *Postal Systems in the Pre-Modern Islamic World* (Cambridge: Cambridge University Press, 2007)

Subrahmanyam, Sanjay, 'Connected Histories: Notes towards a Reconfiguration of Early Modern Eurasia', *Modern Asian Studies*, 31 (1997), 735–62
Vogelin, Eric, 'Mongol Orders of Submission to European Powers, 1245–1255', *Byzantion*, 15 (1940–41), 378–411
Yang Qiao, 'From the West to the East, From the Sky to the Earth: A Biography of Jamāl al-Dīn', *Asiatische Studien — Études Asiatiques*, 71 (2017), 1231–45

CHRISTOPH MAUNTEL
AND KLAUS OSCHEMA

Between Universal Empire and the Plurality of Kingdoms

On the Practical Influence of Political Concepts in Late Medieval Latin Europe

The starting point of this chapter is a quite simple observation: in the medieval Latin-Christian world (or Europe[1]), monarchical rule, i.e. a king's authority over his people, was basically considered to be the 'natural' form of political order.[2] In the eyes of medieval thinkers, the very existence of 'rule' (and by extension a form of political order) was thus intimately connected with the authority of a 'king' over his subjects.[3] This is witnessed, amongst others, by the seventh-century encyclopaedist Isidore of Seville, who stated that 'every nation had had its own reign in its own times'.[4] Bishop Fulbert of Chartres (*c.* 950–1028) echoed this idea on a more structural level, when he defined a 'kingdom' by virtue of three essential elements: a territory, a people, and a king.[5]

Based on these observations, it would seem that the existence of a plurality of peoples inevitably had to lead to the creation of a political landscape that

1 We use the expression for the sake of convenient abbreviation, in spite of all conceptual shortcomings of this notion; see Oschema, *Bilder von Europa*, and Oschema, 'Medieval Europe'.

2 See Schneidmüller, *Grenzerfahrung*, pp. 53–60, 185.

3 For the period between the ninth and thirteenth centuries see the contributions in Schneidmüller and Weinfurter ed., *Ordnungskonfigurationen*.

4 Isidore of Seville, *Etymologiae*, ed. by Lindsay, IX, 3, 1–2: 'Regnum a regibus dictum. Nam sicut reges a regendo vocati, ita regnum a regibus. Regnum universae nationes suis quaeque temporibus habuerunt, ut Assyrii, Medi, Persae, Aegyptii, Graeci, quorum vices sors temporum ita volutavit ut alterum ab altero solveretur'.

5 Fulbert of Chartres, 'Tractatus contra Iudaeos', cols 307–08: 'Tria ergo sunt sine quibus regnum esse non potest, terra videlicet, in qua regnum sit; populus, qui terram ipsam inhabitet; et persona regis electi, qui terram vindicet, et populum regat'. See Blumenkranz, 'À propos du (ou des) Tractatus'.

Christoph Mauntel (christoph.mauntel@uni-tuebingen.de), Eberhard Karls Universität Tübingen, Germany

Klaus Oschema (klaus.oschema@rub.de), Ruhr-Universität Bochum, Germany

Order into Action: How Large-Scale Concepts of World-Order determine Practices in the Premodern World, ed. by Klaus Oschema and Christoph Mauntel, CURSOR 40 (Turnhout: Brepols, 2022), pp. 151–183
BREPOLS PUBLISHERS 10.1484/M.CURSOR-EB.5.123847

consisted of a plurality of political entities. And indeed, a quite famous late medieval source illustrates that such a diversified political order not only existed, but was actually perceived to constitute a natural given and even to be desirable. At least this seems to be a central tenet of the French theologian and Dominican friar John of Paris, who reflected in the early fourteenth century on the relation between imperial and papal rule, and authority.[6] It is not surprising that John explicitly underlined the sovereign status of the kingdom of France: relying on a position that was already well established at the time of his writing, he declared that the French king was neither subject to the pope nor to the Roman Emperor.[7] In this sense, the author rejected any claim of the Roman Emperors to universal suzerainty. What we consider to be more important than this well-known political statement, however, is the systematic argument that he fashions on the basis of his observation and that finally becomes an assertion: Arguing that it was at once natural and desirable that different peoples with diverging customs were governed by individual secular rulers, John invests the idea of multiple secular authorities with normative value. As a consequence, he juxtaposes the desirability of the existence of a single spiritual ruler, i.e. the pope, with the existence and legitimacy of a plurality of secular princes.[8]

In this chapter we argue that the very idea of a plurality of legitimate secular political powers became a central element in late medieval political thinking and that this development enabled and reinforced the creation of specific practices and institutions for the organization of political coordination between different independent realms. Even though the idea might have rarely been expressed as explicitly as in John of Paris's work, late medieval thinkers not only perceived that power and rule were *de facto* distributed in a way that led to the co-existence of several relatively independent realms, but they recognized that this plurality of quasi-sovereign political entities ('realms') could actually be justified and was systematically desirable. Taking this observation as our starting point, we seek to demonstrate that these ideas

---

6 See Bleienstein, *Johannes Quidort von Paris* (with edition and German translation); for an English translation see John of Paris, *On Royal and Papal Power*, trans. by Watt. On John's life and works see most recently the contributions in Jones ed., *John of Paris*.

7 Bleienstein, *Johannes Quidort von Paris*, chap. 15, pp. 150–51, chap. 21, pp. 188–89. See Jones, 'Undefined terms', pp. 326–27, on Jean de Blanot and his famous formula 'rex in regno suo princeps est'; more generally, see Jones, 'Diener zweier Herren?', and Jostkleigrewe, 'Rex imperator in regno suo'. The classical study is Krynen, *L'Empire du roi*; see also Watts, *Making of Polities*, pp. 68–69.

8 Bleienstein, *Johannes Quidort von Paris*, chap. 3, p. 83: 'Primo quidem quia sicut in hominibus est diversitas magna ex parte corporum, non autem ex parte animarum, quae omnes sunt in eodem gradu essentiali constitutae propter unitatem speciei humanae, ita saecularis potestas plus habet diversitatis secundum climatum et complexionum diversitatem quam spiritualis quae minus in talibus variatur. Unde non oportet tantam diversitatem esse in una sicut in alia'. In this perspective, John also concurs with the position Pierre Dubois expressed in his treatise on the recovery of the Holy Land, see 'De recuperatione terrae sanctae', see Oschema, 'No "Emperor of Europe"', pp. 428–29.

and convictions concerning the structure of 'appropriate' political order, which developed and became well established in Europe in the later Middle Ages, had profound consequences for the adaptability of European rulers and their politics beyond their own cultural sphere.

Since our presentation seeks to highlight a quite general phenomenon, we are fully aware that our object of scrutiny is in itself highly elusive. Moreover, our analysis can only provide a first approximation, without any claim to be exhaustive. In spite of these caveats, we consider our subject to be highly relevant in the context of Medieval Studies, especially if they seek to contribute, amongst others, to the larger questions that are discussed under such well-known headings as the 'Great Divergence'.[9] Since sources like John of Paris's treatise are quite well known amongst scholars of the late Middle Ages, some of our observations might seem to be neither new nor original *per se*. At the same time, we believe that the ensuing practical effects and consequences have not yet attracted the attention they deserve.[10] As a consequence, we seek to provide an analysis that connects ideas of political order and pertinent practices in a manner that allows for transcultural comparisons as well as for the insertion of our observations in a larger picture of long-term historical developments on a broader geographical scale.

In order to provide a sound basis for this kind of comparative analysis, we will focus on phenomena that we consider to be characteristic for late medieval 'European' cultures,[11] trying to link ideas and convictions that concern the organization of political order with the correlating practices. Our main interest lies in diplomatic exchanges and the underlying mechanisms on the one hand, and cooperative forms of political cooperation on the other.

---

9 The notion has been coined by Pomeranz, *The Great Divergence*. While Pomeranz focused on the modern period, subsequent studies repeatedly made an effort to demonstrate that (and how) pertinent effects had their roots in earlier periods, see, e.g., Studer, *The Great Divergence Reconsidered*. For a long-term argument on a macro-scale see Morris, *Why the West Rules*. See also the introduction of this volume for further references on the debates concerning the 'Great Divergence' and the intra-European 'Little Divergence'. For older contributions on the development of Europe's alleged 'Sonderweg' and its roots in the medieval period, see e.g. Mitterauer, *Warum Europa?*, who sums up much of the previous debates. For more recent approaches see the contributions in Ertl ed., *Europas Aufstieg*, here esp. Reinhard, 'Europäische Politik'; Drews, 'Politische Theorie', and Jostkleigrewe, 'Expansion – Macht – Legitimität'.

10 See, however, the influential article by Schneidmüller, 'Konsensuale Herrschaft' (English translation: Schneidmüller, 'Rule by Consensus'). Linking theoretical ideas of order with practical consequences, e.g. underlining the long-standing tradition of the subjects' influence on the rulers' politics (p. 69) in what he calls a *Wirkverbund* ('corporate community'), the author's reflections focus on the high and late medieval empire.

11 For a comparison between Europe and Southeast Asia, see the two-volume work by Lieberman, *Strange Parallels*; see also Lieberman, 'Protected Rimlands and Exposed Zones'.

A Striking Example — Franciscan Travellers and the Mongol Claim to Universal Rule

In order to get to the core of our subject, i.e. the connection between theoretical models and ideas of order and their practical effects on people's actions in the political sphere, one might start with a striking example that has repeatedly attracted scholars' attention: in his extraordinary travelogue (that did not reach a broader audience in the author's own time), the Franciscan monk William of Rubruck offered a detailed description of the Mongol court and the ceremonies he witnessed there.[12] William undertook his voyage not only as a missionary, but also as a kind of secret diplomat: King Louis IX of France sent him to the East, where he should visit the unknown people who had ravaged parts of Hungary and Poland in 1241, and gather more information about them and their intentions. After his two-year journey, William wrote a highly interesting account and presented it to the French king in 1255–56. Apart from a huge amount of geographical observations and descriptions of the author's life during the journey, the text contains a wealth of details that express a nearly 'ethnographic' view. Amongst other topics, William also included a vivid description of the audience he was granted by Möngke Khan in August 1254, after several weeks of waiting.

What is of particular interest to us in the present context is neither the fascinating story of William's legation as such, nor the rich details that he provides as one of the first Western travellers to the Mongols. Instead, we would like to underline the short passage in which he describes the Khan's political ideas — and its resonances with the Mongol leader's diplomatic practices as expressed in the context of the above-mentioned audience. According to William, on the occasion of the audience Möngke claimed nothing less than universal authority. He considered himself to be a ruler whose divine mission was to subjugate the entire world — in the words that William puts in the Khan's mouth: 'Like the sun is everywhere, spreading its rays, so my power and the power of this Baatu [i.e. Möngke's co-ruler] spreads everywhere'.[13] This far-reaching claim is further underlined by an additional explanation that follows only slightly later in William's account and aims directly at the heart of our question concerning the relation between theoretical order and

12 On William of Rubruck see most recently Khanmohamadi, *In Light of Another's Word*, esp. pp. 57–87, and Phillips, *Before Orientalism*, here pp. 31–33. For research in German, which Phillips only tentatively includes, see the contributions in Reichert, *Asien und Europa im Mittelalter*. William's text is edited in Guglielmo di Rubruk, *Viaggio in Mongolia*, ed. by Chiesa. On the Mongols' expansion and Latin-Christian reactions see Jackson, *The Mongols and the West*.

13 Guglielmo di Rubruk, *Viaggio in Mongolia*, ed. by Chiesa, xxviii, 18, p. 158: 'Tunc ipse incepit a respondere: "Sicut sol est ubique diffundens radios suos, ita mea potentia et ipsius Baatu diffundit se ubique"'. On the political developments and structures of the Mongol realms see Allsen, *Culture and Conquest*, pp. 17–23.

practical effects. In a short passage, William critically notes that the Mongols thought of themselves as the rightful masters of the world, believing that nobody was allowed to refuse them anything.[14]

And indeed, as a principle, the Mongols did not make peace with the nations they encountered — they only accepted their submission, as another Franciscan traveller, John of Plano Carpini, had already made quite clear in his account only a few years before William:

> It should be known that they do not make peace with any people as long as they don't submit [to the Mongols' rule], since, as has been said above, they have Chinggis Khan's mandate to subdue all nations if they can.[15]

Whereas these observations merely mirror the Mongols' own ideas[16] as seen through European eyes, William goes one decisive step further by contrasting the Mongols' view on politics quite vividly with his own 'European' world-view: if we are to believe his words, he even seized the opportunity to criticize the Khan, at least implicitly, during a second audience. On this occasion, as William tells us, he presented the Christian God as almighty and (missionary that he was) went on to contrast God's divine power with the imperfect character of human nature. On these grounds, he allegedly even rejected the Mongols' claim to superiority: 'No single man can do everything, and that's why there have to be several rulers on earth, because no single person can carry everything'.[17]

Systemic Consequences I — Diplomacy Between Equals or Submission?

These passages from William's account are striking in more than one way — not least, because they actually express a position that seems quite close to the description of the fragmentation (or plurality, depending on the perspective)

---

14 Guglielmo di Rubruk, *Viaggio in Mongolia*, ed. by Chiesa, IX, 3, p. 50: 'Reputant enim se dominos mundi, et uidetur eis quod nichil debeat eis negari ab aliquo'.

15 Giovanni di Pian di Carpine, *Storia dei Mongoli*, ed. by Menestò, pp. 284–85: 'Sciendum est quod cum nullis hominibus faciunt pacem nisi subdantur eis, quia, ut dictum est supra, a Chingiscan habent mandatum et cunctas, si possunt, sibi subiciant nationes'. On John of Plano Carpini see Reichert, *Erfahrung der Welt*, pp. 183–88.

16 See, e.g., *Secret History of the Mongols*, ed. by de Rachewiltz, vol. I, pp. 215–16, and vol. II, pp. 1029–30; cf. Amitai-Preiss, 'Mongol Imperial Ideology', and the contributions by Michal Biran and Donatella Guida in this volume (with further bibliographical references). The ideal of a unified and universal claim to rule coincides with fundamental tenets of premodern Chinese political thought, see, e.g., Pines, *Envisioning Eternal Empire*, p. 26.

17 Guglielmo di Rubruk, *Viaggio in Mongolia*, ed. by Chiesa, XXXIIII, 17, p. 252: 'Respondi: "Noster Deus, preter quem non est alius, est omnipotens et ideo non indiget alicuius auxilio, immo omnes indigemus auxilio eius. Non sic est de hominibus: nullus homo potest omnia, et ideo oportet esse plures dominos in terra, quia nullus potest omnia portare"'.

of political rule that is usually understood to have been formulated only several decades later by John of Paris in such an explicit manner.[18] What is even more important to us, however, is the observation that the Mongols' diplomatic practices — and in particular their claim to universal rule as described by William — conflicted directly with contemporary ideas and practices in Latin Christendom. On the theoretical level of political ideas, the organization of the Latin-Christian world can roughly be described as having relied on the assumption that a plurality of realms existed and that these more or less independent and even sovereign[19] political units were nearly exclusively constituted as monarchies.[20]

While the very existence of these various realms could not and cannot be doubted, it also raised the question of how they should relate to each other? Obviously enough, different actors held divergent ideas, with the popes claiming feudal superiority over realms like England, Aragón, or Sicily,[21] or the Roman-German emperors insisting on their sovereignty over France.[22] However, in a more general perspective, political realities and their theoretical modelling seem to have developed in a different direction, namely towards a system that allowed for complex interactions of more or less equal actors, in spite of the hierarchical elements it retained.

Focusing on medieval Europe, recent contributions have adequately and rightfully described the establishment of widespread ideas about rank and precedence that have been taken very seriously and acted out accordingly in public settings by the representatives of political entities: different opinions about an individual's rank often led to debates and conflicts. The clearest examples can probably be found in the context of the fifteenth-century church councils, which furnished a public stage on which each and every protagonist sought to establish, confirm, and demonstrate his rank.[23] At the same time, these assemblies provided a playing field that was fundamentally characterized by its versatility. In addition, the papal curia tried to prevent potential rivalries and ensuing conflicts by drafting lists of all Christian realms in which they were assigned their proper rank among the European principalities. While these lists might not have been anything more than intellectual pastimes

---

18 For the idea of necessary fragmentation of political rule, see above, n. 8.

19 See above, n. 7.

20 See Schneidmüller, *Grenzerfahrung*, pp. 53–60, 185; cf. in comparative perspective Woodacre and others ed., *The Routledge History of Monarchy*.

21 Wiedemann, 'Super gentes et regna'; Wiedeman, 'Papal Overlordship'.

22 Miethke, 'Politisches Denken', p. 141, pointing to the example of Lupold of Bebenburg.

23 For the example of the Burgundian representatives at the council of Basel and other assemblies, see Müller, *Théâtre de la préséance*; for examples from the context of imperial diets see, e.g., Spieß, 'Rangdenken und Rangstreit im Mittelalter' (1997), and Spieß, 'Rangdenken und Rangstreit' (2017). On the role of rituals and ceremonies in late medieval political assemblies see Peltzer, Schwedler, Többelmann ed., *Politische Versammlungen und ihre Rituale*; on 'rank' as an analytical tool and historical phenomenon in the late medieval Empire, see Peltzer, *Der Rang der Pfalzgrafen bei Rhein*.

from the outset, they could potentially have become relevant in situations in which several Christian princes or their representatives came together in an assembly.[24]

The political landscape of Latin Christianity in late medieval Europe was thus by and large structured by a somehow ordered interplay of rival and sometimes openly antagonistic forces: while the individual rulers tended to underline their 'independence' and individual sovereignty, the sheer multitude of political entities that belonged to the overarching unit of Latin Christianity as well as the concrete necessity to mutually arrange their politics in order to establish more or less peaceful relations, presupposed the creation of ways and forms of cooperation. If these approaches were to furnish a viable option for political coexistence, they had to recognize individual claims to rank and precedence as a given. At the same time, they had to open up a space of (at least ideal) 'equality' and to provide media of communication that allowed for potentially successful negotiations.[25]

It seems to us that this situation of polarized entanglements can aptly be described as a 'family of kingdoms',[26] whose members had in common, above all, the adherence to the Christian faith. They were thus united by a bond that, strictly speaking, lay outside of the sphere of genuinely political factors. Nevertheless, the Roman Church played an important role in a quite practical perspective, since its network of provinces, bishoprics, and parishes furnished the pervasive institutional structure that tied together the multitude of diverse regions and realms.[27] In a more political perspective, contemporaries recognized the symbolic prevalence of the Roman Empire.[28] But while the unity of Christendom and the honorific precedence of the Emperor as the protector of the church continued to be recognized, as early as in the twelfth century the idea of the sovereign rule of each king in his own realm had become a widespread concept that found its most complete formulation in thirteenth-century France with the famous expression *rex imperator in regno suo est* ['the king is the emperor in his own realm'].[29] With this formula, French legists rejected any exterior *political* claims the emperor of the Holy Roman

24 Schneidmüller, *Grenzerfahrung*, pp. 175–76, 185–86; Hack, *Das Empfangszeremoniell.*

25 For a case study concerning the relations between England and France in the high and late Middle Ages see van Eickels, *Vom inszenierten Konsens zum systematisierten Konflikt.*

26 On the formula 'Familie der Könige' ('family of kings') see most recently the critical comments by Brandes, 'Die "Familie der Könige" im Mittelalter'. Elliott, 'A Europe of Composite Monarchies', hinted at the late medieval and early modern phenomenon of the union of crowns, e.g. in England, Spain, or Scandinavia: even if one king ruled over several countries, the different monarchies remained separate units, at least theoretically.

27 See esp. Schmidt, *Kirche, Staat, Nation*; the contributions to Bünz and Fouquet ed., *Die Pfarrei im späten Mittelalter*, only partially address this more structural question. Wetzstein, 'Die Überwältigung des Raumes', is unfortunately not yet available in print; its publication is announced in the series 'Mittelalter-Forschungen'.

28 See most recently Jones, Mauntel, and Oschema ed., *A World of Empires.*

29 See above, n. 7.

Empire might have cultivated, thereby effectively underlining the sovereignty of their own king in his realm.

As early as in 1940, Franz-Josef Dölger introduced the notion of the 'family of kings' in order to describe the Byzantine rulers' political theory and practical approaches towards exterior powers. In an important critical article Wolfram Brandes has argued that this notion was profoundly anachronistic and thus inadequate as a tool to analyse medieval political ideas.[30] While we appreciate Brandes's arguments and agree with his observations concerning the notion's absence from medieval sources, we still consider the metaphor to be a fruitful instrument to apprehend the underlying structures of 'international' politics in late medieval Europe. The expression can serve as a 'fertile anachronism' in the sense established by Peter von Moos:[31] condensed in a familiar and easily understandable motif, it instantaneously conveys a set of different and crucial ideas — the idea of belonging together, the underlying norms of peaceful (and ideally even harmonic) cooperation, and the harsh realities of a non-egalitarian community that are often dominated by conflicts of interest.

The larger unit that overarches the polyphony of political entities might be identified as the *respublica christiana* — a quasi-virtual community, whose very existence frequently led European rulers to coordinate their interests in mutual recognition and that mostly seems to have manifested itself when confronted with exterior rivals. As of today, it seems that we do not really know if there was actually an identifiable common feature beyond the Christian religion that justified and explained the existing network of political relations (such as, for example, a sense of kinship or of belonging to the nobility);[32] in this respect further research seems to be necessary. But no matter what the answer turns out to be, the discernible acceptance of a plurality of political entities made the development of diplomatic practices inevitable. Peaceful (or at least non-violent) exchange and the reconciliation of political interests on a more or less level playing field called for the creation of a reliable framework. On the very practical level of 'foreign politics',[33] we can thus witness the creation and development of a specific set of diplomatic practices.

While these practices could vary enormously in detail, as far as the accompanying 'script' of the ritualized behaviour for the adequate verbal expressions and performative actions is concerned, they all served a common end: to furnish a platform for exchange and communication in mutual understanding

---

30 See above, n. 26.

31 See von Moos, 'Das Öffentliche und das Private im Mittelalter'; Loraux, 'Éloge de l'anachronisme en histoire'.

32 For a number of pertinent contributions see Schwinges, Hesse and Moraw ed., *Europa im späten Mittelalter*.

33 The notion and its applicability to medieval phenomena have been vividly discussed; for a brief overview see Ottner, 'Einleitung'. Among the pioneering works for a renewed application of the concept see Kintzinger, *Westbindungen*, esp. pp. 17–25, and Reitemeier, *Außenpolitik im Spätmittelalter*, pp. 21–24. See also Moeglin and Péquignot, *Diplomatie et 'relations internationales'*.

and recognition. This quest for symbolic equality is, for example, vividly demonstrated by the practices that can be observed during encounters on rivers or bridges. An impressive number of narrative accounts are witness to the practice of princes or kings meeting on the border of their realms, on bridges, or even on boats in the middle of the river — a practice which made sure that no ruler had to enter the other one's territory, thereby contributing to the (certainly idealized) idea that both rulers could symbolically claim to be of equal rank.[34]

Recent studies have intensively scrutinized the ritual arrangements in these contexts, and considerably improved our understanding of many aspects concerning the actors' behaviour, spatial arrangements, and performative actions like specific gestures, etc. One detail that has been less analysed in this particular context, although it attracted a lot of interest around the turn of the last century, is the practice of gift-giving: as several studies made clear, even though they treated the subject rather *en passant*, gifts and gift-giving played a major role in diplomatic contexts, either at the beginning or at the end of the encounters.[35] In fact, gifts seem to have been ubiquitous on these occasions, and they functioned as a sort of communicative 'lubricant' that helped to engage in harmonic exchange and to ascertain the counterpart's benevolence, in spite of tendencies to formalize the value of the gifts that were exchanged and to organize them according to the rank of the receiver.[36] By and large, however, these practices remained profoundly rooted in a culture of reciprocity: while the gift's value depended on the recipient's rank, it equally served to express the donor's material potency and benevolence. It was not supposed to demonstrate overt submission, at least on the level of the idealized discourse of diplomatic encounters. Quite the contrary: if it did endow somebody with obligations, in the eye of medieval Europeans, it was the receiver.

How deeply rooted this sense of reciprocity actually was in the political culture of medieval Latin-Christian Europe becomes particularly perceptible in the context of encounters with political actors that were not part of this tradition. The contrast to the Mongols' interpretation of the diplomatic gifts they received could hardly be starker: in their eyes, foreign envoys' or visitors'

---

34 On the history and ritual aspects of these meetings see, e.g., Schwedler, *Herrschertreffen des Spätmittelalters*; Schneider, 'Mittelalterliche Verträge auf Brücken und Flüssen'; Moeglin and Péquignot, *Diplomatie et 'relations internationales'*, pp. 169–73. The question whether this practice justifies the identification of the chosen locations as 'neutral', as has been proposed by Kintzinger, 'Der neutrale Ort', might need further discussion, see, e.g., Oschema, 'Auf dem Weg zur Neutralität'.

35 For brief overviews see Moeglin and Péquignot, *Diplomatie et 'relations internationales'*, pp. 213–17; Schwedler, *Herrschertreffen des Spätmittelalters*, pp. 24–25, 380–88, and Reitemeier, *Außenpolitik im Spätmittelalter*, pp. 446–47. In a more general perspective that focuses on the gift as 'social fact' see Groebner, *Liquid Assets, Dangerous Gifts*, and the contributions in Algazi, Groebner, and Jussen ed., *Negotiating the Gift*. For the early medieval period, see, e.g., the contributions in Davies, ed., *The Languages of Gift*.

36 See, e.g., Paravicini, 'Der Ehrenwein'.

gifts did equally function as an introduction to ensuing communication, but on an entirely different level. They interpreted them not as voluntary signs of benevolence or of the giver's wealth that could at once ensure harmonic exchange and impress the receiver. Rather, the Mongol rulers asked for gifts that demonstrated the giver's will to subordination and to give tribute. Any ensuing communication did not then take place on the level playing field of diplomatic exchange, but between overlord and subject.[37]

Interestingly enough — and in a quite paradoxical way — the practices of diplomatic communication could not only buy our Franciscan monk William of Rubruck an entry ticket to the Mongol court, but the diverging interpretations by both parties could also open up a productive space of exchange. This fertile 'misunderstanding' was only made possible by the implicit underlying interpretations: what the Latin envoys perceived to be an act of polite encounter and mutual recognition could be interpreted by their Mongol counterparts as something completely different, namely the submissive act of paying tributes. It is interesting to note that the fundamental ambivalence of the practice of gift-giving in the name of a ruler has already been noticed by the earliest travellers to the Mongol court. As a consequence, William of Rubruck did not only scrupulously avoid to be identified as a legate of King Louis of France, who had sent him, but he commented upon this very explicitly and consciously in his narrative.[38] William's strategy even went so far as to not bring any gifts to the Mongol court at all — an approach that threatened to poison the atmosphere at first, until he explained that his status as monk implied an existence without any possessions. While William's narrative repeatedly mentions difficult moments, in which the lack of gifts apparently presented a problem and the situation might have taken a turn for the worse, his Mongol counterparts seem to have ended up accepting his special position due to the monk's religious status.[39]

---

37 Jackson, *The Mongols and the West*, pp. 32, 184, 201–04; cf. Allsen, *Commodity and Exchange*, pp. 28–29 (with a focus on textiles as tribute). In spite of our observations concerning the interpretation of gift-giving in a diplomatic context, it has to be noted that the Mongols developed considerable flexibility as far as the media of communication are concerned, especially the choice of language, see Schmieder, 'Nomaden zwischen Asien, Europa und dem Mittleren Osten', esp. pp. 197–98.

38 Guglielmo di Rubruk, *Viaggio in Mongolia*, ed. by Chiesa, I, 6, p. 12: 'Ego tamen predicaueram publice in Ramis Palmarum apud Sanctam Sophiam quod non essem nuntius nec uester nec alicuius, sed ibam apus illos incredulos secundum regulam nostram' (on his sojourn in Sudak on the Black Sea).

39 Guglielmo di Rubruk, *Viaggio in Mongolia*, ed. by Chiesa, XV, 2–3, p. 72: 'Tunc incepit querere ductor noster quid portaremus ei, et cepit multum scandalizari quando udit quod nichil parabamus ad portandum. [...] Excusaui etiam me quia monachus eram, non habens neque recipiens neque tractans aurum uel argentum uel aliquid preciosum, solis libris et capella, in qua seruiebamus Deo exceptis, unde nullum exennium afferebamus ei nec domino suo: qui enim propria dimiseram, non poteram esse portitor alienorum. Tunc respondit satis mansuete quod bene faciebam, ex quo eram monachus, si seruarem uotum meum, et non indigebat rebus nostris, sed magis daret nobis de suis, si indigeremus'.

Systemic Consequences II — Cooperation and Alliances

What are we to make of these rather pointillist observations on a larger scale? We would like to argue in (at least) two directions. First and foremost, we hold that the fundamental idea of the coexistence of independent political units that operated, if not in the mode of total equality, at least on the same playing field, helps to explain several fundamental features of late medieval political practices in Latin Christianity (present section). Secondly, they also provided a particularly helpful basis for the efficient organization of the expansion of European influence from the thirteenth century onwards (see the following section: 'Systemic Consequences III').

Let us begin with our first hypothesis. Even though the idea of 'empire' and of the desirability of an overarching imperial authority lingered on in the Latin world of the late Middle Ages,[40] political theory and practice in reality reserved only little space for the potential establishment of hegemonic rule or pertinent claims. In order to illustrate this phenomenon, one could cite numerous examples, including the debates about non-German candidatures for the title of Roman-German king (and thus potentially Roman Emperor).[41] For the sake of our argument, we only want to mention one of the most explicit cases: Emperor Henry VII.[42]

On the day of his coronation as Roman Emperor in Rome, 29 June 1312, Henry issued a circular letter to several European monarchs, in which he claimed imperial suzerainty over all kingdoms in a very outspoken and explicit manner. According to him, all human beings, kingdoms, and regions had to be subject to only one ruler (*princeps monarchus*), since the fragmentation of the world into different kingdoms constituted a sin against the divinely ordained world order that followed the ideal of unity.[43] While this claim tied in with the imperial conceptions of the twelfth and thirteenth century emperors from the Hohenstaufen dynasty, the reactions from the letters' recipients clearly demonstrate that it could no longer be enforced in fourteenth-century Europe.[44] Pope Clement V, for example,

---

40 See Jones, Mauntel, and Oschema ed., *A World of Empires*, and Scholl, Gebhardt, and Clauß ed., *Transcultural Approaches*, for further contributions and bibliographical references.

41 See in particular Jones, *Eclipse of Empire?*

42 On his life and career see the contributions in Penth and Thorau ed., *Rom 1312*, and Heidemann, *Heinrich VII.* In a broader perspective, see Scales, *The Shaping of German Identity*, esp. pp. 204–59.

43 *Constitutiones et acta publica*, n° 801, p. 802: 'Sic universi homines distincti regnis et provinciis seperati uni principi monarche subessent, quatinus eo consurgeret machina mundi preclarior, quo ab uno Deo suo factore progrediens sub uno principe moderata'. See Heidemann, *Heinrich VII.*, pp. 170–77; Schneidmüller, 'Kaiser sein', pp. 286–87; Schneidmüller, 'Verklärte Macht', pp. 102–04; Kölmel, *Regimen Christianum*, pp. 498–502. Henry's claim was explicitly rejected by Jean Quidort, see Miethke, 'Politisches Denken', p. 136.

44 Heidemann, *Heinrich VII.*, pp. 170–77, 340–56 (in a broader perspective on ideas of imperial universalism).

simply ignored the letter,[45] while King Edward II of England sent polite but non-committal congratulations nine months later.[46] Philip IV of France was more outspoken: as could be expected, he explicitly refused Henry's claims, underlining that the French king did not recognize any superior in his realm, except God.[47] Finally, King Robert of Naples, a long-term opponent of Henry, even accused the latter of illegitimate imperial aspirations, thus refusing to recognize him as Roman Emperor at all, whatever an emperor's theoretical claims to authority over other rulers might have been.[48]

The attitude of Latin-Christian rulers — religious and secular alike — towards Henry's attempts to renew the imperial claims to universal authority seems thus to have been at least evasive, if not outright inimical. Of course, it would be necessary to draw a much more nuanced picture of the political convictions and ideas that existed during this period. For one, the different reactions to Henry's initiative resulted from profoundly diverging backgrounds: from the perspective of Pope Clement, for example, one would have to underline the influence of the long-standing debates about papal or imperial prerogatives,[49] while the French reaction tied in with the ascent of the Capetian king's authority as ruler over a powerful and centralized monarchy. In addition, even the theoretical positions varied and not every contemporary scholar shared the monarchs' opinion: some political thinkers, but also rulers like Henry VII himself, visibly adhered to the notion that universal authority was not only part of the Roman-German emperors' prerogatives, but indeed a fundamental element of divine world order and thus a normative ideal.[50] Yet it seems that reality had already surpassed these monolithic ideas of universality, especially since the development of politics in the late Middle Ages was increasingly dominated by the growing power of a series of monarchies.[51] Indicators for this development can be found in terminology, but also in the models and realities of political organization.

While some prominent thinkers still discussed the relation between pope and emperor, arguing for the prevalence of one or the other,[52] this discourse had already, at least partly, become disconnected from social and political

---

45 *Constitutiones et acta publica*, n° 810, pp. 811–12; see Heidemann, *Heinrich VII.*, pp. 178–80.

46 *Constitutiones et acta publica*, n° 812, p. 814; see Heidemann, *Heinrich VII.*, pp. 183–84.

47 *Constitutiones et acta publica*, n° 811, pp. 812–14; see Heidemann, *Heinrich VII.*, pp. 180–83.

48 *Constitutiones et acta publica*, n° 1252, pp. 1362–69; see Heidemann, *Heinrich VII.*, pp. 220–27.

49 See, e.g., Mierau, *Kaiser und Papst im Mittelalter*, and Sieber-Lehmann, *Papst und Kaiser*, here pp. 156–62.

50 Amongst the thinkers who supported these claims, Dante must certainly be counted as one of the most outspoken, see Dante Alighieri, *Monarchia*, ed. by Chiesa, Tabarroni, and Ellero; cf. Cassel, *The Monarchia Controversy*. A few decades earlier, Alexander of Roes defended the German claims to imperial rule, see Oschema, 'No "Emperor of Europe"', pp. 427–28; Scales, 'Purposeful Pasts'.

51 Watts, *Making of Polities*, pp. 410–11.

52 For the development of these debates, which continued well into the fifteenth century, see Miethke, *Politiktheorie im Mittelalter*.

practices. This effect is clearly visible in the case of Emperor Charles IV's visit to King Charles V of France in Paris (1378). Both rulers were not only well acquainted, but also closely related: the emperor, a member of the Luxembourg dynasty, was the French king's uncle. Still, the protocol had to be satisfied; but while the French honoured the emperor with lavish banquets and pompous festivities, thereby acknowledging his imperial rank, they also took great pains to avoid any doubt about the sovereignty of the French king over his realm.[53]

Even more important than this kind of symbolic politics is the virtual absence of ideas of imperial superiority from the most productive branches of political thinking and action: in contemporary practice, the fundamental processes of political decision-making were increasingly less determined by the actions of powerful individual princes — popes or kings alike — while techniques of collective decision-making or multi-lateral diplomatic exchange became increasingly important and visible.[54] This might even apply to 'classical' large-scale conflicts acted out between two well-identifiable adversaries, such as the Hundred Years War: this long-lasting series of conflicts, which constitutes a major feature of the history of fourteenth- and fifteenth-century England and France, can of course be described as a succession of wars between the two realms and their rulers.[55] However, such an approach not only neglects the widespread repercussions the conflict had on a European scale, but also the efforts made by exterior powers to end the war through the medium of negotiations.[56]

A particularly revealing example for the practice of collective decision-making is furnished by the series of large ecclesiastical *concilia* in the fifteenth century.[57] Obviously enough, these gatherings were first and foremost organized in order to solve specific problems of the church and the community of the believers: their main *raison d'être* was the problem of the schism that split Latin Christianity into two, then three obediences, from 1378 and 1409 respectively.[58] But the large assemblies of prelates and princes rapidly transformed into something

---

53 See Schwedler, *Herrschertreffen des Spätmittelalters*, pp. 297–317.

54 Watts, *Making of Polities*, pp. 233–38.

55 For a detailed presentation of the events up to 1422 see Sumption, *The Hundred Years War*.

56 For the efforts by the popes and the curia at Avignon and Rome, see e.g. Maleczek, 'Das Frieden stiftende Papsttum'; Müller, 'Konzil und Frieden'; Willershausen, *Die Päpste von Avignon und der Hundertjährige Krieg*. See also Offenstadt, *Faire la paix au Moyen Age*. These initiatives were not limited to clerical actors and institutions, as is attested by the Roman-German King Sigismund's initiative to further initiate negotiations between France and England since 1414, see Kintzinger, *Westbindungen*, pp. 55–139. For the European implications of the Hundred Years' War see Villalon and Kagay ed., *The Hundred Years War*.

57 The relevant literature is too numerous to be cited in detail; for a brief overview (with rich bibliography) see Müller, *Die kirchliche Krise des Spätmittelalters*. See also Müller and Helmrath ed., *Konzilien*, and, for Constance, more recently Signori and Studt ed., *Konstanzer Konzil*. See also Watts, *Making of Polities*, pp. 410–12.

58 See Rollo-Koster and Izbicki ed., *A Companion to the Great Western Schism*. Helmrath and Müller, 'Zur Einführung', pp. 22–23, distinguish between the council's primary and secondary functions; the former consisted of the re-establishment of the unity of the

different: the Council of Constance (1414–18) in particular effectively became a platform for the discussion and resolution of secular political conflicts (at least as far as problems are concerned that could not otherwise be resolved either by peaceful and diplomatic means or through military actions). Matters discussed at Constance include the conflict between the German order in Prussia and the Christian rulers of Lithuania-Poland, but also the murder of Louis of Orléans by the men of Duke John the Fearless of Burgundy (in 1407).[59]

What is most important to us in the present context, however, is the fact that this development was bolstered by theoretical discourses. Protagonists of conciliar theories referred to the model of the early church with its universal or regional synods that were platforms for religious as well as secular decision-making, thereby underlining the importance of corporative policy making.[60] But while the idea of creating platforms for collective coordination and cooperation was by no means entirely new and unheard of, it acquired a new quality when it was revived in the context of the schism of the late fourteenth and early fifteenth centuries.

The road to this kind of thinking had already been paved by an earlier discursive tradition, which linked the dimension of theoretical models of the ancient past with more recent (late medieval) ideas and practices, i.e. the discourse on the recovery of the Holy Land that developed in the aftermath of the loss of Acre in 1291.[61] The majority of treatises that proposed plans to recover the lost territories focused on practical problems of strategy and infrastructure.[62] In addition, they also discussed the necessary political preconditions, all the while leaving ample room for the development of creative and innovative ideas about the means to achieve the goal of the (re)conquest of the holy sites. It is indeed revealing, we believe, that most of these texts did not simply call for the establishment of a central and powerful political figure that could take matters in hand. They certainly recognized the prevalence of particularly important individuals like the emperor, the French king, and of course the pope, who represented the legitimizing institution *par excellence*. But even in the face of what they perceived to be the realm of unbelievers, the authors of pertinent treatises repeatedly explained that the necessary precondition for

---

Church, the question of the faith and the general reform (*causa unionis, causa fidei, causa reformationis*).

59 See briefly Frenken, *Das Konstanzer Konzil*, pp. 252–61; von Moos, 'Das Öffentliche und das Private', pp. 46–74.

60 See, e.g., Oakley, *Conciliarist Tradition*, pp. 60–81, for the ideas of Pierre d'Ailly, Jean Gerson, and Francesco Zabarella; cf. also Walther, 'Konziliarismus', here p. 52. Even when the conciliarists heavily relied on the sentences of canon law, these could refer back to situations of the early church, see e.g. Francesco Zabarella, 'Tractatus de schismate', p. 689, for councils convened by the emperors Constantine and Justinian.

61 For a general overview see, in spite of certain problems, Leopold, *How to Recover the Holy Land*.

62 For an important selection of texts see *Projets de croisade (v. 1290–v. 1330)*, ed. by Paviot. On the history of crusading plans after 1291 see e.g. Housley, *The Later Crusades*, here pp. 421–56, and the contributions in Paviot ed., *Les projets de croisade*; cf. Ertl, 'De Recuperatione Terrae Sanctae'.

a new crusade, i.e. peace in Christendom itself, could only be furnished by reconciling the differences between the Christian princes, thereby preparing a common effort of the united *respublica christiana*.[63]

In other words, the underlying idea of a plurality of sovereign and equal principalities led to practical propositions that favoured not only the creation of alliances, but even the development of institutionalized forms of collective policy making and action. It is true that the most 'innovative' and radical of these voices remained marginal, though, and their propositions, which have sometimes been qualified as 'utopian' by modern historians,[64] were not put into practical application in their own time. Nevertheless, we would argue that they express a more general mind-set that made the development of these ideas possible and had the potential to become more influential in the following centuries.

One author, who is usually credited with having presented some of the most extraordinary and quite revolutionary ideas, was the Norman-French advocate Pierre Dubois. He proposed to establish a union of Christian princes, in which the pope was not to have any decisive role, while the secular princes were expected to cooperate in institutionalized form.[65] Dubois' proposition, probably written around 1306, was indeed extraordinary and it has repeatedly been identified as the first project of a 'European union' of rulers.[66] This latter interpretation is certainly problematic, as it seems rather removed from the historical context and Dubois did not have the slightest interest in 'Europe' at all, whatever the notion might theoretically have meant to him: in fact, not even the word itself appears in his text.[67] The fact that he could come up with the idea of a union of princes, however, is a clear expression of the relevance of concepts of political cooperation.

Fascinating as it might look in the eyes of modern readers, nothing came of Dubois' proposition — for a multitude of different reasons. However, the idea itself seems to have lingered on, continuing to attract the minds of contemporaries. In the 1460s, the Bohemian king George of Podiebrad developed a similar project that his envoy Antonio Marini negotiated in some detail with the French king Louis XI. George's, or rather Marini's, project was even more elaborate than that of Dubois, and it contained details about the institutional organization of the union, including reflections about the location where the seat of the

63 See for example William of Adam, *How to Defeat the Saracens*, ed. and trans. by Constable, pp. 60–62. See also Sanudo Torsello, *The Book of Secrets*, p. 26, calling on the French king to coordinate his plans with the kings of Naples and Sicily and the Byzantine Emperor. For a more general overview on the notion of *respublica christiana* see Kurze, 'La "respublica christiana"'.

64 See Oexle, 'Utopisches Denken im Mittelalter'.

65 On the project see Kéry, 'Pierre Dubois und der Völkerbund'; Rexroth, 'Pierre Dubois und das Projekt einer universalen Heilig-Land-Stiftung'. The text is edited in Pierre Dubois, *De recuperatione Terre Sancte*; for an English translation see Pierre Dubois, *The Recovery of the Holy Land*.

66 See Kéry, 'Pierre Dubois und der Völkerbund', pp. 1–2.

67 Oschema, *Bilder von Europa*, pp. 380–90.

organization was supposed to reside, its collective seal, and its administration.[68] In the end, the idea to form an alliance of 'mutual charity and fraternity', as the text put it, shared the fate of the earlier projects and failed.[69] But even though both projects, Dubois's and Podiebrad's, have not been put into practice, they are witness to the existence of the idea of a pluralistic political order, which they sought to organize in a multilateral structure.

A quite impressive example of the circulation of this idea is furnished by Thomas of Saluzzo's 'Chevalier errant', an allegoric chivalric novel written in the French vernacular during the time of the author's imprisonment in Turin between 1394 and 1396 (and probably revised between 1403 and 1405).[70] In a passage that is highly charged with symbolic allusions, the author describes how the Emperor's herald proclaims the privileges awarded to Gian Galeazzo Visconti, i.e. his establishment as duke of Milan, amidst an assembly of secular and clerical princes. The passage and the accompanying miniatures (see Figures 6.1 and 6.2) are, of course, highly stylized and purely fictitious in their composition, even though they refer to a concrete political act that took place in 1395 (the author erroneously ascribes it to Emperor Charles IV instead of his son and successor Wenceslas).[71] At the same time, the two lavish miniatures in the Paris manuscript, one of two surviving witnesses of the text, clearly demonstrate that — and how — such a kind of princely assembly could be imagined by an early fifteenth-century artist. In an open space that is surrounded by their tents, the princes of the entire world, dressed in stylistically different robes and identified by real as well as imagined coats of arms, are assembled and engage in vivid discussions. While the distribution of the two miniatures on two successive pages, which evokes the structure of a diptych, separates the princes of the Occident and those of the Orient, the dividing line does not coincide with religious differences, since the latter includes not only the (Christian) Greek emperor, but also the (equally Christian) king of Jerusalem.

In a complementary perspective, the idea of a pluralistic political order can equally be traced through terminological observations: At the very

68 The text is edited as 'Tractatus pacis toti christianitati fiendae'; on this project see Monnet, 'Le projet de paix'; Šmahel, 'Antoine Marini de Grenoble et son Mémorandum', and Vaněček, *The Universal Peace Organization*.

69 'Tractatus pacis toti christianitati fiendae', p. 72: 'Ad statum mutue caritatis et fraternitatis unione laudabili deducantur, nos de certa nostra sciencia, matura deliberacione prehibita, invocata ad hoc Spiritus Sancti gracia, prelatorum, principum, procerum, nobilium et iuris divini et humani doctorum nostrorum ad hoc accedente consilio et assensu, ad huiusmodi connexionis, pacis, fraternitatis et concordie inconcusse duraturam ob Dei reverenciam fideique conservacionem devenimus <in> unionem in modum, qui sequitur'.

70 On the author and his work see Fajen, *Die Lanze und die Feder*; Piccat, 'Tommaso III, Marchese errante'.

71 On the illustrations of manuscript BnF, MS fr. 12559, here fols 161^{v}–162^{r}, see Bouchet, *L'Iconographie du 'Chevalier errant'*, pp. 70–74. For the text, see Tommaso III di Saluzzo, *Il Libro del Cavaliere Errante*, pp. 447–64.

same period, the notion of 'empire' (with all its implications of hegemony and universal rule) became somewhat diluted in Latin and vernacular texts. While high medieval authors often thought of the singular Roman tradition when they referred to 'the Empire', many late medieval authors progressively employed the notion in the sense of a generic political category.[72] Hence they addressed a number of different political entities as 'empires' — mostly outside of Europe — thereby implicitly, but effectively stripping the Roman-German Empire of its special and unique status. The most famous chronicler of the already mentioned Council of Constance, Ulrich Richental, provides a striking example: in his effort to list all participants of the Council and thus to potentially cover all realms of the world, he enumerated no less than nine 'empires'. Seven of these were located in Asia, but none in Europe (as King Sigismund was crowned Roman Emperor only after the Council).[73]

Just how deeply ingrained this idea actually was, can be demonstrated by a seemingly remote phenomenon: in the later Middle Ages a number of Latin authors used the expression 'Emperor of Europe', which had hitherto been virtually unknown.[74] But the authors in question did not apply the notion in a positive way, for example identifying or wishing for a hegemonic ruler from inside Europe, who might have united the *respublica christiana* in the fight against its religious adversaries, be they 'Saracens', Mongols, or Turks.[75] Quite the contrary, they referred to an *imperator Europae* in order to conjure up the idea of an external menace, e.g. declaring that the Ottoman sultans, who had already subjected Asia, would now strive to become the rulers of Europe, too.[76] As to the interior developments of Latin Christendom, we can indeed observe that even in moments of massive exterior menace, truly hegemonic political figures were neither called for, nor did they develop. Insofar as the plurality of sovereign kingdoms had become a given political fact, the idea of a single prince who ruled all of Europe was obviously perceived as a menace, not as a solution.[77]

72 See the contributions in Jones, Mauntel, and Oschema ed., *A World of Empires*, esp. Mauntel, 'The "Emperor of Persia"'.

73 Ulrich Richental, *Chronik*, pp. 142–43; see Mauntel, 'The "Emperor of Persia"', pp. 355–56, 377–76.

74 On the following, see in more detail Oschema, 'No "Emperor of Europe"'.

75 The antagonism towards the 'exterior' force of the expanding Ottoman empire did in fact dominate much of the political discourse of the fifteenth century, see most recently Housley ed., *Reconfiguring the Fifteenth-Century Crusade*; Höfert, *Den Feind beschreiben*; Topkaya, *Augen-Blicke sichtbarer Gewalt?*; Helmrath, 'Pius II. und die Türken'.

76 Oschema, 'No "Emperor of Europe"', pp. 425–36.

77 Dante's *Monarchia* represents one of the few exceptions to this general tendency, see n. 50.

FIGURE 6.1. Thomas III of Saluzzo, *Le Livre du Chevalier Errant*: Encampment of the princes of the Occident, convened by Fortune, Paris, Bibliothèque nationale de France, MS fr. 12559, fol. 161v. Circa 1404. © Bibliothèque nationale de France.

FIGURE 6.2. Thomas III of Saluzzo, *Le Livre du Chevalier Errant*: Encampment of the princes of the Orient, convened by Fortune, Paris, Bibliothèque nationale de France, MS fr. 12559, fol. 162r. Circa 1404. © Bibliothèque nationale de France.

Systemic Consequences III — Dealing with the Other

The deeply rooted idea that the concert of Latin-Christian realms could be described in ways that we might understand as the image of a 'family of kingdoms' of ideally equal rank not only led to successful collective forms of negotiation and propositions of institutionalized alliances (even if these mostly remained theoretical). It also had effects on the way Europeans encountered and dealt with political entities that they had hitherto ignored. In order to complete our short — and necessarily sketchy — overview, let us briefly look at the ideas that Latin authors held about the world outside of Europe (or rather Latin Christianity) and how they translated into concrete actions.

Just as the European kingdoms formed alliances amongst themselves, they were also keen on winning additional partners, especially for their fight against the Muslim states in the Near East. What is even more striking is that Christians in the Levant also entered into alliances with Muslim partners on numerous occasions.[78] A famous, but certainly not representative example is furnished by the 'crusade' of Emperor Frederick II that was characterized by negotiations rather than warfare: in 1229, the emperor and the Ayyubid Sultan of Egypt, al-Kāmil, agreed on a treaty that included a ten-year truce.[79]

In a perspective that transcends individual contracts like these, one of the central tasks of the envoys to the Mongols was to ascertain whether the latter would join the Christians in a concerted action against the Muslims in the Near East. The underlying plan was to organize a coordinated attack of Christians and Mongols, possibly after the latter's conversion to Christianity. It took the European courts and rulers some time to realize the futility of this endeavour: the Mongols were not willing to coordinate their wars with anyone. In spite of all the differences between the Latin-Christian world and the Mongols, however, European rulers remained eager to include the Mongol Empire, that they still hoped could be Christianised, into their system of alliances.[80]

Politics and religion were inextricably linked in this context, and diplomatic advances that sought to win the Mongols as allies went hand in hand with efforts to convert them. After all, from a Christian point of view, it was not only desirable to evangelize all peoples of the world, but was also necessary.[81] And so the first travellers, including John of Plano Carpini and William of Rubruck, already tried to fathom the chances of success.

78 For the period of the Crusades, see, e.g., Köhler, *Alliances and Treaties*; Shatzmiller ed., *Crusaders and Muslims*.

79 See for example Takayama, 'Frederick II's Crusade'; Hechelhammer, *Kreuzzug und Herrschaft unter Friedrich II.*

80 For a general overview see Jackson, *The Mongols and the West*, pp. 165–95; Schmieder, *Europa und die Fremden*, pp. 89–122.

81 The Mongols were included in several papal bulls that enumerated the heathen people, which could (or rather should) be Christianised, from 1253 onwards, see Schmieder, '*Cum hora undecima*', p. 262.

In accordance with long-standing practices and experience of mission and conversion, all pertinent efforts in Mongol China targeted the Khan himself, the central figure of the political hierarchy. This orientation reflected the experience of the early and high medieval Christianization of Europe, which had largely been achieved by the conversion of princes and rulers, who more or less served as an example to their people.[82] As is attested by numerous rumours about the Christian inclinations of several Khans or their wives, the hopes to convert the Mongols by converting their political leader lingered on for quite a long time.[83] Drawing on experiences made in Europe, this pattern of thought made several missionaries rush to the Mongol court — a clear expression of the extent to which they misjudged the Mongols' attitude towards 'religion'. As has been stressed by Peter Jackson, the Mongols were quite eager to borrow ideas or practices from different systems of belief, as long as they could benefit from them. But this orientation was primarily concerned with the present life, not the next. Even a potentially visible interest in the Christian God would thus not have implied the acceptance of its monotheistic background. In addition, even if the Khan as a person could have been converted, the pluralistic *pantheon* of the Mongols would have limited the practical effects.[84]

It is not without a touch of irony that European travellers or missionaries overestimated the position of the Khan in this case. At this point, two patterns of thought merged. First, the deeply rooted idea that a ruler's individual religious affiliation mirrored (and at the same time determined) his people's attitude. Second, the conviction that the Mongol Khan was in a certain way an almighty ruler, second to none — except, perhaps, the mythic Prester John, a mighty legendary Christian patriarch and king, who was at the centre of legendary stories that circulated in Europe from the twelfth century onwards.[85]

While European Christians might have been right to imagine the Khan as a most powerful ruler (at least in the thirteenth century), they were quite misguided in their expectations concerning the aims to which a Khan would put his powers into use. Even after Latin-Christian observers had noticed the dissolution of the *one* Mongol Empire into several independent polities, they still adhered to their conviction that the Mongol rulers were extremely

---

82 For an overview see Fletcher, *The Conversion of Europe*; von Padberg, *Die Christianisierung Europas*.

83 See for example Giovanni di Pian di Carpine, *Storia dei Mongoli*, ed. by Menestò, p. 327; Guglielmo di Rubruk, *Viaggio in Mongolia*, ed. by Chiesa, IX, 1, p. 48, and XVII, 2, p. 82. See also Schmieder, *Europa und die Fremden*, pp. 218–22, and the contributions in Tremml-Werner and Crailsheim ed., *Audienzen*.

84 Jackson, *The Mongols and the West*, pp. 270–74; Schmieder, *Europa und die Fremden*, pp. 128–51.

85 For an overview, see the essays in Beckingham and Hamilton ed., *Prester John, the Mongols and the Ten Lost Tribes*; Wagner, *Die 'Epistola presbiteri Johannis' lateinisch und deutsch*. Comfortable access to the sources is provided by *Prester John. The Legend and its Sources*, trans. by Brewer.

powerful. Seen in a broader perspective, this picture reveals two opposite worlds as construed by Latin-Christian authors: while they described Europe as a plurality of kingdoms (and conveyed this image even at the Mongol court),[86] they imagined the 'East' or 'Asia' as being dominated by a limited number of extremely powerful imperial rulers[87] — and they acted accordingly.

Conclusion

To sum up: our argument focused on the entanglement of ideas of political order and diplomatic practices in a primarily Latin-Western perspective. We underlined the specificity of Latin Christianity, where the idea of (secular) political pluralism became an important element from the twelfth century onwards. While we cannot say with certainty which of the two developed first — the ideas of plurality or a plural reality — a growing number of authors and thinkers clearly perceived and described the secular order as multifaceted and plural in a quite early stage of this development.

We argue that this discourse and the ideas it produced reinforced the practices of political organization: Latin-Christian rulers steadily developed diplomatic practices that allowed for exchange and negotiation on an ideally level playing field, and they learned to think and act according to an ideal of 'alliances', regardless of their individual claims to monarchical and sovereign rule inside of their realms. Even though most political entities in Latin Europe were monarchies, the late Middle Ages saw the growing importance of bodies of collective decision-making that led to multipolar political discussions even within the kingdoms. In a complex circle of practical developments, observations, and interpretations that could in turn acquire normative and formative force, Latin Christianity thus developed a set of practices that relied on elaborate ideas about how secular rule should be organized and ordered in its very tangible plurality.

When the envoys of European rulers, like William of Rubruck, travelled to the East, they carried these ideas with them and acted accordingly. The focus on contact with the Mongol rulers makes it possible to pinpoint this specificity of the ideas and convictions concerning political organization in the Latin-Christian world: in their efforts to engage in diplomatic exchange, Western travellers had to realize that their approach was largely incompatible with the Mongols' claims to universal rule. Nevertheless, their own ideas and corresponding practices opened up a 'space of ambiguity' that led to continuous efforts to come to an understanding, even if the Mongols' and the Christian travellers' aims were not compatible. Our argument can finally be condensed to the basic idea that the development of political ideas in Latin Europe (in

86 See above, n. 17.

87 Mauntel, 'The "Emperor of Persia"', pp. 374–78.

the intersection of material realities and theoretical reflections) led to the creation of an accompanying set of diplomatic practices. While these practices alone cannot explain the outward orientation of so-called 'European culture' in the early modern period, they might help to better understand its specific forms and its success — without having to rely on any particular 'European nature' in an ontological sense.

The 'Europeans' had a set of established and well-proven diplomatic techniques at their disposal, which they put into use when they made contact with foreign political entities — and which were deeply entangled with their own ideas of (political) order. One might even assume that, at least in some cases, 'Europeans' accepted other realms' diplomatic and administrative boundaries, as long as their governments staunchly demanded to be recognized — because they were used to doing so from their own cultural context.

This approach did not inevitably lead to success. In an instructive study, Serge Gruzinski analysed the experiences of the Spanish in their encounters with the Aztecs and the concurrent encounters between the Portuguese and China in the 1520s. Comparing both series of events, Gruzinski pointed out striking differences:[88] while the Portuguese in China were confronted with a well-organized imperial bureaucracy that set clear boundaries to foreign visitors, the Spanish encountered an Aztec empire, whose subjects were quite willing to ally with the strangers against the oppressive capital. The Chinese thus systematically limited the Europeans' liberties of action while the Aztecs, on the other hand, were not able to show similar resistance.

This example reminds us, once again, that the fall or survival of entire realms cannot be explained by monocausal theories — in reality, a broad range of different factors played important roles in these contexts, like military strength or medical issues (such as the fatal diseases imported by Europeans to the Americas). This does not mean, however, that we should neglect structural influences that are less prominent and visible, like the one we focused on in this contribution. What we thus want to argue for, is the importance of underlying patterns of thought that inform and (to a certain degree) even steer the way people (re)act.

---

88 Gruzinski, *L'Aigle et le Dragon*.

Works Cited

Manuscripts

Paris, Bibliothèque nationale de France, MS fr. 12559 (Thomas III of Saluzzo, *Le Livre du Chevalier Errant*)

Primary Sources

Bleienstein, Fritz, *Johannes Quidort von Paris. Über königliche und päpstliche Gewalt ('De regia potestate et papali')* (Stuttgart: Klett, 1969)

Constitutiones et acta publica imperatorem et regum, Tomus IV: Inde ab a. MCCXCVIII. ad a. MCCCXIII. Pars II, ed. by Jacob Schwalm, Monumenta Germaniae Historica, Constitutiones, 4,2 (Hanover: Hahn, 1911)

Dante Alighieri, *Monarchia*, ed. by Paolo Chiesa, Andrea Tabarroni, and Diago Ellero (Rome: Salerno, 2013)

Francesco Zabarella, 'Tractatus de Schismate', in *De iurisdictione, autoritate et praeeminentia imperiali, ac potestate ecclesiastica, deque iuribus regni et imperii, variorum authorum, qui ante haec tempora vixerunt, scripta*, ed. by Simon Schardius (Basel: Oporinus, 1566), pp. 688–711

Fulbert of Chartres, 'Tractatus contra Iudaeos', in *Patrologiae cursus completus: series latina*, ed. by Jacques-Paul Migne, CXLI (Paris: Garnier, 1844–64), cols 305–18

Giovanni di Pian di Carpine, *Storia dei Mongoli*, ed. by Enrico Menestò (Spoleto: Centro Italiano di Studi sull'alto Medioevo, 1989)

Guglielmo di Rubruk, *Viaggio in Mongolia (Itinerarium)*, ed. by Paolo Chiesa, Scrittori greci e latini (Rome: Fondazione Lorenzo Valla/Mondadori, 2011)

Isidore of Seville, *Etymologiae sive origines libri XX*, 2 vols, ed. by Wallace Martin Lindsay (Oxford: Clarendon Press, 1911)

John of Paris, *On Royal and Papal Power*, trans. by John A. Watt (Toronto: Pontifical Institute of Mediaeval Studies, 1971)

Pierre Dubois, *De recuperatione Terre Sancte. Traité de politique generale*, ed. by Charles-Victor Langlois, Collection de textes pour servir à l'étude et à l'enseignement de l'histoire, 9 (Paris: Picard, 1891)

——, *The Recovery of the Holy Land*, Records of Civilisation, 51, trans. by Walther I. Brandt (New York: Columbia University Press, 1956)

Prester John: The Legend and its Sources, trans. by Keagan Brewer, Crusade Texts in Translation, 27 (Farnham: Routledge, 2015)

Projets de croisade (v. 1290–v. 1330), ed. by Jacques Paviot, Documents relatifs à l'histoire des croisades, 20 (Paris: Académie des Inscriptions et Belles Lettres, 2008)

Sanudo Torsello, Marino, *The Book of Secrets of the Faithful of the Cross: Liber secretorum fidelium crucis*, trans. by Peter Lock, Crusade Texts in Translation, 21 (Farnham: Routledge, 2011)

The Secret History of the Mongols: A Mongolian Epic Chronicle of the Thirteenth Century, 3 vols, ed. and trans. by Igor de Rachewiltz, Brill's Inner Asian Library, 7 (Leiden: Brill, 2006–13)

Tommaso III di Saluzzo, *Il Libro del Cavaliere Errante (BnF ms. fr. 12559)*, ed. by Marco Piccat and Laura Ramello (Boves: Araba Fenice, 2008)
'Tractatus pacis toti christianitati fiendae', ed. by Jiří Kejř, in *The Universal Peace Organization of King George of Bohemia: A 15th Century Plan for World Peace, 1462/1464*, ed. by Václav Vaněček (Prague: Czechoslovak Academy of Sciences, 1964), pp. 69–82
Ulrich Richental, *Chronik des Konstanzer Konzils 1414–1418*, ed. by Thomas Martin Buck (Ostfildern: Jan Thorbecke, 2010)
William of Adam, *How to Defeat the Saracens*, Dumbarton Oaks Medieval Humanities, ed. and trans. by Giles Constable (Washington, DC: Dumbarton Oaks Research Library and Collection, 2012)

Secondary Studies

Algazi, Gadi, Valentin Groebner, and Bernhard Jussen, ed., *Negotiating the Gift: Pre-Modern Figurations of Exchange*, Veröffentlichungen des Max-Planck-Instituts für Geschichte, 188 (Göttingen: Vandenhoeck & Ruprecht, 2003)
Allsen, Thomas T., *Commodity and Exchange in the Mongol Empire*, Cambridge Studies in Islamic Civilization (Cambridge: Cambridge University Press, 2002 [paperback edn])
——, *Culture and Conquest in Mongol Eurasia*, Cambridge Studies in Islamic Civilization (Cambridge: Cambridge University Press, 2004 [paperback edn])
Amitai-Preiss, Reuven, 'Mongol Imperial Ideology and the Ilkhanid War against the Mamluks', in *The Mongol Empire and its Legacy*, ed. by Reuven Amitai-Preiss and David O. Morgan, Islamic History and Cilization, 24 (Leiden: Brill 1999), pp. 57–72
Beckingham, Charles F., and Bernard F. Hamilton, ed., *Prester John, the Mongols and the Ten Lost Tribes* (Aldershot: Ashgate, 1996)
Blumenkranz, Bernhard, 'À propos du (ou des) Tractatus contra Iudaeos de Fulbert de Chartres', in *Juifs et Chrétiens, patristique et Moyen Âge. Collected Essays*, ed. by Bernhard Blumenkranz (London: Variorum, 1977), pp. 5–51
Bouchet, Florence, *L'Iconographie du 'Chevalier errant' de Thomas de Saluces*, Corpus du Répertoire iconographique de la littérature du Moyen Âge, 3 (Turnhout: Brepols, 2014)
Brandes, Wolfram, 'Die "Familie der Könige" im Mittelalter. Ein Diskussionsbeitrag zur Kritik eines vermeintlichen Erkenntnismodells', *Rechtsgeschichte. Zeitschrift des Max-Planck-Instituts für europäische Rechtsgeschichte*, 21 (2013), 262–84
Bünz, Enno, and Gerhard Fouquet, ed., *Die Pfarrei im späten Mittelalter*, Vorträge und Forschungen, 77 (Ostfildern: Jan Thorbecke, 2013)
Cassel, Anthony K., *The Monarchia Controversy: An Historical Study with Accompanying Translations of Dante Alighieri's 'Monarchia', Guido Vernani's 'Refutation of the "Monarchia" Composed by Dante' and Pope John XXII's Bull 'Si fratrum'* (Washington, DC: The Catholic University of America Press, 2004)
Davies, Wendy, ed., *The Languages of Gift in the Early Middle Ages* (Cambridge: Cambridge University Press, 2010)

Drews, Wolfram, 'Politische Theorie und imperiale Konzepte', in *Europas Aufstieg: Eine Spurensuche im späten Mittelalter*, ed. by Thomas Ertl (Vienna: Mandelbaum, 2013), pp. 34–62

Elliott, John H., 'A Europe of Composite Monarchies', *Past and Present*, 137 (1992), 48–71

Ertl, Thomas, ed., *Europas Aufstieg: Eine Spurensuche im späten Mittelalter* (Vienna: Mandelbaum, 2013)

——, 'De Recuperatione Terrae Sanctae. Kreuzzugspläne nach 1291 zwischen Utopie und "Useful Knowledge"', in *Zukunft im Mittelalter. Zeitkonzepte und Planungsstrategien*, ed. by Klaus Oschema and Bernd Schneidmüller, Vorträge und Forschungen, 90 (Ostfildern: Jan Thorbecke, 2021), pp. 283–312

Fajen, Robert, *Die Lanze und die Feder. Untersuchungen zum 'Livre du Chevalier errant' von Thomas III., Markgraf von Saluzzo*, Imagines Medii Aevi, 15 (Wiesbaden: Reichert, 2003)

Fletcher, Richard, *The Conversion of Europe. From Paganism to Christianity 371–1386 AD* (London: Harper Collins, 1997)

Frenken, Ansgar, *Das Konstanzer Konzil* (Stuttgart: Kohlhammer, 2015)

Groebner, Valentin, *Liquid Assets, Dangerous Gifts: Presents and Politics at the End of the Middle Ages* (Philadelphia: University of Pennsylvania Press, 2002) [German orig.: *Gefährliche Geschenke. Ritual, Politik und die Sprache der Korruption in der Eidgenossenschaft im späten Mittelalter und am Beginn der Neuzeit* (Constance: Universitätsverlag Konstanz, 2000)]

Gruzinski, Serge, *L'Aigle et le Dragon. Démesure européenne et mondialisation au XVI*[e] *siècle* (Paris: Fayard, 2012) [Engl. trans. *The Eagle and the Dragon: Globalization and European Dreams of Conquest in China and America in the Sixteenth Century* (Chichester: Wiley, 2014)]

Hack, Achim Thomas, *Das Empfangszeremoniell bei mittelalterlichen Papst-Kaiser-Treffen*, Regesta Imperii Beihefte, 18 (Cologne: Böhlau, 1999)

Hechelhammer, Bodo, *Kreuzzug und Herrschaft unter Friedrich II. Handlungsspielräume von Kreuzzugspolitik (1215–1230)*, Mittelalter-Forschungen, 13 (Ostfildern: Jan Thorbecke, 2004)

Heidemann, Malte, *Heinrich VII. (1308–1313). Kaiseridee im Spannungsfeld von staufischer Universalherrschaft und frühneuzeitlicher Partikularautonomie*, Studien zu den Luxemburgern und ihrer Zeit, 11 (Warendorf: Fahlbusch, 2008)

Helmrath, Johannes, 'Pius II. und die Türken', in *Europa und die Türken in der Renaissance*, ed. by Bodo Guthmüller and Wilhelm Kühlmann (Tübingen: Niemeyer, 2000), pp. 79–137

Helmrath, Johannes, and Heribert Müller, 'Zur Einführung', in *Die Konzilien von Pisa (1409), Konstanz (1414–1418) und Basel (1431–1449). Institution und Personen*, ed. by Heribert Müller and Johannes Helmrath, Vorträge und Forschungen, 67 (Ostfildern: Jan Thorbecke, 2007), pp. 9–29

Höfert, Almut, *Den Feind beschreiben. 'Türkengefahr' und europäisches Wissen über das Osmanische Reich 1450–1600* (Frankfurt: Campus, 2003)

Housley, Norman, *The Later Crusades, 1274–1580: From Lyons to Alcazar* (Oxford: Oxford University Press, 1992)

——, ed., *Reconfiguring the Fifteenth-Century Crusade* (London: Palgrave Macmillan, 2017)

Jackson, Peter, *The Mongols and the West, 1221–1410*, The Medieval World (Harlow: Pearson Longman, 2005)

Jones, Chris, *Eclipse of Empire? Perceptions of the Western Empire and Its Rulers in Late-Medieval France*, Cursor Mundi, 1 (Turnhout: Brepols, 2007)

——, 'Diener zweier Herren? Jean Quidort und das Problem der königlichen Autorität', *Jahrbuch für Universitätsgeschichte*, 19 (2016), 151–85

——, 'Undefined Terms: Empires and Emperors in Late Medieval French Thought', *The Medieval History Journal*, 20,2 (2017), 319–53

——, ed., *John of Paris: Beyond Royal and Papal Power*, Disputatio, 23 (Turnhout: Brepols, 2015)

Jones, Chris, Christoph Mauntel, and Klaus Oschema, ed., *A World of Empires: Claiming and Assigning Imperial Authority in the Middle Ages*. Thematic issue of *The Medieval History Journal*, 20,2 (2017) (Los Angeles: SAGE, 2017)

Jostkleigrewe, Georg, 'Expansion – Macht – Legitimität. Diplomatie und grenzüberschreitende Kommunikation zwischen "staatlichen" und "nicht-staatlichen" Akteuren', in *Europas Aufstieg: Eine Spurensuche im späten Mittelalter*, ed. by Thomas Ertl (Vienna: Mandelbaum, 2013), pp. 63–83

——, '"Rex imperator in regno suo" — an Ideology of Frenchness? Late Medieval France, Its Political Elite and Juridical Discourse', in *Imagined Communities: Constructing Collective Identities in Medieval Europe*, ed. by Andrzej Pleszczyński and others, Explorations in Medieval Culture, 8 (Leiden: Brill, 2018), pp. 46–83

Kéry, Lotte, 'Pierre Dubois und der Völkerbund: ein "Weltfriedensplan" um 1300', *Historische Zeitschrift*, 283 (2006), 1–30

Khanmohamadi, Shirin A., *In Light of Another's Word: European Ethnography in the Middle Ages*, The Middle Ages Series (Philadelphia: University of Pennsylvania Press, 2014)

Kintzinger, Martin, *Westbindungen im spätmittelalterlichen Europa. Auswärtige Politik zwischen dem Reich, Frankreich, Burgund und England in der Regierungszeit Kaiser Sigmunds*, Mittelalter-Forschungen, 2 (Stuttgart: Jan Thorbecke, 2000)

——, 'Der neutrale Ort: Konstruktion einer diplomatischen Realität. Ein methodisches Experiment', in *Faktum und Konstrukt: politische Grenzziehungen im Mittelalter: Verdichtung – Symbolisierung – Reflexion*, ed. by Nils Bock, Georg Jostkleigrewe, and Bastian Walter, Symbolische Kommunikation und gesellschaftliche Wertesysteme, 35 (Münster: Rhema, 2011), pp. 111–38

Köhler, Michael, *Alliances and Treaties between Frankish and Muslim Rulers in the Middle East: Cross-Cultural Diplomacy in the Period of the Crusades*, The Muslim World in the Age of the Crusades, 1 (Leiden: Brill, 2013) [German orig.: *Allianzen und Verträge zwischen fränkischen und islamischen Herrschern im Vorderen Orient. Eine Studie über das zwischenstaatliche Zusammenleben vom 12. bis ins 13. Jahrhundert*. Studien zur Sprache, Geschichte und Kultur des islamischen Orients, New Series, 12 (New York: de Gruyter, 1991)]

Kölmel, Wilhelm, *Regimen Christianum. Weg und Ergebnisse des Gewaltenverhältnisses und des Gewaltenverständnisses (8. bis 14. Jahrhundert)* (Berlin: de Gruyter, 1970)

Krynen, Jacques, *L'Empire du roi. Idées et croyances politiques en France, XIIIe–XVe siècle* (Paris: Gallimard, 1993)

Kurze, Dietrich, 'La "respublica christiana" et l'Europe médiévale', in *Imaginer l'Europe*, ed. by Klaus Malettke (Paris: Belin, 1998), pp. 11–49

Leopold, Antony, *How To Recover the Holy Land: The Crusade Proposals of the Late Thirteenth and Early Fourteenth Centuries* (Aldershot: Ashgate, 2000)

Lieberman, Victor, *Strange Parallels: Southeast Asia in Global Context, c. 800–1830*, 2 vols (*I: Integration on the Mainland*, 2003; *II: Mainland Mirrors: Europe, Japan, China, South Asia, and the Islands*, 2009) (Cambridge: Cambridge University Press, 2003–09)

——, 'Protected Rimlands and Exposed Zones: Reconfiguring Premodern Eurasia', *Comparative Studies in Society and History* 50,3 (2008), 692–723

Loraux, Nicole, 'Éloge de l'anachronisme en histoire', *Le Genre humain*, 27,1 (1993), 23–39

Maleczek, Werner, 'Das Frieden stiftende Papsttum im 12. und 13. Jahrhundert', in *Träger und Instrumentarien des Friedens im hohen und späten Mittelalter*, ed. by Johannes Fried, Vorträge und Forschungen, 43 (Sigmaringen: Jan Thorbecke, 1996), pp. 249–332

Mauntel, Christoph, 'The "Emperor of Persia": "Empire" as a Means of Describing and Structuring the World', *The Medieval History Journal*, 20,2 (2017), 354–84

Mierau, Heike, *Kaiser und Papst im Mittelalter* (Cologne: Böhlau, 2010)

Miethke, Jürgen, 'Politisches Denken und monarchische Theorie. Das Kaisertum als supranationale Institution im späten Mittelalter', in *Ansätze und Diskontinuität deutscher Nationsbildung im Mittelalter*, ed. by Joachim Ehlers, Nationes, 8 (Sigmaringen: Jan Thorbecke, 1989), pp. 121–44

——, *Politiktheorie im Mittelalter. Von Thomas von Aquin bis Wilhelm von Ockham* (Tübingen: Mohr Siebeck, 2008)

Mitterauer, Michael, *Warum Europa? Mittelalterliche Grundlagen eines Sonderwegs* (Munich: Beck, 2003)

Moeglin, Jean-Marie, and Stéphane Péquignot, *Diplomatie et 'relations internationales' au Moyen Âge (IXe–XVe siècle)*, Nouvelle Clio (Paris: Presses universitaires de France, 2017)

Monnet, Pierre, 'Le projet de paix et d'union chrétiennes de Georges de Podiebrad', in *Histoire du monde au XVe siècle*, ed. by Patrick Boucheron (Paris: Fayard, 2009), pp. 527–32

Morris, Ian, *Why the West Rules — For Now: The Patterns of History and What They Reveal About the Future* (London: Profile Books, 2011)

Müller, Heribert, 'Konzil und Frieden. Basel und Arras (1435)', in *Träger und Instrumentarien des Friedens im hohen und späten Mittelalter*, ed. by Johannes Fried, Vorträge und Forschungen, 43 (Sigmaringen: Jan Thorbecke, 1996), pp. 333–90

——, *Théâtre de la préséance. Les ducs de Bourgogne face aux grandes assemblées dans le Saint-Empire*, Conférences annuelles, 13 (Ostfildern: Jan Thorbecke, 2007)

——, *Die kirchliche Krise des Spätmittelalters*, Enzyklopädie deutscher Geschichte, 90 (Munich: Oldenbourg, 2012)
Müller, Heribert, and Johannes Helmrath, ed., *Die Konzilien von Pisa (1409), Konstanz (1414–1418) und Basel (1431–1449). Institution und Personen*, Vorträge und Forschungen, 67 (Ostfildern: Jan Thorbecke, 2007)
Oakley, Francis, *The Conciliarist Tradition: Constitutionalism in the Catholic Church, 1300–1870* (Oxford: Oxford University Press, 2003)
Oexle, Otto G., 'Utopisches Denken im Mittelalter: Pierre Dubois', *Historische Zeitschrift*, 224 (1977), 293–339
Offenstadt, Nicolas, *Faire la paix au Moyen Age. Discours et gestes de paix pendent la guerre de Cent Ans* (Paris: Jacob, 2007)
Oschema, Klaus, 'Auf dem Weg zur Neutralität. Eine neue Kategorie politischen Handelns im spätmittelalterlichen Frankreich', in *Freundschaft oder amitié? Ein politisch-soziales Konzept der Vormoderne im zwischensprachlichen Vergleich (15.–17. Jahrhundert)*, ed. by Klaus Oschema, Zeitschrift für Historische Forschung. Beihefte 40 (Berlin: Akademie-Verlag, 2007), pp. 81–108
——, 'Medieval Europe — Object and Ideology', in *Ideas of/for Europe: An Interdisciplinary Approach to European Identity*, ed. by Teresa Pinheiro, Beata Cieszynska, and José Eduardo Franco (Frankfurt: Peter Lang, 2012), pp. 59–73
——, *Bilder von Europa im Mittelalter*, Mittelalter-Forschungen, 46 (Ostfildern: Jan Thorbecke, 2013)
——, 'No "Emperor of Europe": A Rare Title between Political Irrelevance, Anti-Ottoman Politics and the Politics of National Diversity', *The Medieval History Journal*, 20,2 (2017), 411–46
Ottner, Christine, 'Einleitung', in *Außenpolitisches Handeln im ausgehenden Mittelalter. Akteure und Ziele*, ed. by Sonja Dünnebeil and Christine Ottner, Regesta Imperii. Beihefte, 27 (Vienna: Böhlau, 2007), pp. 9–20
Paravicini, Werner, 'Der Ehrenwein. Stadt, Adel und Herrschaft im Zeichen einer Geste', in *Residenzstädte der Vormoderne. Umrisse eines europäischen Phänomens*, ed. by Gerhard Fouquet, Jan Hirschbiegel, and Sven Rabeler (Ostfildern: Jan Thorbecke, 2016), pp. 69–151
Paviot, Jacques, ed., *Les Projets de croisade. Géostratégie et diplomatie européenne du XIVe au XVIIe siècle*, Les croisades tardives, 1 (Toulouse: Presses universitaires du Midi, 2014)
Peltzer, Jörg, *Der Rang der Pfalzgrafen bei Rhein. Die Gestaltung der politisch-sozialen Ordnung des Reichs im 13. und 14. Jahrhundert*, RANK: Politisch-soziale Ordnungen im mittelalterlichen Europa, 2 (Ostfildern: Jan Thorbecke, 2013)
Peltzer, Jörg, Gerald Schwedler, and Paul Töbelmann, ed., *Politische Versammlungen und ihre Rituale. Repräsentationsformen und Entscheidungsprozesse des Reichs und der Kirche im späten Mittelalter*, Mittelalter-Forschungen, 27 (Ostfildern: Jan Thorbecke, 2009)
Penth, Sabine, and Peter Thorau, ed., *Rom 1312. Die Kaiserkrönung Heinrichs VII. und die Folgen. Die Luxemburger als Herrscherdynastie von gesamteuropäischer Bedeutung*, Regesta Imperii. Beihefte 40 (Cologne: Böhlau, 2016)

Phillips, Kim M., *Before Orientalism: Asian Peoples and Cultures in European Travel Writing, 1245–1510*, The Middle Ages Series (Philadelphia: University of Pennsylvania Press, 2014)

Piccat, Marco, 'Tommaso III, Marchese errante: l'autobiografia cavalleresca di un Saluzzo', in *Tommaso III di Saluzzo, Il Libro del Cavaliere Errante (BnF ms. fr. 12559)*, ed. by Marco Piccat and Laura Ramello (Boves: Araba Fenice, 2008), pp. 5–26

Pines, Yuri, *Envisioning Eternal Empire: Chinese Political Thought of the Warring States Era* (Honolulu: University of Hawai'i Press, 2009)

Pomeranz, Kenneth, *The Great Divergence: China, Europe, and the Making of the Modern World Economy*, The Princeton Economic History of the Western World (Princeton: Princeton University Press, 2000)

Reichert, Folker, *Erfahrung der Welt. Reisen und Kulturbegegnung im späten Mittelalter* (Stuttgart: Kohlhammer, 2001)

——, *Asien und Europa im Mittelalter. Studien zur Geschichte des Reisens* (Göttingen: Vandenhoeck & Ruprecht, 2014)

Reinhard, Wolfgang, 'Europäische Politik als weltgeschichtliche Ausnahme', in *Europas Aufstieg: Eine Spurensuche im späten Mittelalter*, ed. by Thomas Ertl (Vienna: Mandelbaum, 2013), pp. 17–33

Reitemeier, Arndt, *Außenpolitik im Spätmittelalter. Die diplomatischen Beziehungen zwischen dem Reich und England 1377–1422*, Veröffentlichungen des Deutschen Historischen Instituts London, 45 (Paderborn: Ferdinand Schöningh, 1999)

Rexroth, Frank, 'Pierre Dubois und das Projekt einer universalen Heilig-Land-Stiftung', in *Gestiftete Zukunft im mittelalterlichen Europa. Festschrift für Michael Borgolte zum 60. Geburtstag*, ed. by Wolfgang Huschner (Berlin: Akademie-Verlag, 2008), pp. 309–31

Rollo-Koster, Joëlle, and Thomas M. Izbicki, ed., *A Companion to the Great Western Schism (1378–1417)*, Brill's Companions to the Christian Tradition, 17 (Leiden: Brill, 2009)

Scales, Len, *The Shaping of German Identity: Authority and Crisis, 1245–1414* (Cambridge: Cambridge University Press, 2012)

——, 'Purposeful Pasts: Godfrey of Viterbo and Later Medieval Imperialist Thought', in *Godfrey of Viterbo and his Readers: Imperial Tradition and Universal History in Late Medieval Europe*, ed. by Thomas Foerster (Farnham: Ashgate, 2015), pp. 119–44

Schmidt, Hans-Joachim, *Kirche, Staat, Nation. Raumgliederung der Kirche im mittelalterlichen Europa*, Forschungen zur mittelalterlichen Geschichte, 37 (Weimar: Böhlau, 1999)

Schmieder, Felicitas, *Europa und die Fremden. Die Mongolen im Urteil des Abendlandes vom 13. bis in das 15. Jahrhundert*, Beiträge zur Geschichte und Quellenkunde des Mittelalters, 16 (Sigmaringen: Jan Thorbecke, 1994)

——, '*Cum hora undecima*: The Incorporation of Asia into the Orbis Christianus', in *Christianizing Peoples and Converting Individuals*, ed. by Guyda Armstrong and Ian N. Wood, International Medieval Research, 7 (Turnhout: Brepols, 2000), pp. 259–65

——, 'Nomaden zwischen Asien, Europa und dem Mittleren Osten', in *Weltdeutungen und Weltreligionen, 600 bis 1500*, ed. by Johannes Fried and Ernst-Dieter Hehl, WBG Weltgeschichte, 3 (Darmstadt: Wissenschaftliche Buchgesellschaft, 2010), pp. 179–202

Schneider, Reinhard, 'Mittelalterliche Verträge auf Brücken und Flüssen (und zur Problematik von Grenzgewässern)', *Archiv für Diplomatik*, 23 (1977), 1–24

Schneidmüller, Bernd, 'Konsensuale Herrschaft. Ein Essay über Formen und Konzepte politischer Ordnung im Mittelalter', in *Reich, Regionen und Europa in Mittelalter und Neuzeit. Festschrift für Peter Moraw*, ed. by Paul-Joachim Heinig, Sigrid Jahns, Hans-Joachim Schmidt, Rainer Christoph Schwinges, and Sabine Wefers, Historische Forschungen, 67 (Berlin: Duncker & Humblot, 2000), pp. 53–87

——, 'Kaiser sein im spätmittelalterlichen Europa. Spielregeln zwischen Weltherrschaft und Gewöhnlichkeit', in *Spielregeln der Mächtigen. Mittelalterliche Politik zwischen Gewohnheit und Konvention*, ed. by Claudia Garnier and Hermann Kamp (Darmstadt: Wissenschaftliche Buchgesellschaft, 2010), pp. 265–90

——, *Grenzerfahrung und monarchische Ordnung. Europa 1200–1500* (Munich: Beck, 2011)

——, 'Rule by Consensus: Forms and Concepts of Political Order in the European Middle Ages', *The Medieval History Journal*, 16,2 (2014), 449–71

——, 'Verklärte Macht und verschränkte Herrschaft. Vom Charme vormoderner Andersartigkeit', in *Macht und Herrschaft transkulturell. Vormoderne Konfigurationen und Perspektiven der Forschung*, ed. by Matthias Becher, Stephan Conermann, and Linda Dohmen, Macht und Herrschaft, 1 (Göttingen: Vandenhoeck & Ruprecht, 2018), pp. 91–121

Schneidmüller, Bernd, and Stefan Weinfurter, ed., *Ordnungskonfigurationen im hohen Mittelalter*, Vorträge und Forschungen, 64 (Ostfildern: Jan Thorbecke, 2006)

Scholl, Christian, Torben R. Gebhardt, and Jan Clauß, ed., *Transcultural Approaches to the Concept of Imperial Rule in the Middle Ages* (Frankfurt: Peter Lang, 2017)

Schwedler, Gerald, *Herrschertreffen des Spätmittelalters: Formen, Rituale, Wirkungen*, Mittelalter-Forschungen, 21 (Ostfildern: Jan Thorbecke, 2008)

Schwinges, Rainer C., Christian Hesse, and Peter Moraw, ed., *Europa im späten Mittelalter. Politik–Gesellschaft–Kultur*, Historische Zeitschrift, Beiheft N.F., 40 (Munich: Oldenbourg, 2006)

Shatzmiller, Maya, ed., *Crusaders and Muslims in Twelfth-Century Syria*, The Medieval Mediterranean, 1 (Leiden: Brill, 1993)

Sieber-Lehmann, Claudius, *Papst und Kaiser als Zwillinge? Ein anderer Blick auf die Universalgewalten im Investiturstreit*, Papsttum im mittelalterlichen Europa, 4 (Cologne: Böhlau, 2015)

Signori, Gabriela, and Birgit Studt, ed., *Das Konstanzer Konzil als europäisches Ereignis. Begegnungen, Medien und Rituale*, Vorträge und Forschungen, 79 (Ostfildern: Jan Thorbecke, 2014)

Šmahel, František, 'Antoine Marini de Grenoble et son Mémorandum sur la nécessité d'une alliance anti-turque', in *La Noblesse et la Croisade à la fin du Moyen Âge. France, Bourgogne, Bohême*, ed. by Martin Nejedlý and Jaroslav Svátek (Toulouse: Presses universitaires du Midi, 2015), pp. 205–31

Spieß, Karl-Heinz, 'Rangdenken und Rangstreit im Mittelalter', in *Zeremoniell und Raum*, ed. by Werner Paravicini, Residenzenforschung, 6 (Sigmaringen: Jan Thorbecke, 1997), pp. 39–61

——, 'Rangdenken und Rangstreit. Kurfürsten und Fürsten im spätmittelalterlichen Reich', in *(Un)Gleiche Kurfürsten? Die Pfalzgrafen bei Rhein und die Herzöge von Sachsen im späten Mittelalter (1356–1547)*, ed. by Jens Klingner and Benjamin Müsegades, Heidelberger Veröffentlichungen zur Landesgeschichte und Landeskunde, 19 (Heidelberg: Winter, 2017), pp. 109–22

Studer, Roman, *The Great Divergence Reconsidered: Europe, India, and the Rise to Global Economic Power* (New York: Cambridge University Press, 2015)

Sumption, Jonathan, *The Hundred Years War*, 4 vols (*I: Trial by Battle*, 1999; *II: Trial by Fire*, 2001; *III: Divided Houses*, 2012; *IV: Cursed Kings*, 2015) (London: Faber & Faber, 1999–2015)

Takayama, Hiroshi, 'Frederick II's Crusade: An Example of Christian–Muslim Diplomacy', *Mediterranean Historical Review*, 25,2 (2010), 169–85

Topkaya, Yiğit, *Augen-Blicke sichtbarer Gewalt? Eine Geschichte des 'Türken' in medientheoretischer Perspektive (1453–1529)* (Paderborn: Fink, 2015)

Tremml-Werner, Birgit, and Eberhard Crailsheim, ed., *Audienzen und Allianzen. Interkulturelle Diplomatie in Asien und Europa vom 8. bis zum 18. Jahrhundert*, Expansion, Interaktion, Akkulturation. Globalhistorische Skizzen, 26 (Vienna: Mandelbaum, 2015)

van Eickels, Klaus, *Vom inszenierten Konsens zum systematisierten Konflikt. Die englisch-französischen Beziehungen und ihre Wahrnehmung an der Wende vom Hoch- zum Spätmittelalter*, Mittelalter-Forschungen, 10 (Stuttgart: Jan Thorbecke, 2002)

Vaněček, Václav, *The Universal Peace Organization of King George of Bohemia: A 15th Century Plan for World Peace, 1462/1464* (Prague: Czechoslovak Academy of Sciences, 1964)

Villalon, L. J. Andrew, and Donald J. Kagay, ed., *The Hundred Years War*, 3 vols, History of Warfare, 25, 51, 85 (*I: A Wider Focus*, 2005; *II: Different Vistas*, 2008; *III: Further Considerations*, 2013) (Leiden: Brill, 2005–13)

von Moos, Peter, 'Das Öffentliche und das Private im Mittelalter. Für einen kontrollierten Anachronismus', in *Das Öffentliche und Private in der Vormoderne*, ed. by Gert Melville and Peter von Moos, Norm und Struktur, 10 (Vienna: Böhlau, 1998), pp. 3–83

von Padberg, Lutz, *Die Christianisierung Europas im Mittelalter*, Universal-Bibliothek, 17015 (Stuttgart: Reclam, 1998)

Wagner, Bettina, *Die 'Epistola presbiteri Johannis' lateinisch und deutsch. Überlieferung, Textgeschichte, Rezeption und Übertragungen im Mittelalter. Mit bisher unedierten Texten*, Münchener Texte und Untersuchungen zur deutschen Literatur des Mittelalters, 115 (Tübingen: Niemeyer, 2000)

Walther, Helmut G., 'Konziliarismus als politische Theorie? Konzilsvorstellungen im 15. Jahrhundert zwischen Notlösungen und Kirchenmodellen', in *Die Konzilien von Pisa (1409), Konstanz (1414–1418) und Basel (1431–1449). Institution und Personen*, ed. by Heribert Müller and Johannes Helmrath, Vorträge und Forschungen, 67 (Ostfildern: Jan Thorbecke, 2007), pp. 31–60

Watts, John, *The Making of Polities: Europe, 1300–1500*, Cambridge Medieval Textbooks (Cambridge: Cambridge University Press, 2009)

Wetzstein, Thomas, 'Die Überwältigung des Raumes. Studien zur Kommunikationsgeschichte des europäischen Hochmittelalters' (unpublished habilitation thesis, Ruprecht-Karls Universität Heidelberg, 2009)

Wiedemann, Benedict G. E., 'Papal Overlordship and *protectio* of the King, c. 1000–1300' (London, doctoral thesis, 2017), <https://discovery.ucl.ac.uk/10038385/1/Thesis%20Final.pdf> [accessed 21 June 2021]

——, 'Super gentes et regna: Papal "Empire" in the Later Eleventh and Twelfth Centuries', *Studies in Church History*, 54 (The Church and Empire) (2018), 109–22

Willershausen, Andreas, *Die Päpste von Avignon und der Hundertjährige Krieg. Spätmittelalterliche Diplomatie und kuriale Verhandlungsnormen (1337–1378)* (Berlin: De Gruyter, 2014)

Woodacre, Elena, Lucinda H. S. Dean, Chris Jones, Zita Rohr, and Russell Martin, ed., *The Routledge History of Monarchy* (Abingdon: Routledge, 2019)

DONATELLA GUIDA

Imperial Geography and Fatherly Benevolence

The Chinese World Order and the Construction of its Margins

Introduction

Chinese civilization is often described as monolithic and immutable, despite its long imperial history that started in 221 BCE with the Qin unification and continued for two thousand years until its final collapse in 1911.[1] Actually, as the word 'unification' already suggests, since its beginning it encompassed several populations with different cultures who lived from the third millennium BCE onwards, not only in the Yellow River area, which tradition defines as the cradle of Chinese civilization, but also around the Yangzi River in the south and in the western regions of today's Shaanxi and Sichuan.

Centuries before the unification of the Empire, the first groups of settlers are identified in literary sources as well as in archaeological findings with a form of collective organization that designated itself as the 'Shang Yin' dynasty, whose representatives were said to be direct descendants of the gods.[2] Their technical skills, especially in the creation of bronze artefacts, and their writing system, abundantly preserved on animal bones that were used for divination, gave them clear advantages over their neighbours, whom they fought on several occasions, until they were themselves badly defeated around 1045 BCE by the Western power of Zhou.[3] At this point, the identity of the *Huaxia* 華夏 peoples (i.e. the Chinese in the modern understanding) slowly started to become more defined, not least in the course of confrontations with nearby 'alien' tribes whose habits and languages were different. These

1 For a general overview of Chinese history see Rossabi, *A History of China*, and Vogelsang, *Geschichte Chinas*.

2 For further reading on the Shang Yin, see Keightley, *Sources of Shang History*.

3 Loewe and Shaughnessy ed., *The Cambridge History of Ancient China*, p. 233.

Donatella Guida (dguida@unior.it), Department of Asian, African, and Mediterranean Studies, Università degli Studi di Napoli 'L'Orientale', Italy

Order into Action: How Large-Scale Concepts of World-Order determine Practices in the Premodern World, ed. by Klaus Oschema and Christoph Mauntel, CURSOR 40 (Turnhout: Brepols, 2022), pp. 185–208
BREPOLS PUBLISHERS 10.1484/M.CURSOR-EB.5.123848

alien tribes thus contributed greatly to determine more clearly what was to be considered 'Chinese' and what was not. The need to unite and amalgamate at least three ethnic groups — Shang, the people they subjugated, and Zhou — through a set of common values and beliefs led the new government to worship Heaven (*tian* 天) as the highest authority, which effectively replaced the Shang pantheon. Henceforth, the king received the title 'Son of Heaven' and moral virtue became the criterion that allowed the identification of a true sovereign, whose power could be revoked as soon as his behaviour went against public welfare.[4]

The origin of the Chinese world order thus dates back to the time of the Zhou dynasty, when King Wu's brother, the Duke of Zhou (Zhou gong 周公), who was to become the unsurpassed paragon of virtue of Confucian tradition,[5] developed the theory of the 'Mandate of Heaven' (*tianming* 天命) to substantiate and support his family's claim to the Shang throne:[6] in one of the main sources for this period, the *Book of Documents* (*Shangshu* 尚書, *c.* eighth to third century BCE),[7] Wu (whose name means 'martial') is represented as an extremely virtuous and loyal person. According to this text, he was not so much keen on forceful conquest, but rather acted simply as an instrument in the hands of the heavenly will. Seen from this perspective, Wu appears less as an aggressor or an enemy, who acts violently in order to take

4 Loewe and Shaughnessy ed., *The Cambridge History of Ancient China*, p. 292; Pines, 'Changing Views of *tianxia* in Pre-imperial Discourse', pp. 101–02.

5 Zhou Dan, known also as Zhou Gong, completed the consolidation of his family rule by leading the army to conquer the eastern territories and administered the Zhou state after his brother's death in the name of the latter's son, King Cheng, who was still a minor. As soon as the young king became old enough, the Duke retired peacefully, after six years of intense activity in every field of public affairs. The establishment of a 'feudal' system is credited to him, as well as the construction of an ideal capital city near modern Luoyang. He is considered to have been wise and unselfish, not least because he did not think of depriving his nephew of the throne. Through a close reading of two chapters of the *Book of Documents*, Shaughnessy, 'The Duke of Zhou's Retirement', convincingly demonstrates how this character also became the ideal model for ministers as kings' advisors, a crucial role in Confucian tradition, as the philosopher-advisor's authority is considered to be higher than the sovereign's. Confucius mentions the Duke several times in his *Analects*, e.g. 子曰:「甚矣吾衰也! 久矣吾不復夢見周公。」 (The Master said, 'Extreme is my decay. For a long time, I have not dreamed, as I used to do, that I saw the duke of Zhou'.) (*Lunyu*, I, 5) and 子曰:「如有周公之才之美, 使驕且吝, 其餘不足觀也已。」 (The Master said, 'Though a man have abilities as admirable as those of the duke of Zhou, yet if he be proud and niggardly, those other things are really not worth being looked at'.) (*Lunyu*, VIII, 11).

6 The Duke of Zhou is said to have governed the *Huaxia* realm between 1045 and 1038 BCE. This founding period of Chinese history is dealt with in depth in Loewe and Shaughnessy ed., *The Cambridge History of Ancient China*, pp. 292–351.

7 The *Shangshu* (known also as *Shujing* 書經) is a collection of speeches and orations made by rulers and ministers from mythical times to the Western Zhou dynasty. It has been enlarged and rewritten over the centuries, possibly even by Confucius himself, and its precise dating is very difficult. Some parts have been added after Qin unification, i.e. in Han times; see Yang Weisheng, 'Shangshu'.

possession of the throne, but rather as a hero, who agrees with all his heart to restore proper order and lost harmony. Through the establishment of this new vision of things, the sanctity of the sovereign, which had relied on the belief that he was a direct descendant of heaven, was overcome and replaced by an ideology of sacredness that was derived from the ruler's individual qualities and from his respect for a set of universal norms of behaviour. In fact, the king had to observe these norms just like everybody else; indeed, he was supposed to serve as an example for nobles, soldiers, and the common people alike. Since there is only one sky, the king's (and later the emperor's) dominion came to be the *tianxia* 天下, 'all that is under Heaven', as explicitly stated in the following passage:

> 益曰: 都, 帝德廣運, 乃聖乃神, 乃武乃文。皇天眷命, 奄有四海為天下君。
>
> (Yi said, 'Oh! Your virtue, O Di, is vast and incessant. It is sagely, spirit-like, awe-inspiring, and adorned with all accomplishments. Great Heaven regarded you with its favour, and bestowed on you its appointment. *Suddenly you possessed all within the four seas, and became ruler of all under heaven*'.)[8]

As has been masterfully discussed by Yuri Pines, the evolution of the term *tianxia* is illuminating: until the beginning of the Zhou dynasty, it denoted the Zhou king's dominion and bore a mainly cultural significance. It was only later, namely during the Spring and Autumn period (770–453 BCE), that it started to acquire a more outspoken political value. There are even some passages in the *Lunyu* 論語,[9] the collected sayings of Confucius handed down to posterity by his disciples, that refer to it. In Pines' words:

> The prevalence of the Way clearly refers to common cultural values that are supposed to unify All under Heaven. However, the prevalence of these values is conceived politically, as the restoration of political unity, characteristic of the Western Zhou period. All under Heaven ought to be ruled by the Son of Heaven, suggests Confucius.[10]

In historical and philosophical works from the Warring States period (453–221 BCE), the term *tianxia* became dramatically more recurrent, as conflicts between the states exposed the need for a new kind of political unity

8 *Shangshu* 尚書 (*The Book of Documents*), ed. and trans. by Legge, p. 54 ('Counsels of the Great Yu'), emphasis added.

9 *Lunyu*, 'Ji shi' 季氏 XVI, 2. 天下有道, 則禮樂征伐自天子出; 天下無道, 則禮樂征伐自諸侯出。自諸侯出, 蓋十世希不失矣; 自大夫出, 五世希不失矣; 陪臣執國命, 三世希不失矣。(When the Way prevails under Heaven, rites, music, and punitive expedition are issued by the Son of Heaven; when there is no Way under Heaven, rites, music, and punitive expedition are issued by the overlords. If they are issued by the overlords, few [states] will not be lost within ten generations; if they are issued by the nobles, few will not be lost within five generations; when the retainers hold the destiny of the state, few will not be lost within three generations [trans. by Pines, *Envisioning Eternal Empire*, p. 28].)

10 Pines, 'Changing Views of *tianxia* in Pre-imperial Discourse', p. 104.

and stability. Zhou cultural tradition was beginning to fade — as is, for example, attested by burial rites — due to the increasing importance of the peripheral cultures of Qin and Chu, in order to mention just the most important ones. 'All under Heaven' was meant to be a wider and more structured construct, which would eventually be defined by the incredibly rich writings of political thinkers that backed the foundation of the first unified empire by Qin Shi Huangdi in 221 BCE.[11]

As a consequence, according to the established order and ideology, no major or fundamental differences were to be made between the inner territory, i.e. China proper, and outer countries, which ideally owed the same respect to the universal monarch. As the *Liji* 禮記 (*The Record of Rites*) puts it 天子不言出 (i.e. the Son of Heaven should not be spoken of as 'going out [of his state]').[12] This is the basic concept that lies behind China's self-designation as the 'Middle Kingdom', because it perceives itself as being located in the centre of the inhabited world. In fact, the role of the centre was considered to be so important that the Chinese tradition knew of five cardinal points, not four, since the model explicitly included the centre.[13] The central territory was mostly thought to be surrounded by the Four Seas, which constituted the limits of the world, similarly to the Pillars of Hercules in the Greco-Roman tradition. The world was thus imagined as being square, while the Heaven above was round; ships that ventured to the edge of the ocean were thought to run the risk of falling into a sort of maelstrom, or vortex called *weilü* 尾閭, a hole where all the waters converged and that marked the edge of the human world (not unlike the experience Ulysses was said to have made in the *Divina Commedia*).[14] Beyond this border was the underworld, it was imagined. In these regions, the unknown merges into the realm of fear and the unconscious, as the exotic slowly becomes imaginary.

The fundamental 'order' (*zhi* 治) of the entire world that belongs to Heaven is to be obtained and enforced through extensive use of a proper ritual (*li* 禮) that classifies each person, family, territory, and behaviour, thus showing the uninterrupted link between Heaven and Earth, Sovereign and People, Man and Nature. As a consequence, 'China' and the world are equated with each other, since the basic principle of unity dominates Chinese history and

---

11 For a critical reconstruction of this fascinating process, see Yuri Pines' seminal works: Pines, *Envisioning Eternal Empire*; Pines, *The Everlasting Empire*.

12 *Liji*, ed. and trans. by Legge, p. 113. *The Record of Rites* is a collection of norms with long descriptions of ritual matters, written around the Warring states period (fifth century BCE).

13 For a comparison of Chinese, Latin-Christian, and Arab-Islamic cartographic ideas, see Mauntel, Oschema, Ducène, and Hofmann, 'Mapping Continents'.

14 Dante Alighieri, *La Divina Commedia. Inferno*, XXVI, 90–142, pp. 282–85. Dante reports a medieval legend about the last adventure of the Homeric hero: he is said to have left Circe with some companions to continue his experiences of the known world, but, having gone further than any human being, the party arrived in sight of Purgatory to be immediately caught in a powerful whirlpool and submerged by the sea.

philosophy, leading to a profound obsession against disorder (*luan* 亂) as opposed to proper conduct in both the inner and the outer sphere, i.e. man's inner world and human society.

In the previously mentioned *Book of Documents*, more precisely in the chapter called *The Tribute of Yu* (*Yu gong pian* 禹貢篇) the structure of the territory that constitutes the physical world is described in a quite precise way:

> 五百里甸服 [...] 五百里侯服: 百里采, 二百里男邦, 三百里諸侯。五百里綏服: 三百里揆文教, 二百里奮武衛。五百里要服: 三百里夷, 二百里蔡。五百里荒服: 三百里蠻, 二百里流。
>
> (Five hundred *li*[15] constituted the Domain of the Sovereign. [...] Five hundred *li* (beyond) constituted the Domain of the Nobles. The first hundred *li* was occupied by the cities and lands of the (sovereign's) high ministers and great officers; the second, by the principalities of the barons; and the (other) three hundred, by the various other princes. Five hundred *li* (still beyond) formed the Peace-securing Domain. In the first three hundred, they cultivated the lessons of learning and moral duties; in the other two, they showed the energies of war and defence. Five hundred *li* (remoter still) formed the Domain of Restraint. The (first) three hundred were occupied by the tribes of the Yi; the (other) two hundred, by criminals undergoing the lesser banishment. Five hundred *li* (the most remote) constituted the Wild Domain. The (first) three hundred were occupied by the tribes of the Man; the (other) two hundred, by criminals undergoing the greater banishment.)[16]

This text defines an ideal concentric structure (see Figure 7.1) with the Chinese sovereign at its centre and specific categories of people at a proper distance, which is inversely proportional to their respective virtue: the more uncultivated and wild they are, the further away they are to be relegated.[17] The structure is, of course, somewhat elastic and mobile, because anyone can improve, foreign 'barbarians' included, as we shall see.

The quoted excerpt from the *Book of Documents* actually deals with a semi-mythological figure, namely 'Yu the Great', who allegedly lived roughly a thousand years before the establishment of the Zhou dynasty. The fact that this pattern is said to have been established so early, gives us a clear idea of how a tradition needed to be backdated in order to meet present needs,

15 A *li* 里 is a unit of length, equal to approximately half a kilometre.

16 *Shangshu* 尚書 (*The Book of Documents*), ed. and trans. by Legge, pp. 142–47 (*The Tribute of Yu*).

17 Lewis, *The Construction of Space in Early China*, argues convincingly that the relation between the human body, family, and household, but also village, region, and the world, was equally imagined as a concentric structure; for the latter dimension, see esp. pp. 245–302 (chap. 5). *The Tribute of Yu* is one of earliest and fundamental sources that defined this concept, together with the *Shanhai Jing* 山海經 (*Classic of Mountains and Seas*).

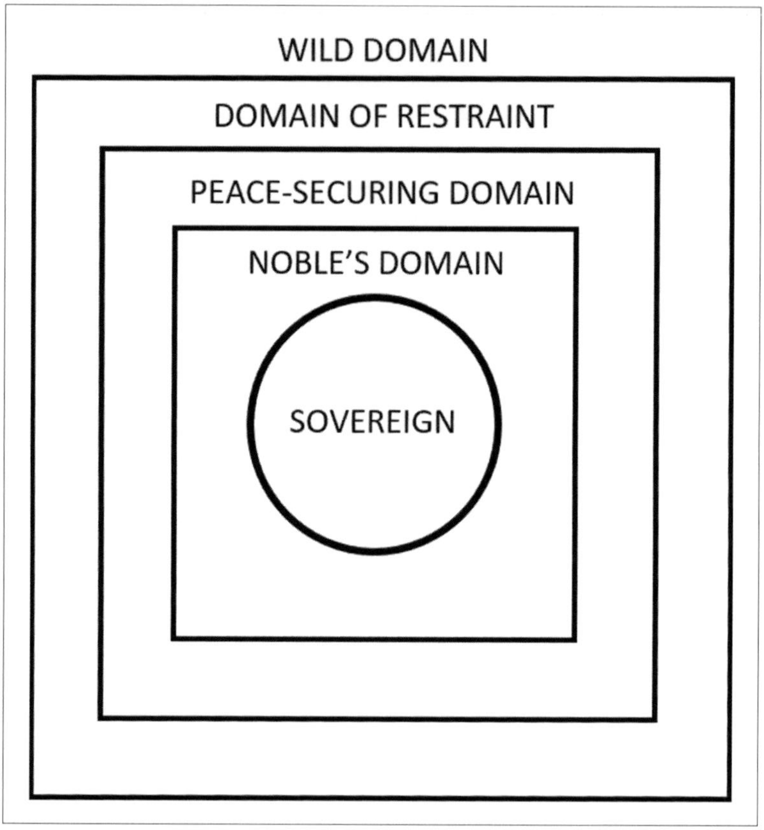

FIGURE 7.1. The concentric structure of the world as described by *The Tribute of Yu*. Drawing by the author.

mostly in the sense of conveying additional legitimacy. Besides, the *Book of Documents*, written several centuries after the events it relates (this chapter was actually redacted between the Warring States and Qin-Han periods, i.e. from the fifth to the second century BCE) and altered several times until the Han dynasty (206 BCE–220 CE), attests to an ideological vision (fully imperial by then), which tends to read the events of the past in an ethical perspective in order to strengthen the principles of Confucian philosophy.

Geography and Visual Representations

Although accurate maps of the territory had been produced and disseminated with the help of new printing techniques since the Song dynasty (960–1279 CE),[18] Chinese scholars concurrently continued to reproduce other kinds of visual representations that served political and ideological goals. Actually, until the nineteenth century cartographers were literati rather than skilful technicians.[19] Their representations were usually flat and no attention was given to factual accuracy — not so much because these literati lacked appropriate skills or knowledge, but rather because they preferred to stick to a model of the past that could be traced all the way back to *The Tribute of Yu*. As can be seen in the map below (Figure 7.2), the Chinese mainland was often represented as a square that was surrounded by the Four Seas, while foreign countries were depicted either as islands or as distant shores beyond this mainland.

Another characteristic feature of this kind of map consists in the casual combination of real and imaginary lands: in the east, for example, Japan lies next to the 'island of the Dwarfs' (which is actually an alternative, derogatory name for the same country), while on the opposite side the 'Country of Western Women' is not far from the 'Reign of the Great Qin', the name under which the Roman Empire was known in earlier sources. Even further beyond, the 'Country of Gentlemen' lies north of the 'Kingdom of the Pierced Hearts'; there is also the 'Country of the Horse Hooves' and the 'Kingdom of Pigmies'. All these names were handed down from the *Shanhai Jing* 山海經 (*The Classic of Mountains and Seas*)[20] and the *Bowuzhi* 博物志 (*Vast Records about Different Topics*),[21] two well-known ancient sources of mythical geography that date between the third century BCE and the third century CE. Many centuries later, Chinese scholars still used the terms that figured in these texts, even after the massive production of maps and geographical books by the Jesuits between the end of the sixteenth century and Qing times, because the new visual representations with meridians and parallels clashed with the traditional world image, since it made China look much smaller in comparison with the rest of the world (Figure 7.3). As Richard J. Smith puts it:

18 De Weerdt, 'Maps and Memory', p. 152, retraces the first map that includes both Chinese and non-Chinese peoples (*Huayi tu*, now lost) back to Jia Dan in 801, during the reign of Emperor Dezong of the Tang dynasty. However, it was only after 1100 that the drawing of maps assumed a political meaning in the sense of establishing the memory of past glory and of providing a stimulus to political action against the overwhelming presence of foreign powers. It is hardly surprising that maps consciously distorted 'real' spatial relations in this case.

19 Smith, *Mapping China and Managing the World*, p. 52.

20 There are several translations of this early source, see e.g. *Shanhai Jing* 山海經 (*The Classic of Mountains and Seas*), ed. and trans. by Birrell.

21 The *Bowuzhi* is a collection of short stories written by Zhang Hua 張華 in the third century CE, see Bai Huawen, 'Bowuzhi 博物志'.

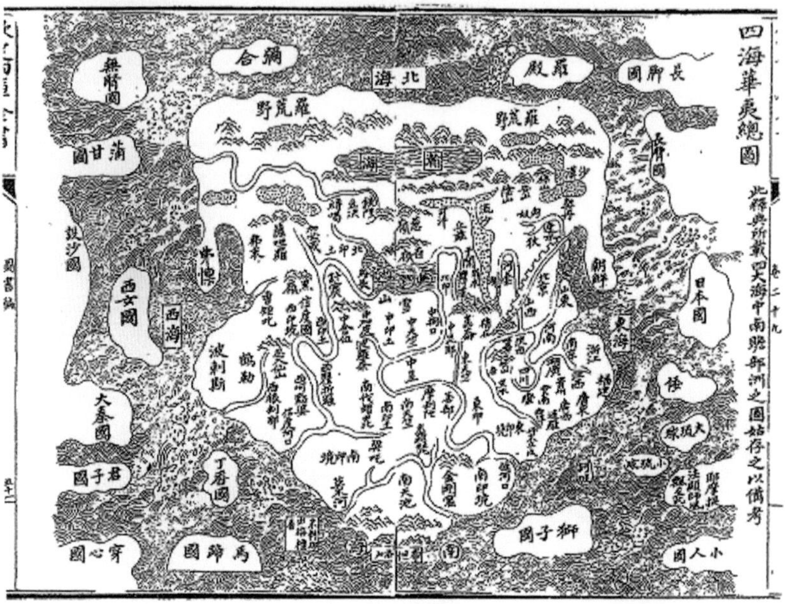

FIGURE 7.2. *Sihai HuaYi Zongtu* 四海華夷總圖 (*General Map of Chinese and Barbarian Lands within the Four Seas*), undated, from Zhang Huang 章潢, *Tushu bian* 圖書編 (1613), *juan* 29, in *Siku Quanshu*.

> It is not surprising, then, to find that a number of Chinese scholars bitterly attacked the Jesuits for misrepresenting the world and China's place in it. According to one Ming scholar, Wei Jun, Ricci's map not only contained 'fabulous and mysterious' information that could not be verified, but in locating China to the west of center and inclined to the north, it dislodged the 'Central Kingdom' from its rightful position at 'the center of the world'.[22]

It is worth noting that, as stated before, both representations or maps (in Chinese *tu* 圖) are contained in the same source, the *Tushu bian* (*Compendium of Illustrations and Writings*, 1613),[23] a cosmological treatise that is included in the philosophy section (*zi* 子) of the great late imperial collection *Siku quanshu* 四庫全書 (*Complete Books of the Four Storehouses*, 1781). Figure 7.4, also from the *Tushu bian*, further clarifies the centrality of the Chinese territories: on this map, the borders are well defined, again in the shape of a square, and some placenames are written in neat rectangles. Exterior territories, on the other hand, appear as if they were located in an indefinite space, represented only by their names and thus remaining pure toponyms (even though one has to

22 Smith, *Mapping China and Managing the World*, p. 65; see also Ch'en, 'Matteo Ricci's Contribution'.

23 Zhang Huang 章潢, *Tushu bian* 圖書編 (1613), in *Siku Quanshu*.

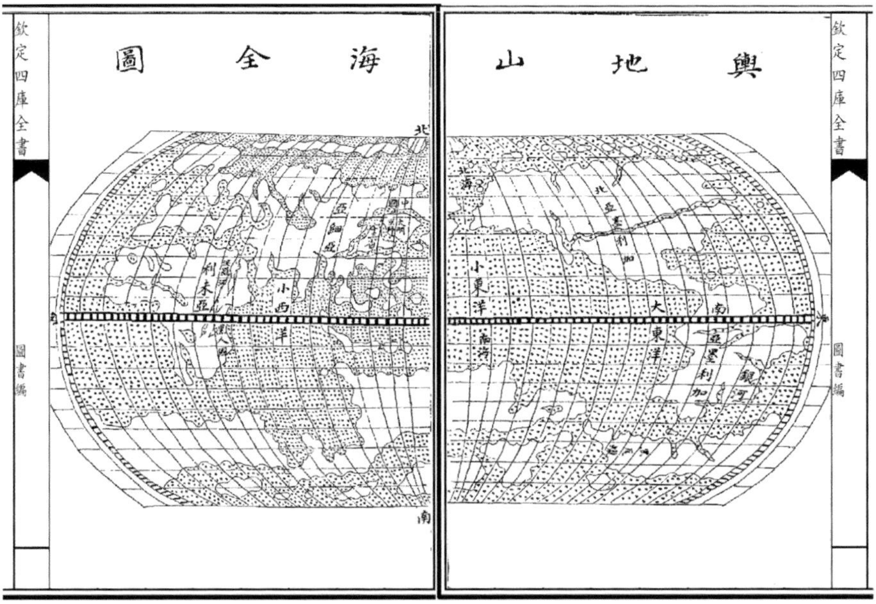

FIGURE 7.3. *Yudi Shanhai quantu* 輿地山海全圖 (*Complete Map of Mountains and Seas*), from Zhang Huang 章潢, *Tushu bian* 圖書編 (1613), *juan* 29, in *Siku Quanshu*.

take into account that in the Chinese tradition the written word is considered to be of higher value than a figurative representation). The makers of this map apparently felt that no indication of borders was needed, choosing to give only some information about the respective countries' position in the Chinese world order — mainly focusing on the question whether they could be considered to be tributary countries or not.

Among the Chinese emperor's duties was the obligation to spread civilization and virtue to all mankind, and in this perspective the 'foreign' powers were requested to acknowledge the supremacy of China through rituals that resemble those performed by the aristocrats who had been enfeoffed by the Zhou king. In principle, the whole world was perceived to belong to the Chinese emperor and he graciously entrusted his domain to foreign kings — exactly as the king had delegated his powers to nobles who were put in charge of peripheral areas in Zhou times.

Foreign princes expressed their acceptance of this proposition in two 'symbolic' ways: by presenting ritual tribute (*gong* 貢, or *chaogong* 朝貢) of typical products of their territory (*fangwu* 方物) to the emperor and by performing the *koutou* 叩頭 (kneeling three times, each time bowing their head to the ground three times). In turn, they received gifts, such as different kinds of precious silks and — more importantly — the Chinese calendar as well as an umbrella, which was considered to be a symbol of sovereignty, transmitted to them by the emperor. The calendar had to be adopted by

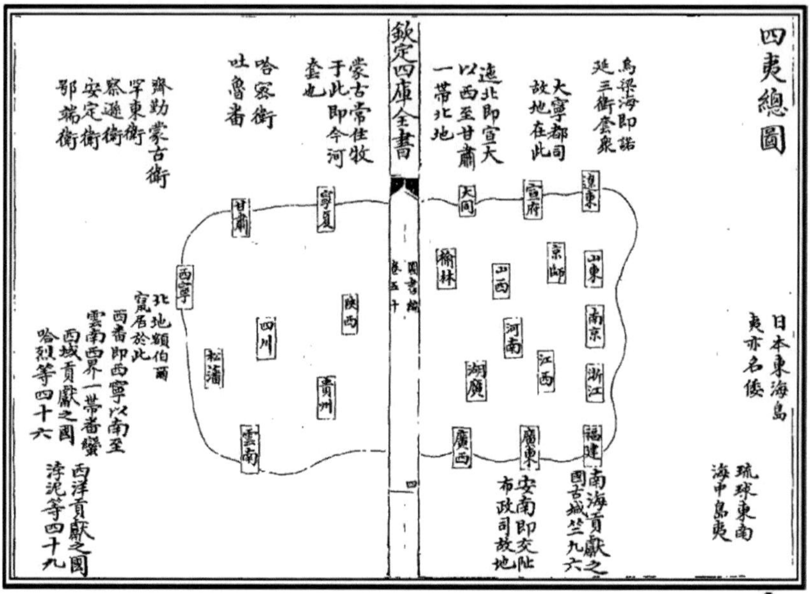

FIGURE 7.4. *Siyi zongtu* 四夷總圖 (*General Map of the Four Barbarians*), from Zhang Huang 章潢, *Tushu bian* 圖書編 (1613), *juan* 50, in *Siku Quanshu*.

foreign kings in order to express their faith in the Heavenly Emperor, who magnanimously shared with his distant sons his superior knowledge of the universe. At least in the official documents, the years had to be named and numbered according to the Chinese system, or else foreign documents were to be rejected and delegations sent back with disfavour and even anger. According to its merit, each country was entitled to a certain number of visits to the Court, ranging from three times a year to once every five years.[24] Complex regulations prescribed the number of people for each delegation as well as the gifts that had to be bestowed upon each member and which varied according to the individuals' rank. If the foreign king proved to be respectful, he would be granted additional benefits and moved up the ladder of virtue, thereby getting closer to the empire.

24 Very distant countries were never asked to officially visit the court more than once for each reign, i.e. each individual emperor's rule, see e.g. *Ming Taizu shilu*, pp. 1696–97 (chap. 100): 'The Grand Master for Thorough Counsel Ruan Ruojin and others, who had been sent by Chen Tuan of Annam, came to enquire of the Court the required frequency of tribute. The Emperor ordered the assembled ministers to deliberate and they jointly advised: "In ancient times, the various marquis sent a minor embassy to the Son of Heaven every year and a major embassy once every three years. However, the *fan* states and distant countries only needed to come to Court once every reign (世見而已)".' See also *Ming Huidian*, pp. 1–4 (chap. 76).

This ritual, which started to be performed by some foreign representatives during the Han dynasty in the second century BCE (although it was by no means the only way of dealing with what we would call international relations in Han times)[25] and reached its apex in Ming times (1368–1644), was obviously very important, not least because of its impact on domestic policy: tributary products that arrived from all corners of the world were considered to be evidence of the emperor's possession of the Mandate of Heaven, and the variety of exotic animals and goods clearly demonstrated how far the mighty emperor's aura reached. A new emperor — or better still, the founder of a new dynasty — unfailingly used to send messengers to neighbouring countries in order to inform them about his accession to the Chinese throne and to solicit their visit and homage. For instance, when the founder of the Ming dynasty, Zhu Yuanzhang 朱元璋, ascended the throne in 1368, after a century of Mongol domination, he sent several letters to Korea, Japan, Vietnam, Sri Vijaya, Java, and other countries, to inform their rulers about his re-establishment of a dutiful Chinese sovereignty and his firm will to follow the way of the ancient tradition, as in the following passages:

> 朕聞順天者昌, 逆天者亡。此古今不易之定理也。粵自古昔帝王居中國而治四夷。
>
> > (It is my belief that those who are obedient to heaven prosper, while the disobedient perish. This has been an immutable principle from ancient times. From antiquity, the emperor, enthroned in China, has ruled over foreign peoples of all the four directions.)[26]
>
> 朕之使已在途矣。朕之遣使, 正欲報王知之。曩者, 我中國為胡人竊據, 百年遂使夷狄布滿四方, 廢我中國之彝倫。 朕是以起兵討之垂, 二十年芟夷既平。 朕主中國天下, 方安恐四夷未知故遣使以報諸國。 [...]
>
> > (My ambassadors are already on their way. I sent them because I want to inform the king of this: in the past, our kingdom was occupied by the northern foreigners for a hundred years; they were able to extend their rule in all directions, destroying the cardinal relationships of our Middle Kingdom. Therefore, I have taken up arms to fight them and, after twenty years, I have managed to exterminate the foreigners. Now everything is peaceful, and I rule the Chinese world. Fearing that the foreign kingdoms were not aware of this, I sent ambassadors to inform everyone.)[27]

---

25 For an informative and thought-provoking discussion concerning foreign relations and tribute in Han times, see Selbitschka, 'Early Chinese Diplomacy', which includes a very useful summary of the most important publications on the subject.

26 *Ming Taizu shilu*, p. 987 (chap. 50: letter to the king of Japan).

27 *Ming Taizu shilu*, p. 783 (chap. 39: letter to Champa, i.e. Southern Vietnam).

In order to enhance the legitimation of his new dynasty, Zhu emphasized native traditions and the ethnic difference between the previous dynasty of Mongol origin and his government: 北逐胡君，肅清華夏，復我中國之舊疆。(The foreign lords have been banished to the north, the *huaxia* territory has been cleaned up and I restored the old territory of China).[28]

Therefore, it is not surprising that the ancient sources for rituals, like the previously mentioned *Liji*, divide even foreign peoples outside the boundaries of the Chinese realm into specific categories according to both their geographical location and the intensity of their relationship with the empire. These peoples are identified with collective terms that are sometimes slightly derogatory, such as *Di* 狄 (the 'northern barbarians', with the 'dog'-radical), *Rong* 戎 in the West, *Man* 蠻 (with the 'insect'- or 'worm'-radical) in the South and *Yi* 夷 in the East,[29] and have nothing to do with their real names, i.e. the designations they used for themselves. In fact, these terms could even apply to different peoples, as the Chinese empire expanded in all four directions: *Man*, for instance, was also used to refer to Yunnan tribes during the Tang period (618–907),[30] while its use was limited to Southeast Asia in Ming times, because Yunnan had become a southern province of the empire in the meantime. The model was thus clearly adjusted to reality. At the same time, it represented a carefully ordered universe, which had the emperor at its centre and on its hierarchical top. In the official sources, the 'satellite countries' were in fact arranged in a rigid hierarchical system that consisted of circles or concentric bands, which surrounded the Middle Kingdom in a series of layers: the first one was Korea, followed by Vietnam and by Japan (that disappeared in war times), because these were the countries that could proudly claim to have the longest history of fruitful relations with China and to have adopted its language and culture much more deeply than any other.[31]

Southeast Asia in Late Chinese Imperial Sources

Being a pacific territory, devoid of any particular strategic value or concern — whereas the northern and western regions, on the contrary, were always troubled by the attacks of nomadic peoples — Southeast Asia as described in Chinese sources provides an interesting case study for setting out the complex dynamics of the diplomatic relations as outlined above.[32] Several episodes concerning Southeast Asian countries may be taken as illuminating examples of imperial rhetoric and practices.

---

28 *Ming Taizu shilu*, p. 750 (chap. 37: letter to Korea). For a discussion about ethnicity and legitimation in early Ming discourse, see Guida, 'Ming Taizu on the Yuan dynasty'.

29 *Liji*, ed. and trans. by Legge, p. 111.

30 *Xin Tangshu*, pp. 6267–96 (chap. 222).

31 See e.g. the relevant section in the *Ming Shi*, comp. by Zhang Tingyu and others, pp. 8279–627 (chaps 320–32).

32 For a detailed study, see Guida, *Nei Mari del Sud*.

To begin with, the tomb of a Borneo king, discovered in 1958 near Nanjing and dating back to 1408, provides insights into the close ties between China and the tributaries that pledged to go to the capital to pay tribute and to present their 'gifts' in the kinds and quantities prescribed by the code. The funeral monument bears a long inscription that narrates the events, which took place in the sixth year of the Yongle Emperor [1408]. According to the inscription, King Ma-na-re-jia-na of Borneo[33] arrived in the capital Nanjing at the head of a delegation of 150 people, in order to offer his tribute visit. Grateful for the welcome and hospitality received, he allegedly declared:

> 天以覆我, 地以載我, 天子以乂寧我。我長我幼, 處有安居, 食有和味, 衣有宜服, 利用備器, 以資其生；強不敢凌弱, 眾不敢欺寡, 非天子孰使之然也?
>
> (The Heaven covers me, the Earth sustains me, the Son of Heaven gives me peace. In my country the big and the small have good food to eat, beautiful clothes to wear, the strong does not dare to insult the weak, people do not dare to deceive widows; without the Son of Heaven, how could it be so?)[34]

After a banquet, however, the king suddenly fell ill. Shortly before dying, he called his wife and eldest son, telling them that he would die without regrets because he had been so fortunate as to see the great light of the emperor. In addition, said the king, a proper burial in China would surely be granted to him. 'I will not be treated like a foreign ghost!' (*yigui* 夷鬼), he exclaimed, adding: 'I want you to swear that the benevolence of the Son of Heaven will never be forgotten, for ever and ever'.

The satisfaction and pride of being part of such an important cultural unity accompanies the king even on his deathbed (at least according to this official narrative): he knows that the imperial ideology ensures inalienable privileges, while excluding all those who reject it. The latter live in the darkness of ignorance and they will be relegated to this place outside of the ideal boundaries of the empire for as long as they continue to reject true civilization. The official history of the Ming duly records this episode, listing all the lavish gifts that were given by the emperor to his rightful subjects. The text mentions the emperor's deep grief and the three days of mourning that were ordered following the king of Borneo's death. After the proper ceremonies and burial with a 'spirit way' (*shendao* 神道)[35] in stone, just as his rank deserved, King Ma-na-re-jia-na's son, the Crown prince,

---

33 Boni 浡泥 probably refers to the Brunei region; see Chen Jiarong, Xie Fang and Lu Junling ed., *Gudai nanhai diming huishi*, p. 672.

34 The full text of the stele is edited in Ji Shijia, 'Boniguo wang mu he Boniguo zhu wenti yanjiu', pp. 54–56. Unfortunately, there is no evidence that the reported statements were actually pronounced by the king of Boni, as no Bornean sources of the same period survived.

35 A 'spirit way' is a series of stone statues, usually set in couples, that ornament the road leading to an emperor's or an official's tomb; see Sullivan, *The Arts of China*, p. 246.

was immediately recognized as the new king by the Chinese emperor, from whom all legitimacy emanated.[36]

In the 'Champa' chapter of the *Ming History*, we find the following interesting episode:

> 三年 遣使往祀其山川, 尋頒科舉詔於其國。初, 安南與占城構兵, 天子遣使諭解, 而安南復相侵。四年, 其王奉金葉表來 朝, 長尺餘, 廣五寸, 刻本國字。館人譯之, 其意曰:「大明皇帝登大寶位, 撫有 四海, [...], 欽蒙遣使, 以金印封為國王, 感戴忻悅, 倍萬恆情。惟是安南用兵, 侵擾疆域, 殺掠吏民。伏願皇帝垂慈, 賜以 兵器及樂器、樂人, 俾安南知我占城乃聲教所被, 輸貢之地, 庶不敢欺陵。」帝命 禮部諭之曰:「占城、安南並事朝廷, 同奉正朔, 乃擅自構兵, 毒害生靈, 既失事 君之禮, 又乖交鄰之道。已咨安南國王, 令即日罷兵。本國亦宜講信修睦, 各保疆 土。所請兵器, 於王何吝, 但兩國互構而賜占城, 是助爾相攻, 甚非撫安之義。樂 器、樂人, 語音殊異, 難以遣發。爾國有曉華言者, 其選擇以來, 當令肄習。
>
> > (In the third year of Hongwu [1370] [the Emperor] sent his ambassadors to offer sacrifices to the mountains and rivers; shortly after, he promulgated the examinations system and bestowed it on this country.
> >
> > In the beginning, Annam [i.e. northern Vietnam] was at war with Champa [southern Vietnam]. The Son of Heaven then sent ambassadors with an edict inviting them to overcome their discord, but Annam again invaded the territory of Champa. In the fourth year [1371], the king of Champa came to the Court to offer a gold-leaf document over a foot long and eight inches wide engraved with an inscription in the language of that country. The interpreters translated it; it read: 'The Emperor of the Great Ming sits on a precious seat, educating all the four seas [i.e. the world] […]. We are grateful to His Majesty for sending ambassadors with gold seals, and granting us the title of king of our country, we nurture gratitude and respect [toward the empire] and a constant feeling of joy [pervades us]. Still, Annam attacks us, invades our territory, killing our officials by surprise. Prostrating ourselves, we invoke the benevolent condescension of Your Majesty to bestow upon us gifts of weapons, musical instruments and musicians: this way, Annam will know that we were enlightened by civilization, and they will not dare any longer to oppress a tributary state of the Empire'.
> >
> > The emperor ordered the Ministry of Rites to issue an edict that read: 'Annam and Champa are two separate countries that have both received the official calendar. Nevertheless, they make war without authorization, doing violence to their people, forgetting the Emperor's precepts. They both insist on disturbing their neighbour.

36 *Ming Shi*, comp. by Zhang Tingyu and others, p. 8412 (chap. 325).

I have already sent an official communication to Annam, ordering to immediately withdraw its troops; this country has said it wants to cement peaceful relations with good faith and will, and agrees to respect each other's territory and borders. Therefore, I will not satisfy your request for weapons not because I cannot, but because, as the two countries are at war, giving weapons to Champa would contribute to mutual hostility, and prevent justice and peace. As for the musical instruments and musicians, your language is different from ours, and it would be especially hard to comply with for those who should be sent. In your country there are people who know Chinese language, do select some to come here to learn'.)[37]

In this narrative, the Son of Heaven generously acts as a benevolent father, who bestows precious gifts to his subjects and brings peace and stability everywhere. The small states, on the other hand, are described as greedy and mutually hostile — while the emperor's perfect behaviour might serve as an example for them to reform their ways.

Let us turn to a third and last example, concerning the Malay Peninsula, which was crucial for Chinese trade and expansion in Ming times. The official history records the beginning of its tributary relations as follows:

永樂元年十月遣中官尹慶使其地，賜以織金文綺、銷金帳幔諸物。其地無王，亦不稱國，服屬暹羅，歲輸金四十兩為賦。慶至，宣示威德及招徠之意。其酋拜裡迷蘇剌大喜，遣使隨慶入朝貢方物，三年九月至京師。帝嘉之，封為滿剌加國王，賜誥印、彩幣、襲衣、黃蓋,覆命慶往。其使者言:「王慕義，願同中國列郡，歲效職貢，請封其山為一國之鎮。」帝從之。制碑文，勒山上.

(In the tenth month of the first year, Emperor Yongle [1403] sent the eunuch Yin Qing to this country, bringing gifts of golden silk curtains with gold characters and various other objects. [At that time] this country had no king, and it could not be considered a kingdom [in itself], as it was subjected to Xianluo [i.e. present-day Thailand], to which it had to pay forty *liang* of gold annually as tribute. [Yin] Qing came showing dignity and virtue and affirmed that he wanted to establish a relationship of friendship [in the name of the emperor]. The chief of this country Bai-li-mi-su-la was very pleased and sent ambassadors to go to court with [Yin] Qing to pay tribute. In the 9th month of the 3rd year Yongle [1405] [Malacca's ambassadors] arrived in the capital. The Emperor appreciated [such behaviour] and officially appointed him king, giving him an official seal, silk, money, a robe, a yellow umbrella, and ordered [Yin] Qing again to go to that country. The [Malaysian] ambassador said: 'The king admires justice, and wants to become like the many subjects of the Middle Kingdom.

37 *Ming Shi*, comp. by Zhang Tingyu and others, p. 8384 (chap. 324).

> He will offer tributes every year, so we beg you to enfeoff out our mountains as a true kingdom'. The Emperor agreed and wrote the text of an inscription to be erected on the mountains.)[38]

Once again, the Emperor addresses the King of Malacca as a father, generous of gifts for a son who acts according to the proper norms and fulfils his social role. The king, in turn, must take care of his person, because a celestial task has been entrusted to him: to represent the emperor in a distant country, which needed his enlightened guidance. The king knew that, if he needed it, the emperor would always be willing to help him. In fact, when Xianluo repeatedly tried to invade Malacca, his former vassal, in the following years, it was the empire's responsibility to remind him of the respect due to this kingdom, which had become a tributary of equal dignity.

This general impression could easily be confirmed by further sources, hence the image of a compassionate, tender-hearted father who distributes gifts and good advice also emerges from the following passages from the official Canon of the Ming dynasty as well as from a fifteenth-century local gazetteer (*Guangdong tongzhi* 廣東通志):

> 瀕行, 賜宴奉天門, 再賜玉帶、儀仗、鞍馬、黃金百、白金五百、鈔四十萬貫、錢二千六百貫、錦綺紗羅三百匹、帛千匹、渾金文綺二、金織通袖膝襴二;妃及子侄陪臣以下, 宴賜有差。禮官餞於龍江驛, 復賜宴龍潭驛。

> (When [the Malay delegation] was about to leave, they were invited to a banquet at Fengtianmen, and there the Emperor again bestowed them official insignia, jade belts, saddled horses, one hundred pieces of yellow gold, five hundred of white gold, four hundred thousand banknotes, 2600 coins, three hundred rolls of brocade, silk woven diagonally, gauze and thin silk, a thousand rolls of another silk fabric, two rolls of silks wholly woven with gold characters, and two *lan* dresses woven with gold. The queen, her son, grandchildren and other ministers received gifts according to their rank. An official of the Ministry of Rites gave a banquet for them at Longjiangyi and again they were offered a farewell dinner at Longtanyi.)[39]

> 王涉海數萬里至京師, 坦然無虞, 蓋王之忠誠, 神明所祐。朕與王相見甚驩, 固當且留;但國人在望, 宜往慰之。今天氣向寒, 順風南帆, 實維厥時, 王途中善飲食、善調護, 以副朕睠念之懷。

> (The imperial decree [issued at the time of the departure of] the delegation said: 'You, O king, travelled ten thousand *li* to the capital with a tranquil mind, without fear, driven by your loyalty and with heavenly help. We met with great joy, I would be happy to let you

---

38 *Ming Shi*, comp. by Zhang Tingyu and others, p. 8416 (chap. 325).

39 *Ming Shi*, comp. by Zhang Tingyu and others, pp. 8416–17 (chap. 325); see also *Ming Huidian*, pp. 5b–7b (chap. 98).

> stay here for a little longer, but your people need you; you must go back to take care of them. Now the temperature is falling, the wind is favourable to your sails and to your departure. During the journey you have to eat and drink well, take good care of your health: This is my wish and desire'.)[40]

There are also some episodes of violence that show how the emperor was able to react if challenged, as happened in Java in 1406, when 170 Chinese soldiers were killed. Emperor Yongle (r. 1402–24) had the king and his entourage held captive and asked for a huge quantity of gold, only to give it back later, in order to demonstrate that the Son of Heaven did not care for material compensation.[41]

Several other episodes illustrate the precise procedure of Chinese ritual to be followed by foreign envoys as well as the implicit acceptance of its basic principle of factual, heavenly supremacy. Smaller kingdoms in Southeast Asia readily submitted themselves, not only because they were afraid of the powerful neighbour, but also in order to ease their trade in the area, as Chinese goods were very precious and could be sold for profit quite easily. On the other hand, the commercial aspect was always neglected by the Chinese side, or at least it was not officially mentioned as it did not fit into the ideological framework. Any suspicion that tributary envoys had commercial motivations could effectively cause their rejection, as is mentioned in a chapter of the Ming History about Xianluo (Thailand). This passage reports that a group of people appeared on the shores of Guangdong in 1373, claiming to have suffered a shipwreck. Local officials welcomed them and helped them in every way, learning to their great amazement that they were tributary envoys from Xianluo who intended to proceed to the capital to present some goods to the Emperor. Since they did not have a list of the official gifts and seemed completely unaware of the procedure, 'they were suspected to be just foreign merchants. Order was given to reject them'.[42] After this episode, the emperor issued the following decree:

> 古諸侯於天子, 比年一小聘, 三年一大聘。九州之外, 則每世一朝, 所貢方物, 表誠敬而已。惟高 麗頗知禮樂, 故令三年一貢。他遠國, 如占城、安南、西洋瑣裡、爪哇、浡泥、三 佛齊、暹羅斛、真臘諸國, 入貢既頻, 勞費太甚。今不必復爾, 其移牒諸國俾知之。」
>
> (In the past, the nobles of our country made a minor visit to the Son of Heaven every second year and a major visit every third year. Outside the Nine regions (i.e. China), there was only one visit to the throne once in a reign period. Submission of local products signifies that they are sincere and respectful and nothing else. Only Korea knows ritual

40 *Guangdong tongzhi*, p. 4b.
41 *Ming Shi*, comp. by Zhang Tingyu and others, p. 8403 (chap. 324).
42 *Ming Shi*, comp. by Zhang Tingyu and others, p. 8397 (chap. 324).

> and music well enough, so I order them to send tribute mission once every third year. As the other remote countries like Champa, Annam, Southern India, Soli, Java, Borneo, Srivijaya, Thailand, Cambodia, since their tribute missions come incessantly, the toil and cost are too heavy. Now it is not necessary for them to resume their tribute missions.)[43]

In this decree, the Hongwu Emperor established an explicit parallel between the feudatories of ancient China, who were asked to visit every third year, and Korea, his closest tributary kingdom. 'The other remote countries' were equated to the foreigners of older times, who were only asked to show their respect and obeisance once for each emperor. The same cosmological pattern is thus mirrored on a larger scale, and a concrete action must follow the fundamental cosmic order defined by the Celestial will, as I tried to demonstrate through some fragments of Chinese official sources. The Emperor is represented as a wise, patient, ideal father, whose sole activity is to educate the people and to care about their well-being. If the correct principles of behaviour are observed and put into practice by every subject of the Son of Heaven, from the highest ranks of his inner court to the farthest, unknown population that belongs to the human sphere, then all the inhabited world will be in peace, and universal harmony will be reached. The first act of this process is the ritual submission to the Emperor, to be performed according to detailed rules and procedures.

In this frame, it is not surprising that Hongwu's fourth son, Zhu Di, who became the Yongle ('Eternal Happiness') Emperor, spent time and resources on the organization of impressive maritime expeditions to the Western Ocean.[44] Yongle ascended the throne in 1402 by means of a *coup*, attacking the imperial palace of Nanjing where his nephew Jianwen had succeeded Hongwu four years earlier. As a consequence, he needed to demonstrate the possession of the heavenly mandate more than anyone else. After sending letters and emissaries to foreign kings, just as his father had done, he thus ordered the preparation of a magnificent fleet for imperial ambassadors who were then sent to the tributary countries, where they should spread the good news of his ascent.

It was the largest fleet ever seen: around two hundred vessels, equipped in a modern way, with about twenty-eight thousand men, including sailors, soldiers, technicians, artisans, interpreters, officials of different categories, and scribes who could narrate the unrepeatable undertakings for posterity.[45]

---

43 *Ming Shi*, comp. by Zhang Tingyu and others, p. 8397 (chap. 324; trans. by Grimm, 'Thailand in the light of Official Chinese Historiography', p. 4, slightly modified).

44 The bibliography about Zheng He's expeditions is huge. Over the last centuries, it has attracted the interest of both Western and Chinese scholars, who celebrated the 600th anniversary of the first journey in 2005 with conferences, books, exhibitions, and even commemorative stamps. Zheng He is considered a national hero. Dreyer, *Zheng He: China and the Oceans*, provides a good synthesis by a well-known historian of the Ming dynasty; see also Salmon and Ptak, eds, *Zheng He: Images and Perceptions*. There is also a great number of specific studies on the sailing techniques and shipbuilding.

45 See the translations by Mills, *Ma Huan Yingyai Shenglan. The Overall Survey of the Ocean's*

The fleet left in 1405 and came back two years later, after having reached the countries of Champa, Thailand, Sumatra, Palembang, Sri Lanka, and Calicut. These reigns enthusiastically confirmed their faith in the Celestial Emperor, renewing their visits with gifts in the following years. The fleet was to depart Chinese soil five more times,[46] heading towards several countries of the Southern Seas (*Nanyang* 南洋), as Southeast Asia is still called in Chinese, and further west, to India and even the Arabian Peninsula as well as African shores, where the 'Ambassador' Zheng He and his ships made landfall for the first time in 1414.

In the following years, the delegations from these foreign countries multiplied and many exotic animals and objects, sometimes extremely valuable, were delivered to the court, in turn receiving gifts that were deemed suitable to their status. Among those *mirabilia*, it is worth mentioning a giraffe from Malindi that was brought to the Yongle Emperor and was recorded as a 'unicorn' (*qilin* 麒麟), the mythical animal that was supposed to appear when a new, rightful sovereign seated on the dragon throne.[47] The more foreign embassies came to the court, the more the emperor's virtue was confirmed — and as a result the officialdom became increasingly willing to support the emperor's wishes. The homages by foreign countries triggered the same mechanism previously described for King Wu of Zhou, thereby putting Yongle's *coup* in a very different light.

Was this the only objective of these magnificent expeditions? Zheng He's biography in the official 'History of the Ming' mentions two specific motives. On the one hand, the emperor was said to have worried about his nephew, his ill-fated young predecessor, who was rumoured to have escaped from the Palace, disguised as a Buddhist monk, and to have fled to the Southern Seas. On the other hand, Yongle's intention was said to have been 'to display his soldiers in strange lands in order to make manifest the wealth and power of China'. They 'went to the various foreign countries proclaiming the edicts of the Son of Heaven and giving gifts to their rulers and chieftains. Those who did not submit were pacified by force'.[48] Even for this strong army the successful retrieval of the Jianwen emperor, whose body was nowhere to be found, was certainly not likely. However, these journeys represented a promising strategy to secure the seas and neighbouring countries. In this

---

Shores, and Mills, *Fei Xin, Hsing-cha sheng-lan*.

46 The expeditions' dates of departure and return are as follows: 1407–09, 1409–11, 1413–15, 1417–19, 1421–23. After the death of Yongle in 1424 and of his successor Hongxi in 1426, Yongle's grandson Xuande sent the fleet only once more, the seventh expedition, in 1431–33.

47 The *qilin*, usually translated as unicorn, is one of the four mythical animals, or Four Spirits of Chinese tradition, together with the phoenix, the dragon and the turtle. It is described as possessing the body of a deer, the tail of an ox and one horn. The idea that it represents a benevolent ruler whose reign is approved by heaven, is mentioned in several ancient sources, the most famous of which is the close of the *Spring and Autumn Annals* (XIV year of Duke Ai's reign, 477 BCE). A unicorn is also said to have appeared at Confucius' birth, bearing a jade in his mouth, thereby announcing the extraordinary life of the 'crownless king'.

48 *Ming Shi*, comp. by Zhang Tingyu and others, pp. 7766–67 (chap. 304).

sense, the closing sentence of the quoted passage is especially revealing: the ideal order had to be put into action by any means, echoing at the same time the Mongols' ways of ensuring allies (or, better, subordinates),[49] and thus confirming the enduring heritage of the previous rulers. If a reaction from the celestial army was needed in order to 'pacify' the territory, as was the case in the Java episode of 1406, the Chinese would have been in a position to strike without hesitation.[50]

Conclusion

The official sources, written 'by officials for officials',[51] tend to create an image of the Chinese Empire that is generally characterized by long-standing unity, wisdom, and morally irreproachable behaviour — and one that must be associated with the Son of Heaven, as described in the classics. In the same way as feudal princes of ancient times, foreign kings were supposed to recognize the indisputable moral sovereignty of the Chinese through specific actions of a deep ritual significance. The so-called tributary system was enforced and exalted during the Ming dynasty (1368–1644) because — after a century of Mongol domination — the dynasty's founder, Zhu Yuanzhang, needed to win the support of the Chinese bureaucracy. As a consequence, he emphasized the return to the old values as required by the neo-Confucian Jinhua school, which he had chosen to rely upon before becoming emperor.[52] Therefore, although the Emperor was a man of humble origins and had some personal grudges against the literati class, the ritual became stricter than ever before, as the long chapters of the 'Ming Collected Statutes' demonstrate.[53] The larger numbers of tributary embassies that were registered in the official sources were interpreted as evidence of the order and stability the world enjoyed; at the same time, they contributed greatly to the interior legitimation of the new dynasty in the eyes of its ruling class. A specific office of the Ministry of Rites, the Bureau of Receptions (*zhuke qingli si* 主客清吏司), was in charge of the foreign dignitaries at court, instructing them about the proper behaviour and ritual actions to perform. Just as planets or satellites revolve around the

49 See the contributions by Michal Biran as well as by Klaus Oschema and Christoph Mauntel in this volume.

50 Some scholars have highlighted strong commercial interests that could have been the hidden motivation of the later journeys of the fleet. This interpretation conflicts, however, with the firm opposition of Xia Yuanji, the Minister of Finance, who convinced the Hongxi Emperor to decree the 'precious ships' should be dismantled in September 1424, when his father Yongle had been dead for only a month; cf. *Ming Shi*, comp. by Zhang Tingyu and others, p. 4153 (chap. 149). The details of the question concerning the motivation behind the expeditions are beyond the scope of this chapter.

51 See Balazs, 'L'Histoire comme guide de la pratique bureaucratique'.

52 See Dardess, *Confucianism and Autocracy*.

53 *Ming Huidian*, chaps 55–102.

sun in ordered orbits, small kingdoms had to follow a specific route in order to maintain the cosmic order.

At the same time, this very sophisticated model remained remarkably versatile: if any specific event did not entirely fit into the framework, it could easily either be omitted or modified for the sake of stability. This happened, for example, in the case of the infamous British delegate Lord Macartney in 1793, who sternly refused to *koutou*, claiming that he would not do anything more than what he usually did before his own king, George III, i.e. kneeling on one knee. Besides, kneeling on both knees was to be done only before God, he explained. Chinese official histories, however, do not record this detail. They merely labelled the British delegation as tributary and implicitly reported that everything had been done in the proper way.[54]

One may wonder what is left today of Chinese world order: in the Beijing National Museum in Tian'anmen Square there used to be a huge permanent exhibition called 'State Gifts: Historical Testament to Friendly Exchanges' that displayed

> a selection of 611 representative gifts [which] Party and government leaders received in their diplomatic activities since the founding of New China. The number of countries with which China has diplomatic relations has increased from 18 shortly after the founding of New China to 172 at present. These gifts are a testament to the brilliant success of our country's diplomacy over the past 60-plus years, an expression of the friendly feelings between the Chinese people and other countries.[55]

This exhibition was much more successful in terms of the number of Chinese visitors than the rooms dedicated to the exquisite art objects on display on the lower floors of the museum, demonstrating that even today the recognition and homage by foreign states is crucial for government stability. Not many foreigners venture to visit it, but I believe that is beyond its main scope. It is no coincidence that Confucianism has resumed an important position over the last twenty years and that classical quotations as well as the claim of unity appear quite often in the party leaders' slogans. The (glorious) past serves political needs also today.

---

54 *Qingshi Gao* 清史稿 (*The Draft History of the Qing Dynasty*), p. 4516 (chap. 154). For a detailed analysis, see Hevia, *Cherishing Men from Afar*. The Qing dynasty's foreign policy was not exactly the same as the previous dynasty's, though.

55 Zhang Ying, 'State Gifts'.

Works Cited

Primary Sources

Dante Alighieri, *La Divina Commedia. Inferno*, ed. by Natalino Sapegno (Florence: La Nuova Italia, 2004)

Guangdong tongzhi 廣東通志 (*Gazetteer of Guangdong Province*), in *Gujin tushu jicheng* 古今圖集成 (*Complete Collection of Pictures and Books of Old and Modern Times*) (Bianyidian 邊裔典: Foreign countries, 1726)

Liji 禮記 (*Record of Rites*) [*The Li ki, I–X*], ed. and trans. by James Legge, The Sacred Books of China, 4 / The Texts of Confucianism, 3 (Oxford: Clarendon Press, 1885)

Lunyu 論語 (*The Analects*), ed. and trans. by James Legge, The Chinese Classics, 1 (London: Trubner, 1865)

Mills, J. V. G., transl., *Ma Huan Yingyai Shenglan. The Overall Survey of the Ocean's Shores* (London: Cambridge University Press, 1970)

——, transl., *Fei Xin, Hsing-cha sheng-lan. The Overall Survey of the Star Raft* (Wiesbaden: Harrassowitz, 1996)

Ming Huidian 明會典 (*Collected Statutes of the Ming Dynasty*) [1509], in *Siku Quanshu* 四庫全書 dianziban (Shanghai: Renmin, 2000)

Ming Shi 明史 (Ming History) [1739], comp. by Zhang Tingyu and others (Beijing: Zhonghua shuju, 1974)

Ming Taizu shilu 明太祖實錄 (*Veritable Records of the Ming Dynasty*) (Taipei: Zhongyang yanjiuyuan, 1962–68)

Qingshi gao 清史稿 (*The Draft History of the Qing Dynasty*) [1922] (Beijing: Zhonghua shuju, 1977)

Shangshu 尚書 (*The Book of Documents*), ed. and trans. by James. Legge, The Chinese Classics, 3 (London: Trubner, 1865)

Shanhai Jing 山海經 (*The Classic of Mountains and Seas*), ed. and trans. by Anne Birrell (London: Penguin, 1999)

Xin Tangshu 新唐書 (*New History of the Tang Dynasty*) [1060], ed. by Song Qi and others (Beijing: Zhonghua shuju, 1975)

Zhang Huang 章潢, *Tushu bian* 圖書編 [1613], in *Siku Quanshu* 四庫全書 dianziban (Shanghai: Renmin, 2000)

Secondary Studies

Bai Huawen 白化文, 'Bowuzhi 博物志', in *Zhongguo da baike quanshu* 中國大百科全書, *Zhongguo wenxue* 中國文學, vol. 1 (Beijing: Zhongguo da baike quanshu chubanshe, 1986), pp. 46–47

Balazs, Étienne, 'L'Histoire comme guide de la pratique bureaucratique (les monographies, les encyclopédies, les recueils des statuts)', in *Historians of China and Japan*, ed. by William G. Beasley and Edwin G. Pulleyblank (London: Oxford University Press, 1961), pp. 78–94

Ch'en, Kenneth [Chen Guansheng], 'Matteo Ricci's Contribution to and Influence on Geographical Knowledge in China', *Journal of the American Oriental Society*, 59 (1939), 325–59

Chen Jiarong 陈佳荣, Xie Fang 谢方, Lu Junling 陆峻岭, ed., *Gudai nanhai diming huishi* 古代南海地名汇释 (Beijing: Zhonghua shuju, 1986)

Dardess, John, *Confucianism and Autocracy: Professional Elites in the Founding of the Ming Dynasty* (Berkeley: University of California Press, 1983)

De Weerdt, Hilde, 'Maps and Memory: Readings of Cartography in Twelfth- and Thirteenth-Century Song China', *Imago Mundi*, 61,2 (2009), 145–67

Dreyer, Edward L., *Zheng He: China and the Oceans in the Early Ming dynasty, 1405–1433* (New York: Pearson Longman, 2007)

Grimm, Tilemann, 'Thailand in the Light of Official Chinese Historiography: A Chapter in the History of the Ming Dynasty', *The Journal of the Siam Society*, 49 (1961), 1–20

Guida, Donatella, *Nei Mari del Sud. Il viaggio nel Sud-est asiatico tra realtà e immaginazione: storiografia e letteratura nella Cina Ming e Qing* (Roma: Edizioni Nuova Cultura, 2007)

——, 'Ming Taizu on the Yuan Dynasty: Between Ethnicity and Legitimation', *Archiv orientální*, 86,1 (2018), 137–60

Hevia, James, *Cherishing Men from Afar: Qing Guest Ritual and the Macartney Embassy of 1793* (Durham, NC: Duke University Press, 1995)

Ji Shijia, 'Boniguo wang mu he Boniguo zhu wenti yanjiu', in *Zheng He Xia Xiyang Lunwenji* 郑和下西洋论文集, ed. by Li Zhizhong 李执中, 2 vols (Nanjing: Nanjing Daxue chubanshe, 1985), vol. 1, pp. 52–59

Keightley, David, *Sources of Shang History: The Oracle-Bone Inscriptions of Bronze Age China* (Berkeley: University of California Press, 1978)

Lewis, Mark, *The Construction of Space in Early China* (Albany: State University of New York Press, 2006)

Loewe, Michael, and Edward L. Shaughnessy, ed., *The Cambridge History of Ancient China: From the Origins of Civilization to 221 B.C.* (Cambridge: Cambridge University Press, 1999)

Mauntel, Christoph, Klaus Oschema, Jean-Charles Ducène, and Martin Hofmann, 'Mapping Continents, Inhabited Quarters, and The Four Seas: Divisions of the World and the Ordering of Spaces in Latin-Christian, Arabic-Islamic, and Chinese Cartography, 12th–16th Centuries — a Critical Survey and Analysis', *Journal of Transcultural Medieval Studies*, 5,2 (2018), 295–376

Pines, Yuri, 'Changing Views of *tianxia* in Pre-imperial Discourse', *Oriens Extremus*, 43,1–2 (2002), 101–16

——, *Envisioning Eternal Empire: Chinese Political Thought of the Warring States Era* (Honolulu: University of Hawai'i Press, 2009)

——, *The Everlasting Empire: The Political Culture of Ancient China and Its Imperial Legacy* (Princeton: Princeton University Press, 2012)

Rossabi, Morris, *A History of China* (Oxford: Wiley Blackwell, 2014)

Salmon, Claudine, and Roderich Ptak, eds, *Zheng He: Images and Perceptions* (Wiesbaden: Harrassowitz, 2005)

Selbitschka, Armin, 'Early Chinese Diplomacy: Realpolitik vs. the So-Called Tributary System', *Asia Major*, 3rd Series, 28,1 (2015), 61–114

Shaughnessy, Edward L., 'The Duke of Zhou's Retirement in the East and the Beginnings of the Ministerial-Monarch Debate in Chinese Political Philosophy', *Early China*, 18 (1993), 41–72

Smith, Richard J., *Mapping China and Managing the World: Culture, Cartography and Cosmology in Late Imperial Times* (London: Routledge, 2013)

Sullivan, Michael, *The Arts of China* (Berkeley: University of California Press, 2008)

Vogelsang, Kai, *Geschichte Chinas* (Stuttgart: Reclam, 2012)

Yang, Weisheng 楊渭生, 'Shangshu 尚書', in *Zhongguo da baike quanshu* 中國大百科全書 *Zhongguo wenxue* 中國文學, vol. 11 (Beijing: Zhongguo da baike quanshu chubanshe, 1986), p. 694

Zhang, Ying, ed., 'State Gifts: Historical Testament to Friendly Exchanges', n.d., <http://en.chnmuseum.cn/exhibition/past_exhibitions/201911t20191120_171614.html > [accessed 21 June 2021]

MICHAEL WINTLE

The Advent of the Black Magus

*Moving towards a Continental Hierarchy**

Introduction

In the Ancient world, many writers, politicians, and soldiers knew about the three continents of Africa, Asia, and Europe, but these were just convenient geographical labels, and very little more. There are some remarks about Asia in particular in some of the Ancient sources, to do with despots and slavishness, but there is almost no evidence of any sense of a European identity.[1] By the time of the Renaissance, however, and certainly by the later sixteenth century, a hierarchy of the parts of the world had come into being in European minds, with Europe at the top, Asia in the middle and Africa (plus the new continent, America) at the bottom.[2] It has since become a way of ordering the world in terms of power and virtue, alongside spatial geography.[3]

---

* This chapter derives from a paper presented to the international conference on 'Order into Action. How large-scale concepts of world-order determine practices in the premodern world', held at Heidelberg University, 10–12 November 2016. I am grateful to the organizers for the invitation to present, and to many of the participants for the excellent comments and suggestions they provided. The redrafted and expanded version in this chapter relies heavily on my earlier work on the Magi in Wintle, *The Image of Europe*, pp. 191–216 (chap. 4.4). There are many new examples here, a new framing in accordance with the themes of this volume, and some response to reviews and criticism. But the basic thesis remains the same, and some passages have been partially reproduced here, albeit in modified wording.

1 For some of those sparse references, see Wintle, *The Image of Europe*, pp. 84–87.

2 This was a European rather than a global imagined hierarchy; for example, it was not even remotely shared in China (see the chapter in this collection by Donatella Guida, on the Chinese imperial world order, which certainly gave no special status to Europe). Much later, when the European colonial empires were at their height, there was an element of hegemony through which much of the rest of the world subscribed to the idea of hierarchy, but at the time of the Renaissance it was not shared outside Europe.

3 Lewis and Wigen, *The Myth of Continents*, has now become a standard work on that continental hierarchy.

Michael Wintle (M.J.Wintle@uva.nl), Department of European Studies, University of Amsterdam, The Netherlands

Order into Action: How Large-Scale Concepts of World-Order determine Practices in the Premodern World, ed. by Klaus Oschema and Christoph Mauntel, CURSOR 40 (Turnhout: Brepols, 2022), pp. 209–235
BREPOLS PUBLISHERS 10.1484/M.CURSOR-EB.5.123849

This chapter is concerned with what happened in between, in the Middle Ages: how did this transition from almost a lack of awareness of Europe to a prevalent Eurocentrism come about? And what were the mechanisms of the creation of that hierarchy, with all the concomitant assumptions and political implications? In accordance with the general aims of this volume, we shall endeavour to locate, where possible, concrete examples of how new ideas interacted with new political situations: how did the discourse evolve, did it give rise to any tangible consequences, and who played what role?

The focus will fall on a single aspect of that broad issue, and it involves the visual arts. We shall confine ourselves to one of the great stories of the Christian religion, the adoration of the Magi, or the worship of the three kings or wise men, at the birth of Christ. It emerged from being a few lines in the Gospel of St Matthew to become the ubiquitous story we see all over our Christmas cards and in our art galleries today: along with the Annunciation, the Adoration of the Shepherds, and the Crucifixion itself, it is perhaps the most widely repeated fable in Western Christian thought. It has been current for almost two millennia, and has been wildly popular in the West for much of that time. One commentator has even referred to the story as 'the prime socio-organizational icon of Christianity during the European Middle Ages'.[4]

In the course of the early fifteenth century, something extraordinary happened: one of the kings became a black man. It occurred quite suddenly, with few precedents; by 1500 the portrayal of the black Magus had become very widespread. Since then, more often than not, one of the Magi has been illustrated as a black and so presumably African prince, with the concomitant implication that the other two kings represent Asia and Europe, making up the three known continents. This enabled European artists to project their ideas about their own continent, and indeed about the other continents in relation to their own. They could and did begin to develop an ordering or hierarchy of the continents, with themselves at the top.

It will be maintained here that this change took place not simply as a result of the whim of a couple of painters or because of arbitrary artistic fashion: it was caused by a number of important political and cultural forces in Europe in the late Middle Ages, and it had significant implications for developing an idea of the hierarchy of the continents, and even for the crystallization of modern ideas of racism. I am aware that claiming to unearth the origins of Eurocentrism and racism is an inflated ambition. Of course, the black Magus was not the only factor involved, but it was an important one, and for that reason this chapter is devoted to it, and to the way in which the mechanism of change operated.[5]

---

4 Trexler, *The Journey of the Magi*, p. 36.

5 There are a number of standard works on the history of the black Magus in European art, all of which are useful and which I have gratefully consulted. Kehrer, *Die heiligen drei Könige*, is dated but still useful on the history of the visual image of the Magi; Hofmann, *Die heiligen*

There is considerable discussion in academia about the timeframe in which race and racism became forces to be reckoned with in the West. It used to be held that in Antiquity, cultural difference and indeed skin colour were not grounds for fundamental prejudice: the Romans were said to be quite positive about black people. Now we are less sure. However, Francisco Bethencourt has pointed out that even if a concept of 'race' existed with the Ancients, there was little or no discrimination accompanying it (which is axiomatic for his definition of 'ra*cism*': 'prejudice concerning ethnic descent coupled with discriminating action').[6] Much the same applies to the medieval period: concepts equivalent to race were certainly present and sometimes acted upon, as shown in the work of Geraldine Heng.[7] While this was not what we understand by a modern biological racism, a field of discourse which has been called 'proto-racism' evolved in the course of the Middle Ages, with input from Antiquity and from the increasing contact with different ethnic groups from outside Europe.[8] The general medieval view of the world was one of monogenesis, that is to say one which assumed that all humans, all over God's earth, had been generated from the same biological source, and this view continued in Europe into the sixteenth and seventeenth centuries. Recent studies have been able to pick out elements of race and racism in that early modern period, which did not amount to a coherent system and which were severely hindered by other ideologies like Christian universalism, but a 'proto-racism' does seem to have existed, all of which helped and underpinned the development of what would eventually become scientific racism in the nineteenth and twentieth centuries.[9] Here we are concerned with a growing relationship during the Middle Ages between the concept of race, and the hierarchy of the continents.

The chapter will proceed by looking at the ways in which various factors influenced the rise of the black Magus in the fifteenth century. First to be covered are what might be called external factors, like the increasing European interest

---

drei Könige, handles the history of the cult of the Magi; Kaplan, *The Rise of the Black Magus*, deals specifically with the question of the appearance of the black king; Bugner ed., *The Image of the Black*, embraces the much wider subject of the role of black people generally in Western art; and Trexler, *The Journey of the Magi*, examines the way in which various interest groups have used the story throughout history. Trexler's detailed account pays particular attention to the way in which various princes had themselves portrayed as Magi in visual art up to the sixteenth century (p. 118), and to the issue of gender: the Magi are always male, though (according to Trexler) the third Magus, also when given a dark skin, has strong feminine qualities (pp. 93–95, 108–15). This argument is used to bolster one of his principal theses, namely that there is a dichotomy between the youngest and the two older Magi (pp. 95–101).

6 Bethencourt, *Racisms*, pp. 1, 3, 14, 271–72. Amongst a very large literature, see also Painter, *The History of White People*, and Eliav-Feldon and others ed., *The Origins of Racism*.

7 Heng, 'The Invention of Race'; and Heng, *The Invention of Race*.

8 Miramon, 'Noble Dogs, Noble Blood'.

9 Wheeler, *The Complexion of Race*, p. 9; see also Eliav-Feldon and others ed., *The Origins of Racism*, pp. 24, 31.

in the continent of Africa and in black people, not least by means, eventually, of the slave trade. Then we shall look briefly at some written traditions of the Magi story, from the gospels up to the chronicles and popular history fables circulating in the late Middle Ages. Next it will be the turn of the powerful: the princes, the popes, the prelates, the emperors, who all saw something to be gained in propaganda terms by bending the Magi story, with or without its black king, to their various causes. And finally, we shall consider that most important acting force: the artists themselves. The interaction between the motives and actions of the artists over the centuries and those of the secular and religious powers of the day are therefore at the heart of the investigation. An attempt will be made to see what that interaction had to do with the creation of this new order of the continents as a hierarchy of culture and power and race, with Europe at the top, Asia somewhere in between, and Africa and America at the bottom.

The crucial change and contrast in Magi imagery between 1300 and 1450 becomes crystal clear with the assistance of the two initial illustrations in Figures 8.1 and 8.2. The first (Figure 8.1) shows a typical early fourteenth-century portrayal, from Cologne: the Virgin and child are on the right, with a star of Bethlehem above them, while the three kings — old, middle-aged and young (their facial hair shows their age) — bring their gifts. The oldest one kneels, and the second points out the star to the youngest, who has no beard. This is an absolutely standard medieval portrayal, typical of the period from 800 CE up to about 1400; age is the only badge of seniority among the kings (and a very important one at that).

Contrast that with the representation in Figure 8.2 from 1444, a century later, by the Master of the Polling altarpiece, painted for a church in Bavaria. The old man is now hook-nosed and (arguably) stereotypically Semitic (Asia), the middle-aged king is ruddy-haired and vigorous (Europe), while the third, youngest king is, in his gorgeous finery, a stereotypical black African man.[10] This transformation, this change from the Magi representing just the ages of man, to representing the three separate continents of the world, took place in the middle of the fifteenth century. So, the question begs: what was the reason for that transformation?

10 There are few if any empirical grounds for linking particular physical facial features with a racial type. Neither does skin colour bear any relationship to intelligence: see Conley and Fletcher, *The Genome Factor*, especially chap. 5. However, there is no denying the power of the stereotype, especially in popular art, and we shall not ignore its significance. See Van Leeuwen and Jewitt ed., *Handbook of Visual Analysis*, p. 107. From the sixteenth century on, the word used by the Portuguese and others to describe these black Africans was 'negro', meaning 'black'. Since the 1960s 'negro' has become an offensive term in English, and so is seldom used.

FIGURE 8.1. 'The Adoration of the Magi', detail (bottom left-hand panel) of Triptych with depiction of the Salvation Story, Cologne, 1340–50. Collection of Ferdinand Franz Wallraf, Wallraf Richartz Museum Cologne, inv. no. WRM 0001. Photo: © Rheinisches Bildarchiv / Sabrina Walz, rba_d032478_01. By kind permission.

FIGURE 8.2. 'The Adoration of the Magi', The Polling altarpiece (*Marienaltar*), 1444. Munich, Alte Pinothek, inv. no. 1360. © bpk 50009563 | Bayerische Staatsgemäldesammlungen. By kind permission.

External Circumstances

First, there were geopolitical events taking place. From the twelfth century onwards, much more interest was taken by Europeans in portraying black people, partly because of the propaganda needs of the Hohenstaufen court (see below), but also because of the renewed ambitions of Christian power in the Mediterranean area, in the context of a centuries-long struggle with Islam, which had by no means always gone Europe's way in the Middle Ages.[11] There was a large Jewish population in Asia, and also a very considerable Nestorian Christian Church, knowledge of which was to be had in the West from pilgrims to Crusader Jerusalem.[12] In 1402 Ethiopian ambassadors arrived in Venice, and a further delegation went to Rome in 1402–07. Increasing contact with sub-Saharan Africa by means of exploratory voyages down the west coast of Africa, and the growth of the Genoese slave market at the end of the fourteenth and beginning of the fifteenth centuries, meant that black (and other) slaves were much more common all over Italy, and indeed elsewhere.[13] There was more contact with Copts and Ethiopians in the 1440s, and in the 1450s the popes themselves were trying to contact the mythical black Christian potentate Prester John, as part of a search for potential allies against Islam. It was even thought that John might be descended from one of the Magi.[14]

Written Sources

The original story of the Magi was related by the Evangelist St Matthew (Matthew 2. 1–12); the details were very sparse. The wise men, or Magi (a word connected with an ancient Persian or Anatolian cult), came from the East to worship the Christ-child as King of the Jews and to bring him gifts of gold, frankincense, and myrrh; these items helped to fulfil Old Testament prophecies in Exodus and Isaiah.[15] King Herod got wind of their mission and attempted to eliminate the threatened claim to his throne by ordering the Massacre of the Innocents, which prompted the Holy Family's flight into Egypt. The early biblical commentators, as they so often did, added to the story a great wealth of detail, including the rank of the Magi as kings, their names, and their number. St Augustine contributed that the kings came from the various corners of the earth, not just from the East, and this was repeated in the

11 Sanders, *Lost Tribes and Promised Lands*, pp. 17, 52; Kiernan, *The Lords of Human Kind*, pp. 15–16; Nederveen Pieterse, *White on Black*, pp. 26–27. On Europe and Islam through the ages, see Wintle, 'Islam as Europe's Other'.

12 Hamilton, 'Prester John and the Three Kings of Cologne', pp. 178–79.

13 Kaplan, *The Rise of the Black Magus*, pp. 13–14, 103; Wintle, *The Image of Europe*, p. 199.

14 Kaplan, *The Rise of the Black Magus*, pp. 103–06; Whitaker, 'An Historical Explanation of the Asiatic Myths of Prester John'; Hamilton, 'Prester John and the Three Kings of Cologne', pp. 180–81.

15 Warner, *Alone of All Her Sex*, p. 6.

sermons of Pope Leo the Great in the mid-fifth century.[16] Other commentators amplified the ecumenical flavour of the story: the Venerable Bede (English, *c.* 700) confirmed that they came from further afield than just 'the East', and the later Pseudo-Bede (probably Irish, later eighth century) added that there was a difference in the ages of the three Magi, representing the three ages of mankind: elderly, middle-aged and young.[17] He added some further details about their names, ages and gifts:[18] Melchior was the eldest, and gave gold; Caspar was young, red-haired, and beardless, carrying incense; while Balthasar had a full beard, brought myrrh, and — crucially — was 'dark' (*fuscus*).[19]

It seems that this description — whether or not it was intended to apply to his skin colour — was an important source for what became an enduring and portentous detail: one of the Magi had a dark skin.[20] According to Robert McNally, Pseudo-Bede's commentary on Matthew is a 'representative example of the early medieval understanding of the universalism of the Magi':[21] this Irish scribe's interpretation of the Magi as representing all corners of God's earth was important to the discourse about the kings in the later medieval period, out of which grew the Renaissance labelling of the three kings as 'Caucasian, Semite and Negro'.[22] Many other strands were involved in the convoluted growth and evolution of the written versions, including nursery stories and popular myths. One of these texts is John of Hildesheim's *Historia trium regum* of about 1370, which added a great range of highly imaginative background and detail to the story, including the separate origin of the kings, their various attributes, their life after the Epiphany, and the story of Prester John, the black king allegedly descended from a Magus. The *Historia trium regum* was widely circulated and translated, with a considerable impact, and was the first really influential source to state without prevarication that one of the Magi was a 'blak Ethiope'.[23] By means of these monastic and popular-literary

16 Köllmann and Wirth, 'Erdteile', cols 1130–31; Kaplan, *The Rise of the Black Magus*, pp. 20–27. On Leo's third sermon on the Epiphany, § 2, see Stracke, 'Epiphany', who cites: 'In the three Magi let [...] God be known not in Judea alone, but in all the world'.

17 Trexler, *The Journey of the Magi*, pp. 37–38.

18 Vezin, *L'Adoration et le cycle des Mages*, p. 63. Their names were already familiar to some, e.g. in the Ravenna mosaics of *c.* 620, in Figure 8.5.

19 Pseudo-Bede's text is quoted in Latin and English by Kaplan, *The Rise of the Black Magus*, p. 26.

20 Kaplan, *The Rise of the Black Magus*, pp. 20–27; Mâle, *L'Art religieux*, pp. 215–16. In later traditions, from the mid-fifteenth century on, the youngest, beardless Magus is almost always the black one, although there were exceptions. For more recent reflections on the perception of skin colours in the Middle Ages see Groebner, 'Haben Hautfarben eine Geschichte?'; Braude, 'The Sons of Noah'; Pastoureau, *Une histoire symbolique*, pp. 193–98; and Heng, *The Invention of Race*, chap. 4, pp. 181–230.

21 McNally, 'The Three Holy Kings in Early Irish Latin Writing', pp. 676–77. The 'universalism' refers to a wish to make access to Christianity universal, rather than a universe-wide or global belief.

22 See McNally, 'The Three Holy Kings in Early Irish Latin Writing', p. 677. His article was published in 1970, by which time the term 'Negro' was becoming less and less acceptable.

23 John of Hildesheim, *The Three Kings of Cologne*, ed. by Horstmann, pp. IX, XV, 72–73.

FIGURE 8.3. 'Coats of arms attributed to the Magi', Brussels, *c.* 1360; adapted and recorded in Köllmann and Wirth, 'Erdteile' (1967), col. 1116.

sources, the notion that one of the three kings was a black man spread out through Germany and beyond.

Now this emerging, occasional suggestion, in the interests of the universal appeal of the Church and Christianity, that the third Magus was dark-skinned and therefore might represent the continent of Africa, appears to have gained a great deal of credence from a particular and important late medieval source. The drawing in Figure 8.3 is taken from an extensive lemma by Erich Köllmann and Karl-August Wirth in an authoritative and scholarly encyclopaedia of German art history dating from the 1960s, who claim to have drawn it from fourteenth-century manuscript sources, recorded in a nineteenth-century heraldic compendium which drew on medieval codices.[24] Its authenticity is not beyond doubt, as we shall see very shortly. But as a didactic aid to help us through the highly complex evolution of the story of the Magi, the growing number of their attributes and their eventual emergence as a codified support for a specific hierarchy of the continents in the Renaissance, it has an exemplary function. It shows three imaginary coats of arms, which are fourteenth-century inventions, with the names of the Magi (also from the medieval sources), and the names of the continents in square brackets, thus linking each continent with a specific set of iconographical attributes, and finally with a continent. The attributes are as follows: the arms of Balthasar on the right are formed by a shield surmounted by the head of a young man with tight curly hair, an upturned nose and protruding lower lip; in the fourteenth-century source he is coloured in a dark brown, and all these features lead us to identify the iconography as a 'moor's head' (a long-standing feature in heraldry signifying Africans, or Muslims). There is also a standing moor with the same facial features, with a staff or spear, appearing on the

24 Köllmann and Wirth, 'Erdteile', col. 1131.

shield. The central figure, 'Kaspar', is represented by an old man with a full beard, and caricature-Semitic facial features, who rises out of the helmet; the shield is decorated with a crescent (linked to Islam) and a six-pointed star (of David and so Judaism) on the shield. And on the left there is Melchior. There is no head above the shield and helmet in his case, but a Bethlehem star (eight-pointed, often used in Epiphany scenes), and there is a crown on the helmet slightly larger than the others.[25] There are six further stars on his shield, each with six points (it is possible that these stars, of Bethlehem and David, might conceivably refer to Christianity rather than Judaism). In this example extracted from medieval heraldry, there appears to be a close link expressed in the iconography between the old Magus and the ancient Semitic peoples of Asia with their Jewish and Muslim religions, between the young one and the population of Africa, and between Europe and the middle Magus; this is confirmed by the labelling in square brackets showing the names of the three known continents.[26]

Now there are some significant reservations to be posed about this apparently eloquent manifestation in Figure 8.3 of the association between the Magi and the continents. The German medievalist Klaus Oschema, with considerable erudition, has recently demonstrated that the coats of arms in Figure 8.3 are drawn from imaginary devices ascribed to the three kings, illustrated in various German manuscripts of the fifteenth century, and in particular from a book of heraldry known as the Gelre Armorial, compiled at the end of the fourteenth century by Claes Heinenzoon, a herald in the service of the Duke of Guelders. Oschema noticed that Köllmann and Wirth had made an important alteration when adapting the medieval manuscript for the encyclopaedia: they added the names of the continents (in Figure 8.3 in square brackets), which had not appeared in the original manuscript of the turn of the fourteenth and fifteenth centuries. (In addition, Caspar's position was switched with that of Melchior, so that Melchior/Europe was now on the left).[27] On the basis of this and other evidence, Oschema is moved to deny that these illustrations in their medieval form refer to the individual continents at all, and — more significantly — that there was any continental hierarchy involved in the conception of the three Magi in the Middle Ages. Köllmann and Wirth's insertion of the names of the continents is therefore condemned as an anachronism, which has led some historians into seeking Eurocentric sentiments at work in the Middle Ages.[28]

25 For detailed references, see Köllmann and Wirth, 'Erdteile', col. 1131.

26 In other fourteenth-century heraldic collections from the Low Countries, similar associations are made: see Kaplan, *The Rise of the Black Magus*, pp. 91–92.

27 Oschema, *Bilder von Europa im Mittelalter*, p. 497 and plates 30–33.

28 This is one of Oschema's principal theses, and indeed an ably defended one. Oschema, *Bilder von Europa im Mittelalter*, p. 21 and throughout, esp. p. 320: 'The hierarchical assessment [*Einschätzung*] of the continents remained vague [*unklar*] until the later Middle Ages' (my translation). Oschema has thereby specifically challenged (e.g. at pp. 494–99)

However, even without the continental labels, the iconography and especially the facial features, which are certainly drawn accurately from the Gelre Armorial, seem to make clear the associations of the three kings with the three known continents. These were early and by no means unequivocal examples, but Köllmann and Wirth did add some evidence of occasional recognizable (if not categorical) signs of associations between the continents and the Magi in the Middle Ages. They cited St Augustine's original suggestion of the kings' separate geographical origins, and asserted that it was inserted into the canon by (amongst others) the Frankish scholar (H)Rabanus Maurus (*c.* 780–856), who eventually became Archbishop of Mainz. By the time of the later Middle Ages, they went on to claim, the link was no longer just an *interpretatio posterior*, but a frequent (though not universal) assertion in heraldry and medallions or coinage.[29] In view of what was to occur shortly with the painting industry of the German lands and the Low Countries, it is probably an indication of such associations beginning to form in Europeans' minds. These associations, vague and incidental at first, were the 'building blocks' of what was to become a Eurocentric world order, at least partially based on skin colour, and so eventually on race.

To conclude this discussion about the association between the Magi and the continents in medieval iconography, it is pleasing to note that there is one (single) undeniable manifestation of that link dating from the end of the medieval period, between 1457 and 1480. There exists an elaborate monstrance, which was made at that time as an offering from the French king Louis XI to St Martin's church in Halle, near Brussels. The central feature is an inverted (west at the top) T-O model of the world, or *orbis*, with a label for each of the continents to designate each of the three spaces, hanging on small chains. On one side of the labels appear the names of the continents — Europe, Africa, and Asia — and on the other there is engraved the name of a Magus: Melchior, Caspar, and Balthasar (respectively).[30] This gives a certain satisfying closure, but I would contend that the presence of this link, which would be so significant later on, had been an incipient part of the discourse for several centuries by the time of the 1450s.

---

my own work on the rise of Eurocentrism in *The Image of Europe*. It is true that I have enthusiastically welcomed the implications of Köllmann's and Wirth's addition of the names of the continents to the Magi coats of arms. Actually, I have no quarrel with Oschema's view, and only wish to qualify it by showing how the late medieval period contained a discourse which, at the time of the Renaissance, developed into a full-blown Eurocentric conception. Intriguingly, Paul Kaplan's analysis of the Gelre Armorial did not link the Magi directly with the continents; he suggested that they might refer possibly to Byzantium, France and the Holy Roman Empire: see Kaplan, *The Rise of the Black Magus*, pp. 91–92.

29 Köllmann and Wirth, 'Erdteile', cols 1130–31.

30 Oschema himself brings this example to light: see Oschema, *Bilder von Europa im Mittelalter*, p. 508 and plates 41–42.

The Power of Princes

So much for the power of the written word and heraldry; now let us consider issues related to the power of princes and prelates. There was also a political side to the growth of the cult of the Magi, and to the inclusion of a black prince amongst them, and it was part of the struggle for dominance between the emperors and the popes, which had begun in the eleventh century with the so-called Investiture Controversy, and which continued into the High Middle Ages with imperial members of the Hohenstaufen dynasty. During extended military operations in northern Italy, Emperor Frederick Barbarossa (r. 1155–90) was campaigning near Milan in 1158, when a set of bones alleged to be those of the Magi was 'discovered' at the church of St Eustorgius on the outskirts of the city. The Archbishop of Cologne, Rainald von Dassel (*c.* 1120–67), who also became Frederick's Chancellor, 'translated' them to Cologne, where they were later installed in the cathedral as holy relics of the highest order. They became an important pilgrimage destination, which was one of the most popular (and so lucrative) in the Christian world, and which continues to this day.

There was another reason for the translation, alongside the economic gain and religious kudos which Cologne and the Empire would attract. In the words of Bernard Hamilton, 'it was a piece of propaganda. The shrine of the Three Holy Kings was intended to become the centre of a cult of Christian kingship', where kings would enjoy a status much higher than that attributed to them by popes such as Alexander III.[31] The story of the Magi, and especially its visual representation, was a manifestation of great secular lords or kings, crowned and clothed in finery appropriate to their status, interacting directly with Christ and his parents, without the presence of any intermediary or priest of any sort. Alongside their crucial function of witnessing the birth of the Saviour and bringing gifts in recognition of that momentous event, it was as if their status as kings, crowned and powerful, was being confirmed by the solemnity of the occasion, and indeed by the presence of Christ himself and his mother. Potentially then, it could support a concept of temporal authority which was sanctioned by the Almighty, but which was not required to be blessed by the priesthood, or any other intermediary, and certainly not by a pope: this was a direct 'divine right' to rule, as it were, without papal interference. At the same time the Empire could use the story, with its iconography of all ages of mankind from all corners of the world to further its own claims of universal empire, with or without the sanction of Rome.[32] At this stage there was not necessarily a widely recognized link between any specific continent and one specific Magus (though such allusions were clearly in the air), but

31 Hamilton, 'Prester John and the Three Kings of Cologne', pp. 182–83.

32 It is perhaps significant that around this time, certain people at the Hohenstaufen court began to refer to the Empire as the 'Holy Roman Empire': see Weinfurter, 'Um 1157: Wie das Reich heilig wurde'. I am grateful to Christoph Mauntel for pointing out this reference.

from the late twelfth and thirteenth centuries the cult of the Magi could play felicitously into the hands of the Hohenstaufen court.[33]

The portrayal of black people was of potential interest in claims to universal empire by the Hohenstaufens, well before the appearance of the black Magus in the fifteenth century, for example by Barbarossa's descendant Frederick II (Emperor 1220–50), who had black servants in his service. Black *attendants* began to crop up in renderings of the retinue of the Magi in the thirteenth century: the most famous early example is the portrayal of the Magi on the wondrous pulpit in the *duomo* in Siena, carved by the sculptor Nicola Pisano in the 1260s. According to Paul Kaplan, by including two stereotypically sub-Saharan attendants in that scene, Pisano 'explicitly identified the biblical figures of the Magi with the Hohenstaufen rulers'.[34]

It was not only the Hohenstaufens who were launching claims to universal empire. The succeeding Habsburgs were also interested in faraway Christians, especially Frederick III (r. 1452–93), who gave a particular boost to the rise of the black Magus.[35] The Roman Catholic Church had always been implicitly universal, and in the later fourteenth and fifteenth centuries was revitalizing its aspirations, for example at the Councils of Basel and Ferrara-Florence (1438–45), at which two Ethiopians were present in 1441,[36] and which witnessed the optimistic campaign to reunify the Greek and Latin Churches in 1439. Contact was being sought with Prester John in the 1450s.

A study of the various ways in which the cult of the Magi has been 'used' down the ages, Richard Trexler's *The Journey of the Magi* sees the story as having been variously portrayed in order to encourage and officially sanction donations to the church by all, to celebrate papal glory, to show the essential role of secular princes in recognizing the birth of Christ and accessing the deity directly, to compete 'over and against the clergy' and, finally, to raise the profile of Cologne as a centre for pilgrimage and for supporting the crusades.[37] Many secular potentates, and some clerical ones, had themselves painted in as the Magi in the late Middle Ages and the early Renaissance: amongst many others, the Burgundian dukes Philip the Good and Charles the Bold, emperors Charles IV and Maximilian, members of the Baglioni clan which ran Perugia, and of course the Medici, not least in frescoes in their Florence *palazzo* painted by Benozzo Gozzoli in about 1460.[38] This is further evidence of an interaction between specific political actors, and the promotion of a myth which would in

---

33 See John of Hildesheim, *The Three Kings of Cologne*, ed. by Horstmann, pp. xiii, xvii–xviii; Bugner ed., *The Image of the Black*, vol. ii part i, pp. 131–38; Kaplan, *The Rise of the Black Magus*, pp. 29–30; and the carefully researched Bisgaard, 'A Black Mystery'. On Hohenstaufen claims of empire, see Folz, *The Concept of Empire*, pp. 99–100.

34 Kaplan, *The Rise of the Black Magus*, pp. 10–12.

35 Kaplan, *The Rise of the Black Magus*, pp. 98, 103–06.

36 Northrup, *Africa's Discovery of Europe*, p. 4; Northrup provides a catalogue of early African visitors to Europe.

37 Trexler, *The Journey of the Magi*, respectively pp. 23, 28–31, 93, and 73–74.

38 See Wintle, *The Image of Europe*, pp. 209–10; Trexler, *The Journey of the Magi*, pp. 80–91. On

the end help establish a Eurocentric hierarchy of the continents. These powerful men were using the story to further their own interests and campaigns and prestige, while contributing to the eventual establishment of a world order. An image which originated as a way of bringing a certain 'order' and symmetry to the Christian world was being employed by powerful patrons as a means of 'action' in support of their various political ends.

The Artists

What was the role of the artists in the promotion of the Magi cult by means of visual representations, especially in painting? What was the degree of agency on their part in the introduction of the black Magus? How did they influence the differentiation between the three separate Magi on the basis of their age and their geographical origins?

From the third century CE there were visual representations of the Magi legend placed in Christian tombs, for example in the cemeteries and catacombs of Rome.[39] One wall-painting from the Capella Graeca, in Rome's Catacomb of St Priscilla and possibly dating from around 300 CE, shows three shadowy figures above an arch, more or less identical and all moving left to right towards Mary and the Christ-child, bearing gifts. This must be one of the oldest depictions of the Magi. Another example dates from some time in the fourth century, and is on a fragment of a Roman sarcophagus from the cemetery of Saint Agnes in Rome. This version is in finely sculpted marble, and shows three identical, beardless young men, with lowered hoods rather than crowns, approaching the Madonna and child from right to left, with camels in the background, and bearing gifts, lit by a star.[40]

Figure 8.4 shows another of these early representations of the Magi from around 300 CE, also from the catacombs in Rome. The three Magi are identical here, all quite young, approaching the Madonna and child, with Joseph (or possibly a prophet) standing behind, and a star in the heavens: this is a version straight from Matthew 2. 11. The inscription asks that the dedicatee, Severa, may live in God (*in deo vivas*). All the Magi have flowing capes and a kind of eastern Phrygian bonnet, and are carrying gifts: the two outside ones each have a plate, and the central figure has a bag of something, possibly money or gold. No crowns are to be seen;[41] there are gifts and a star, but no other distinction between the visitors.

Gozzoli's work see Cardini, *The Chapel of the Magi*; and de Koomen ed., *Benozzo Gozzoli*. On the cult of the Magi in Florence in the Renaissance, see Hatfield, 'The Compagnia de' Magi'.

39 Many are documented in Vezin, *L'Adoration et le cycle des Mages*, who provides a thorough analysis of the iconography in the very early material, especially in Italy and France.

40 Now in the Vatican Museums, Museo Pio Cristiano, inv. 31459. For details, see Harley-McGowan and McGowan, 'The Magi and the Manger'.

41 Crowns replaced bonnets around the time of the tenth century; see Vezin, *L'Adoration et le cycle des Mages*, pp. 109, 114.

FIGURE 8.4. Stone sealing the loculus (niche tomb) of Severa, marble, with the Magi. From the cemetery of Priscilla on the Via Salaria, Rome, *c.* 250–325 CE. Vatican City, Musei Vaticani, cat. 28594. © 2020, Photo Scala, Florence.

The depiction in Figure 8.5 takes us on to early Byzantine-style mosaics, from the renowned Basilica of Sant' Apollinare Nuovo in Ravenna, dating from about 620 CE, by which time it was already a Roman Catholic church. The Magi all have identical expressions and postures, but have now (perhaps for the first time in visual art) acquired names: Balthasar, Melchior and Caspar. Even more importantly, they have differentiated facial hair: on the right, we have an older greybeard, leading the group towards the Madonna and child; on the left we have a vigorous-looking middle-aged man with a dark beard, and in the middle, there is the young, beardless Magus. Here we have represented the ages of man: young and old all are welcome to Christ and in the Church. But they are all still geographically anonymous: they are probably, as the Evangelist had reported, 'from the East'.

We need therefore to ask when the Magi first became associated in art with separate and distinctive continents, by means of the depiction of their skin colour and other physical features. There are some early, somewhat strange examples, almost certainly later forgeries (see below). Less spuriously, in the Christian East there is an icon at the monastery of St Catherine on Mount Sinai, dating from *c.* 1300, apparently portraying a black Ethiopian as the third Magus. It might have been made to commemorate a visit by an African potentate on his way to Jerusalem, where there were many Ethiopians by that time. There may perhaps be other examples; apparently there was a more developed awareness of the dark-skinned Other in Eastern than in Western Christianity at this early stage, at least in the Holy Land. And as we have noted, from about 1250 there was also a certain optimistic hope that black Africans might be an ally against the forces of Islam.[42] We have seen that there were black *servants* shown in Tuscan church sculptures from the thirteenth

42 Hunt, 'Skin and the Meeting of Cultures', pp. 98–100. This may be the same image noted in Folda, *Crusader Art*, p. 321, which tentatively identifies the dark Magus as a Mongol, representing Oriental alongside Middle Eastern and Western Christianity, possibly in the

FIGURE 8.5. Mosaic of the three Magi, Basilica of Sant' Apollinare Nuovo, in Ravenna, *c.* 620 CE. <https://commons.wikimedia.org/wiki/File:RavennaMosaico.jpg> public domain [accessed 21 June 2021].

century, and that the development was linked to Hohenstaufen ambitions.[43] The artists seem to have been emulating each other, and developing their styles and conventions, all the way from all-white kings, through black attendants, to the black Magus himself.

In Western European art, among the contenders for the first black Magus, there are a number of possibilities from the early fifteenth century.[44]

---

person of a Nestorian Mongol general, Kitbogha, who commanded the Mongol forces in Syria in the late 1250s.

43 It is possible to chart the progress of the adoption of the motif of the black attendant in Magi sculpture in various Tuscan churches from the twelfth to the fifteenth century, ending up eventually on Ghiberti's baptistery doors in Florence (*c.* 1405): see Wintle, *The Image of Europe*, pp. 199–203. They can also be found in Italian and Burgundian/French paintings of the fourteenth and early fifteenth centuries, e.g. a panel by a Franco-Flemish master, 'The Adoration of the Magi with St Anthony Abbott', *c.* 1390–1410, Los Angeles, Getty Center, n° 2004.68. One of the first Tuscan renderings of the black Magus himself was actually from the workshop of a Flemish-born sculptor Giambologna (1529–1608), in a sixteenth-century bronze panel on the main doors of the Duomo in Pisa.

44 See, e.g., a decorated capital letter initial in the *Missale secundum usum ecclesiae s. Floriani*, fol. 4^{r}, *c.* 1400 (Sankt Florian, Stiftsbibliothek, Cod. III.205); detail of an altarpiece wing from Friedburg church (Rhineland), *c.* 1410, now in the Museum Catharijneconvent, Utrecht (described in the next paragraph); altar panels from Staufen church, *c.* 1420, Freiburg im

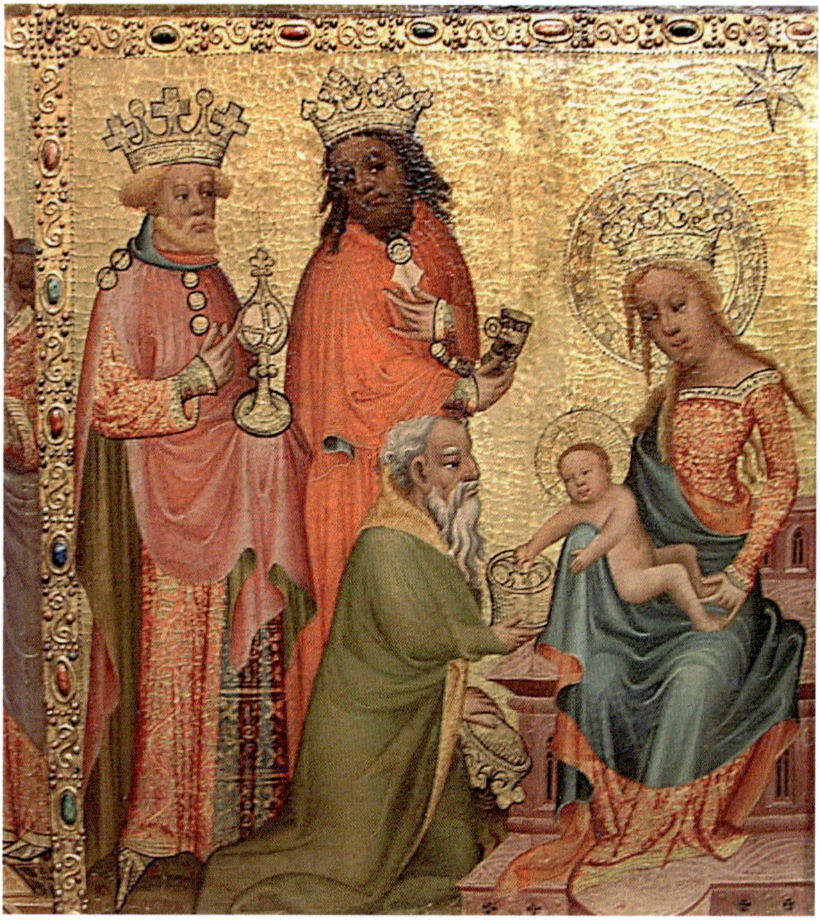

FIGURE 8.6. Meister Bertram von Minden, 'The Adoration of the Kings'. Panel of a double-winged altarpiece from the Petrikirche in Buxtehude, inside left wing of the altar, *c.* 1390/1415. Hamburg, Kunsthalle, inv. no. HK-501a–4; collection: Alte Meister. © bpk image 00032686. By kind permission.

In Figure 8.6 we see a black Magus as a part of a group painted on a German altarpiece, which is dated 1410 by the Kunsthalle in Hamburg: the youngest, beardless Magus in the centre is brown-skinned. The second king with a

---

Breisgau, Augustinermuseum. All cited in Bugner ed., *The Image of the Black*, vol. II part II, pp. 37–38; on the Magi in the *Missale* from Sankt Florian see most recently Avkiran, 'Das rassifizierte Fremde im Bild', pp. 52–53. Trexler, *The Journey of the Magi*, p. 102, mentions the 1360s for the date of the first black king, but his authority is Kaplan, *The Rise of the Black Magus*, p. 10, who is actually referring to black attendants, not kings.

yellow beard, who is middle-aged, is pointing at the star, as in the traditional stylized versions. The old king has taken off his crown and is on his knees. This is a foreshadowing of the new pattern.

There is another German painting of the Adoration, in the Museum Catharijneconvent in Utrecht, which forms part of a large altarpiece, also dated to 1410.[45] The artist portrays the kneeling older king with his crown on the step before him, a middle-aged king with reddish-blond hair and beard, holding his crown in his free hand, and a young beardless black king with stereotypical sub-Saharan features and hair, with his crown on his head, but third in line and junior in age.

Further north, there is also a fine painted carving of the Adoration, part of the elaborate Lüderskooper Altar, in Cuxhaven-Lüdingworth on the German North Sea coast.[46] In the delightfully ornate parish church there, this late Gothic altar was carved in the 1430s in limewood. In the imaginative and playful adoration scene, at which not one child but several are present, the elderly Magus kneels, while the central figure of the middle (or European) king is enlarged and adorned with an enormous brown (not white) beard, adding to his importance in the composition. The black king to his rear is playing a game with another child, and may have a hint of a light beard.

The established authority on the black Magus, Paul Kaplan, decided that amongst these various candidates, the famous 1437 Wurzach altarpiece, by Hans Multscher, should hold the title for the first undisputed painting of the black king.[47] In that image, we can identify the different ages of the kings, but the glittering magnificence of the youngest king, as usual towards the back, must have been all the more astonishing because his face was painted as dark-skinned, the effect amplified by the black attendant who stood behind him. However, that king's facial features bear no traces of the stereotypical black man; his luxuriant hair is black and unruly under his crown, but not tightly curled.

After these early manifestations, the black Magus spread like wildfire, first through the German lands, and the Low Countries, and then beyond. An influential example we saw in Figure 8.2, painted by the Master of the Polling altarpiece in 1444.[48] We noticed above how the facial features here could without much imagination on the part of the informed onlooker be linked to the continents: these are stereotypes which have now become clichéd, but would have been recognizable even then. Much is familiar from

45 Panel of the Adoration of the Magi, on a retable from Middle Rhine or Westphalia, *c.* 1410. Museum Catharijneconvent, Utrecht, ABM S25–28 and 156–58, interior panel n° 4. This is presumably the piece mentioned by Bugner, see above n. 44.

46 St Jacobi Kirche in Cuxhaven-Lüdingworth, *c.* 1430s; see Wintle, *The Image of Europe*, pp. 204–05.

47 Kaplan, *The Rise of the Black Magus*, p. 85. Hans Multscher (1400–47), *The Adoration of the Magi*, 1437, panel, 148x40 cm, wings of the *Wurzacher Altar* with scenes of the passion of Christ. Berlin, Gemäldegalerie, cat. 1821 D-G.

48 See also Kaplan, *The Rise of the Black Magus*, p. 99.

the standard medieval formula: the eldest Magus kneels bareheaded, and offers gold to Jesus. The second king looks at the third one, and is pointing at the Christ-child. A six-pointed star twinkles above. The third, youngest king pays attention.

But for the first time in a thousand years of graphic visual portrayals of the Magi in Christian art, these new-style depictions have taken an enormous step on the path towards an emerging European image of the world and its component parts. The crucial difference is of course that the third king is black, and increasingly is being given clear sub-Saharan facial features. There can be little doubt that he represents Africa in the Polling painting, in his exotic white and silver gown. The old king is deserving of respect; he stands for Asia, and for the Semitic peoples. The second king is in the prime of life. His reddish hair and his clothing make him recognizably European, and though he must defer in age and status before Christ to the older king, he is the vigorous and vibrant one amongst the Magi: in the terrestrial world he is the main force, as his central location and importance in the composition emphasizes. It is as if the artist is moving towards recognizing the potent agency of the middle king as representative of Europe, and his status as a dominant force in the world alongside the venerable piety of the older king and the fascinating exoticism of the younger one. The Polling Master is following closely many of the medieval conventions in portraying the Magi, but he is also marking a trailblazing route forward to a more Eurocentric age in the Renaissance.[49]

Mass Production

In the second half of the fifteenth century, the new fashion had spread to the Low Countries, where it was adopted and mass-produced in what have been called 'art factories',[50] and by 1500 it had become almost universal in European art. Virtually all of the greatest (and other) artists of the next couple of centuries, from Dürer to Rubens, and eventually right through into the twentieth century, produced their own versions (often several) of the classic Christian tableau, with their fascinating displays of the rich and exotic, juxtaposed with the sacred simplicity of the Bethlehem stable. It had been a familiar image for a millennium, and now with the enormous proliferation of the pictures and the addition of the black Magus, it became even more of a common reference point. The paintings adorned the palaces of the secular and priestly aristocracy, but also were introduced into churches all over Christendom, from the most magnificent cathedrals to the humblest of village churches. The new form of the Magi also appeared in more weather-resistant

49 The new Eurocentrism of the Renaissance period is documented in Hale, *The Civilization of Europe in the Renaissance*, chap. 1; Wintle, 'Renaissance Maps and the Construction of the Idea of Europe'; and Wintle, *The Image of Europe*, chap. 5.

50 Bugner ed., *The Image of the Black*, vol. II part II, p. 168.

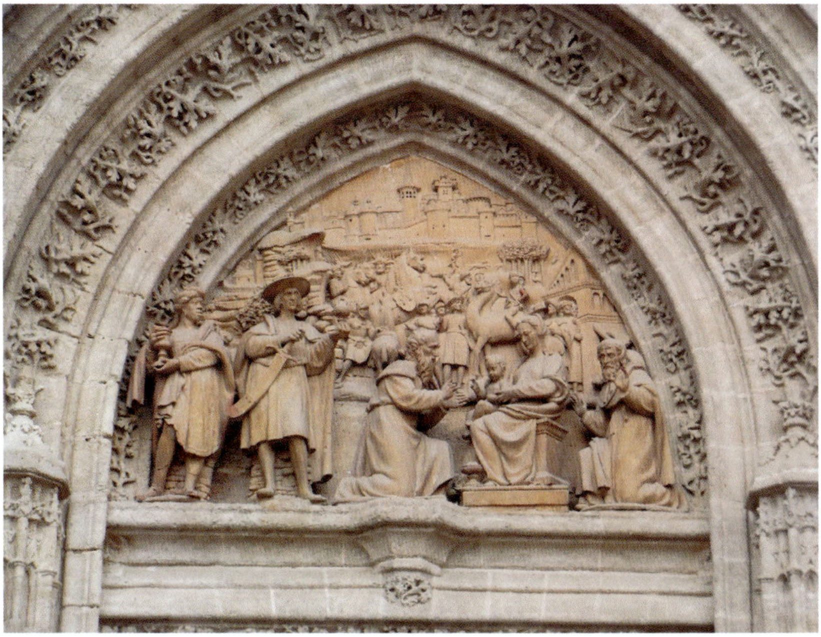

FIGURE 8.7. Miguel Perrin (sculptor), 'The Adoration of the Magi', in the tympanum above the Puerta de los Palos, Cathedral of Seville, 1520–23. Author's photograph.

form on the outside of buildings, especially of great churches, carved on the doors and in the tympani above the portals.

One very eloquent copy, for example, could (and can still) be found above the *Puerta de los Palos* of Seville cathedral, the main doors of which open onto the principal square of the city (Figure 8.7). This is where the teeming masses thronged in the city which received the precious treasure from the Indies fleets, and so was one of the most important public spaces in Europe. Miguel Perrin sculpted his Adoration there in terracotta in 1520–23, and it too shows a young stereotypical black Magus, a middle-aged one in the form of a Humanist European prince, and a kneeling bearded sage. The reach of the concept and its iconography was panoramic.

All this shows us that the artists were gradually moving towards the inclusion of the black Magus. Were they doing so under instructions, were they acting on their own initiative, or was agency a result of a discourse between the patrons and the artists — and perhaps even the public? There are two areas which can cast additional light on that issue. We have already seen that black attendants had been portrayed as part of the Magi's retinue as early as the mid-thirteenth century, which played to the ambitions of the Hohenstaufens and others, but it also indicated a willingness on the part of the artists themselves to take up that challenge, considerably before the appearance of the black Magus himself. The other is the question of later forgeries. There are several examples of black Magi before 1400 which can be seen to have been crudely altered at a later date to turn an originally white king into a black Magus.[51] The painters or graffiti artists who executed these later changes were clearly conforming to an asserted doctrine *after the fact*. They may have been acting under instructions, but they were certainly carrying out the alterations themselves. By blackening and so 'Africanizing' the third Magus, whether in new images of the fifteenth century or in disfigurements of earlier works, they were actively complying with new notions which had evolved so far as to demand conformity to the new orthodoxy. There were three Magi, three ages of man, and three continents. And the junior one was black, from Africa. What motivated the artists in their shared agency? Their patrons did, in all probability, and there were also external events like the appearance in Europe of more black people. But in addition, there was a fascination with these extravagant black princes, whom they could dress up as wildly exotic and gorgeous in their almost outlandish finery: the opposite of everything that was European. That Othering process was a very important part of the advent of the black Magus.

Othering, Identity, Interaction

'Othering' is an important contribution to the formulation of identity, where defining what one is *not* can be an essential and often relatively easy step in forging one's own identity, or that of one's group.[52] Although certain overarching identities were probably developing in the medieval period, it can be convincingly argued that a European identity evolved principally in the period of the Renaissance, and that the 'discovery' of the Americas and the increased interaction with other continents in that period were important contributions to that process.[53] That identity formation did not, of course, start overnight in 1492, and there were already developments underway — such as the advent of the black Magus — which had helped to assemble some of the 'building blocks' which would later underpin notions of Europeanness, weak though they were for most of the medieval period. But it is important to understand that 'Othering' does not necessarily mean defining your enemies (though of course it sometimes can): *difference* is the key concept, and the

51 See various examples, from Catalonia in the twelfth century, Germany in the fourteenth, and north-western Spain also in the fourteenth century: Wintle, *The Image of Europe*, pp. 198–99; Bugner ed., *The Image of the Black*, vol. II part I, p. 137, and vol. II part II, pp. 19, 20–27. See also Mâle, *L'Art religieux*, p. 216 n. 3.

52 On 'Othering' in a theoretical context, including at European level, see Corbey and Leerssen ed., *Alterity, Identity, Image*; Gifford and Hauswedell ed., *Europe and its Others*; Stråth ed., *Europe and the Other and Europe as the Other*.

53 See Wintle, *The Image of Europe*, pp. 219–81 (chap. 5).

black Magus was very different indeed from the European self-image. The picture drawn of the dark-skinned Magus was in the medieval and early modern period invariably positive: he was almost always the youngest and therefore the most junior; in some more countryside churches he might even be shown as playful, or perhaps even a bit naughty, as in the Cuxhaven portrayal mentioned above, or in a Danish mural of the Adoration in the village church of Søndersø on Funen, of about 1500.[54] The third Magus can thus sometimes be shown to be perhaps a little immature. But this is more in line with the age hierarchy, and is certainly not denigratory towards black kings or black people in general.[55] There is a pecking order of seniority in years, which was centuries old, and an emerging differentiation to show origins from different parts of the world. But the hierarchy of the Magi was not used to degrade Africa or its 'king'; again, difference was the key and, if anything, it was the virtues of the European Magus which were being developed at this stage. It would be the rise of Atlantic slaving in the seventeenth and especially the eighteenth centuries that would turn the sentiments of Europeans about black people in such a negative direction.

The third Magus was almost always identified with black Africa; however, there were also very rare examples of him representing other parts of the world. There is a suggestion that the early dark Magus in the Sinai monastery of about 1300 may not have been Ethiopian but a Mongol, and so Asian;[56] there is a representation of the third Magus as an American Indian in a panel of the Adoration of between 1500 and 1506 in the cathedral of Viseu in Portugal.[57] Later, in the seventeenth century, there was an Adoration by the Rubens School in the collection of the Duke of Sutherland, with the third Magus displayed as a figure from the Orient or Far East, rather than an African.[58] In spite of these exceptions, nearly all the dark kings were linked to Africa, and an important part of their function was to lend their alterity, their difference, to assist in the process of European self-definition.

Amongst the enormous range of sumptuous Magi paintings of the fifteenth century which are to be seen all over the Western world,[59] the

---

54 It may be by a north German artist. Jerusalem and Golgotha are in the background. The young Magus has a slightly darker skin, and his facial features might be described as 'African'.

55 Sachs, 'L'Image du Noir', p. 891; Knipping, *Iconography of the Counter Reformation*, vol. I, p. 201; Bugner ed., *The Image of the Black*, vol. II part II, pp. 175–78; Kaplan, *The Rise of the Black Magus*, p. 119.

56 See above, n. 42, and especially Folda, *Crusader Art*, p. 321.

57 Honour, *The European Vision of America*, ill. 4. This possibly represents the first portrayal of an American in European art.

58 Knipping, *Iconography of the Counter Reformation*, vol. I, p. 226.

59 Among the most striking from this period are those by Andrea Mantegna (*c.* 1464, now in the Uffizi), Francesco Botticini (*c.* 1495, now in the Art Institute of Chicago; the painting is in the form of a *mappa mundi*), and Jeroen Bosch (*c.* 1500, now in the Prado). All these and many more are beautifully illustrated in Bugner ed., *The Image of the Black*, vol. II part II, pp. 131–85.

FIGURE 8.8. Master of the Prado, 'Adoration of the Magi', free copy of the central panel of the *Columba Triptych* by Rogier van der Weyden in Munich (Alte Pinakothek), in the style of Hans Memling, 1460s. © Madrid, Museo Nacional del Prado, inv. P01558. By kind permission.

example chosen for display here is an Adoration of the 1460s by an anonymous artist, copying Rogier van der Weyden in the style of Hans Memling (Figure 8.8). It typifies the portrayal of a familiar scene of the nativity with the relatively humble figures of the holy family and the animals in the stable, contrasted with the exquisite finery of the exotic potentates from the East: the effect is one that has continued to be impressive for 650 years. In the visual luxuriating there is no figure more fascinating than the young black prince in the rear (here we also see a black attendant, glancing across at his young master). None of the three kings has facial hair in this version but their differing age and seniority are quite clear from the portrayal of their faces. They have caps or hats rather than crowns, all removed in reverence. There is no evidence of 'Semitic' features in the face of the senior, kneeling Magus, though at the front of the group of attendants to the right there is a 'stage' Semite, apparently holding the fur-trimmed hat of the second, middle-aged, 'European' king, who has distinctive reddish-blond hair. The show is stolen of course by the third Magus, who combines the beauty and posture of youth with a display of finery unequalled in the whole scene, holding a bejewelled cap aloft in one hand and his gift in the other. It is a stunning spectacle, and — amongst many other sentiments — represents the tactile, caressing exploration by these Renaissance artists, eventually all over Europe, of these imagined paragons of youthful humanity from the other side of the world.

The primary message continued to be one of ecumenical universality: all ages and origins are welcome in Christianity.[60] But at the same time, we can witness in growing numbers of portraits of the Magi a gradual movement towards (re)defining a European identity.[61] The increasingly adopted new conventions were 'rarely executed without some thought and interest on the part of the maker'. In Kaplan's words, the entry of the black Magus can be seen as one of those 'complex processes by which social experience and aspirations are transformed and articulated in works of art'.[62] From the twelfth century onwards, as a result of increased interaction with West Africa, and as a spin-off from the politics of Empire and Papacy, we see more interest in black people on the part of some European artists. This interest in what might be called 'race' was probably not an exercise in 'rac*ism*', but more to do with curiosity about new phenomena, in a monogenetic context.[63]

However, within the generally benign context, there was room for a hierarchy to emerge: the two white, older Magi were distinct from the black one, and increasingly the virtues of an obvious European Magus were extolled in some of the visual presentations. The artists of the fifteenth century responded to all the impetus and sources available, and publicized the association between one continent — Africa — and one of the kings. Again, if one was Africa, and there were three continents, then one of the others had to be Europe. The veneration for the elderly, ancient Asia continued and, almost by default, it became clear to some that there was scope for portraying Europe in the figure of the second Magus. Euro-assertion was not universal, and it did not imply a negative portrayal of either Asia or Africa. But from the moment the third king became black, the implication was clear. The black Magus assisted in the formulation of a European identity in the Renaissance period, and 'offers a

60 Knipping, *Iconography of the Counter Reformation*, vol. II, p. 365.

61 Benjamin Schmidt denies that the images of the Magi or the Sons of Noah were 'codified' as representing the continents in either the Middle Ages or the Renaissance, for he is concerned to reserve that role for Dutch artists of the seventeenth century; see Schmidt, *Innocence Abroad*, p. 125. While the codification later became perhaps more rigid, it has been shown here that it was certainly initially launched in the medieval period.

62 Kaplan, *The Rise of the Black Magus*, pp. 2–3.

63 Sanders, *Lost Tribes and Promised Lands*, pp. 17, 52; Nederveen Pieterse, *White on Black*, pp. 26–27. On the existence of 'race' in the Middle Ages, see Heng, *The Invention of Race*.

fascinating mirror', which can provide us with 'a highly instructive picture of the European mentality'.[64]

We should not avoid the implicit conclusion that, despite the absence of a racist hierarchy of the continents in the Middle Ages and for much of the Renaissance period, elements of the discourse of racial hierarchy were rising to the surface, and would be used as arguments in the full-blown racist conceptions of the later seventeenth century, the Enlightenment, and beyond. Even in the later Middle Ages, although the black man was an object of theoretically innocent interest and fascination, he had to be 'accommodated [...] to European — and therefore superior — social patterns'; the Other needed to be fitted into emerging Eurocentric views of the world.[65] Not to put too fine a point on it, the black Magus contained some of the seeds of a continental hierarchy, and of a concomitant racism, despite its initial innocence.[66]

Conclusion

The advent of the black Magus was one of the ways in which, through the medium of visual art and through the shared agency of the artists, an emerging European identity was made concrete. There were other visual media and genres as well: for example, maps, pictures of Noah and his three sons, and the legend of Europa and the Bull.[67] All of them, together with other factors, contributed to an emerging hierarchy of the continents based on notions of civilization and virtues. In this heady mix of moving towards more recognizably 'modern' attitudes, political events influenced the way artists expressed themselves in their patrons' commissions. Those expressions in turn affected the thought and mentality of a wide public, and of those who drove political events — the princes and prelates — and may well have encouraged or even justified the powerful in their attitudes and actions. The hypothesis seems legitimate that, in this period of the later Middle Ages as well as in the more obvious manifestations in the Renaissance, there was a constant interaction between nascent Eurocentric thinking about the ordering of the world in continents, and the work of cultural actors in the form of artists and their patrons.

64 Bugner ed., *The Image of the Black*, vol. II part II, p. 175.
65 Bugner ed., *The Image of the Black*, vol. II part II, p. 226.
66 See Bastide, 'Color, Racism and Christianity'; and Kaplan, *The Rise of the Black Magus*, p. 119.
67 See Wintle, *Image of Europe*, pp. 102–49, 163–90.

Works Cited

Primary Sources

John of Hildesheim, *The Three Kings of Cologne: An Early English Translation of the Historia Trium Regum by John of Hildesheim*, ed. by Carl Horstmann (London: EETS, 1886)

Secondary Studies

Avkiran, Melis, 'Das rassifizierte Fremde im Bild. Zur Genese differenzbildender Konzepte in der Kunst des 15. Jahrhunderts am Beispiel des Malers Hans Memling', *Image. Zeitschrift für interdisziplinäre Bildwissenschaft*, 28 (2018), 40–74, <http://www.gib.uni-tuebingen.de/own/journal/pdf/IMAGE%20 28_Themenheft.pdf> [accessed 21 June 2021]

Bastide, Roger, 'Color, Racism and Christianity', in *Color and Race*, ed. by J. H. Franklin (Boston: Houghton Mifflin, 1968), pp. 34–49

Bethencourt, Francisco, *Racisms: From the Crusades to the Twentieth Century* (Princeton: Princeton University Press, 2013)

Bisgaard, Lars, 'A Black Mystery: The Hagiography of the Three Magi' (unpublished paper at the conference Medieval History Writing and Crusading Ideology, Rome, January 2001)

Braude, Benjamin, 'The Sons of Noah and the Construction of Ethnic and Geographical Identities in the Medieval and Early Modern Periods', *The William and Mary Quarterly*, 54,1 (1997), 103–42

Bugner, Ladislas, ed., *The Image of the Black in Western Art*, 2 vols in 3 parts (Cambridge, MA: Harvard University Press, 1976–79) [second printing, 1991]

Cardini, Franco, *The Chapel of the Magi in Palazzo Medici* (Florence: Mandragora, 2001)

Conley, Dalton, and Jason Fletcher, *The Genome Factor: What the Social Genomics Revolution Reveals about Ourselves, our History, and the Future* (Princeton: Princeton University Press, 2017)

Corbey, Raymond, and Joep T. Leerssen, ed., *Alterity, Identity, Image: Selves and Others in Society and Scholarship* (Amsterdam: Rodopi, 1991)

Eliav-Feldon, Miriam, Benjamin Isaac and Joseph Ziegler, ed., *The Origins of Racism in the West* (Cambridge: Cambridge University Press, 2009)

Folda, Jaroslav, *Crusader Art in the Holy Land, from the Third Crusade to the Fall of Acre 1187–1291* (Cambridge: Cambridge University Press, 2005)

Folz, Robert, *The Concept of Empire in Western Europe from the Fifth to the Fourteenth Century* (London: Edward Arnold, 1969)

Gifford, Paul, and Tessa Hauswedell, ed., *Europe and its Others: Essays on Interperception and Identity* (Oxford: Bern, 2010)

Groebner, Valentin, 'Haben Hautfarben eine Geschichte? Personenbeschreibungen und ihre Kategorien zwischen dem 13. und dem 16. Jahrhundert', *Zeitschrift für Historische Forschung*, 30 (2003), 1–18

Hale, John, *The Civilization of Europe in the Renaissance* (London: Harper Collins, 1994)

Hamilton, Bernard, 'Prester John and the Three Kings of Cologne', in *Studies in Medieval History Presented to R. H. C. Davis*, ed. by Henry Mayr-Harting and Robert I. Moore (London: Hambledon, 1985), pp. 179–91

Harley-McGowan, Felicity, and Andrew McGowan, 'The Magi and the Manger: Imaging Christmas in Ancient Art and Ritual', *The Yale ISM Review*, 3,1 (2016), Article 2, <http://ismreview.yale.edu/article/the-magi-and-the-manger-imaging-christmas-in-ancient-art-and-ritual-2/> [accessed 21 June 2021]

Hatfield, Rab, 'The Compagnia de' Magi', *Journal of the Warburg and Courtauld Institutes*, 33 (1970), 107–61

Heng, Geraldine, 'The Invention of Race in the European Middle Ages', parts I & II, *Literature Compass*, 8,5 (2011), 258–74 and 332–50

——, *The Invention of Race in the European Middle Ages* (Cambridge: Cambridge University Press, 2018)

Hofmann, Hans, *Die heiligen drei Könige: zur Heiligenverehrung im kirchlichen, gesellschaftlichen und politischen Leben des Mittelalters* (Bonn: Röhrscheid, 1975)

Honour, Hugh, *The European Vision of America* (Cleveland: Cleveland Museum of Art, 1975)

Hunt, Lucy-Anne, 'Skin and the Meeting of Cultures', in *Images of Otherness in Medieval and Early Modern Times: Exclusion, Inclusion and Assimilation*, ed. by Anja Eisenbeiß and Lieselotte E. Saurma-Jeltsch (Berlin: Deutscher Kunstverlag, 2012), pp. 89–106

Kaplan, Paul H. D., *The Rise of the Black Magus in Western Art* (Ann Arbor: UMI Research Press, 1985)

Kehrer, Hugo, *Die heiligen drei Könige in Literatur und Kunst*, 2 vols (Leipzig: Seemann, 1908–09)

Kiernan, Victor G., *The Lords of Human Kind: European Attitudes to the Outside World in the Imperial Age* (Harmondsworth: Penguin, 1972)

Knipping, John B., *Iconography of the Counter Reformation in the Netherlands: Heaven on Earth*, 2 vols (Leiden: Sijthoff, 1974)

Köllmann, Erich, and Karl-August Wirth, 'Erdteile', in *Reallexikon zur deutschen Kunstgeschichte*, vol. V, ed. by Otto Schmitt and others (Stuttgart: Metzler, 1967), cols 1107–1202

Koomen, Arjan de, ed., *Benozzo Gozzoli, ca 1420–1497* [special issue of *Kunstschrift*, 54,4 (Aug.–Sept. 2010)] (Amsterdam: Kunst en Schrijven, 2010)

Leeuwen, Theo van, and Carey Jewitt, ed., *Handbook of Visual Analysis* (London: Sage, 2001)

Lewis, Martin W., and Kären E. Wigen, *The Myth of Continents: A Critique of Metageography* (Berkeley: University of California Press, 1997)

Mâle, Émile, *L'Art religieux du XIIIe siècle en France: étude sur l'iconographie du Moyen Age et sur ses sources d'inspiration*, 8th edn (Paris: Armand Colin, 1948)

McNally, Robert E., 'The Three Holy Kings in Early Irish Latin Writing', in *Kyriakon: Festschrift Johannes Quasten*, ed. by Patrick Granfield and Josef A. Jungmann, 2 vols (Münster: Aschendorff, 1970), vol. II, pp. 667–90

Miramon, Charles de, 'Noble Dogs, Noble Blood: The Invention of the Concept of Race in the Late Middle Ages', in *The Origins of Racism in the West*, ed. by Miriam Eliav-Feldon, Benjamin Isaac, and Joseph Ziegler (Cambridge: Cambridge University Press , 2009), pp. 200–16

Nederveen Pieterse, Jan, *White on Black: Images of Africa and Blacks in Western Popular Culture* (New Haven: Yale University Press, 1992)

Northrup, David, *Africa's Discovery of Europe 1450–1850* (New York: Oxford University Press, 2002)

Oschema, Klaus, *Bilder von Europa im Mittelalter*, Mittelalter-Forschungen, 43 (Ostfildern: Jan Thorbecke, 2013)

Painter, Nell Irvin, *The History of White People* (New York: Norton, 2010)

Pastoureau, Michel, *Une histoire symbolique du Moyen Âge occidental*, La librairie du xxie siècle (Paris: Seuil, 2004)

Sachs, Ignacy, 'L'Image du Noir dans l'art européen', *Annales ESC*, 24,4 (1969), 883–93

Sanders, Ronald, *Lost Tribes and Promised Lands: The Origins of American Racism* (Boston: Little, Brown, 1978)

Schmidt, Benjamin, *Innocence Abroad: The Dutch Imagination and the New World, 1570–1670* (Cambridge: Cambridge University Press, 2001)

Stracke, Richard, 'Epiphany: The Adoration of the Magi', 2015, revised 2016, <https://www.christianiconography.info/magi.html> [accessed 21 June 2021]

Stråth, Bo, ed., *Europe and the Other and Europe as the Other* (Brussels: Peter Lang, 2000)

Trexler, Richard C., *The Journey of the Magi: Meanings in History of a Christian Story* (Princeton: Princeton University Press, 1997)

Vezin, Gilberte, *L'Adoration et le cycle des Mages dans l'art chrétien primitif: étude des influences orientales et grecques sur l'art chrétien* (Paris: Presses Universitaires de France, 1950)

Warner, Marina, *Alone of All Her Sex: The Myth and the Cult of the Virgin Mary* (London: Weidenfeld and Nicholson, 1976)

Weinfurter, Stefan, 'Um 1157: Wie das Reich heilig wurde', in *Die Macht des Königs. Herrschaft in Europa vom Frühmittelalter bis in die Neuzeit*, ed. by Bernhard Jussen (München: C. H. Beck, 2005), pp. 190–204

Wheeler, Roxann, *The Complexion of Race: Categories of Difference in Eighteenth-Century British Culture* (Philadelphia: University of Pennsylvania Press, 2000)

Whitaker, Ian R., 'An Historical Explanation of the Asiatic Myths of Prester John', *The Asiatic Review*, 48 (1952), 74–79

Wintle, Michael, 'Renaissance Maps and the Construction of the Idea of Europe', *The Journal of Historical Geography*, 25,2 (1999), 137–65

——, *The Image of Europe: Visualizing Europe in Cartography and Iconography Throughout the Ages* (Cambridge: Cambridge University Press, 2009)

——, 'Islam as Europe's Other Throughout History: Some Discontinuities', *History*, 101,344 (2016), 42–61

MARK HORTON

Beyond Eurasia — the African Contribution to the Premodern World

Examining the Global and the Local in the Kilwa Sultanate, East Africa

Introduction

In the many studies of global history in premodern times, the role of Africa is often neglected. Europe's connections with Asia, and in particular the Mongol Empire, are often discussed, while the tentative expansions into the Atlantic islands are characterized as a continuation of the *Reconquista* and by extension, of the ideology of the crusades.[1] Rarely discussed is Africa itself — the continent also connected to the Eurasian landmass, and readily accessible both by sea and desert caravan.[2] There were no Marco Polos or William of Rubrucks to leave European narratives of sub-Saharan Africa, and the 'first' European to leave a detailed eyewitness account of the African interior was Leo Africanus (*c.* 1494–1554) in the early sixteenth century.[3] Devoid of these European historical narratives, the states south of the Sahara are often seen as 'black boxes' and lacking any significant agency in the emerging global economy, making it near impossible to understand how they may have been influenced by external social, religious, or economic forces.

Recently, archaeological research has enabled us to fill out the details of these African states, and to expand on the often-fragmentary documentary sources, to understand in more detail their inner workings. This chapter takes an African-centric perspective of one particular state, that of Kilwa,

1 Abu Lughod, *Before European Hegemony*; Fernández-Armesto, *Before Columbus*; Russell, *Prince Henry 'the Navigator'*, pp. 34–35. The capture of Ceuta in 1415 is often seen as the start of the process of Portuguese maritime expansion, given a crusading ideology by its greatest sponsor, Prince Henry and his 'caravels of Christ'.

2 Phillips, *The Medieval Expansion of Europe*, pp. 143–63.

3 Leo Africanus, *The History and Descriptions of Africa*.

Mark Horton (mark.horton@rau.ac.uk), Cultural Heritage Institute, Royal Agricultural University, Cirencester, UK

Order into Action: How Large-Scale Concepts of World-Order determine Practices in the Premodern World, ed. by Klaus Oschema and Christoph Mauntel, CURSOR 40 (Turnhout: Brepols, 2022), pp. 237–262
BREPOLS ✠ PUBLISHERS 10.1484/M.CURSOR-EB.5.123850

located on the East African coast, which between the twelfth and sixteenth centuries, became the key location for the export of southern African gold and other luxuries. In doing this, we will trace how ideas of *order* — economic, social, and religious — often borrowed from the wider Islamic world were employed in the sultanate to cement the pre-eminence of Kilwa among the many competing port cities of the coast. We will examine how one individual, Hasan ibn Sulaiman, through the deliberate borrowing of foreign architectural forms, Islamic culture, and the adoption of foreign titles, was briefly able to assert Kilwa's position, and control the monsoon trade and its merchants. However, in the longer term, this stratagem failed, and a more indigenous order was reasserted, in the face of both the decline of the Indian Ocean trade networks, and the collapse of the town's gold supply from southern Africa.

Historiography

There are inherent difficulties in reconstructing African history during the pre-colonial period with the poor survival of indigenous documents, and often, only narratives of oral history to rely on. External accounts of sub-Saharan Africa are found in Arabic, Persian, and Chinese sources, but these are often highly filtered and biased.[4] Few of these are eyewitness accounts, but hearsay recorded in the Middle East or the ports of southern China. For the East African coast, the particular focus of this chapter, there are only two genuine eyewitnesses from outside Africa: al-Masudi, who last visited the area in 916, and Ibn Battuta in 1331 before the arrival of Vasco da Gama's ships in 1498.[5]

With this lack of external historical data, recent historians and archaeologists have been slow to connect their work to the emerging narratives of global history.[6] They have been often influenced by post-colonial historiographies of indigenous cultural achievements, rather than accepting agency with the long-distance connections between Europeans, Asians, and other African

4 *Corpus of Early Arabic Sources*, ed. by Levtzion and Hopkins; Freeman-Grenville, *The East African Coast. Select Documents*; Filesi, *China and Africa*; Duyvendak, *China's Discovery of Africa*.

5 For Masudi: Freeman-Grenville, *The East African Coast. Select Documents*, pp. 14–17. For Ibn Battuta: Ibn Battuta, *Travels*, ed. by Gibb, pp. 373–82; Freeman-Grenville, *The East African Coast. Select Documents*, pp. 27–32. For Vasco da Gama: *Journal of the First Voyage of Vasco da Gama*, ed. by Ravenstein, pp. 32–46; Freeman-Grenville, *The East African Coast. Select Documents*, pp. 50–63; Newitt, *East Africa*, pp. 1–20, contains a useful digest of the early Portuguese contacts with East Africa.

6 Bayly, 'Archaic and Modern Globalization', p. 52, sees African participation in 'archaic' globalization only from the seventeenth century onwards. Accounts of connections between Europe and Asia omit substantive mention of the African contribution; see Chaudhuri, *Trade and Civilization*; Chaudhuri, *Asia before Europe*. Others, with an African perspective, have accepted global connections between Africa and the wider world, see, e.g., Sheriff, *Dhow Cultures of the Indian Ocean*; Mitchell, *African Connections*, pp. 99–133. Horton and others, 'Eastern Africa and the Early Indian Ocean', discusses many of these issues.

states, through the exchange of ideas, technologies, and commodities. Where contact existed, it was to exploit and impoverish African society.[7] One particular area of debate concerns the role of migration: to what extent did foreign people move around and settle in these distant places? The role of foreigners in African history is a particularly sensitive one as they were often seen as colonizers or the carriers of 'advanced' culture seemingly lacking within indigenous African societies.[8] Arguments about the role of foreigners — in particular 'Arabs' — in the creation of urban societies in both West, East, and southern Africa have intensified in recent years. The prevailing view is that social complexity and urbanization processes were wholly indigenous and driven by internal state-formation.[9]

But in this rethinking of African urbanization, external connections tend to be relegated to lesser importance. Yet African societies supplied some of the key commodities that underpinned the European economy — especially gold from both western and southern Africa, slaves, and a number of precious materials, such as ivory and crystal, that adorned the palaces and churches of the Christian west.[10] Fluctuations in the supply of these into the Mediterranean had important and significant economic consequences[11] — and ultimately were the economic motive for European maritime expansion into the Atlantic and Indian Oceans.

In the emerging methodologies for understanding this big picture, it has often been helpful to contrast the global with the local. To what extent were African states passive players in global networks, or did they exercise real agency, establishing connections with suppliers and understanding distant markets and consumption patterns? While Eurasian knowledge of these African states may have been limited, how much did Africans understand and how much were they influenced by the markets that they were supplying? There is for example archaeological evidence that African communities were resident more widely in the Indian Ocean, especially in Arabian ports from the tenth century, ports that were connected through to the Mediterranean world, as is clear from letters of Jewish traders, preserved in the Cairo Geniza documents.[12] Globalized networks were maintained through long-distance

---

7 Rodney, *How Europe Underdeveloped Africa*.

8 Chittick, 'The East Coast, Madagascar and the Indian Ocean', provides a recent synthesis of the external colonization model.

9 Horton and Chami, 'Swahili Origins', pp. 135–37; MacDonald, 'Before the Empire of Ghana'; McIntosh and McIntosh, *Prehistoric Investigations in the Region of Jenne*; LaViolette and Fleisher, 'Archaeology of Sub-Saharan Urbanism'; Monroe, 'Power and Agency'.

10 Horton and others, 'East Africa as a Source for Fatimid Rock Crystal'; Horton, 'Swahili Corridor'.

11 Day, *Medieval Market Economy*, pp. 35–38, 123–25, on the interruption in the supply of West African gold and the 'great bullion famine'. The Portuguese explorers' main interest in Africa was to locate fresh sources of gold.

12 Goitein and Friedman, *India Traders of the Middle Ages*. Rougeulle, *Sharma*, pp. 216–27, and Whitcomb, 'The Archaeology of Oman', p. 148, fig. 9 d–f, contain illustrations of African

connections — caravans and maritime trade, which included not only commodities but also information.

This chapter looks in particular at East Africa, and the port cities that emerged along its coast. In this perspective, I will examine the Sultanate of Kilwa, located on the Tanzanian Coast, one of the few East African states for which we have a small amount of historical evidence, bracketed by a visit by Ibn Battuta in 1331, and the arrival of Vasco da Gama in 1502,[13] but there is also supplementary evidence in the survival of indigenous chronicles, one written down in Portuguese, one in Arabic, and several in Swahili, that narrate the history of Kilwa from a date of around 1000 CE until the arrival of the Portuguese, and in the Swahili chronicles, into the eighteenth century.[14] Coins are known from the sultanate that name a few of the rulers and provide some historical validation for these chronicles.[15]

Prompted by this historical and numismatic record, Kilwa was chosen as the location of a long-running excavation directed by Neville Chittick and the British Institute in Eastern Africa during the early 1960s.[16] The results of Chittick's work have never been fully challenged, in spite of some fifty years of further research on the East African coast. In 2016, the present author returned to Kilwa for a much smaller-scale excavation, employing micro-archaeological recovery methods not undertaken in the earlier work, adjacent to one of Chittick's original sondages in the centre of the site.[17] There has also been a major project at the nearby fifteenth-century urban centre of Songo Mnara and regional surveys of both the terrestrial and maritime landscape around Kilwa.[18] In addition, much archaeological work has been undertaken in

---

earthenware pottery (Tana) found on the Arabian coast; see also Horton, 'East Africa, the Global Gulf'.

13 The first Portuguese visitor was Pedro Alvares Cabral, who passed by in 1500, and noted the town's importance. Vasco da Gama, who missed Kilwa during his famous voyage of 1498/99, made a deliberate attempt to visit Kilwa, with its famed control of the gold trade, during his second voyage of 1502.

14 Freeman-Grenville, *Medieval History*, sets the translated texts of the Arabic History (hereafter referred to as *History*), and the Portuguese Chronicle (hereafter referred to as *Chronicle*) alongside each other. For the publication of the original Arabic text see Strong, 'The History of Kilwa'; for the Portuguese Chronicle see *Records of South-Eastern Africa*, ed. by Theal, pp. 4, 233–34; 240–44. Both versions are reprinted in Freeman-Grenville, *The East African Coast. Select Documents*, pp. 31–49, 90–95. For the Swahili version and later genealogies see Freeman-Grenville, *The East African Coast. Select Documents*, pp. 221–26; Freeman-Grenville, *French at Kilwa Island*, pp. 28–38. Another version, not known to Freeman-Grenville, is Chittick, 'Early History of Kilwa Kivinje'.

15 Walker, 'History of Coinage'; Freeman-Grenville, 'Coinage in East Africa'; Chittick, *Kilwa*, II, pp. 269–301; Perkins, *Coins of the Swahili Coast*; Perkins, 'Indian Ocean'.

16 Chittick, *Kilwa*.

17 The investigation was part of the Songo Mnara project, directed by Stephanie Wynne-Jones and Jeff Fleisher; Wynne-Jones and others, 'Dating Kilwa Kisiwani'. The trench at Kilwa was located on the south side of Chittick's trench numbered ZLL, Chittick, *Kilwa*, I, pp. 36–43.

18 Wynne-Jones, *Urbanisation at Kilwa*; Chami, 'Archaeology of Pre-Islamic Kilwa'; Pollard, *Archaeology of Tanzanian Coastal Landscapes*, pp. 69–144; Fleisher and Wynne-Jones,

southern Africa, the source of the ivory and gold that underpinned Kilwa's wealth.[19] With this new data, it is possible to begin a reassessment of the Kilwa sultanate and its role in the global economy.

This chapter will examine the rise of Kilwa as the preeminent port city of the coast, the East African equivalent to Mali but very much less well known.[20] It was the entrepôt for the supply of gold and ivory from southern Africa between the thirteenth and fifteenth centuries, but unlike the Saharan kingdoms was never part of a great empire, but a mercantile centre that was able to accumulate its wealth through long-distance trade connections that spanned the Mediterranean, the Gulf, southern India, Southeast Asia and China. In the medieval period, Kilwa captured the southern African gold trade for a while from other Swahili towns and used this resource to enrich itself, its architecture, and its global standing.[21] It is therefore an ideal case study to observe how the global forces influenced the local order and how the local order responded to them.

The Swahili of the East African Coast

Kilwa is one of a series of port cities located along the East African coast, from southern Somalia to Mozambique and the offshore islands of Pemba, Zanzibar, and the Comoros. There never was a Swahili 'empire', but this area was inhabited by an interconnected and fairly uniform cultural grouping, known to modern scholars as the Swahili.[22] These communities were connected through a common language, ki-Swahili, similar forms of social organization and marriage alliances, adherence to Islam, and a livelihood based around maritime trade and the exploitation of maritime resources. Monsoon winds blow along the coast, with biannual reversal, allowing for rapid communication by sea along a corridor that was over three thousand kilometres in length. Sea currents also helped in rapid transits between north and south that extended to western Madagascar and the southern African coast.

The Swahili emerged in the seventh century as a distinctive cultural group that has been identified through their ceramics (known as Tana / TIW, i.e. Triangular-Incised Ware), which show a remarkable uniformity along the 'Swahili corridor' as well as the coastal hinterland.[23] This ceramic tradition

---

'Archaeological Investigations at Songo Mnara, 2009 Field Season'; Fleisher and Wynne-Jones, 'Archaeological Investigations at Songo Mnara, 2011 Field Season'; Horton, Fleisher, and Wynne-Jones, 'Mosques of Songo Mnara'.

19 Pwiti, 'Southern Africa and the East African Coast'; Coutu and others, 'Earliest Evidence'.

20 Mali was well known in Europe, on account of the famous pilgrimage of its ruler Mansa Musa to Mecca in 1324. He was celebrated in a series of *mappae mundi*, as a seated ruler holding a nugget of gold; Sutton, 'The African Lords', pp. 220–25.

21 Sutton, 'The African Lords', pp. 232–33.

22 Horton and Middleton, *The Swahili*; Wynne-Jones and LaViolette, *The Swahili World*.

23 Horton, 'Swahili Corridor'; Horton, *Shanga*; Fleisher, and Wynne-Jones, 'Ceramics and

maps closely onto the distribution of NE Coastal Bantu languages, of which ki-Swahili forms a component. Initially, these Swahili communities were small fishing and foraging communities, but by the eighth century, several centres emerged in the Lamu archipelago (Shanga and Manda), Pemba (Mtambwe Mkuu, Ras Mkumbuu, and Tumbe), and Zanzibar (Unguja Ukuu), that had international trading connections with imported material from the Middle East, India, and China and substantial populations. The largest of these emerging urban sites is likely to have been Unguja Ukuu, on Zanzibar, covering around twenty hectares, and a population that was several thousands. Over ten per cent of the ceramics from Unguja Ukuu, between the eighth and tenth centuries, were imports.[24]

While these communities have African roots, they also embraced Islam from an early date. Direct evidence for this comes from Shanga, a site in the Lamu archipelago, where mosques have been found, burials from *c.* 780, and locally minted coins from the early ninth century.[25] Initially mosques were made from timber and thatch, with mud floors, but by the tenth century they were being built in stone. Other early mosques have been suggested on Pemba island, at Unguja Ukuu, and at Sima (Comoros). One reason why Islam seems to have had such rapid take-up may have been the East African slave trade, since it would have furnished a (limited) insurance against capture by slavers. Substantial numbers of 'Zanj' slaves were taken to the Gulf during the eighth and ninth centuries. Another principal trade item seems to have been ivory, well known from the first century, but particularly important by the ninth century, according to al-Masudi. There are also records for the export of timber, particularly mangrove poles, for the large-scale building projects in the Abbasid Middle East.[26]

Kilwa

The Kilwa archipelago lies to the south of these early centres of Swahili activity in the Zanzibar and Lamu archipelagos. Its strategic location was close to the southern limit of the seasonal monsoons, where a reliable return journey could be made with the Middle East and Gulf regions and therefore a key access point to southern Africa. There are few major hazards in reaching Kilwa; the ships would typically leave Arabia in November and return in April or May. A graphic account of the one of the last traditional voyages was recorded by Alan Villiers in 1939, leaving Kuwait, and making for the Rufiji delta, a few

---

the Early Swahili'; Walsh, 'Swahili Language and its Early History'; Nurse and Hinnebusch, *Swahili and Sabaki*.

24 Priestman, 'Quantitative Evidence'; Priestman, 'A Quantitative Archaeological Analysis'; Horton, *Zanzibar and Pemba*.

25 Horton, *Shanga*; Horton, 'Early Islam on the East African Coast'.

26 Horton, 'East Africa and Oman'.

miles north of Kilwa to collect mangrove poles, that were still in demand in the Gulf until the late twentieth century.[27]

South of Kilwa there is a distinct wind pattern and currents that can take ships much further south to the Mozambique coast and South Africa. From Kilwa, the voyage was southwards though the Mozambique channel to the coasts of south-east Africa, to the 'Land of Sufala' and its access to the gold-bearing rocks of southern Africa, as well as the open savannah plains that yielded high quality ivory. Kilwa was located not only between the African and the Indian Ocean worlds, but also between the northern and southern Indian Oceans. Its merchants were therefore able to grow rich as middlemen in the long-distance trade in high-value luxuries.

The archipelago comprises a number of drowned valleys, formed from an ancient African river, with three low-lying islands, Kilwa, Songo Mnara, and Sanje ya Kati, comprising coral bedrock and dune sand.[28] It is protected by a fringing coral reef, and the channels between the islands are calm and full of maritime resources, as well as mangroves for timber. The main entrances from the Indian Ocean are through the reef between Kilwa island and the mainland and between Kilwa and Songo Mnara, both leading into natural and safe anchorages.

Each of the three islands has archaeological sites — Songo Mnara (largely fifteenth century), Sanje ya Majoma (fourteenth and fifteenth century), Sanje ya Kati (late eleventh and twelfth century), and Kilwa Kisiwani (ninth century to the present day). While there is some evidence for Early Iron Age occupation (*c.* 100–500 CE) in the Kilwa area, the oldest Tana / TIW levels are found at Kilwa Kisiwani, *c.* 800.[29] The 2016 excavations that reopened a four-metre-deep sondage from the 1960s, in the presumed oldest part of the site, located these early levels. These were modest in scale, with a heavy reliance on fish and shellfish, and virtually no imports. From these beginnings, the site grew to cover at least fifty hectares at its peak in the fourteenth and fifteenth centuries, with numerous stone houses, mosques, and tombs. While sacked by the Portuguese in the early sixteenth century, Kilwa Kisiwani was never abandoned, and revived its prosperity in the late eighteenth century with a local slave trade — which led to new buildings and the robbing of the older medieval ones for building materials.[30] Nowadays a village occupies part of the area of the archaeological site (which is designated a World Heritage Site), that grew out of the eighteenth-century settlement. The last 'sultan' of Kilwa, Hasan bin Sulaiman, was described as a nonentity with an empty title in the 1840s.[31]

27 Villers, *Sons of Sinbad*.

28 Pollard, *Archaeology of Tanzanian Coastal Landscapes*, pp. 69–72.

29 Chami, 'Archaeology of Pre-Islamic Kilwa'; Wynne-Jones, 'Urbanisation at Kilwa', p. 104; Wynne-Jones and others, 'Dating Kilwa Kisiwani', p. 281; Horton and others, 'The Chronology of Kilwa Kisiwani'.

30 Freeman-Grenville, *French at Kilwa Island*; Chittick, *Kilwa*, 1, pp. 206–12.

31 Freeman-Grenville, *French at Kilwa Island*, p. 33.

Origins of the Kilwa Sultanate

The archaeological record from Kilwa suggests that it was first established on a short peninsula of dune sand around the beginning of the Common Era, as a small fishing settlement surrounding a well in the dunes. It is not the earliest site on the coast, or indeed in these levels the most prosperous, with import ratios of less than 0.5 per cent compared to other ports that range from 3 to 12 per cent. During the tenth century, but particularly in the eleventh century, the site's prosperity increased, although the settlement was built of daub and timber buildings. The highest proportion of imports, at 3.5 per cent, was recorded in the early twelfth century, after which there was a levelling off at around 2 per cent.

Kilwa is first mentioned by name in the *Book of Curiosities of the Sciences and Marvels for the Eyes*, written in Fatimid Egypt in *c.* 1060, as part of an itinerary of places down the African coast towards Sufala.[32] The first stone architecture dates to around 980, and the 2016 excavations located a large monumental tower (possibly a tomb tower) which was completely destroyed a generation later. The oldest mosque buildings date to around this period also. In these same levels come the earliest silver coins, locally minted, and bearing the name Ali bin al-Hasan. These coins are significant as they seem to connect with the earliest dynasty that ruled here, known as the Shirazi dynasty, on account of their claimed origins from Shiraz in Iran. Coins of both Ali and Daud ibn al-Hasan (possibly his brother) are known in copper and seem to have continued in use for many centuries. Silver coins (with another nine names) are known from Mtambwe Mkuu on Pemba where they formed a hoard, with deposition dates after 1066, as well as Unguja Ukuu and Kisimani Mafia — in levels also dating to the eleventh century.[33] The *History of Kilwa* names the first ruler as Ali ibn al-Husain (*sic*) ibn Ali, most likely one of the producers of these silver coins, and while they claimed to have come from Shiraz, they are probably locally converted Swahili Muslims who moved from the northern coastal area. It is likely they were Shia and were at Kilwa and the adjacent islands in the eleventh century for around two generations.[34]

Reconciling the different versions of the Kilwa chronicle remains a complex task, but there is a single external reference to an Ibadi community at Kilwa in *c.* 1115, and this may correspond to a takeover of Kilwa, mentioned in the

32 *An Eleventh-Century Egyptian Guide*, ed. by Rapoport and Savage-Smith, pp. 444–45; Horton, 'The Swahili Corridor Revisited'.

33 Horton and others, 'Mtambwe Hoard'; Horton, *Zanzibar and Pemba*.

34 Freeman-Grenville, 'Shi'i Rulers'; Freeman-Grenville, *Medieval History*, p. 78. Husain / Hasan has created considerable difficulties in the two versions, and reconciliation with the coin evidence. The *History* gives Hasan as the father (p. 75) and Ali ibn al-Husain ibn Ali as his son (p. 78). The *Chronicle* gives 'Hocen' as the father, and Ali as his son. Walker, 'History of Coinage', thought that the Ali ibn al-Hasan coins were associated with a fifteenth-century sultan, but the excavations at Kilwa clearly showed that they were much earlier, and associated with the Shirazi dynasty, Chittick, '"Shirazi" Colonization'.

Kilwa Chronicle, by the 'Matamandalin', possibly the rival town of Sanje ya Kati, for a period of around thirty-nine years, controlled by Ibadi Muslims.[35] The Shirazi regained control of Kilwa around 1140 and one ruler, al-Hasan ibn Daud ibn Ali, was apparently the grandson of the Shirazi founder, placing him within a credible time-frame. At this point the Arabic and Portuguese versions diverge, with an additional nine rulers in the Portuguese version, of which the second, Daud ibn Sulaiman, is recorded as having commenced the gold trade with Sufala, having personal knowledge of the region, and apparently displacing the Somali town of Mogadishu, whose merchants sailed directly and secretly to the Sufala coast.[36] The Arabic version omits these nine rulers, and it is unclear why the founders of Kilwa prosperity were written out of its history, or whether the extra dynasty was a duplication of later rulers in order to make the chronology 'fit'.[37] In any case, the likely time that this gold trade developed in the hands of the Kilwans was during the middle of the twelfth century.

According to the *Chronicle*, '[i]n the course of time, by means of the trade which the Moors had with these Kaffirs, the rulers of Kilwa became absolute masters of the gold trade'. Sailing south to the Mozambique coast was difficult, with not only unreliable monsoon winds, but also the Mozambique channel current, which when it flows makes it difficult to return north.[38] Recent studies of the current, using surface drones, have shown that rather than a single south-flowing current, it is a series of anticyclonic currents, which allow counter currents to be followed along the Madagascan west coast, facilitating a return voyage. Considerable skill was clearly needed to undertake this voyage safely, and the Kilwans seem to have mastered this. One of the key indicators of the degree of penetration of Indian Ocean trade into the interior is the distribution of glass beads, which can be chemically characterized, and connected to assemblages on the coast.[39]

The Mahdali Dynasty and Hasan ibn Sulaiman

A significant shift of the commercial activity of Kilwa can be observed in the mid-thirteenth century, with the appearance of imported pottery, known as black-on-yellow ware, which was made near Aden in southern Arabia, displacing sgraffiato wares from the Makkran at the entrance to the Gulf.[40]

35 Wilkinson, 'Oman and East Africa'; Horton, 'Ibadis in East Africa'.
36 Freeman-Grenville, *Medieval History*, pp. 88–90.
37 Wilkinson, 'Oman and East Africa'; Chittick, '"Shirazi" Colonization'.
38 Few Kilwan ships sailed south of Cape das Correntes, notorious for its currents and sand banks; Freeman-Grenville, *The East African Coast. Select Documents*, p. 84.
39 Wood and others, 'Zanzibar and Indian Ocean Trade'; Wood, *Interconnections*; Denbow and others, 'The Glass Beads'; Sinclair, 'Chibuene'; Sinclair and others, 'Trade and Society'.
40 Horton, *Shanga*; Chittick, *Kilwa*, II, pp. 303–04.

This shift coincides with a new dynasty in Kilwa known as the al-Mahdali — a dynasty that took its *nisba*, or surname, from a family of Sayyids from the Wadi Surdad in the Hadramaut in Yemen.[41] This family may originally have come to Kilwa as part of the general conversion of the coastal population to Sunni Islam (away from Shia and Ibadism, which survived in places into the thirteenth century) and was able to assume power through their religious connections, possibly through their appointment as amirs and wazirs to the legitimate Kilwa ruler. The first ruler was named as al-Hasan ibn Talut, 'who with the help of his people seized the kingdom by force'.[42] This took place around 1277.

While this new dynasty was Sunni / Shafi, they were keen to claim connections to the founders of Kilwa, the Shirazi (and likely Shia) rulers of the late tenth and eleventh centuries. This is evident in their resumption of coining that seems to have been abandoned for some two hundred years. These coins are similar in style to that of Ali and Daud and represent the first four of the al-Mahdali rulers[43] of Kilwa, between *c.* 1277 and 1356. One of the most important recent discoveries has been of five gold coins found in Zanzibar, but minted in Kilwa in the 720s H (1320–29 CE) by Hasan ibn Sulaiman, the third of the Mahdali rulers (*c.* 1310–33), and grandson of the founder of the dynasty.[44] One has the inscription set within a square — a typical Rasulid feature, from southern Arabia — in which he takes the titles al-Malik al-Mansur, 'the conquering king', an echo of the ancient Caliph's titles, as well as the 'father of gifts and lion of the faith'. In the use of these, he styled himself as a great Islamic ruler, and fully part of the Islamic world. According to the *History*, the title of the ruler was not sultan, but Abu al-Mawahib, 'the giver of gifts', a title often employed by Sufi scholars.[45]

The *History* gives considerable detail about Hasan ibn Sulaiman's education.[46] He travelled to Arabia when his father was still alive, stayed at Aden to study spiritual science and 'excelled in all branches of knowledge'.[47] Then he made his pilgrimage to Mecca when he was sixteen, shortly after returning to Kilwa to inherit the throne, where his brother had been regent. He was also the ruler, when Ibn Battuta visited in 1331, perhaps towards the end of his reign.[48] Here he is described as making numerous gifts, and being very humble, he 'sits

41 Martin, 'Arab Migrations', p. 373.

42 Freeman-Grenville, *Medieval History*, p. 93. Saad, 'Kilwa Dynastic Historiography'.

43 Al-Hasan bin Talut, Sulaiman bin al-Hasan, al-Hasan bin Sulaiman, and Daud bin Sulaiman.

44 Brown, 'Three Kilwa Gold Coins'.

45 Freeman-Grenville, *Medieval History*, p. 95.

46 Freeman-Grenville, *Medieval History*, p. 96.

47 Freeman-Grenville, *Medieval History*, p. 96.

48 Ibn Battuta, *Travels*, ed. by Gibb, pp. 379–82. Freeman-Grenville, *Medieval History*, p. 69, computes his dates as 1310–33, which are probably accurate to within a year or two. Chittick, '"Shirazi" Colonization', p. 281 and table II, dates the beginning of the Mahdali dynasty to *c.* 1300, so Ibn Battuta would have visited at the start of his reign. Freeman-Grenville's chronology makes more sense with the discovery of the dated gold coins, not known to Chittick.

with poor brethren and eats with them and greatly respects men of religion and noble descent'.[49] He also recalls a lengthy account of giving his clothes to a beggar on his return from Friday prayers. Ibn Battuta contrasts his brother, Daud ibn Sulaiman, who succeeded him, as mean, although the *History* states he was a devout king and a master of theological argument.[50]

Mahdali Architecture

The accession of the Mahdali seems to have precipitated the construction of new and unusual buildings.[51] From the eleventh century onwards, the only stone buildings that we can be certain of, were mosques. The Friday mosque was rebuilt in the late eleventh or early twelfth century over a slightly smaller eleventh century mosque, using undersea-mined coral blocks and lime mortar.[52] Tombs may also have been built of stone. All the houses, however, seem to have been constructed in daub and timber, with thatched roofs, although one stone building, of undersea coral, that is not a mosque and is probably twelfth century, was found in the excavations.[53] When Ibn Battuta visited in 1331, he remarked that Kilwa was built of timber and roofed with reeds, and this is probably an accurate description of the domestic buildings.[54]

The Mahdali were however responsible for three outstanding public buildings in stone: the Great Mosque extension, Husuni Kubwa, and Husuni Ndogo.

The oldest of these constructions is probably the Great Mosque extension, a huge southern addition to the earlier twelfth-century mosque, comprising four rows of columns supporting thirty vaults.[55] These were supported on monolithic coral columns. In the south-east corner, there was a covered praying space for

---

49 Ibn Battuta, *Travels*, ed. by Gibb, p. 381.

50 Freeman-Grenville, *Medieval History*, p. 109.

51 Sutton, 'The African Lords', pp. 230–31, and Sutton, 'Kilwa', p. 127, suggest that these buildings may all have been constructed by al-Hasan ibn Sulaiman, rather than during the reigns of his two predecessors, al-Hasan and Sulaiman (who also minted coins). Only Husuni Kubwa has an inscriptional link to al-Hasan ibn Sulaiman. The *Chronicle* attributes the building of 'a fortress of stone and lime, with walls towers and other houses' to Sulaiman Hasan, the son of Daud, the fabled initiator of the gold trade in the twelfth century; Freeman-Grenville, *Medieval History*, p. 90. This seems to be a reference to the Husunis, but may be a confusion with the work of the later Mahdalis, possibly even Sulaiman ibn al-Hasan, the father of al-Hasan ibn Sulaiman.

52 Horton, 'Early Islam on the East African Coast', p. 266. Chittick, *Kilwa*, I, pp. 18 and 34, placed the construction of the mosque in his period II, dating from around 1200.

53 Chittick, *Kilwa*, I, p. 57.

54 Ibn Battuta, *Travels*, ed. by Gibb, p. 380. Freeman-Grenville, *Medieval History*, p. 107, suggested the text should be changed from *min al-khashb* (of wood) to *min al-hasb* (with elegance); Chittick, *Kilwa*, I, p. 247, rejected this. The archaeological evidence suggests that in 1330, the bulk of the houses were in mud and thatch, and that the use of coral rag in domestic building dates from the middle or later fourteenth century; Horton, *Shanga*, p. 242.

55 Chittick, *Kilwa*, I, pp. 64–65.

the sultan himself. This was entered through a private south-east door, with its own small washing tank, and a vaulted antechamber. The space under a single great dome was around 3.5 m, an exceptionally large area, and unique in East Africa until the colonial era. The *History* describes this 'famous dome under which he was wont to pray', and the construction remains largely intact today.[56] This was not the fate of the remainder of the mosque that collapsed during the reign of al-Hasan ibn Sulaiman, when the monolithic columns used to support the vault failed; the present vaulted mosque extension dates to its rebuilding in the early fifteenth century. According to the *History*, the 'mosque remained in ruins and the people prayed under shelters and tents until the time of Sultan Sulaiman ibn al-Malik al-Adil (*c*. 1421–42).[57] The mosque-collapse most likely occurred after the visit of Ibn Battuta in 1331 (who describes him coming out of the mosque after Friday prayers) but before the death of the sultan in *c*. 1333.

Two miles east of the town, on a virgin site, perched high on a cliff, facing the sea, a substantial building project was attempted — two completely new palaces, known as Husuni Kubwa and Husuni Ndogo. Husuni Kubwa can be attributed to al-Hasan ibn Sulaiman on the basis of an inscription[58] found in the palace court, that details al-Hasan ibn Sulaiman, and provides his title, also used on his gold coins, al-Malik al-Mansur. Very few datable finds were found in the excavation, but they included coins of the Mahdali sultans and a fine example of a Qingbai-glazed bottle of the Yuan dynasty, dating to *c*. 1300.[59]

Husuni Kubwa was a vast building in two halves. That on the northern, seaward side was the private accommodation, set around three courts, designed as the palace, domestic and audience courts, with the fourth area given over to an octagonal ornamental pool, entered through semi-circular steps. The four inscriptions were all found in the palace court area, as well as ornamental stonework. The palace area was entered via a stairway that was built up from the beach and landing place. At the base of this stair, and next to the sea (and so a supply of water), is the only suggestive evidence for a private mosque, 2 m by 2.8 m. The domestic or residential block, with its own landward entrance on the east side of the palace, was surrounded by parallel rows of rooms. On the west side was a pavilion that faced the audience court. This was a large sunken area, the walls of which have multiple niches that may have housed lamps. The pool, 7.5 m across, would have held water to a depth of between 2 and 1.6 m. Curiously, access between the four areas was limited, raising issues of privacy and court ceremonial.

56 Freeman-Grenville, *Medieval History*, p. 96.

57 Freeman-Grenville, *Medieval History*, pp. 96–97.

58 Garlake, *Early Islamic Architecture*; Chittick, *Kilwa*, I, pp. 174–95; II, p. 260. In translation, in carved coral, using *Naski* script: 'Verily God is the helper of the Commander of the Faithful, al-Malik al-Mansur al-Hasan b. Sulaiman, may Almighty God grant him success'.

59 Chittick, *Kilwa*, I, p. 179, pl. 149. It is very similar to a bottle in the Metropolitan Museum in New York (25.215.6), attributed to the Jingdezhen kilns. Sutton, 'Kilwa', p. 43 wrongly describes it as celadon.

The southern half of the complex was almost entirely cut off from the northern part, save for a single small doorway that led off from the pavilion. It is a large quadrangle, 48 m × 42 m × 45 m × 46 m, flanked by double rows of rooms, probably eight individual units on each side (giving thirty-two apartments) entering the courtyard. In the centre of the courtyard was a large unfilled pit, possibly an unfinished well or cistern. Those on the north-east and north-west sides were built with an upper story that overlooked the courtyard and was roofed in barrel or conical domed roofs. These more elaborate apartments, perhaps fourteen in total, each had a distinctive dome, either barrel, conical, or tent shaped octagonal vaults supported on pseudo-pendentives, as well as carved coral mouldings. The courtyard had three public entrances, one leading to the sea, that was probably reached by steps, one to the town and one to Husuni Ndogo. It seems that the basement rooms were used for storage and the upper rooms for the accommodation of merchants, who were privately entertained by the sultan.

The third building, Husuni Ndogo, is a huge enclosure 69.5 m by 51 m (possibly 134 × 100 cubits of 518 mm) entered from the south, with seven six-sided polygonal half towers in the sides and eight-sided three-quarter towers at the four corners.[60] The centre of the west wall has a projecting platform rather than a tower. Within it were some puzzling and probably later structures, as well as a massive well and octagonal tank, but some original internal structures were uncovered in the southeast corner, as well as projecting walls from the east and west walls. The enclosure is entered from the south with an internal entrance building, with a right-angled passageway that would have obscured the view of the interior from the outside. The excavator thought it might be a mosque, because of unconvincing traces of an apse in the north wall.[61] Very few finds were found in its excavation, but the earliest are contemporary with Husuni Kubwa, from the early fourteenth century, with some evidence of reuse in later centuries.

The 'New Architecture' at Kilwa and Mahdali Commercial Strategy

These three buildings were revolutionary in terms of local architectural styles but have long presented a challenge to explain them.[62] In terms of how they are built, the use of vaults and sunken courtyards as well as construction using terrestrial coral rag rather than mined undersea coral was innovatory. Finding parallels for their form in the Islamic world has hitherto proved fruitless as they seem to include multiple elements from different structures.

---

60 Chittick, *Kilwa*, i, pp. 196–205.

61 Chittick, *Kilwa*, i, p. 200; Garlake, *Early Islamic Architecture*, p. 112.

62 Garlake, *Early Islamic Architecture*, p. 113, described Husuni Kubwa as the 'fountainhead of all of post thirteenth century architecture on the coast'.

Husuni Ndogo might reflect Umayyad desert palaces, but also a tradition that continued into the Abbasid period as mosques, such as at Raqqa or Samarra. The Caliphal palace of al-Mutasim at Samarra (836) as noted by Garlake[63] has some similarities in plan to Husuni Kubwa, entered via a monumental stairway from the river, which is organized as a series of axial courts. There is also a bastioned enclosure, known as 'the barracks', that might echo Husuni Ndogo. Some of the stucco decoration from Samarra, including the fleur-de-lys, is also found in carved coral at Husuni Kubwa. None of these parallels are convincing, not least because they are buildings hundreds of years earlier.[64]

A better explanation is that Husain ibn Sulaiman was modelling himself on the Seljuk court, whose sultans, shortly before his time, were the most powerful Islamic rulers in the world and whose architecture spanned an area from Anatolia to northern India. The Seljuk, strongly Sunni, and ultimately of nomadic origin from Central Asia, controlled a huge area of the Middle East and the Gulf, from Turkey to Central Asia during the eleventh and twelfth centuries. The enfeebled Abbasid Caliph was often under Seljuk control, in Baghdad and southern Iraq, until the arrival of the Mongols and killing of the last Caliph, al-Mustasim in 1258. With the arrival of the Mongols, the power of the Seljuks waned, although they survived as the Sultanate of Rum in Anatolia until 1308. Even though the caliphate was no more, it seems that the Mahdalis' use of caliphate titles on their gold coins and inscriptions in Husuni Kubwa still echoed caliphate aspirations of a former golden age that had come to an end within living memory.

The Mahdali sultans went beyond the adoption of honorific titles to stress their prestige and Islamic antecedents, but also sought out architecture to emulate in East Africa that was an expression of these political ideologies. This architecture was not, however, a slavish copy of Middle Eastern originals, but an eclectic and original mix of forms and plans.

The use of domes, much used by the Seljuk architects, would have been familiar to any visitor to Kilwa. In particularly the conical 'tent' domes, supported on pendentives, found at Husuni Kubwa, are similar to vaults in tower tombs with their conical roofs, that ultimately go back to nomadic tent designs.[65] They are also found in a group of thirteenth-century Seljuk monuments in Anatolia known as *hans* such as Sultan Han,[66] and it is these caravanserai that

63 Garlake, *Early Islamic Architecture*, p. 113.

64 Garlake, *Early Islamic Architecture*, pp. 113–14; fig. 72 h; Creswell, *Short Account*, pp. 333–39, fig. 215.

65 These conical domes are otherwise only known in East Africa, at the Mosque of Fakhr ad-Din in Mogadishu, which is dated to late thirteenth or early fourteenth century; Garlake, *Early Islamic Architecture*. Another connection between this mosque in Mogadishu and Kilwa is the use of a marble plaque in the mihrab, imported from Gujarat; other examples of the marble are found in the Sultan Mausoleum at Kilwa; Lambourn, 'The Decoration of the Fakhr al-Dīn Mosque'.

66 Hillenbrand, *Islamic Architecture*, p. 349, fig. 6.45; Crane and Korn, 'Turko-Persian Empires', pp. 338–42, fig. 13.4.

perhaps offer the closest comparisons for both the Great Mosque extension and Husuni Ndogo. Located on main trading routes, they were charitable foundations, of which at least eight were established by the Seljuk Rum sultan. They often form two elements, a vaulted and covered hall, normally five bays wide and between five and seven bays long (the Great Mosque extension was five by six bays), with a central conical vault. These halls were entered through an open enclosure, with vaulted side rooms, and entrance rooms and baths. Several examples, such as Karatay Han (1231–40) and Sultan Han (1229), have side half towers and corner three-quarter towers, identical to Husuni Ndogo. Karatay Han has a private mosque under a 4 m-wide dome, also similar to the Kilwa example. The foundation deed for the *han* survives as an inscription and directs that services such as food and drink, medicines, shoeing of horses and candles for light should be provided for free. Both Husuni Ndogo and the Great Mosque extension would have been familiar to any trader from the Middle East, who presumably would also have expected the same hospitality.

Husuni Kubwa may have served similar functions — as the residence of the sultan and for the accommodation of merchants — within a familiar Islamic landscape. The survival of palaces from this period is rare and it is difficult to cite direct parallels from the Islamic world.[67] The most eye-catching feature of Husuni Kubwa is undoubtedly the octagonal pool with its eight semi-circle steps that are often found in contemporary Mamluk houses in Egypt. Two undated fountains are reconstructed in the Coptic museum, Cairo, and there is a fifteenth-century example in the Aga Khan Museum, Toronto. These fountains may derive from pools found in madrasas (qur'ānic schools) that are often octagonal or square and form a central feature of the courtyards. An example, a little earlier than Husuni Kubwa, of an octagonal pool with semi-circular steps, is the Madrassa al-Firdaus, in Aleppo (1235–41).[68] Madrassas as an architectural type were developed by the Seljuks in the late twelfth century, and like the Kilwa architecture made much use of domed courtyards.[69]

The Mahdali sultans (and most likely Hasan ibn Sulaiman in particular) were therefore explicitly setting out to create an Islamic landscape at Kilwa that would have been recognizable to any Middle Eastern visiting merchant. Along with their caliphate titles and the resumption of local coinage derived from the Shirazi rulers two hundred years previously, they were proclaiming both their African ancestry and their Islamic legitimacy. The precision with which these buildings were laid out suggests formal architectural knowledge, generally not found in East Africa. Here they were determined to create an order, and thus a connection with the Islamic world, that was not present in traditional African architecture (that was much more free form).

---

67 Hillenbrand, *Islamic Architecture*, pp. 316–18.

68 Hillenbrand, *Islamic Architecture*, pp. 188–89 and 509, fig. 4.20.

69 Crane and Korn, 'Turko-Persian Empires', pp. 332–33.

The creation of this order had a specific commercial function: the Mahdali sultans wished to construct a familiar architectural landscape to lure maritime traders to Kilwa, away from the other port cities of the coast. But they also wished to enrich themselves at the cost of the other Kilwa merchants. In traditional Swahili society trade was conducted through sponsorship. Ibn Battuta describes this on his visit to Mogadishu — how small boats surround any new arrival, offering food and claiming the merchants as their guest.[70] The host then provided accommodation and protection, and in exchange monopolized all of the merchant's trade. These practices were widespread and continued until recent times. Swahili stone houses of the eighteenth and nineteenth centuries often had specific guest rooms for the visitors, known as *sabule*, that performed a similar function.[71] The Husunis may have been intended as grand guest houses for the visiting merchants, who were entertained by the sultan, but who as a result could only trade with him, ensuring that he was able to capture vast wealth.

While these grand buildings made a definite statement, they were ultimately a failure. It is likely that the Husunis were never fully completed, or occupied, while the Great Mosque extension collapsed shortly after its completion, *c.* 1331–33.[72] Very few finds were made in either of the Husunis, and much of the southern courtyard of Husuni Kubwa was left unfinished. The absence of a mosque large enough to accommodate those merchants may also indicate that the whole project was abandoned. When Ibn Battuta visited in 1331, there is no mention of the Husunis, and the sultan seems to have moved back into the town, if he ever left. Rather than being a great builder, at the end of his reign Hasan ibn Sulaiman is described by Ibn Batutta as 'a man of great humility; he sits with poor brethren and eats with them and greatly respects men of religion and noble descent'.[73] He was accompanied by at least three Husainid sharifs from Mecca and Medina.

The attempt to create an Islamic state at Kilwa ultimately failed. One cause may have been local resistance by the local merchants who saw their prosperity being captured by the ambitious sultans. But another factor may have been the changing global economics of the Indian Ocean which had an equally important effect on the fortunes of the Kilwa sultans.

---

70 Ibn Battuta, *Travels*, ed. by Gibb, p. 374.

71 Horton and Middleton, *The Swahili*, pp. 91 and 117; Middleton, 'Merchants'. Middleton, *African Merchants*, pp. 83–86, describes how exchange 'was a complex system of building wide-scale and long-term relationships between many societies of Africa and Asia centred on the Swahili towns along this remote coastline'.

72 Freeman-Grenville, *Medieval History*, p. 96: 'During the reign of al-Hasa b. Sulaiman, the Friday Mosque collapsed, there remains nothing save the famous dome in which he was wont to pray. The mosque remained in ruins and the people prayed under shelters until the time of Sultan Sulaiman al-Malik [...]'. As the mosque was clearly intact when Ibn Battuta visited, this would date the collapse at the very end of his reign, *c.* 1331–33.

73 Ibn Battuta, *Travels*, ed. by Gibb, p. 381.

Slaves and Gold

Ibn Battuta suggests that the source of Kilwa's wealth was slaves and gold. Of slaves, he describes raids by the sultan into the interior—'its people engage in jihad because they are on a common mainland with the heathen Zanj people, and contiguous to them'—adding that the sultan 'used to engage frequently in expeditions to the land of the Zanj people raiding them and taking booty, and he would set aside a fifth part of this to devote to objects prescribed for it in the Book of God Most High'.[74] This statement is a fairly precise rendition of the Ibadi *Jami ibn Ja'far* of the late ninth century, which sets out the rules for raiding in the *dar al-harb* where slaves and booty (*ghanima*) could be freely taken, providing that the expedition was authorized by the Imam.[75] Clearly there was a demand for some slaves on the East African coast, and the scale of construction of the Husunis would only have been possible with slave labour.[76] However it is also likely that Kilwa was a significant supplier of slaves into the Indian Ocean world, as it was in the late eighteenth century.

Ibn Battuta's account of the gold trade is more difficult to understand. He describes Sufala as half a month's journey from Kilwa, mentioning that gold dust is brought from Yufi in the country of the Limis to Sufala, a further month's journey away. The bay of Sufala is around 1500 km from Kilwa, so the trip might take two weeks when sailing 120 km a day. From Sufala, there is a direct route to the Zimbabwe Plateau and the Great Zimbabwe complex, 400 km away (15 km a day for twenty-eight days), that sits at its eastern side, controlling the routes to the centre and north-west where the gold-bearing reefs are mostly situated. Ibn Battuta's Limis (possibly LamLam) and Yufi (Ife) are actually located in West Africa, and it is likely that he was geographically confused.[77]

Gold had been mined in southern Africa on a small scale since the tenth century, and gold artefacts are known from thirteenth-century royal burials on Mapungubwe Hill, close to the Limpopo and at the southern end of the gold reefs. It has been argued that the Mapungubwe state moved north to Great Zimbabwe towards the end of the thirteenth century, neatly coinciding with the rise of Mahdali Kilwa and a shift in trade goods from ivory to gold. However, recent work at Mapela Hill, 120 km north of Mapungubwe, and located closer to the gold reefs, has identified another possible state centre that is a more convincing antecedent to Great Zimbabwe (that was itself an important place before *c.* 1270).[78] The close relationship between Great

---

74 Ibn Battuta, *Travels*, ed. by Gibb, p. 380.

75 Wilkinson, 'Oman and East Africa', p. 279.

76 In both Husunis, massive square wells, both over 4 m in size and over 16 m deep, were constructed through the bedrock, on a scale never found again in East Africa; Chittick, *Kilwa*, I, pp. 194 and 196.

77 Sutton, 'The African Lords', pp. 232–33.

78 Chirikure and others, 'Zimbabwe Culture before Mapungubwe'; Chirikure and others, 'A

Zimbabwe and Mahdali Kilwa (and indeed a single coin of al-Hasan ibn Sulaiman has been found at Great Zimbabwe) has long been noted.[79]

Global economic forces may help to explain the thirteenth-century rise of Great Zimbabwe and Mahdali Kilwa. Southern African gold must have been increasingly valuable after the decline of the Nubian gold mines in the Wadi al-Allaqi in the 1130s, and an ensuing crisis in gold bullion supply in the 1160s that had impacted the India trade, which was heavily reliant on gold.[80] However it was fresh supplies of West African gold in the mid-thirteenth century that allowed the Italian mercantile cities of Venice, Genoa, and Florence to issue gold coinage between 1252 and 1284, for the first time since Late Antiquity, much of which found its way into the Indian Ocean world to pay for spices and silks.[81] The Kilwa / Zimbabwe gold should be seen as part of a global shift towards a gold-based economy that was booming both to the west and east of the Red Sea from the mid-thirteenth to early fourteenth century.

The vulnerability of Kilwa to global markets became evident in the fourteenth century when a series of catastrophes affected the European economies. First came the ending of the medieval warm period, and a series of wet summers, which led to a northern European famine between 1315 and 1322.[82] This was followed by the Black Death from 1348 onwards; both significantly reduced the population. One consequence was the Great Bullion Famine, where economic historians have detailed how prices fell, bimetallic ratios fluctuated widely, and gold and silver reserves collapsed.[83] For periods, mints closed down because they could not issue coins, and economic activity slowed. The rise of credit and banking systems in the later Middle Ages was partly a response to this crisis, although limited by a reluctance to move away from a bullion-based system. The causes of the crisis seem to have been many — the collapse of European and Eurasian mining in the wake of labour shortages due to the Black Death, the continued demand for spices that meant that there was an inbuilt balance of payments deficit between East and West, with an outflow of bullion (especially gold) through Mamluk Egypt into the Indian Ocean world. It seems that the supply of gold from both western and southern Africa was greatly reduced.

The fate of Great Zimbabwe matched that of Kilwa. The traditional end-date of *c.* 1450 has now been challenged, and the site may have continued into the sixteenth century, although the majority of radiocarbon dates cluster within the period 1200–1400, and it is unclear whether it was still involved in international

---

Baysian Chronology for Great Zimbabwe', p. 870.

79 Garlake, *Great Zimbabwe*; Sutton, 'The African Lords', fig. 7.

80 Power, 'The Red Sea', p. 5.

81 Phillips, *Medieval Expansion of Europe*, pp. 103–04. Blanchard, *Mining, Metallurgy and Minting in the Middle Ages*, p. 1335, sees the revival of Indian Ocean gold trade as part of the 'Persian Gulf Climatic cycle of 1235/50–1332 to 1432–52'.

82 Jordan, *The Great Famine*.

83 Day, *Medieval Market Economy*, pp. 35–38 and 123–25.

trade after around 1400.[84] The fifteenth century saw the rise of alternative state-centres in the region, Torwa at Khami and Mutapa in Zambezia, that produced and traded gold on a more modest scale; gold seems to have been supplemented by copper, both from the Zimbabwe mines and the Zambian copper belt. By the end of the fifteenth century, the southern African gold trade seems to have been largely over. When Vasco da Gama visited Kilwa in 1502, he collected tribute of a modest 1200 mithqals of gold (around 5 kg) which was later worked into a golden monstrance for the Jerónimos monastery in Bélem, in Lisbon, having been presented in a triumphal procession as a basin full of coins.[85] A Portuguese eyewitness in 1506 estimated that the gold trade was formally valued at 1,300,000 mithqals a year (over 5000 kg), but this is almost certainly an exaggeration. At present it is estimated that only 50,000 mithqals (around 200 kg) were exported through Angoche.[86] The Portuguese were ultimately disappointed that the region produced so little gold — maybe as little as 1000 kg a year by the late sixteenth century — and switched their commercial attention towards ivory.[87]

Order in Action

The story of Kilwa provides a case study of intersecting worlds. We can map the rise of an urban community, with very little territory, from modest origins as a fishing community located on an exposed sand dune, to the pre-eminent port city of the East African coast. While not so famous globally, it was noted as the source (and possibly the main producer) of gold and ivory into the Indian Ocean world, at least for a period in the thirteenth and early fourteenth century. The merchants living in Kilwa saw themselves as successful Muslim traders, civilized, and part of the Islamic world, *dar al-Islam*.

The Kilwans were not Arabs or Persians or Indians, but Africans, and it was this that enabled them to be successful traders. The sources of ivory and gold were at least 1500 km away, and then 400 km inland from Kilwa, and to obtain these successfully, they had to undertake negotiations with distant shores, states, and traders. How they did this is unclear, but their access to Indian Ocean commodities — cloth and glass beads — must have been critical. Judging by later practice, these exchanges were probably cemented by kinship bonds, and complex webs of obligation and negotiation.

At the centre of this stands the great architectural monuments of Husuni Kubwa, Husuni Ndogo, and the Great Mosque extension. Conceived at the height of the gold trade, they represent an attempt to create an Islamic state

---

84 Chirikure and others, 'A Baysian Chronology for Great Zimbabwe', p. 870; compare Pikirayi, *Zimbabwe Culture*, p. 153.

85 Freeman-Grenville, 'Apropos the Gold of Sofala', p. 101.

86 Freeman-Grenville *The East African Coast. Select Documents*, p. 123.

87 Pikirayi, *Zimbabwe Culture*, p. 153; Pearson, *Port Cities*, pp. 49–50 and 104–05.

centre to accommodate visiting Muslim merchants, in the style of the grandest Seljuk caravanserai. Along with the production of coinage and claimed titles, the Sultan saw himself as a great Islamic ruler, who was able to make himself rich on the trade by monopolizing the merchants into his own household. The fact the experiment failed may have been due to local resistance to such grand schemes and expenditure, so explicitly Islamic, or perhaps because the gold economy on which it was based collapsed in the aftermath of the Black Death.

Kilwa survived for another 150 years, and rediscovered its prosperity during the fifteenth century, although on a more modest scale. The neat order of the earlier era had now given way to a more confused society, without ambitious architecture schemes, where the politics were less clear and continuously disputed. It was then left to the Portuguese to blunder into a trading system that they did not understand and to exploit what they could, while destroying its foundations. Within a decade, the most famous town in East Africa was left as village, surrounded by the ruins of past glories.

Works Cited

Primary Sources

Corpus of Early Arabic Sources for West African History, ed. by Nehemia Levtzion and John F. P. Hopkins, Fontes Historiae Africanae. Series Arabica, 4 (Cambridge: Cambridge University Press, 1981)

An Eleventh-Century Egyptian Guide to the Universe: The Book of Curiosities, ed. by Yosef Rapoport and Emilie Savage-Smith (Brill: Leiden, 2014)

Ibn Battuta, *The Travels of Ibn Battuta*, II, ed. by Hamilton Gibb, (Cambridge: Hakluyt Society, 1962)

A Journal of the First Voyage of Vasco da Gama, ed. by Ernest George Ravenstein (London: Hakluyt Society, 1898)

Leo Africanus, *The History and Descriptions of Africa and Notable Things therein Contained*, 3 vols, ed. by Robert Brown and John Pory (London: Hakluyt Society, 1896)

Records of South-Eastern Africa, VI, ed. by George McCall Theal (Cape Town: Government Printer, 1898–1903 [repr. Cape Town: C. Struik, 1964])

Secondary Studies

Abu Lughod, Janet, *Before European Hegemony: The World System AD 1250–1350* (Oxford: Oxford University Press, 1989)

Bayly, Christopher A., 'Archaic and Modern Globalization in the Eurasian and African Arena', in *Globalization in World History*, ed. by Antony G. Hopkins (London: Pimlico, 2002), pp. 47–73

Blanchard, Ian, *Mining, Metallurgy, and Minting in the Middle Ages*, III: *Continuing Afro-European Supremacy, 1250–1450* (Stuttgart: Franz Steiner, 2005)

Brown, Helen W., 'Three Kilwa Gold Coins', *Azania*, 26 (1991), 1–4

Chami, Felix, 'The Archaeology of Pre-Islamic Kilwa Kisiwani (Island)', *Studies in the African Past*, 5 (2006), 119–50

Chaudhuri, Kirti N., *Trade and Civilization in the Indian Ocean: An Economic History from the Rise of Islam to 1750* (Cambridge: Cambridge University Press, 1985)

——, *Asia before Europe* (Cambridge: Cambridge University Press, 1990)

Chirikure, Shadreck, Munyaradzi Manyanga, A. Mark Pollard, Foreman Bandama, Godfrey Mahachi, and Innocent Pikirayi, 'Zimbabwe Culture before Mapungubwe: New Evidence from Mapela Hill, South-Western Zimbabwe', *PLoS ONE*, 9,10 (2014) e111224, <https://doi.org/10.1371/journal.pone.0111224> [accessed 21 June 2021]

Chirikure, Shadreck, A. Mark Pollard, Munyaradzi Manyanga, and Forman Bandama, 'A Bayesian Chronology for Great Zimbabwe: Re-threading the Sequence of a Vandalised Monument', *Antiquity*, 87,337 (2013), 854–72, <https://doi.org/10.1017/S0003598X00049516> [accessed 21 June 2021]

Chittick, H. Neville, 'The "Shirazi" Colonization of East Africa', *Journal of African History*, 6 (1965), 275–94

——, 'The Early History of Kilwa Kivinje', *Azania*, 4 (1969), 153–54

——, *Kilwa: An Islamic Trading City On the East African Coast*, 2 vols, British Institute in Eastern Africa, Memoir, 5 (Nairobi: British Institute in Eastern Africa, 1974)

——, 'The East Coast, Madagascar and the Indian Ocean', in *Cambridge History of Africa*, vol. III, ed. by Roland Oliver (Cambridge: Cambridge University Press, 1977), pp. 183–231

Coutu, Ashley, Gavin Whitelaw, Petrus le Roux, and Judith Sealy, 'Earliest Evidence for the Ivory Trade in Southern Africa: Isotopic and ZooMS Analysis of Seventh–Tenth Century AD Ivory from KwaZulu-Natal', *African Archaeological Review*, 33,4 (2016), 411–35

Crane, Howard, and Lorenz Korn, 'Turko-Persian Empires between Anatolia and India', in *A Companion to Islamic Art and Architecture*, ed. by Finbarr Barry Flood and Gülru Necipoglu (Hoboken: Wiley Blackwell, 2017), pp. 327–55

Creswell, Keppel Archibald Cameron, *A Short Account of Early Muslim Architecture* (rev. and suppl. ed. by J. W. Allen) (Aldershot: Scholar Press, 1989)

Day, John, *The Medieval Market Economy* (Oxford: Blackwell, 1987)

Denbow, James, Carla Klehm, and Laure Dussubieux, 'The Glass Beads of Kaitshàa and Early Indian Ocean Trade into the Far Interior of Southern Africa', *Antiquity*, 89,344 (2015), 361–77

Duyvendak, Jan Julius Lodewijk, *China's Discovery of Africa* (London: Probsthain, 1949)

Fernández-Armesto, Felipe, *Before Columbus: Exploration and Colonisation from the Mediterranean to the Atlantic, 1229–1492* (Philadelphia: University of Pennsylvania Press, 1987)

Filesi, Teobaldo, *China and Africa in the Middle Ages* (London: Frank Cass, 1972)

Fleisher, Jeff, and Stephanie Wynne-Jones, 'Archaeological Investigations at Songo Mnara, Tanzania 2009 Field Season' (unpublished Report to Department of Antiquities, 2010)

——, 'Ceramics and the Early Swahili: Deconstructing the Early Tana Tradition', *African Archaeological Review*, 28 (2011), 245–78

——, 'Archaeological Investigations at Songo Mnara, Tanzania 2011 Field Season' (unpublished Report to Department of Antiquities, 2013)

Freeman-Grenville, Greville Stewart Parker, 'Coinage in East Africa before Portuguese Times', *Numismatic Chronicle* (6th series), 17 (1957), 151–79

——, *The East African Coast. Select Documents from the First to the Earlier Nineteenth Century* (London: Clarendon Press, 1962)

——, *The Medieval History of the Coast of Tanganyika*, Veröffentlichungen des Instituts für Orientforschung, 55 (Berlin: Akademie-Verlag, 1962)

——, *The French at Kilwa Island* (Oxford: Clarendon Press, 1965)

——, 'Shi'i rulers at Kilwa', *Numismatic Chronicle* (7th series), 18 (1978), 187–90

——, 'Apropos the Gold of Sofala', in *Threefold Wisdom — Islam, the Arab world and Africa*, ed. by O. Hulac and M. Mendel (Prague: Academy of Sciences of the Czech Republic, Oriental Institute, 1993), pp. 89–106

Garlake, Peter, *The Early Islamic Architecture of East Africa* (Oxford: Oxford University Press and British Institute for History and Archaeology in East Africa, 1966)

——, *Great Zimbabwe* (London: Thames & Hudson, 1973)
Goitein, Shlomo Dov, and Mordechai A. Friedman, *India Traders of the Middle Ages*, 2 vols (Leiden: Brill, 2011)
Hillenbrand, Robert, *Islamic Architecture: Form, Function, and Meaning* (New York: Columbia University Press, 1994)
Horton, Mark, 'The Swahili Corridor', *Scientific American*, 257,3 (1987), 86–93
——, *Shanga: The Archaeology of an Early Muslim Trading Settlement on the Coast of East Africa* (London: British Institute in Eastern Africa, 1996)
——, 'Ibadis in East Africa: Archaeological and Historical Evidence', in *Studies in Ibadism and Oman*, vol. II: *Oman and Overseas*, ed. by Michaela Hoffmann-Ruf, Abdulrahman al-Salimi, and Heinz Gaube (Hildesheim: Olms, 2013), pp. 93–106
——, 'Early Islam on the East African Coast', in *A Companion to Islamic Art and Architecture*, ed. by Finbarr Barry Flood and Gülru Necipoglu (Hoboken: Wiley Blackwell, 2017), pp. 250–74
——, 'East Africa and Oman c. 600–1856', in *The Ports of Oman*, ed. by Abdulrahman al-Salimi and Eric Staples (Hildesheim: Olms, 2017), pp. 255–79
——, 'East Africa, the Global Gulf and the New Thalasssology', in *Gulf in World History: Arabia at the Global Crossroads*, ed. by Allen Fromherz (Edinburgh: Edinburgh University Press, 2018), pp. 160–81
——, 'The Swahili Corridor Revisited', *African Archaeological Review*, 35,2 (2018), 341–46
——, *Zanzibar and Pemba, the Archaeology of an Indian Ocean Archipelago* (British Institute in Eastern Africa / Routledge, forthcoming)
Horton, Mark, Nicole Boivin, Alison Crowther, Ben Gaskell, Chantel Radimilahy, and Henry Wright, 'East Africa as a Source for Fatimid Rock Crystal: Workshops from Kenya to Madagascar', in *Gemstones in the First Millennium AD: Mines, Trade, Workshops and Symbolism*, ed. by Alexandra Hilgner, Susanne Greiff, and Dieter Quest, Römisch-Germanisches Zentralmuseum, Tagungen, 30 (Mainz: Römisch-Germanisches Zentralmuseum, 2017), pp. 103–18
Horton, Mark, Alison Crowther, and Nicole Boivin, 'Eastern Africa and the Early Indian Ocean: Understanding Mobility in a Globalising World', *Journal of Egyptian History*, 13 (2020), 380–408
Horton, Mark, Helen W. Brown, and W. Andrew Oddy, 'The Mtambwe Hoard', *Azania*, 21, (1986), 115–23
Horton, Mark, and Felix Chami, 'Swahili Origins', in *The Swahili World*, ed. by Stephanie Wynne-Jones and Adria LaViolette (Abingdon: Routledge, 2018), pp. 135–46
Horton, Mark, Jeffrey Fleisher, and Stephanie Wynne-Jones, 'The Mosques of Songo Mnara', *Journal of Islamic Archaeology*, 4,2 (2017), 163–88
Horton, Mark, and John Middleton, *The Swahili: The Social Landscape of a Maritime Society* (Oxford: Blackwells, 2000)
Horton, Mark, Jesper Olsen, Jeffrey Fleisher, and Stephanie Wynne-Jones, 'The Chronology of Kilwa Kisiwani, AD 800–1500', *African Archaeological Review* (forthcoming)
Jordan, William Chester, *The Great Famine: Northern Europe in the Early Fourteenth Century* (Princeton: Princeton University Press, 1996)

Lambourn, Elizabeth, 'The Decoration of the Fakhr al-Dīn Mosque in Mogadishu and Other Pieces of Gujarati Marble Carving on the East African Coast', *Azania*, 34 (1999), 61–86

LaViolette, Adria, and Jeffrey Fleisher, 'The Archaeology of Sub-Saharan Urbanism: Cities and Their Countrysides', in *African Archaeology*, ed. by Ann Stahl (Oxford: Blackwell, 2005), pp. 327–52

MacDonald, Kevin, 'Before the Empire of Ghana', in *Transformations in Africa*, ed. by Graham Connah (Leicester: Leicester University Press, 1998), pp. 71–99

McIntosh, Susan Keech, and Roderick J. McIntosh, *Prehistoric Investigations in the Region of Jenne, Mali*, 2 vols, British Archaeological Reports. International Series, 89 (I–II) / Cambridge Monographs in African Archaeology, 2 (Oxford: British Archaeological Reports, 1980)

Martin, Bradford G., 'Arab Migrations to East Africa in Medieval Times', *International Journal of African Historical Studies*, 7 (1974), 367–90

Middleton, John, 'Merchants: An Essay in Historical Ethnography', *Journal of the Royal Anthropological Institute*, 9,3 (2003), 509–26

——, *African Merchants of the Indian Ocean* (Long Grove: Waveland, 2004)

Mitchell, Peter, *African Connections* (Walnut Creek: AltaMira, 2005)

Monroe, J. Cameron, 'Power and Agency in Precolonial African States', *Annual Review of Anthropology*, 42 (2013), 17–35

Newitt, Malyn, *East Africa: Portuguese Encounters with the World in the Age of Discoveries* (Aldershot: Ashgate, 2002)

Nurse, Derek, and Thomas J. Hinnebusch, *Swahili and Sabaki: A Linguistic History*, Publications in Linguistics, 121 (Berkeley: University of California Press, 1993)

Pearson, Michael N., *Port Cities and Intruders: The Swahili Coast, India, and Portugal in the Early Modern Era*, The Johns Hopkins Symposia in Comparative History, 23 (Baltimore: Johns Hopkins University Press, 1998)

Perkins, John, 'The Coins of the Swahili Coast, c. 800–1500' (unpublished doctoral thesis, University of Bristol, 2013)

——, 'The Indian Ocean and Swahili Coast Coins, International Networks and Local Developments', *Afriques*, 6 (2015), <https://journals.openedition.org/afriques/1769> [accessed 21 June 2021]

Phillips, John Roland Seymour, *The Medieval Expansion of Europe* (Oxford: Oxford University Press, 1990)

Pikirayi, Innocent, *The Zimbabwe Culture: Origins and Decline of Southern Zambezian States* (Walnut Creek: AltaMira, 2001)

Pollard, Edward, *The Archaeology of Tanzanian Coastal Landscapes in the 6th to 15th Centuries AD* (Oxford: British Archaeological Reports, 2008)

Power, Timothy, 'The Red Sea Under the Caliphal Dynasties, c. 639–1171', *History Compass*, 16 (2018), <https://doi.org/10.1111/hic3.12484> [accessed 21 June 2021]

Priestman, Seth, 'A Quantitative Archaeological Analysis of Ceramic Exchange in the Persian Gulf and Western Indian Ocean, AD c. 400–1275' (unpublished doctoral thesis, University of Southampton, 2013)

——, 'Quantitative Evidence for Early Long-Distance Exchange in Eastern Africa: The Consumption Volume of Imported Ceramics', in *The Swahili World*, ed. by Stephanie Wynne-Jones and Adria LaViolette (Abingdon: Routledge, 2018), pp. 472–84

Pwiti, Gilbert, 'Southern Africa and the East African Coast', in *African Archaeology*, ed. by Ann Stahl (Oxford: Blackwell, 2005), pp. 378–91

Rodney, Walter, *How Europe Underdeveloped Africa* (London: Bogle-L'Ouverture, 1972)

Rougeulle, Axelle, *Sharma. Un entrepôt de commerce médiéval sur la côte du Hadramawt (Yémen, ca. 980–1180)*, British Foundation for the Study of Arabia monograph, 17 (Oxford: Archaeopress, 2015)

Russell, Peter, *Prince Henry 'the Navigator': A Life* (New Haven: Yale University Press, 2000)

Saad, Elias, 'Kilwa Dynastic Historiography: A Critical Study', *History in Africa*, 6 (1979), 177–207

Sheriff, Abdul, *Dhow Cultures of the Indian Ocean* (New York: Columbia University Press, 2010)

Sinclair, Paul, 'Chibuene — An Early Trading Site in Southern Mozambique', *Paideuma*, 28 (1982), 149–64

Sinclair, Paul, Anneli Ekblom, and Marilee Wood, 'Trade and Society on the South-East African Coast in the Later First Millennium AD: The Case of Chibuene', *Antiquity*, 86,333 (2012), 723–37

Strong, Arthur, 'The History of Kilwa', *Journal of the Royal Asiatic Society*, 27 (1985), 385–430

Sutton, John, 'The African Lords of the Intercontinental Gold Trade before the Black Death: Al-Hasan bin Sulaiman of Kilwa and Mansa Musa of Kilwa', *Antiquaries Journal*, 77 (1997), 221–42

——, 'Kilwa: A History of the Ancient Swahili Town with a Guide to the Monuments of Kilwa Kisiani and Adjacent Islands', *Azania*, 33 (1998), 113–67

Villers, Alan, *Sons of Sinbad* (London: Hodder & Stoughton, 1940)

Walker, John, 'The History of the Coinage of the Sultans of Kilwa', *Numismatic Chronicle* (5th series), 16 (1936), 43–81

Walsh, Martin, 'The Swahili Language and its Early History', in *The Swahili World*, ed. by Stephanie Wynne-Jones and Adria LaViolette (Abingdon: Routledge, 2018), pp. 121–30

Whitcomb, Donald S., 'The Archaeology of Oman: A Preliminary Discussion of the Islamic Periods', *Journal of Oman Studies*, 1 (1975), 123–57

Wilkinson, John C., 'Oman and East Africa: New Light on Early Kilwan History from the Omani Sources', *International Journal of African Historical Studies*, 14,2 (1981), 272–305

Wood, Marilee, *Interconnections: Glass Beads and Trade in Southern and Eastern Africa and the Indian Ocean 7th to 16th centuries AD*, Studies in Global Archaeology, 17 (Uppsala: Department of Archaeology and Ancient History, 2011)

Wood, Marilee, Serena Panighello, Emilio F. Orsega, Peter Robertshaw, Johannes T. van Elteren, Alison Crowther, Mark Horton, and Nicole Boivin, 'Zanzibar and Indian Ocean Trade in the First Millennium CE: The Glass Bead Evidence', *Archaeological and Anthropological Sciences*, 9,5 (2017), 879–901, <https://doi.org/10.1007/s12520-015-0310-z> [accessed 21 June 2021]

Wynne-Jones, Stephanie, 'Urbanisation at Kilwa' (unpublished doctoral thesis, University of Cambridge, 2005)

Wynne-Jones, Stephanie, and Jeff Fleisher, 'Archaeological Investigations at Songo Mnara, Tanzania 2009', *Nyame Akuma*, 73 (2010), 2–9

Wynne-Jones, Stephanie, Mark Horton, Jeff Fleisher, and Jesper Olsen, 'Dating Kilwa Kisiwani: A Thousand Years of East African History in an Urban Stratigraphy', in *Urban Network Evolutions: Towards a High Definition Archaeology*, ed. by Rubina Raja and Søren M. Sindbak (Aarhus: Aarhus University Press, 2018), pp. 277–85

Wynne-Jones, Stephanie, and Adria LaViolette, ed., *The Swahili World* (Abingdon: Routledge, 2018)

VERONICA STRANG

Seeing Through the Rainbow

*Aboriginal Australian Concepts of an Ordered Universe**

Introduction

Drawing on long-term ethnographic research in Australia's Cape York, with Kunjen, Yir Yoront, and Kokobera language groups on the Mitchell River,[1] this chapter considers the world order of one of the world's most enduring indigenous communities, and how this maintained particular lifeways for millennia. Aboriginal people arrived on the Australian continent in several migratory waves 40,000–60,000 years ago, crossing the narrow straits to the north, possibly when lower sea levels created a window of opportunity.[2] Their hunting and gathering society consisted of small language groups and, over time, several hundred of these and their subsidiary clans formed a network across the continent. The richly resourced tropical northern areas and river estuaries around the coast supported denser populations, while in the inner, drier areas, communities were more sparsely arranged. But each traded resources and people systematically with contiguous groups, and with longer exchange routes. Thus, hundreds of small language groups were located within larger social and economic systems.

Such incrementally extended exchange networks are typical of hunter-gatherers,[3] but their everyday existence was necessarily intensely focused on local environments and organized in concert with ecological events to

* I would like to acknowledge the collaborative engagement in this research of the Aboriginal language groups in Kowanyama, North Queensland, and in particular the Kunjen elders' generosity in guiding me through their cultural landscape. My long-term research with indigenous communities in Australia has been funded, at different stages, by the ESRC, the Royal Anthropological Institute, the University of Auckland, and the Australian Research Council.

1 1988, 1991–1995, 2003–2008, 2011.

2 Bednarik, 'The Earliest Evidence of Ocean Navigation'; Oppenheimer, *Out of Africa's Eden*.

3 Peterson, 'Territorial Adaptations'.

Veronica Strang (veronica.strang@durham.ac.uk), Department of Anthropology, Durham University, United Kingdom

Order into Action: How Large-Scale Concepts of World-Order determine Practices in the Premodern World, ed. by Klaus Oschema and Christoph Mauntel, CURSOR 40 (Turnhout: Brepols, 2022), pp. 263–289
BREPOLS PUBLISHERS 10.1484/M.CURSOR-EB.5.123851

FIGURE 10.1. Alma Wason at a long-term campsite on the Mitchell River, Cape York, Queensland. Photo: Veronica Strang.

take advantage of resource opportunities within clan estates or 'country'. In Cape York, for example, extreme wet and dry seasons encouraged clans to conform to a pattern of long-term camps on ridges in the Wet when resources were plentiful, and, in the Dry, to move between key sites and resources, and to hold meetings to enable exchange (Figure 10.1).[4]

Hunting and gathering makes use of just about everything in the local environment. It requires a vast lexicon of knowledge about the landscape, flora and fauna, water sources, and seasonal changes. Every aspect of the local ecosystem must be closely observed. Thus Aboriginal terminologies for seasonal changes recognize the complex relationalities within the environment: for example, the flowering of certain trees will signal that the crocodiles will be laying their eggs, or when 'fat fish season' arrives, clans will gather for communal fishing activities.[5]

Such attention to local ecological details, and collective methods of gathering resources, provided a highly diverse diet, and for millennia it sustained a population which, according to the first European explorers, appeared to be in excellent health.[6] The highly intimate relationship with local environments

4 Alpher, *Yir-Yoront Texts*; Strang, *Uncommon Ground*.
5 Strang, *Uncommon Ground*; see also Morphy, *Ancestral Connections*.
6 See Flannery, *The Explorers*.

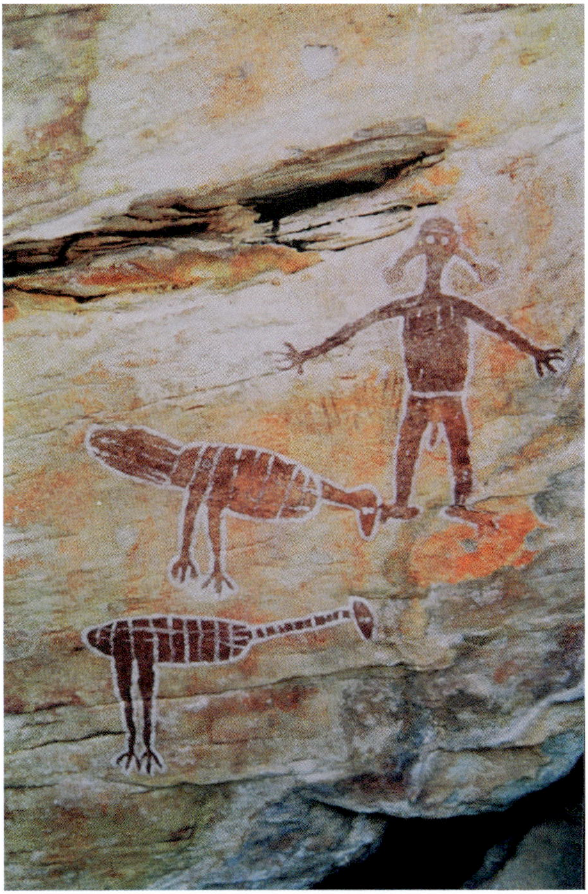

FIGURE 10.2. Rock art depicting ancestral figures, Cape York, Queensland. Photo: Veronica Strang.

maintained by indigenous Australians also provided the basis for a cosmological 'world order' in which the land and its waters were central to and mediated all aspects of life.

Cosmological Order

What did an orderly world look like in pre-colonial Aboriginal Australia? (Figure 10.2) Rock art, material culture and ethnographic accounts record a unique cosmos: a world composed in the Dreamtime, or the 'Story Time' as it is called in Cape York.[7] The Dreamtime is generally represented as an earlier creative era. Ancestral beings emerged, usually from water sources, into a flat, featureless landscape. They appeared most often as birds and animals, but also other things — hollow logs, clouds, floodwaters. They lived as hunter-gatherers, fishing, hunting, and moving from one place to another. As they did so, their actions transformed the landscape and made the world as it is. When they dug holes, these became water sources; they opened dilly [string] bags to release flying foxes into the world; they stuck spears into the ground that became forests.

For example, at a sacred site near the Mitchell River, at Emu Lagoon, when the ancestral Emu and Brolga fought because Emu killed some of Brolga's

7 Flood, *Rock Art of the Dreamtime*; Taçon, Wilson, and Chippendale, 'Birth of the Rainbow Serpent'.

chicks, Brolga burned Emu's wings off, so that emus never flew again. A Kunjen elder, Lefty Yam continues the story:

> He[8] [Brolga] said, 'You can't fly like me fly', he tell that old Emu, you know ... 'you just run along the ground. You can't fly'. He talk to old Emu. All his arms are burnt off ... He only got little arms now, about that long. He big, Emu, eh, but he got little small arm. But Brolga got long [arms], he fly ... Today, he's still flying, Brolga. And Emu, he running, you see.[9]

Brolga was still not satisfied though: he picked Emu up and dropped him from a great height:

> take him way up, must be two hundred feet! Let him go from top then, and he fall right here, in the middle here. Drop him right there.[10]

Where Emu fell, the imprint of his fall created a creek:

> He wasn't creek there, not till that old bird bin come. He never change, still the same. He had really Emu shape, that little creek, when he was down the end of the waterhole. That's where Emu [fell].[11]

Through thousands of such stories, the ancestral beings formed the land, its features, its inhabitants, and their particular characteristics and behaviours. Then, having completed their journeys, they 'sat down' back into the land, and became the totemic ancestors of human clans.[12] There they remained, in a sentient landscape, watching, nurturing human groups, providing their clan members with resources, and withholding these from strangers.

Transmitted inter-generationally through stories, songs, dances, rituals, and material culture, the stories about the ancestral beings therefore provide accounts of local environments and the living beings inhabiting them. This knowledge constituted what Aboriginal people call 'the Law'. This is, in effect, a whole body of cultural knowledge which contains details about everything: not only how to recognize and make use of key species and places, but also how to manage resources and people in relation to each other; how to compose networks of kin and exchange relationships within and beyond these; how to live and act morally; and how to understand the world.

8 Aboriginal English generally refers to both genders as 'he' although — as they have chicks — the protagonists in this story are probably female. Similarly, plurals are often rendered as singular; and past and present tense are often conflated.

9 Lefty Yam (Strang fieldnotes 1992). These and other quotes from Kunjen elders are from ethnographic fieldwork conducted as part of a cultural mapping project with the Kunjen community 1991–1994. This research entailed visiting each sacred site with the elders and recording all key information about it, including the associated ancestral story.

10 Lefty Yam (Strang fieldnotes 1992).

11 Lefty Yam (Strang fieldnotes 1992).

12 Morphy, 'Myth, Totemism and the Creation of Clans'.

Coming from the Rainbow

The major ancestral figure in this creative genesis is the Rainbow Serpent or Rainbow, which, like water, or more accurately *as* water, is seen as the source of all life. It was from this being that others emerged. Thus, the Rainbow Serpent features as the main actor in ancestral stories: it tears through the land, making rivers and lakes; spits or spews — or sometimes excretes — whole populations of animals, fish, birds, plants. It makes the sacred water places at which the ancestral forces are most accessible. It remains, in multiple serpentine forms, within many such places, watching, enforcing the Law, and sometimes swallowing miscreants who fail to respect ritual prohibitions. It is present in all places, permeating them, as the underlying power of life and death, as a fundamental ordering principle, and as the source of life.[13]

Human spiritual being is believed to come from this vital source of power, 'jumping up' from water places to enervate the foetus in a woman's womb. This locates each person with a spiritual 'home' place within the clan estate, and within a network of kin. It confers upon them inalienable rights to collective land and resources, and situates them in a social world with highly specific rules and obligations. Traditionally these included systematic marriage arrangements, which ensured the orderly circulation of people between local clans.

The Law thus presents the relationship between people and places as inalienable. This is the ideal, although populations did move somewhat over time in response to environmental changes. For example, suggesting considerable potential for longevity in oral history,[14] there are persistent ancestral stories about floods and resettlement all around the 'top end' of Australia, where sea levels rose about 10,000 years ago and formed the Gulf of Carpentaria.[15] These describe ancestral efforts to dam the floods. Thus, in a Cape York story, the Two Brothers, *Antujil*, during a fight with their grandfather, cut down a giant tree to make poles from its branches, which they 'threw to the west', forming the sand ridges along the coast:

> They put two pole[s] up to stop that water from coming, overflowing the country, so that land and the sea go one side and lagoon separate. When big rain came they still here. Sink it down, just like a big yam stick, you know — with a sharp end … they had to stick that places to block that water, that flood to spread around that country.

13 Strang, *Life Down Under*.

14 Similar continuities over time are suggested by recurrent rock art images and other archaeological indicators. More anecdotally, like other anthropologists involved in recording cultural stories over long periods of time, I found that there was strong consistency in the retelling of such stories over a number of decades. Given that the traditional aim for indigenous Australians, according to the Law, is to 're-live' the lives of the ancestors, it is not surprising to find high levels of conservatism in narrative forms.

15 Smart, 'Late Quaternary Sea-level Changes'.

> That's why today we don't have flood much, otherwise we could be drowned ... They stopped the sea coming this way: they put all them tree along that hill country ... Stopped that sea ... And this way down here [to the west] it can't climb up that way, you know. He bit high, you know, this ground here's high.[16]

The brothers' grandfather lifted up the giant tree and threw it to the east, making the mountains that run down the other coast of the peninsula:

> Lift him. Chuck him way over there [to the east] ... That's where he bin block that sea, you know. He bin chuck that tree from there to Cairns ... Now we got hill that side, top side [east] stopping all that sea ... He don't want the sea to come in here.[17]

But, while encompassing long-term changes in population and in the land itself, such movements recreated a way of life which still assumed that all individuals would have a permanent home place, from which they could never be fully separated. This provides insights into the passion and commitment that has underpinned Aboriginal efforts to reclaim their land in recent decades. It also highlights an important deterrent to population mobility and expansion. This intense sense of location was illustrated by a Kunjen elder, who explained how a person's spirit is sung ritually back to its birthplace from wherever they have died. Asked where he thought white people's spirits would go, his response was that they must go home: that they must *have* a home place somewhere (though clearly this was somewhere else).

Within this traditional cosmological frame, the moral object of human existence was to live according to the blueprints of the Law: hunting and gathering; 'caring for country'; acquiring secret sacred knowledge over time, and — eventually — becoming 'closer to the ancestors' in wisdom and knowledge, so that upon death the spirit could be sung back to its place of origin and reunited with its totemic 'mate' in a common pool of ancestral force.

Progress towards reunification with the ancestors was believed to come with key transitional stages in human lives: rites of passage in which sacred knowledge was imparted with increasing depth and sophistication. It was possible to go further: those willing to risk the dangers of engagement with the powerful Rainbow might submit to a classic swallowing and regurgitation ritual which involved immersion at a sacred water place. 'Passing through the Rainbow' allowed the initiate to acquire deep secret knowledge, and thus to become (in Aboriginal English) a 'clever doctor'.[18]

From this account it can be seen that the Rainbow Serpent had a central role as a source of authority and order: all knowledge about how to live — the Law — was believed to emerge continuously from the ancestral forces held

16 Colin Lawrence and Lefty Yam, cited in Strang, *Kunjen Country*, p. 168.

17 Colin Lawrence and Lefty Yam, cited in Strang, *Kunjen Country*, p. 169.

18 Strang, *Life Down Under*, see also Taylor, 'Of Acts and Axes'.

within the land, and most particularly from the Rainbow itself. Knowledge — especially secret sacred knowledge — was the most vital source of power, and its acquisition at different life stages upheld the gerontocratic governance of Aboriginal society. All individuals — men and women — became elders and thus leaders in their communities, comprising what was probably one of the flattest and most egalitarian political structures in the world.[19] That is not to suggest that there were no inequalities. Traditional gender roles differed, with the major responsibilities for hunting lying with men, and those focused on gathering with women. But there were key indicators of relative gender equality: all clan members, men and women, co-owned land and resources in a classic example of what Ostrom has described as a 'common property regime'.[20] Kinship systems were as likely to be matrilineal as patrilineal (though this is not a guarantee of gender equality). Men and women had different secret and sacred 'business', but both were important. And political status and involvement in decision-making was located in all elders. European settlers tried to pinpoint male 'kings' of groups, and even went to the trouble of making 'king plates' — neck ornaments — to try to reify such positions (Figure 10.3). But an ethic of collectivity prevailed, and it is still considered questionable for people to put themselves forward as individual leaders.

As this implies, Aboriginal relationships, internally, and also with the non-human world, were very different from those introduced by the European settlers. The egalitarian political structures of Aboriginal groups were echoed in their relationships with non-human beings. With non-human totemic ancestors, and each person having a 'bush name' identifying them with these, there was no dualistic vision of Culture and Nature, or a sense that humankind was above or differentiated from non-human kinds.[21] Order was not imposed on 'Nature' from an elevated position of 'God-given' dominion.[22] It was based, instead, on a reciprocal partnership between people and country. This was not some kind of romantic 'harmony with Nature'[23] but a highly pragmatic

19 This system does give leadership to older people, of course, although power is acquired at various life stages. But with decisions made collectively by all elders, it is more inclusive than any representational democracy creating a political superstructure. There is also a different philosophy of leadership, in which it is believed that holding authority is inextricably linked to a responsibility to nurture.

20 Ostrom, *Governing the Commons*; see also Agrawal, 'Sustainable Governance of Common Pool Resources'.

21 Strang, 'Knowing Me, Knowing You', pp. 25–56.

22 Plumwood, *Feminism and the Mastery of Nature*, and Plumwood, *Environmental Culture*.

23 There has been a strong critique of representations suggesting that indigenous people enjoy a Utopian harmony with their environments, see Hames, 'The Ecologically Noble Savage Debate'. Such communities have indeed inspired environmentalists, who may have idealized them. But this should not obscure a reality that traditional hunter-gatherers had relationships with the material world and non-human beings that were conceptually and practically sustainable, and radically different from those of societies adopting other lifeways.

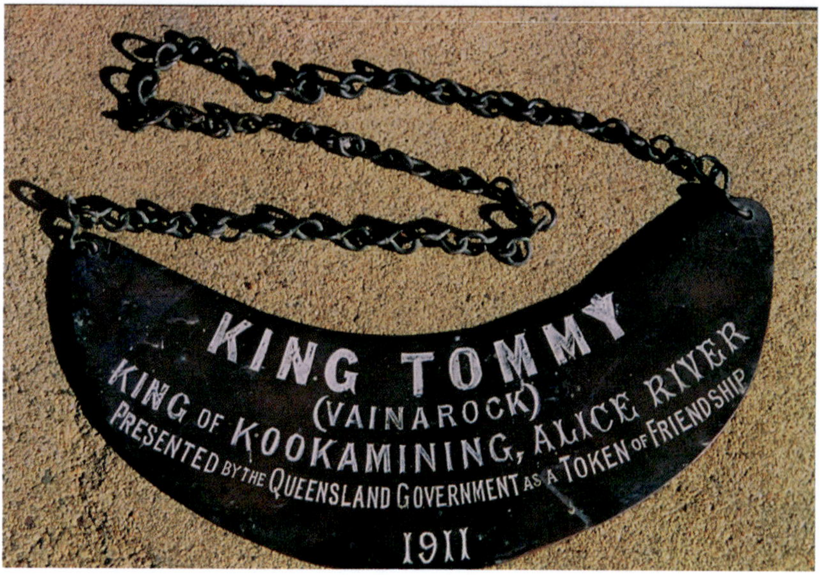

FIGURE 10.3. King plate, Kowanyama, Cape York. Photo: Veronica Strang.

relationship, founded on radically different beliefs and values, in which the non-human world was engaged with rather than merely acted upon.[24]

According to the most fundamental tenets of Aboriginal Law, it was the responsibility of the local clans to care for their country, and its human and non-human inhabitants, both practically — using resources sustainably, and keeping the landscape 'clean' through fire management — and ritually, by maintaining communication with the ancestors and ensuring that they, in turn, would take care of the clan and continue to meet its needs. What emerges, therefore, is a co-operative partnership between human and non-human worlds, in which order comes from a system of knowledge held mutually by humans, by non-human ancestral beings, and a sentient landscape. It comes with a vision of the future that looks precisely like the past, with people maintaining permanent, inalienable relationships with their clan estates, and upholding the Law. In this sense, Aboriginal culture was deeply conservative, both ideologically, and materially.

Material Order

Cosmological world-views and their ordering principles are invariably expressed in material form. This is a recursive relationship: enacted upon

24 Strang, *Gardening the World.*

a cultural landscape, material expression serves to represent and maintain particular ideas and practices over time, concretizing concepts of order and upholding traditions. In indigenous Australia, a belief that the Law required individuals to replicate the lives of their ancestors was expressed in a range of practices designed to ensure this continuity. Aboriginal communities carefully manipulated the physical environment. Land management involved the systematic use of fire to clear scrub and allow the growth of 'green pick' (new grass) which would advantage game, as well as reducing the risks of walking through tall grass containing numerous species of poisonous snakes.[25] Over millennia 'firestick management' transformed much of the Australian landscape into open savannah or thin forest, which favoured some plant and animal species more than others. But it was a slow and subtle process, and therefore highly sustainable in terms of supporting both human and non-human populations.

The Law demanded the meticulous management of resources so that these would be replenished. In gathering yams, for example, it was vital to return part of the root to the soil so that the plant would continue to grow. In harvesting spear rods, enough of the tree would be left that it could regenerate and continue to supply these. Increase rituals — the use of sympathetic magic to intensify particular resources — were common, and aimed at maintaining these at sustainable levels.

There was very little imposition of physical order on the environment. Small fish weirs and other traps might be built in streams. Thus, a Kunjen elder described how they used to make a 'fish bed' in a stream with high banks at the western edge of Emu Lagoon:

> Used to make a bed here, for fish … deep there — make a bed there, got high bank there … Used to cut a big log, bed log, down there, put another one there, put another one crossways, 'nother one crossways, cut a little stick, all the way up. We get a bark [a section of bark from a tree], put him on top of them stick, and the water go underneath. When the fish come … he gotta jump straight into that bed.[26]

In some areas, small irrigation channels were made to encourage the growth of useful plants such as taro. There was some planting of food and medicinal plants around campsites. But such practices were aimed at maximizing gains from existing ecological processes, rather than introducing infrastructures or technologies that would radically reorder these to serve human interests. Some scholars have suggested that these kinds of activities may have constituted a form of early agriculture,[27] but the line between the domiculture around long-term campsites and small-scale agriculture is not hard and fast. It is

25 Lewis, 'Ecological and Technological Knowledge of Fire'.
26 Lefty Yam, cited in Strang, *Kunjen Country*, p. 38.
27 Gerritsen, *Australia and the Origins of Agriculture*; see also Pascoe, *Dark Emu*.

FIGURE 10.4. Carved 'passport' sticks, with clan designs. Photo: Veronica Strang.

clear that indigenous Australian land management gradually transformed the environment over time,[28] but it did not involve the enclosure of fields, or changes in types of property ownership, and it did not follow a trajectory of expansion and intensification.

Nor did Aboriginal society expand its population. Long-term breast feeding helped to limit fertility, and unwanted pregnancies were reportedly aborted through the use of 'giddee-giddee' seeds and other bush medicines.

There was of course some change: within this conservative ideal, groups expanded and contracted with social and environmental shifts, and there were some changes in practices over time. But overall, the basic tenets of Aboriginal social and spatial organization pertained with remarkable consistency, keeping the population firmly located in place.

That is not to say that people never travelled away from their homes, though going further afield generally required permission from local clans. Carved wooden 'passports' were used to demonstrate the traveller's clan identity and thus their home location (Figure 10.4). People typically spoke three or four languages which, though they might be geographically contiguous, were often quite different. The ownership of land and resources was defined by sacred

28 Gammage, *The Biggest Estate on Earth*.

FIGURE 10.5. Traditional humpy, wooden frame with cabbage palm leaves, Cape York, Australia. Photo: Veronica Strang.

sites (ancestral story places with high concentrations of power), but there were no territorial boundaries as such — simply a detailed understanding between long-term exchange partners about who owned or had rights to which land and resources. Notably, the dispersal of people across the landscape had — and required — no geographic centre, no focus from which a more centralized form of governance might emerge. Nor were there defined 'regions' as such, which might acquire distinctive identities in relation to each other

Social Order

In the ancestral stories cautionary tales often focus on failures to respect sacred sites, or on 'wrong way' marriage and its consequences. The systematic exchange of partners through specific patterns of marriage maintained the social and spatial arrangement of people in relation to land and resources. So, rather than policing territorial boundaries, the Law tended to uphold the right social choices about who to marry, and to point to the price of 'wrong way' choices.

An example is provided by a story about a Ghost ancestor in Cape York. This relates how the Ghost built a humpy [shelter] and, while he was away hunting, two women came looking for water lily roots and, finding the humpy abandoned, decided to camp there (Figure 10.5). When he returned, he saw the fire they had made in the doorway.

> He found them two lady was there — he had no wife I suppose — and he wanted to join them two there ... he was so happy, he was glad! Yeah, he was so glad, he wanted to get in the humpy, and have sex with those two woman ... But them two old ladies wouldn't let him come in ... He try to have a sweet talk with them, you see. Tried to make out he was their husband, he said, 'Oh listen, don't be cheeky with me, I'm your husband, I just gone out hunting, see. I come back here to camp'... He tried all night, tried to get in there ... He tormented them all night. Yeah, all night. Till daylight.
>
> As soon as that daylight bin come ... they come out and chased him with a yam stick ... They didn't want him to be with them. So by daylight they got out and got into him, and he took off then, he took off, took off, fright! He had a *womera* [spearthrower] with him, and he took off like that. And that *womera* hook there ... got caught on a vine, and he was trying to pull that, get it down from that vine, but no, them two ladies probably catching up with him. He took off ... he keep on running, left that *womera*, gone! ... That's why he left that womera behind. That's why that place named *Errwont* — that mean 'hooked up *womera. Womera* hook'. ... He never worry about that *womera*, he left him behind, he that much fright![29]

The story is humorous (the 'womera' possibly being a euphemism for a more personal appendage), but it is also a parable about the need to retain the 'right way' marriages and exchanges necessary to ensure a sustainable circulation of people. This was one area in which there was some conflict between groups. Discussing the Yolngu in north-east Arnhem Land, Howard Morphy notes historical accounts of fierce inter-group conflicts over the movements of women, raids to capture them from other groups, and some violent interactions.[30] Some of this history is still related in dance and ritual. But, although some tensions of this kind were evident, communities generally maintained regular exchanges with contiguous groups and, by extension, with larger networks across the continent.

Spatial Order

Aboriginal groups employed multiple methods of producing detailed maps of 'country'.[31] These are integral, for example, in the ancestral stories describing

29 Colin Lawrence, Ivan Jimmy, and Lefty Yam, cited in Strang, *Kunjen Country*, p. 75.

30 Pers. comm.

31 As David Max Moerman (New York) observed during the conference at Heidelberg

the activities of the ancestors as they travelled across the landscape composing ancestral 'tracks' or 'songlines'. Such accounts often contain details about water sources, resources, and topography. Thus, the Brolga ancestor, having dispensed with Emu near the Mitchell River, decided to go back to his home in the Coleman River:

> When he killed him … him fly from there, Brolga, keep them two little kids *bla*[32] him, go way up there, go way down thataway.[33]

Brolga flew west to a place which, in the colonial era, was named Surprise Yard, where he sat down for a while, leaving a 'poison place' [a powerful sacred site] on an island in the lagoon:

> He land there for a while. Land there, have a look around, 'no, not good enough'. He went here, there, just landed, have look around … Just look round, he don't want to stay there, so he went thataway … To Coleman now, to Coleman River, 'I'm going to my home now'.[34]

In returning to the ancestral domain he was transformed into a large rock in the middle of the river:

> He still in there in the Coleman: that's where he ended up. That's where he turn into rock … Today you see a stone, in the middle: that Brolga Story, he still there. *Korrokorr ampungk, errk elampungk* [Brolga home, the home place of his image].[35]

As this suggests, songlines are not confined to particular clan estates, but run across and between them, with clans *en route* focusing on the relevant sections of the story. This provides another set of links between groups, and — as some songlines run for great distances — binds many of them together.

Ancestral stories are transmitted intergenerationally, not just in songs and stories, but also in bark paintings; carvings; body art; painting on shields and boomerangs, and in coloured sand (now translated into acrylic paintings and other artworks employing new techniques and materials). Each clan has its own patterns and designs, often depicting local plants or animals. In Arnhem Land, for example, the cross-hatching seen in bark paintings usually represents grassland, while a diamond pattern might signify the back of an ancestral crocodile that features in local stories. Through layers of condensed symbols, all such images are maps of highly specific relationships between particular places and people.[36] Most importantly,

---

(see Mauntel's and Oschema's introduction to this volume), map-making has various performative elements, and is readily meshed with forms of ritual worship.

32 'Belonging to'.

33 Lefty Yam and Charlie Pindi, cited in Strang, *Kunjen Country*, p. 148.

34 Lefty Yam and Charlie Pindi, cited in Strang, *Kunjen Country*, p. 148.

35 Lefty Yam and Charlie Pindi, cited in Strang, *Kunjen Country*, p. 148.

36 Morphy, *Journey to the Crocodile's Nest*.

they are still believed to embody ancestral power: the shimmering dots and patterns (*bir'yan*) emanates ancestral force, which acts upon the viewer and thus shapes their thinking and behaviour.[37]

The centrality of the Rainbow Serpent in generating this force underlines the point that spatial order in Aboriginal terms is not merely horizontal. Western societies generally represent the landscape as a conceptually horizontal material foundation to activities, but in an indigenous Australian cosmology it is more the point at which the material and non-material domains meet and interpenetrate each other. Below the overarching figure of the visible Rainbow is the other, invisible, half of a circle within the land, composing a hydro-theological cycle in which the Rainbow carries living beings from the invisible non-material ancestral domain, into material being, and then back again. It is for this reason that the terms for the spirit emerging from the ancestral domain generally translate as 'becoming material' or 'becoming visible',[38] and a person's spiritual home, in Kunjen, is called their *errk elampungk*, which can be translated as 'the home place of your image'.[39]

This classic hydro-theological cycle therefore introduces into the equation a vertical conceptual order in which movement is simultaneously from inside to outside. It is accompanied by a traditional concept of time which, unlike the one-way arrow of Western thinking, is fundamentally cyclical. Material and non-material dimensions and their temporalities co-exist, and the Dreamtime is not a time but a place, to the extent that Aboriginal elders would usually say 'where' rather than 'when' in referring to it. There are useful resonances here with Pre-Colombian belief systems in Latin America, which similarly posit alternative generative dimensions.[40]

In this cosmological frame, temporal, spatial and social order all depend on the cyclical flows of persons and things through the Rainbow. These cycles are multiple in scale: considerable attention is paid to local movements of water and the annual wet and dry seasons. Each water place is a generative well from which people and resources arise as well as a potential entry to the invisible domain beneath. But on a larger spatial scale — reflecting the movements of water at a meteorological level — the Rainbow Serpent is also seen to link earth and sky. In Australia, the Milky Way is highly visible, and it is often described as a 'sky river' populated by ancestral beings. Totemic animals, the Emu, the Brolga, form celestial constellations. There are stories in which ancestors ascend 'sky ladders' or giant trees into the sky. Thus, on a vertical as well as a horizontal plane, a focus on local systemic movements opens out into a larger-scale vision of flows across much larger distances.

37 Morphy, *Ancestral Connections*, and Morphy, 'Not Just Pretty Pictures'.
38 Morton, 'The Effectiveness of Totemism'.
39 Strang, *Uncommon Ground*.
40 See the contribution by Sachse in this volume; see also Reichel-Dolmatoff, 'Cosmology as Ecological Analysis'.

This cosmological spatiality is therefore rather like a sacred site: its primary focus is at a local level, but it is not boundaried, and allows an imaginative extension into larger spatial and temporal arrangements. Aboriginal songs, stories, and maps have an intensely local focus that matches, to some extent, the scale of clan estates, but at the same time they clearly compose a mosaic of a larger vision of the world, as a potentially indefinite network which extends not only to the shores of the continent, but beyond. This includes stories about ancestral beings coming from across the sea, and notions that, upon death, a part of the person's spirit will 'go west' across the sea.

There is considerable evidence of trade with people from across the sea. For example, rock art images depicting Makassan *perahu*, and other archaeological records, show that Aboriginal groups on the northern coast had long-term trading relationships with Makassan trepangers (sea cucumber fishers) from South Sulawesi in Indonesia, exchanging with them turtle shells, pearls, and cypress pine, and gaining in return access to technologies for making dugout canoes.[41] In Arnhem Land, some Yolngu even worked with the Makassans as trepangers, and accompanied them back to their homelands.

There are diverse views about the relative harmony of this larger overseas relationship. Bradley maintains that it was a fair and equal trading arrangement characterized by 'mutual trust and respect'.[42] Other anthropologists suggest that contact resulted in a period of 'social upheaval',[43] and that relationships deteriorated in the latter stages of the trade as 'the Aborigines began to feel that they were being exploited'.[44] Over several centuries it is possible that relations varied, but it is clear, at any rate, that there was significant long-term exchange between Australia and Indonesia.

Contact with other groups and their economic practices produced some changes: acquiring the technology for making dugout canoes enabled some expansion of saltwater fishing in Arnhem Land; further south, there were some minor irrigation practices reminiscent of those found across South-East Asia and the Pacific to support taro gardens. There is evidence that some Islamic influences seeped into local Aboriginal stories and ritual practices, and may have had some effect on indigenous communities' treatment of women. Thus, Macknight notes that Allah, coming from the Makassans, was adopted into Aboriginal pantheons of deities, much as the Christian God was later incorporated into indigenous religious beliefs across Australia.[45] Aboriginal Australians therefore had access to larger scales of social and political contact, and to other, very different, cultural contexts.

---

41 May, McKinnon, and Raupp, 'Boats on Bark'; Russell, 'Aboriginal-Makassan Interactions'.

42 Bradley, 'Interview'.

43 McIntosh, 'Islam and Australia's Aborigines?', p. 76.

44 Berndt and Berndt, 'Arnhem Land', p. 110; cited in McIntosh, 'The Birrinydji Legacy. Aborigines, Macassans and Mining in North-east Arnhem Land', p. 81.

45 Macknight, 'Macassans and the Aboriginal Past'; Peterson, 'Territorial Adaptations'.

Yet, despite these links, indigenous lifeways remained largely consistent and indeed very resilient. Even in the twentieth century, when indigenous communities were driven away from their land and forced to seek sanctuary in Christian missions, they accepted the larger, more abstract Christian ideas as a larger religious umbrella, and God as a powerful being, but retained their own beliefs and practices in their everyday lives. While missionaries pushed them to adopt horticultural practices, they continued to hunt and gather. And those who managed to stay on their own land by working for the cattle stations continued, while mustering cattle, to visit their sacred sites, conduct rituals, manage the landscape and make use of their own resources.

Conserving Order

The conservatism which stabilized Aboriginal Australia cannot be said to stem from a single factor, but from a range of linked ideas and practices, and particular environmental limits and opportunities. Though it would have been possible for Aboriginal people to adopt or develop agricultural methods to intensify food production, and so to support a larger human population, they refrained from doing so (Figure 10.6). Possibly the adoption of different forms of food production was discouraged, in part, by the realities of a material environment prone to severe droughts and major floods, with delicate friable soils that were easily eroded. Rather than simply overriding such environmental limitations unsustainably, as many other societies (including European settlers in Australia) chose to do, they retained a vision of order more focused on the long-term well-being of all participants, including the non-human inhabitants of the landscape, and its ecosystems. This required both a deep philosophy of conservation, and practices that would actively support such values.

A willingness to limit population growth was obviously stabilizing. Combined with reciprocal rather than exploitative human-environmental relationships, this reproduced a sustainable hunter-gatherer economy with little need to adopt riskier and more demanding economic practices. Social as well as economic stability was supported by common property regimes and exchange relationships maintaining the steady movement of people and resources between groups. With clans owning land and resources collectively, and every individual inheriting equal rights of access and use, there was little to generate internal competition for these. Though some language groups maintained a moiety system (dividing into two halves), and all had subsidiary clans, these were complementary relationships rather than being competitive with each other.

Gerontocratic political structures, based on equality and power-sharing, discouraged the appearance of the 'big men' and larger tribalization that characterized indigenous societies in nearby Papua New Guinea and New Zealand. Maintaining small language groups, rather than larger tribes, left little

FIGURE 10.6. Elder cooking wallaby in *cup mari* [sand oven]. Photo: Veronica Strang.

room for the creation of hierarchies and elites, and prevented the higher levels of internecine warfare that sometimes emerged between tribal groups elsewhere.

Egalitarian relationships between people (and with non-human beings) were further expressed in and maintained by religious beliefs knitting people firmly into place, socially and spatially. A rich ritual life further communicated and affirmed these principles. And although there was some religious diversity, in ritual performance, or in styles of narrative and representation, Aboriginal communities across Australia broadly shared a particular cosmological understanding. The Rainbow Serpent, bringing spiritual, social and economic life into holistic coherence, represented 'joined up' thinking which appears to have been uncontroversial, and which therefore avoided movement towards pluralism and cultural divergence.

There was a related lack of pressure for outward movement. Although (unlike the delicate bark canoes only suitable for wetlands)[46] dugout canoes allowed people to fish further from shore, these were not used to make forays further afield. Even with experience of travelling to Indonesia, Aboriginal Australians did not embark upon the kinds of canoe expeditions that were carried out, for example, by Māori groups across the Pacific. It may be that they were keenly aware that boomerangs, spears and *womeras* could not match

46 As Bednarik points out, migration to Australia possibly involved the use of bamboo rafts, and 'the lack of large bamboo species in Australia may well explain why a seafaring ability acquired over hundreds of millennia became limited to coastal navigation', see Bednarik, 'The Earliest Evidence of Ocean Navigation', p. 188.

Makassan cannons, and that small clan groups would be easily outnumbered if they ventured across to areas inhabited by large tribal groups. But, more to the point, there was little need or motivation to move outwards. A small population living sustainably generated little pressure to seek new land and resources elsewhere, or to pull up social and psychological roots so deeply embedded in 'home' places.

Driving Hegemony

The conservative lifeways of Aboriginal society, which enabled it to maintain stable, non-expansive lifeways for so long, challenge reductive assumptions about 'natural' human inclinations towards growth and expansion, or the notion that humankind is driven by evolutionary/biological tendencies towards aggressive competition.[47] This should not surprise us: although Aboriginal Australians represent one of the few societies maintaining traditional hunter-gatherer lives into the 1900s, globally, this highly sustainable way of being in the world has comprised most of human history and, as Bateson has observed, assumptions that evolution has been a purely competitive scrabble for supremacy are insufficient: human evolution has, throughout, also been demonstrably dependent upon cooperation.[48]

Cultural beliefs and values can be extremely resilient. Zvelebil draws attention to archaeological evidence in the Baltic regions suggesting that, although hunter-gatherers' practices of sharing, egalitarianism and common ownership came under pressure in the late Mesolithic era, 'brought about by development of delayed-return technologies, an increase in social competition, social differentiation, and, later, contact with farming communities', some groups shifted into farming, but others chose to domesticate reindeer and retain their particularly lifeways.[49] In Africa, the !Kung San, famously described by Marshall Sahlins as 'the original affluent society', showed similar resilience in retaining their hunter-gatherer practices, even after long engagement with Bantu pastoralists.[50] As Sahlins observed, such affluence arose from maintaining limited needs, and thus having ample capacity to live within resource constraints. Similarly, although European missionaries and pastoralists in Australia forced Aboriginal communities to adopt horticulture and participate in cattle farming, they retained a major focus on hunting and gathering, which required relatively small investments of labour and left much time for ritual and creative practices.

But it took only a few millennia for many societies to choose otherwise. In the last short stretch of human history there has been a rapidly accelerating

---

47 Dawkins, *The Selfish Gene*.

48 Bateson, *Steps to an Ecology of Mind*.

49 Zvelebil, 'Innovating Hunter-Gatherers', p. 58.

50 Sahlins, 'Notes on the Original Affluent Society'.

spiral of change and movement towards more intensive modes of production, and the emergence of vastly more competitive and hegemonic societies. The factors that clearly helped to stabilize Aboriginal society throw into relief those that may have an opposite effect.

Jared Diamond points to agriculture as the primary culprit, describing it as 'humanity's worst mistake': a shift that pushed societies onto a slippery slope and created not only increasingly unsustainable environmental relationships, but also social inequalities and a greater emphasis on boundaries and territories.[51] Did agriculture's capacity to support population growth and economic intensification bring with it the seeds of competitive hegemonic expansion and a focus on larger-scale visions of world order?

Such tendencies are not immediately evident in early shifts to small-scale horticulture and pastoralism. As Barnard points out: 'Foraging culture does not die the moment a collector picks up a hoe and becomes a cultivator … mode of thought is more resilient than means of production'.[52] But even in common property regimes, growing crops required the investment of time and labour in clearing land, planting, and making fences to exclude animals. Similarly, the domestication of non-human species generally required containment of some sort, and/or the need for secure grazing. It is therefore logical to infer that such activities probably introduced more particular notions of territoriality. Still, where population numbers remained stable, and activities did not exceed the local environment's carrying capacities, such small-scale collective arrangements were able to pertain for long periods, particularly when mixed with other forms of resource use.

Less economic diversity and a stronger dependence upon agriculture, while generating more food and supporting greater population density, introduced significantly higher levels of risk. Reliance on a few staple crops could go rapidly awry in years of drought, and a single crop disease or insect infestation could be devastating. Even when rendered steadily productive, land, soil, and water are finite resources: population growth represented a rise in risk, and a reality that, at some point, more land or more resources would be needed. As Diamond has shown, a pattern of overly rapid growth and collapse has occurred many times in human history.[53]

There is a limited range of solutions to unsustainable economic practices: internally, the only choices are a reduction in population and/or its requirements, or an increase in production efficiency which may well externalize the costs to other species and have only short-term viability. The alternative is to look outwards, seeking either to negotiate trade with other societies, or to gain access to more land and resources by expanding or moving into new areas. It is worth noting that, even without the occupation of new lands, the externalization of costs to others — human and non-human — constitutes

---

51 Diamond, 'The Worst Mistake in the History of the Human Race'.

52 Barnard, 'The Future of the Foraging Mode of Thought'.

53 Diamond, *Collapse*.

FIGURE 10.7. Contemporary crop irrigation in Queensland. Photo: Veronica Strang.

a form of hegemony, as such externalization appropriates their resources and the environments upon which they depend.

Larger-scale agriculture had significant effects on social and political relationships between people, and between societies and their environments (Figure 10.7). By imposing more directive managerial engagement upon the material world, it contributed to a dualistic differentiation between Culture and Nature, and so to a conceptual separation between human societies and the non-human world. Such separation helped to promote a view that humankind should enjoy 'dominion' over Nature.[54] This later extended to notions of dominion over groups of people who missionaries and colonists felt able to categorize as 'the children of Nature'.[55]

With the settlement and the domestication of land and non-human species, agriculture defined 'wild' and 'domesticated' categories and made a further division between outside/work/public spaces and inside/domestic/private

54 Harrison, 'Subduing the Earth'.

55 Attwood, *The Making of the Aborigines*, and Reynolds, *The Law of the Land*.

spaces. Gender roles and their location in these spaces changed accordingly, supporting male dominance in the public and political realm. New and more exclusive forms of property and enfranchisement took land and resources out of collective forms of ownership and placed them, over time, in fewer and fewer hands.[56]

Enlarging societies developed new technologies and urban areas, introducing rural-urban divides, centralization, and steeper political hierarchies. Elite classes emerged, with attendant inequalities in power and in the agency and perceived value of different social groups. Trade routes extending around the world opened up vistas of other continents, and the flow of goods and ideas from afar made it possible to imagine distant lands as objects of desire.

Following a Durkheimian logic, that societies create their gods in their own images,[57] religious beliefs in agricultural societies moved away from ideas about reciprocal partnerships with multiple 'nature beings', such as totemic ancestors, towards the worship of hierarchical pantheons of increasingly humanized gods, and then to patriarchal monotheisms.[58] These are not mere changes in form: they are also changes in scale, representing a conceptual delocalization and abstraction of ideas and an outward shift in imaginative focus to larger-scale visions of the world.

Growth and development were normalized in many societies, providing a sense of forward movement and momentum and introducing a concept of 'progress' that represented a critical shift away from 'steady state' economies and stable social practices. Modernity has so internalized concepts of progress and growth that it is now counterintuitive to frame these in other than positive terms. Countermovements promoting conservation and 'degrowth economics' have little traction in relation to overwhelming assumptions that growth and development are good and necessary.[59] But growth can only be sustained if there is sufficient room for it. Where there is not, hegemonic expansion, in one form or another, becomes imperative.

Several common threads run through these developments. One is concerned with scale and how this affected populations, and their social, political, and economic institutions. With a move away from close kin networks, face-to-face exchange relationships, and deeply rooted attachment to specific places, increases in scale led to widening differentiations in class, identity, gender, property ownership, and power relations within and between human societies. Religious differentiation became difficult to avoid, as illustrated by the challenges that pluralistic societies experienced in the medieval period, despite the marriage of politics and religion that attempted to unite diverse realms.[60]

56 Hann, *When History Accelerates*.

57 Durkheim, *The Elementary Forms of the Religious Life*.

58 Strang, 'Lording it Over the Goddess'.

59 Illich, 'The Shadow Our Future Throws'.

60 See the contribution by Oschema and Mauntel in this volume.

A failure to maintain sustainable practices produced a pressure for technical advances to intensify production, which in turn accelerated material and social change. People's lives could no longer be predictably inherited and prescribed according to ancestral Law, but became more self-directed and competitive. This suggests another important thread: a movement from collectivity to individuation and from cooperation to competition. Such shifts must surely have eased the way towards hegemonic ambitions.

There is also a recurrent theme of agency. The above comparisons reveal a major contrast in the extent to which different societies have sought to impose human agency onto their environments, and to transform these in accord with their particular needs and interests. The low-key environmental management of Aboriginal communities might be described as 'light touch': a 'working with' rather than 'acting upon' which is radically different from, for example, the clearing of land for arable crops, the construction of vast dams and irrigation schemes, or the extraction of oil and minerals. It is also possible to frame this difference in terms of order: for indigenous Australians 'world order' is drawn *from* the world, from ecological processes, other species and, symbolically, from the Rainbow that encapsulates all of these. This contrasts sharply with lifeways that are directed towards imposing human order, by force if necessary, upon an objectified material environment, and upon non-human kinds as subjects. Nowhere is this more visible than in the construction of major infrastructures that, for example, redirect water flows into irrigation at the expense of ecosystems.[61] In a more competitive world this has also, increasingly, entailed more powerful societies imposing their order hegemonically on others. The result is rising global conflict and disruption, widening inequalities, and the displacement of previously stable small-scale social groups. Moran suggests that:

> The exponential increase in all of these measurable phenomena is tied most fundamentally to two factors: the increase in the human population and our consumption habits. Indeed one must think of these two factors in tandem. One Euroamerican citizen consumes 25 times the resources than one average citizen from India, Guatamala, or another less-developed country does.[62]

Conclusion

Our glimpse into the unique world order of indigenous Australians suggests a complex relationship between multiple domains of human life: economic practices; social and political organization, cosmological and religious understandings; technologies and forms of environmental engagement.

61 Rodgers and O'Neill, 'Infrastructural Violence'.

62 Moran, *People and Nature*, pp. 2–3.

The drivers to hegemonic expansion, and to larger visions of world order, lie in the form that these take, and the beliefs, values, and practices that they promote.

It may be heuristically useful to consider this as a continuum, with Aboriginal Australians at one end of the spectrum: localized, low-key, and so cosmologically and socially conservative as to maintain sustainable lifeways for millennia. Close beside them sit small-scale horticultural and early agricultural modes of living, which retained localized religious systems, common property regimes, and sustainable limits in human populations and their resource use. We might then look at societies that intensified their modes of production and allowed population growth, and which consequently increased their levels of risk to the extent that droughts, or simply exceeding the limits of local ecosystems, forced them to move elsewhere or collapse. At the other extreme of the continuum sit the most aggressively expansive societies: the Romans; the Mongolian tribes; the Byzantine Empire; European colonial empires. Systematic comparison across this continuum illuminates the factors that either discourage or create a propensity for hegemonic expansion and aspirations for 'world domination'.

A comparative view also suggests that, while it is easy for societies to enter into unsustainable spirals of growth, this is very difficult to reverse. Even those communities who have retained egalitarian and sustainable lifeways, have now found themselves, through colonial hegemony, with unsustainable practices and technologies; social, political and religious hierarchies; and matching belief systems thrust upon them by larger societies whose visions of order are more globally oriented.

They — indeed all of us — now inhabit a world in which competition for land, water, and resources is intense and still rising. Hegemony is becoming not merely an expression of desire for greater affluence by the most powerful societies, but an increasingly urgent imperative for them, with commensurate costs not only for other human societies, but also for the planet's non-human species, which are now experiencing an anthropogenically caused mass extinction.[63]

Aboriginal lifeways are not replicable on a larger scale, but they, and other small-scale place-based societies with common property regimes, are probably the clearest exemplars we have of alternate, more sustainable, ways of thinking. They illustrate the utility of having strong affective attachments to place, as well as to principles of equality and respect, not only between humans, but also between humans and the non-human species that are co-dependent upon shared ecosystems.[64] Their lifeways illustrate the efficacy of a strong ethic for population control and more sustainable use of resources, achieved through collaborative modes of engagement, rather than through competition.

63 International Union for the Conservation of Nature, *Species Extinction*.

64 Strang, 'Re-imagined Communities'.

In providing a usefully comparative model, they therefore help us to understand the drivers of hegemonic expansion. They open up alternative choices, and opportunities to build the consensus and cooperation that are needed to co-create a more sustainable 'world order'.

Works Cited

Secondary Studies

Agrawal, Arun, 'Sustainable Governance of Common Pool Resources: Context, Methods, and Politics', *Annual Review of Anthropology*, 32 (2003), 243–62

Alpher, Barry, *Yir-Yoront Texts* (Victoria: Deakin University, 1998)

Attwood, Bain, *The Making of the Aborigines* (Sydney: Allen & Unwin, 1989)

Barnard, Alan, 'The Future of the Foraging Mode of Thought' (unpublished conference paper presented at the Eighth International Conference of Hunting and Gathering Societies, Osaka, 1998)

Bateson, Gregory, *Steps to an Ecology of Mind: Collected Essays in Anthropology, Psychiatry, Evolution and Epistemology* (Northvale, NJ: Jason Aronson Inc., 1987 [orig. 1972])

Bednarik, Robert, 'The Earliest Evidence of Ocean Navigation', *International Journal of Nautical Archaeology*, 26,3 (1997), 183–91

Berndt, Ronald, and Catherine Berndt, *Arnhem Land: Its History and its People* (Melbourne: F. W. Cheshire, 1954)

Bradley, John, Interview in *Janak Rogers* 'When Islam came to Australia', *BBC News Magazine* (24 June 2014), <https://www.bbc.co.uk/news/magazine-27260027> [accessed 21 June 2021]

Dawkins, Richard, *The Selfish Gene* (Oxford: Oxford University Press, 1976)

Diamond, Jared, 'The Worst Mistake in the History of the Human Race', *Discover Magazine*, May 1987, 64–66

——, *Collapse: How Societies Choose to Fail or Succeed* (New York: Viking, 2005)

Durkheim, Emile, *The Elementary Forms of the Religious Life* (London: Allen & Unwin, 1968 [orig. 1915])

Flannery, Tim, *The Explorers: Epic First Hand Accounts of Exploration in Australia* (London: Phoenix, 1998)

Flood, Josephine, *Rock Art of the Dreamtime: Images of Ancient Australia* (Sydney: Angus and Robertson, 1997)

Gammage, Bill, *The Biggest Estate on Earth: How Aborigines made Australia* (Crow's Nest, NSW: Allen & Unwin, 2011)

Gerritsen, Rupert, *Australia and the Origins of Agriculture*, British Archaeological Reports. International Series, 1874 (Oxford: Archaeopress, 2008)

Hames, Raymond, 'The Ecologically Noble Savage Debate', *Annual Review of Anthropology*, 36 (2007), 177–90

Hann, Chris, ed., *When History Accelerates: Essays on Rapid Social Change, Complexity and Creativity* (London: The Athlone Press, 1994)

Harrison, Peter, 'Subduing the Earth: Genesis 1, Early Modern Science, and the Exploitation of Nature', *The Journal of Religion*, 79,1 (1999), 86–109

Illich, Ivan, 'The Shadow Our Future Throws', *New Perspectives Quarterly*, 16,2 (1999), 14–18

International Union for the Conservation of Nature, *Species Extinction: The Facts*, <https://www.iucn.org/sites/dev/files/import/downloads/species_extinction_05_2007.pdf> (2017) [accessed 21 June 2021]

Lewis, Henry, 'Ecological and Technological Knowledge of Fire: Aborigines Versus Park Rangers in Northern Australia', *American Anthropologist*, 91 (1989), 940–61

Macknight, C. C., 'Macassans and the Aboriginal Past', *Archaeology in Oceania*, 21,1 (1986), 69–75

May, Sally, Jennifer McKinnon, and Jason Raupp, 'Boats on Bark: An Analysis of Groote Eylandt Aboriginal Bark-Paintings Featuring Macassan *Praus* from the 1948 Arnhem Land Expedition, Northern Territory, Australia', *The International Journal of Nautical Archaeology*, 38,2 (2009), 369–85

McIntosh, Ian, 'Islam and Australia's Aborigines? A Perspective from North-East Arnhem Land', *Journal of Religious History*, 20,1 (1996), 53–77

——, 'The Birrinydji Legacy: Aborigines, Macassans and Mining in North-East Arnhem Land', *Aboriginal History*, 21 (1997), 70–89

Moran, Emilio, *People and Nature: An Introduction to Human Ecological Relations* (Oxford: Blackwell, 2006)

Morphy, Howard, *Journey to the Crocodile's Nest: An Accompanying Monograph to the Film Madarrpa Funeral at Gurka'wuy* (Canberra: Australian Institute of Aboriginal Studies/Humanities Press, 1984)

——, 'Myth, Totemism and the Creation of Clans', *Oceania*, 60,4 (1990), 312–28

——, *Ancestral Connections: Art and an Aboriginal System of Knowledge* (Chicago: Chicago University Press, 1991)

——, '"Not Just Pretty Pictures": Relative Autonomy and the Articulations of Yolngu Art in its Contexts', in *Ownership and Appropriation*, ed. by Veronica Strang and Mark Busse (Oxford: Berg, 2010), pp. 261–86

Morton, John, 'The Effectiveness of Totemism: Increase Rituals and Resource Control in Central Australia', *Man*, 22 (1987), 453–74

Oppenheimer, Stephen, *Out of Africa's Eden: The Peopling of the World* (Johannesburg: Jonathan Ball, 2003)

Ostrom, Elinor, *Governing the Commons* (Cambridge: Cambridge University Press, 1990)

Pascoe, Bruce, *Dark Emu. Black Seeds: Agriculture or Accident?* (Broome: Magabala Books, 2014)

Peterson, Nicholas, 'Territorial Adaptations among Desert Hunter-Gatherers: The !Kung and Australians Compared', in *Social and Ecological Systems*, ed. by Philip Burnham and Roy Ellen (London: Academic Press 1979), pp. 111–29

Plumwood, Val, *Feminism and the Mastery of Nature* (London: Routledge, 1993)

——, *Environmental Culture: The Ecological Crisis of Reason* (London: Routledge, 2002)

Reichel-Dolmatoff, Geraldo, 'Cosmology as Ecological Analysis: A View from the Rain Forest', *Journal of the Royal Anthropological Institute*, 11,3 (1976), 307–18

Reynolds, Henry, *The Law of the Land* (London: Penguin, 1987)

Rodgers, Dennis, and Bruce O'Neill, 'Infrastructural Violence: Introduction to the Special Issue', *Ethnography*, 13,4 (2012), 401–12

Russell, Denise, 'Aboriginal-Makassan Interactions in the Eighteenth and Nineteenth Centuries in Northern Australia and Contemporary Sea Rights Claims', *Australian Aboriginal Studies*, 1 (2004), 3–17

Sahlins, Marshall, 'Notes on the Original Affluent Society', in *Man the Hunter*, ed. by Richard Lee and Irven DeVore (New York: Aldine, 1968), pp. 85–89

Smart, J., 'Late Quaternary Sea-level Changes, Gulf of Carpentaria, Australia', *Geology*, 5,12 (1977), 755–59

Strang, Veronica, *Kunjen Country: Aboriginal Landscape in the Alice-Mitchell Rivers National Park Area* (North Queensland: Kowanyama Community Council, 1994)

——, *Uncommon Ground: Cultural Landscapes and Environmental Values* (Oxford: Berg, 1997)

——, *Life Down Under: Water and Identity in an Aboriginal Cultural Landscape*, Goldsmiths College Anthropology Research Papers, 7 (London: Goldsmiths College, 2002)

——, 'Knowing Me, Knowing You: Aboriginal and Euro-Australian Concepts of Nature as Self and Other', *Worldviews*, 9,1 (2005), 25–56

——, *Gardening the World: Agency, Identity, and the Ownership of Water* (Oxford: Berghahn, 2009)

——, 'Lording it Over the Goddess: Water, Gender and Human-Environmental Relations', *Journal of Feminist Studies in Religion*, 30,1 (2014), 83–107

——, 'Re-Imagined Communities: The Transformational Potential of Interspecies Ethnography in Water Policy Development', in *The Oxford Handbook on Water Politics and Policy*, ed. by Ken Conca and Erika Weinthal (Oxford: Oxford University Press, 2017), pp. 142–64

Taçon, Paul, Meredith Wilson, and Christopher Chippendale, 'Birth of the Rainbow Serpent in Arnhem Land Rock Art and Oral History', *Archaeology in Oceania*, 31 (1996), 103–24

Taylor, John, 'Of Acts and Axes: An Ethnography of Socio-cultural Change in an Aboriginal Community, Cape York Peninsula' (unpublished doctoral thesis, James Cook University, 1984)

Zvelebil, Marek, 'Innovating Hunter-Gatherers: The Mesolithic in the Baltic', in *Mesolithic Europe*, ed. by Geoff Bailey and Penny Spikins (Cambridge: Cambridge University Press, 2008), pp. 18–59

FRAUKE SACHSE

Translating Otherworlds

*The Encounter of Mesoamerican and European Cosmologies in Colonial Missionary and Indigenous Texts from Highland Guatemala**

Introduction

The European 'discovery of the Americas' in 1492 led to a confrontation of entirely different conceptual systems of world order. While the invaders were driven by Christian expansionism,[1] the native cultures of the 'New World' had to defend and negotiate their cosmological understanding of the world amidst the arrival of strangers that had no prior place in precontact systems of political-religious order. Christianization became the motor for establishing the new social order. While history provided the template for integrating the non-Christian world into Christendom,[2] the 'religious conquest' had to be adapted to the social and spatial realities of the newly subjected provinces.

The process of religious conversion is encapsulated in the Spanish concept of *reducción* (reduction) that was explained by Hanks to imply the 'persuasion' and establishing of 'order' in a life guided by the principles of *policía cristiana* (Christian civility). Hanks subdivides the process of *reducción* into three main objectives: The first and original meaning of the term *reducción*, as it

* This chapter is based on research undertaken during my fellowships at the Dumbarton Oaks Research Library (2012–13) and the Library of Congress (2016–17) in Washington as well as during my research time as a consulting scholar at the American Section of the University of Pennsylvania Museum (2013–16). I am indebted to all three institutions for their support and would furthermore like to thank Garry Sparks for his valuable comments and suggestions on the chapter as well as Allen J. Christenson and Louise Burkhart for influencing my line of thinking.

1 See e.g. Phillips, 'European Expansion'; König, *Arabic-Islamic Views*, pp. 268–69, characterizes the entire late Middle Ages as a period of 'Latin-Christian expansionism'.

2 On the notion and its appellative use in the Middle Ages see the contribution by Berend in this volume.

Frauke Sachse (sachsef01@doaks.org), Dumbarton Oaks Research Library, Harvard Trustees.

Order into Action: How Large-Scale Concepts of World-Order determine Practices in the Premodern World, ed. by Klaus Oschema and Christoph Mauntel, CURSOR 40 (Turnhout: Brepols, 2022), pp. 291–317
BREPOLS PUBLISHERS 10.1484/M.CURSOR-EB.5.123852

was applied by the Church and the missionaries in New Spain, regarded the ordering of space by 'reducing' the number of residential units and gathering the indigenous population into new settlements, so-called *congregaciones* (congregations). This policy of resettlement facilitated the effective control of the people, the extraction of labour and tribute, and it shifted the boundaries of inhabited and uninhabited space. Secondly, *reducción* implied the ordering of social practice with the intention to convert people to a new belief system by changing their social conduct. This implied participation in the new colonial administration and church organization and the practice of daily prayer and recitation of the catechism. Thirdly, the term *reducción* is introduced by Hanks to refer to the ordering of language as a means of conversion. The description of the indigenous languages and translation of Christianity into the Amerindian vernacular was fundamental to the process of the Christian conversion and the creation of 'new' and 'civilized' colonial citizens.[3]

A particularly well-suited area for studying the cultural encounter and the establishment of this new Christian order by means of translation is Highland Guatemala. The K'iche' with their seat governance at Q'umarkaj (Utatlán) were the second political power on the American continent to be conquered by the Spanish after the fall of Tenochtitlán in 1521. Between 1524 and 1529, Pedro de Alvarado led a military campaign that was of unparalleled cruelty and devastation and wiped out a large percentage of the Highland Maya population. By the 1530s, the Eastern highlands were still resisting the invasion. The Spanish and their Central Mexican allies had led several military campaigns to no avail and named the region Tezulután ('Land of War'). To avoid further bloodshed, the Dominican Bartolomé de las Casas, who had been instituted as *protector universal de todos los indios de las Indias* (universal protector of all Indians of the Indies) by the Crown in 1516, strove to bring the resisting regions under Spanish control by means of evangelization. He gathered the greatest language talents of his order to compose texts and songs on the Christian doctrine, from the creation of the world to the apocalypse, in the language of Guatemala. With the help of indigenous converts, a small group of Dominicans entered the 'Land of War' to preach and sing the gospel to the local ruler and his subjects in their own language, winning them over for the new God and, consequently, the new king.[4]

Highland Guatemala was thus one of the first regions in the Americas where missionaries translated the Christian world order into the local languages. The doctrinal literature of the region is particularly copious and includes catechisms, sermons, songs, theological treatises, and other missionary text genres. Missionaries also produced descriptions of the languages in the form of grammars and dictionaries, which provide us today with ample data on the translation of Christian cultural concepts into K'iche'. The creation of Christian discourse and missionary literature met a living native tradition

3 Hanks, *Converting Words*, pp. 39–58.

4 Remesal, *Historia de la Provincia de S. Vicente de Chiapa y Guatemala*, III, chap. XI–XV.

of writing and record keeping in the form of bark paper books, or codices. Indigenous authors soon adopted alphabetic writing and modified Spanish text genres to record their own narrative traditions. One of the most extensive bodies of doctrinal and missionary texts has been preserved for K'iche', the dominant language of the Maya Highlands. The combination of missionary and indigenous written resources makes Highland Guatemala a particularly appropriate place for analysing the colonial encounter of two religious systems and world-views.

This chapter examines how missionaries communicated the concepts of the Christian world-view and analyses how these new conceptualizations of 'Heaven' and 'Hell' mapped onto Mesoamerican notions of cosmology and otherworld dimensions. I will show that missionaries accommodated terminology from K'iche' ritual discourse, while indigenous authors modified and embedded doctrinal discourse into their written traditions, which helped to preserve and reinforce concepts of K'iche' cosmology within the framework of the new Christian order. I will argue that this hybridization is indicative of K'iche' elites actively contributing to the process of Christianization and instrumentalizing the new religion to maintain political influence within the colonial system.

Creating Christian Discourse

Missionary writings from Highland Guatemala are today mostly found in libraries and archives in the United States and Europe. While the nineteenth-century collectors who purchased these documents in Guatemala saw them as valuable resources on the history of Mayan languages, later researchers have shown little interest in colonial Christian texts that were authored for the conversion.[5] Most sources remain to date unpublished and it is only recently that their potential for analysing the process of conversion and cultural change in the wake of the encounter is being recognized.

The mendicant orders brought their greatest language talents from Spain to serve in the mission. Mastering the vernaculars was the prerequisite for the conversion in the indigenous languages, and the translation of catechisms and sermons went hand in hand with the grammatical description of the language and the compilation of dictionaries. Language description and religious prescription were a simultaneous process, in the course of which doctrinal and descriptive materials were constantly corrected, modified, and refined.

5 The largest number of K'iche' manuscripts that we know of today were acquired by the collectors Charles Etienne Brasseur de Bourbourg (1814–74) and William E. Gates (1863–1940). Most manuscripts from Brasseur's collection are today housed at the *Bibliothèque nationale de France*, while Gates' collection of manuscripts and the photographic copies that he produced himself are distributed over a number of different libraries in the United States, see Weeks, *Mesoamerican Ethnohistory*.

The strategies of translation that were applied by the friars to express the abstract concepts of the Christian faith (e.g. 'salvation' or 'confession') in K'iche' are identical to those found in other parts of the world. Translation could either be realized by the introduction of loan words from Spanish or Latin (e.g. *santo, misa*), loan translations (e.g. the Hebrew term *amen*, i.e. 'so be it', was literally rendered in K'iche' as *keje' chuxoq* (so may it be)), as descriptive paraphrases that communicated the practice or value associated with a Christian concept (e.g. baptism = *uqajik uja' Dios* [descending the water of God]) as well as by appropriation of terminology from K'iche' ritual discourse. The reuse of K'iche' ritual terminology in a Christian context involved either a complete change or at least the extension of semantic reference of the term. For example, the term *q'ijilaj* (to count time) that refers to the indigenous religious practice of divination with the 260-day Highland Maya calendar was reused to translate the Christian concept of 'worship'.[6]

These four translation strategies were used rather differently in the missionary texts and seem to depend to some extent on the theological tradition of the respective authors. Franciscans and Dominicans developed different theological positions on translating the Christian doctrine into the indigenous languages and even entered into fierce disputes about this issue.[7] While descriptive and doctrinal writings of Franciscan origin show a clear tendency to translate Christian concepts by creating neologisms in the form of loans, loan translations, or descriptive paraphrases, Dominican authors appropriated more terms from K'iche' ritual discourse to express concepts of Christian faith and divinity.[8] The distinct approaches to translation reflect quite clearly in the doctrinal texts that were created by both orders. The Spanish term *gloria*, for instance, was translated by Dominican authors with the term *q'anal raxal* (yellowness-greenness), a concept that is attested in several Mayan languages to refer to 'abundance of food' and is connected to the ritual petitioning for a good maize harvest, or with the term *tepewal* (majesty) that is used in indigenous texts as an epithet of Mesoamerican deities. Franciscan authors instead used the Spanish term *gloria* or paraphrases such as 'joy', which describe the state associated with the 'glory of God'.[9]

The Dominican preference for appropriating Maya religious terminology was strategic and reflected. It was not only the logical consequence of a

---

6 Sachse, 'The Expression of Christian Concepts', pp. 97–102.

7 García-Ruíz, 'El misionero'.

8 Sachse, 'The Expression of Christian Concepts', pp. 102–05.

9 Entries for the term *gloria* in colonial K'iche' missionary dictionaries include, among others: <canal raxal>, <tepeual> (Basseta, *Diccionario de Basseta*, ed. by René Acuña, fol. 75^{v}), <raxal canal> (Ximénez, *Primera parte del Tesoro*, ed. by de Santa Maria, fol. 162^{r}); <quijcotem> (Cambridge, Tozzer Lib., MS Spec. Col. C.A.6 V 85, fol. 108^{v}), <gloria> (Cambridge, Tozzer Lib., MS Spec. Col. C.A.6 V 85, fol. 3^{r}), <ꜫicotem> (Princeton, Firestone Lib., MS GGMA C0744 160, p. 83).

realist scholastic tradition and humanistic approach as it was taught at the University of Salamanca, where most Dominican missionaries had been trained.[10] It also reflected Las Casas' open and unprejudiced approach to the cultures of the New World and his intention to find the commonalities rather than differences in human cultures. This view shaped the early Dominican mission and is manifested particularly in one text that had a significant impact on the formation and establishment of Christian discourse in Highland Guatemala.

The *Theologia Indorum* (Theology for the Indians) was written by the Dominican friar Domingo de Vico between 1550 and 1554 and counts as the Americas' first Christian theology. Originally comprising two volumes of 217 lengthy chapters that cover more than 700 folios, it is the longest colonial text that was ever composed in an Amerindian language. Although the first volume includes mostly contents from the Old and the second volume contents from the New Testament, the *Theologia Indorum* is not a Bible translation but a detailed summary of the Christian doctrine that explains the concepts and terminology of the faith to an indigenous readership. The text was written entirely in K'iche' and widely disseminated in the colonial highlands, which seems to be indicated by the large number of surviving copies from the sixteenth and seventeenth century, including versions in the other Highland languages of Kaqchikel, Tz'utujil and Q'eqchi'.[11]

In his comprehensive study of the *Theologia Indorum*, Sparks shows that Vico strategically adopted K'iche' ceremonial discourse with its parallelisms and couplets to communicate the new religion in a style that was familiar to the converts.[12] Vico also appropriated K'iche' terminology and metaphors, including the name of the highest K'iche' creator deity *Tz'aqol B'itol* (framer former) as a formal reference to the Christian god. Rather than simply using these terms, Vico dedicates entire chapters of his opus to individual Christian concepts and explains how the K'iche' terminology relates to these ideas. To illustrate this with the given example, Vico describes *Tz'aqol B'itol* as the only creator god and explains to the K'iche' that they had practised monotheism in their past and needed to return to this practice.[13]

The *Theologia Indorum* must have had a significant impact on the conversion in the highlands. It can be assumed that Vico worked with native K'iche'

---

10 Sparks, 'How 'Bout Them Sapotes?', pp. 215–17; Sparks, 'The Use of Mayan Scripture', pp. 398–99.

11 The most detailed and extensive work on the *Theologia Indorum* has been undertaken by Garry Sparks, see Sparks, *Xalqat B'e*. The present paragraph summarizes results published in: Sparks, *Rewriting Maya Religion*; Sparks, 'The Use of Mayan Scripture'; Sparks, 'How 'Bout Them Sapotes?'; Sparks and others, *The Americas' First Theologies*.

12 Sparks, *Rewriting Maya Religion*, pp. 151–52, 179–81; Sparks, 'The Use of Mayan Scripture', p. 406; Sparks and others, *The Americas' First Theologies*, pp. 9–21.

13 Sparks, *Rewriting Maya Religion*, pp. 154–55, and Sparks and others, *The Americas' First Theologies*, pp. 113–14.

converts who were fluent in both languages and influenced the process of translation.[14] A quarter of a century after the Spanish invasion, these K'iche' collaborators had received a Christian education and were literate. The Highland Maya tradition of keeping books for divination and records of historical events was continued in the colonial office of town scribes, who held notary positions in the colonial administration and were responsible for composing official documents, such as testaments, deeds, property sale contracts, legal and community records as well as church and confraternity registers. Only shortly after Vico had finished his work on the *Theologia Indorum* did the K'iche' nobility in the local communities begin to produce documents of indigenous historiography that were based on Spanish genres but amalgamated these with Mesoamerican mytho-historical narratives.

The most famous of these texts is certainly the *Popol Vuh*, which describes the creation mythology and origin of the K'iche' people.[15] The term *popol wuj* means 'book of the council/community' and likely refers to a divinatory almanac that was used by the K'iche' rulers at Q'umarkaj in pre-conquest times.[16] The anonymous authors explicitly state that they are writing their account 'under Christianity' in order to preserve the ancient knowledge, as the book of the ancestors had been lost. Originally written between 1554 and 1558, the *Popol Vuh* can be seen as resistance literature that was composed as a

14 Sparks suggests that Vico worked with members of the K'iche' nobility, in particular with Diego Reynoso from Totonicapán who was trained by missionaries and is also associated with the authorship of the *Título de Totonicapán*, see Sparks, *Rewriting Maya Religion*, pp. 100, 116, 171–73, 217, 246–49, 266; Sparks, 'The Use of Mayan Scripture', p. 402; Sparks, 'How 'Bout Them Sapotes?', pp. 218–34, and Sparks and others, *The Americas' First Theologies*, pp. 211–36.

15 The text of the *Popol Vuh* was copied in the early eighteenth century by the Dominican friar Francisco Ximénez in Chichicastenango from an earlier original that was most likely written between 1555 and 1558 by members of the surviving K'iche' nobility of Q'umarkaj. The *Popol Vuh* contains the most detailed account of the creation of world and humanity, foundational mythologies, and the history of the K'iche' up to the Spanish conquest. The *Popol Vuh* is generally seen as a window into Mesoamerican mythology and commonly drawn on to reconstruct Classic Maya religion. There are various text editions and translations from the original K'iche' available, including the two English translations by Christenson and by Tedlock that are referenced in the present contribution.

16 The *Popol Vuh*, vol. II, ed. and trans. by Christenson, p. 315 (fol. 52^r), and the *Título de Yax*, ed. and trans. by Carmack and Mondloch, p. 69 (fol. 9^v), include identical statements about a divinatory book that was in the possession of the K'iche' rulers of Q'umarkaj: 'They knew, when there would be conflict. It was clear to them all, they would see, whether death, whether hunger, whether war would happen, they just knew it. They had a "means of vision", there was a book, *pop wuj* it was called by the ancestors' (translation by the author). Codices including pictorial almanacs for calendrical divination are known to have existed in Highland Guatemala, as pointed out by Christenson, *Burden of the Ancients*, p. 77, and it is likely that the authors are referring to such a type of book. However, it needs to be emphasized that the known text of the *Popol Vuh* is not an almanac but a textualization of mythologies and oral traditions, although it cannot be excluded that these traditions may have been recited based on a pictorial codex that may have served as a mnemotechnic device. For a more detailed argument and citations see Sachse, 'Metaphors of Maize'.

refutation of Christianity and as a direct indigenous response to the concept of the *Theologia Indorum* as a central dogmatic text.[17] While the authors of the *Popol Vuh* consciously rejected the new religion, other indigenous documents deliberately embedded Christian discourse. There are more than two dozen sixteenth-century documents that are generally referred to as *títulos*. These documents were based on the Spanish text genre of a land title and were issued by the indigenous nobility to state territorial or political legitimacy by means of demonstrating the origin and historical achievements of the local ruling line.[18] Many K'iche' *titulos* reference Christian discourse and weave biblical narratives into their historiographic accounts. In particular the *Título de Totonicapán* integrates entire paragraphs from the *Theologia Indorum*.[19] That Vico's book had a wide dissemination in the highlands is also suggested by explicit mentions of the *Theologia Indorum* and its author in the *Título de Ilocab* and the *Titulo de Pedro Velasco*.[20]

Christian discourse in native documents has traditionally been interpreted as a strategic means to attain the desired goal by conforming to *policía cristiana*, but more recently it has been seen as a simple reflection of the colonial reality, in which indigenous converts became the agents of conversion and willingly reproduced and reconfigured both Christian discourse and native narrative traditions.[21] While the *Popol Vuh* and the *títulos* are our prime sources for the cultural history of the pre-conquest highlands and have been routinely drawn upon to reconstruct even the history, concepts, and practices of Classic Maya culture, they need to be seen first and foremost as products of and responses to the colonial encounter. We have to consider that indigenous discourse may have become influenced by Christian conceptualizations. And although the *Popol Vuh* seems to refute Christianity, the process of textualization alone may have transformed the native mythologies by adapting them to the template of biblical linearity.

---

17 Sparks, *Rewriting Maya Religion*, pp. 168–69, 182, 223–24, and Sparks, 'Primeros folios', pp. 108–16. The argument that the *Popol Vuh* was written as a response to Christianity has been made by Dürr, 'Strategien indianischer Herrschaftslegitimierung', and by Tedlock in *Popol Vuh*, ed. and trans. by Tedlock, p. 30.

18 Similar documents are known from Central Mexico and Oaxaca, though the Guatemalan *títulos* are the earliest of their kind. The exact purpose of the *títulos* has been a vivid debate in the field of Mesoamerican Studies and suggestions range from written testimonials for the colonial administration to a function on local community level. For traditional and more recent treatments of the genre of the *títulos* see Carmack, *Quichean Civilization*, pp. 11–79; Quiroa, 'Revisiting the Highland Guatemala Títulos', and Matsumoto, 'Recording Territory'.

19 The use of Christian narratives in the *Título de Totonicapán* is discussed in Acuña, 'La Theologia Indorum'; Bredt-Kriszat, 'La Theologia Indorum'; Carmack and Mondloch, 'Introducción', pp. 18–19, 210; Sparks, *Xalqat B'e*, pp. 198–200; Sparks, 'How 'Bout Them Sapotes?', pp. 218–24; Sparks and others, *The Americas' First Theologies*, pp. 219–36.

20 Sparks, *Xalqat B'e*, pp. 124–26, and Sparks and others, *The Americas' First Theologies*, pp. 260–61, 265–68, 276.

21 Hanks, *Converting Words*, pp. 338–64.

Sparks has argued that the *Theologia Indorum* (1553), the *Título de Totonicapán* (1554), and the *Popol Vuh* (1554–58) are intertextually related.[22] He shows that Vico references K'iche' deities and narratives from the *Popol Vuh*, suggesting that some written version of this mythology must have been available to him or that the same indigenous collaborators may have been involved in the production.[23] In this scenario native K'iche' may have been the agents who introduced Highland Maya ritual discourse into the language of Christianization while at the same time taking this new Christian discourse and strategically modifying and adapting it in their own literary narratives. This hybridization of doctrinal K'iche' discourse mirrors the attempt of the K'iche' elites to integrate *policia cristiana* and Mesoamerican cosmology and negotiate their political position within this new system of world order. Translation and textualization thus became means for indigenous authors to actualize the cultural encounter and to partake in shaping their new reality.

These mutual adaptations make the hermeneutics of colonial K'iche' texts rather challenging. Besides the expected historical change that K'iche' underwent in the course of five centuries, which includes the loss of a number of grammatical markers and significant shifts in semantic referents of lexemes and metaphors, it is problematic to tell surviving Mesoamerican conceptualizations from those that have been created in the context of linguistic conversion. To comprehend the way missionaries and K'iche' authors negotiated and integrated elements from both religious traditions, the intertextualities of the sources need to be analysed and disentangled. This requires both a systematic diachronic and cross-Mesoamerican comparative approach to the sources, and a more diligent analysis of the thematic contents of doctrinal texts and the creation of Christian discourse that the indigenous authors responded to. In the following sections, I attempt to do this for concepts from the semantic domain of cosmology and examine how the process of translation negotiated two entirely different concepts of the world.

Highland Maya Cosmology

The reconstruction of Highland Maya cosmology requires a diachronic approach to the data. In order to assess the information from the indigenous text sources that were produced in the context of conversion, we need to draw on comparative data from ethnographic studies and the archaeological, written, and pictorial records from the pre-conquest era. Furthermore, it needs to be taken into account that the indigenous text sources reflect a strong cultural influence from Central Mexico in the Postclassic Maya Highlands. The

22 Sparks and others, *The Americas' First Theologies*, p. 209.

23 Sparks, *Rewriting Maya Religion*, pp. 114–15, 180–83, 277–78, and Sparks and others, *The Americas' First Theologies*, pp. 104–05, 107.

following outline of Highland Maya cosmology is based on the *Popol Vuh* as the main source and references data from other sources; it is limited by the scope of the chapter and does not attempt to be in any way comprehensive.

In Mesoamerican belief, the world is perceived as a living thing that was conceived by creator deities at the dawn of time. According to the creation account in the *Popol Vuh*, the earth was born from a womb-shaped sky filled with the water of the primordial sea:

> Xa utukel kaj k'olik, mawi q'alaj uwach ulew, xa utukel remanik palo, upa kaj ronojel ... Ta xkalaj, ta xkik'u'xlaj kib'. Xewi saq ta xkalaj puch winaq.
>
>> (Just alone the sky exists, the face of the earth is not clear yet, just alone the calm sea, all is in the womb of the sky ... Then they gave birth, then they remembered themselves. [There was] just light when they gave also birth to people.)[24]

The birth is the result of the interaction of the deities *Uk'u'x Kaj* (Heart of Sky) and *Tepew Q'ukumatz* (Sovereign Quetzal Serpent) who have both female and male aspects. The first of these creator deities who is otherwise referred to as the storm deity *Juraqan* (One-legged) is invoked in traditional prayers until the present day in a fourfold aspect: *Uk'u'x kaj, Uk'u'x ulew, Uk'u'x cho, Uk'u'x palow* (Heart of Sky, Heart of Earth, Heart of Lake, Heart of Sea). The four elements *kaj, ulew, cho,* and *palow* define the concept of the cosmos which consists of a four-cornered sky and land that is surrounded by freshwaters and saltwaters.

The world was laid out in a quadrangle shape like a maize field. The *Popol Vuh* describes the *kaj tz'uk, kaj xukut* (four corners, four angles) that are measured and outlined with a cord measure, like traditional farmers do when they clear the forest and lay out their maize field:[25]

> Ukaj tz'ukuxik, ukaj xukutaxik, retaxik, ukaj che'xik, umej k'a'amaxik, uyuq k'a'amaxik, upa kaj, upa ulew.
>
>> (Four cornerings, four anglings, measurings, four stakings, doublings over cord measurement, stretching of the cord measurement, of the inside of the sky, the inside of the earth.)[26]

The four corners are a central element of Mesoamerican cosmology and correspond to the cardinal directions. Classic Maya site layouts, iconographic programmes, and written texts underline the mythological importance of directional orientation towards east, north, west, and south, and there are

24 *Popol Vuh*, vol. II, ed. and trans. by Christenson, p. 264 (fol. 1^{v}); translation by the author. All transcriptions of the *Popol Vuh* text are presented here in modernized spelling. Both transcriptions and translations are originally based on *Popol Vuh*, vol. II, ed. and trans. by Christenson, with modifications and changes by the author of this chapter.

25 *Popol Vuh*, ed. and trans. by Tedlock, p. 220; *Popol Vuh*, ed. and trans. by Christenson, p. 65.

26 *Popol Vuh*, vol. II, ed. and trans. by Christenson, p. 264 (fol. 1^{v}); translation by the author.

various pictorial representations of mythological trees marking the four cardinal corners and the centre of the world.[27]

In Classic Maya and Central Mexican imagery, the land is depicted as a large crocodile or turtle that floats in the midst of the sea. While indigenous sources from Highland Guatemala do not give explicit descriptions of this 'earth monster', the conceptualization is mythologically represented in the *Popol Vuh* in form of the mythic protagonist Sipakna who is described as the 'sustainer of the mountains'. The name is a loan from Nahuatl *cipactli* (crocodile).[28] The *Popol Vuh* relates that Sipakna and his brother Kab'raqan, the 'wrecker of the mountains', had to be defeated by two culture heroes to calm and stabilize the earth.[29] These so-called Hero Twins are central figures in Highland Maya mythology. The main episode from the *Popol Vuh* that is also referenced by missionaries and in other Spanish accounts relates the descent of the Hero Twins into the underworld and their victory over the Lords of Death, whereby they define a new world order and create the conditions for human life on earth.

The K'iche' referred to the underworld as *Xib'alb'a*, a locative derivation of an abstractive noun with the root *xib'* (fear, fright) that literally translates as 'place of fearing, or fright'. The term is often used to refer to the Maya underworld in general, although it needs to be noted that the Classic Maya underworld is only known to us through pictorial representations and a hieroglyphic term has never been identified. The Colonial Yukatek Maya used the term *metnal*, which is possibly a Mayanised form of the Nahuatl term *mictlan* (land of the dead).[30] Among the Tzeltal and Tzotzil of Chiapas the underworld is called Katinbak.[31] The most detailed description of the Maya underworld is found in the *Popol Vuh*, where Xib'alb'a — the realm of the lords of death and disease — is a dark place underneath the surface of the earth that is reached through caves, ravines, and rivers.

As in other religions, cosmological conceptualizations and eschatological belief are inextricably interwoven and the aforementioned Hero Twin narrative in the *Popol Vuh* defines the parameters for the human relationship with the

27 The earliest of these representations are found in the Preclassic murals of San Bartolo, see Saturno, Taube and Stuart, *The Murals of San Bartolo*. Iconographic programmes on Classic Maya architecture also commonly feature images of directional trees. More concrete depictions of cosmograms with directional trees in the corners are found in Postclassic codices, such as the *Codex Dresden*, pp. 25–28, and the Central Mexican *Codex Fejérváry-Mayer*, p. 1, see Sachse, 'Over Distant Waters', pp. 151–52.

28 The *Popol Vuh* contains many references to Central Mexican mythological tradition, including names, toponyms and entire narrative episodes that are integrated in and adapted to local Maya mythology, see Sachse, 'Metaphors of Maize'.

29 The term *Kab'raqan* literally means 'two-legged'. The mythological protagonist describes himself as *in yojol juyub'* (I am the wrecker of mountain). The translation follows *Popol Vuh*, ed. by Christenson, p. 108.

30 Thompson, *Maya History and Religion*, p. 300.

31 Pitarch Ramón, 'Almas y cuerpos', p. 28; Pozas Arciniega, *Chamula*, pp. 232–40.

underworld. The episode begins with the tale about the father of the twins who along with his brother is summoned by the lords of Xib'alb'a, who challenge him to a ballgame, defeat, and behead him. His head is placed in a calabash tree in Xib'alb'a. When the daughter of an underworld lord comes too close to the tree, she gets pregnant and escapes to the surface of the earth, where she gives birth to the Hero Twins. Once grown up, the twins are likewise summoned to Xib'alb'a to play ball with the lords. But unlike their father they are not defeated. They sacrifice themselves in a fire and re-emerge from the waters of Xib'alb'a to kill the lords by trickery before rising to the sky as sun and moon. This narrative of defeat, death, and subsequent regeneration is closely connected to Mesoamerican maize mythology.[32]

Maize was first domesticated in Mesoamerica and is still the most important staple crop. The Maya refer to themselves as 'maize people'. The text of the *Popol Vuh* describes several unsuccessful attempts of the gods to create humans until they discover maize and shape the human body from maize dough. Human existence is seen in analogy to the growth-cycle of maize and the terms that describe the stages of the plant are applied to the phases of human life. Children are 'sown', 'sprout', and 'grow' into mature plants who have ten fingers and ten toes like the ideal maize plant has twenty leaves. They procreate and die and the bones of the deceased are buried, like dried maize seeds are planted in the earth to sprout and grow into a new maize plant that gives life to the next generation.[33] This idea of intergenerational exchange is represented in the Hero Twin myth in the figure of the father, whose decapitated head becomes the fruit of a calabash tree, and thus primordial food that generates offspring.[34] The myth constitutes the basis of Highland Maya eschatology: it is the human fate to be buried and regenerated in the underworld to give life to one's own descendants. In the indigenous sources, Xib'alb'a thus is not exclusively a 'place of fear'. In the *Memorial de Sololá* we find a positive connotation of the underworld in the phrase *raxa xib'alb'ay q'ana xib'alb'ay* (green Xib'alb'a, yellow Xib'alb'a'). The metaphor of *rax q'an* (green-yellow) stands for an 'abundance in food' and may in this case refer to an otherworldly Mountain of Sustenance as the origin place of humanity.

Most mythological accounts in the indigenous sources from Highland Guatemala relate an origin of the people from a mythical, paradisiacal place on the other side of the sea that is called *Tulan*:

> Keje k'ut kipetik wae ch'aqa cho, ch'aqa palow pa tulan pa sewan.
>
> > (Like this was their arrival, across the lake, across the sea from Tulan, from Siwan.)[35]

32 Taube, 'The Classic Maya Maize God'; Braakhuis, 'The Tonsured Maize God'.

33 Carlsen and Prechtel, 'The Flowering of the Dead', pp. 28–36.

34 Martin, 'Cacao in Ancient Maya Religion', p. 165.

35 *Título de Totonicapán*, ed. and trans. by Carmack and Mondloch, p. 71 (fol. 8^{r}); translation by the author.

In the *Popol Vuh* and other sources, this place is also identified as *wuqub' pek, wuqub' siwan* (seven caves, seven canyons). Since *Tollan* and *Chicomoztoc* (seven caves) are mythological origin places in Aztec sources, these statements in the K'iche' sources have traditionally been interpreted as indications of the Mexican origin of K'iche' noble ancestry and the phrase *ch'aqa palow* (across the sea) as a reference to a migratory route across the Gulf of Mexico. However, ethnographic accounts from Guatemala suggest that the phrase 'on the other side of the sea' is a metaphor that refers to an abode of the dead as an otherworldly place of creation and rebirth.[36]

The role of the sea as an element of passage to the underworld is also known from the Classic Maya hieroglyphic texts, where the verb phrase *ochi ha'* (to enter the water) is used as an expression to denote the death of a ruler. Contemporary oral traditions from Highland Guatemala relate that figures of saints and other sacred objects have been brought across the sea on the backs of serpents or deer.[37] This otherworld place of death and place of origin 'across the sea' is connected with the here and now through the path of the sun. The K'iche' sources locate Tulan, the place of origin of their ancestors, in the east, *releb'al q'ij* (where the sun emerges):

> B'alam K'itze, B'alam Aq'ab', Majukutaj, Iki B'alam, e nab'e winaq, xepe chila' ch'aqa palo chi releb'al q'ij.
>
> (B'alam K'itze, B'alam Aq'ab', Majukutaj and Iki B'alam were the first people, who came from across the sea where the sun emerges.)[38]

In Mesoamerican cosmology, the sun revolves around the earth, dying each evening in the Pacific Ocean, passing through the underworld at night and rising again as a bringer of life in the East. The daily descent and rebirth of the sun constituted a basic conceptual metaphor for the cycle of life.[39] The solar cycle turns the underworld into a place of death and re-emergence, which is also manifested in the Aztec belief in a celestial paradise in the East from where the souls of warriors who die in battle are reborn. The *Memorial de Sololá* illustrates that the otherworld was conceptually divided into different locations by the path of the sun. The text specifies the existence of four Tulans that are located in the east, the west, in Xib'alb'ay, and thus nadir, and in K'ab'owil at the zenith of the sky:[40]

> kaji' k'a xpe wi winäq pa Tulan: chi releb'al q'ij jun Tulan, jun chik k'a chi Xib'alb'ay, jun chik k'a chi ruqajib'al q'ij, chi ri' k'a xojpe wi chi ruq'ajib'al q'ij, jun chik wi k'a chi K'ab'owil

36 Sachse, 'Over Distant Waters', pp. 133–34, 145.

37 Hutcheson, *Cultural Memory*, pp. 176–79.

38 *Popol Vuh*, vol. II, ed. and trans. by Christenson, p. 311 (fol. 48^{r}); translation by the author.

39 Chinchilla Mazariegos, 'Tecum, the Fallen Sun', pp. 699–701.

40 The Kaqchikel term *k'ab'owil* originally refers to any kind of deity and its use in reference to a celestial place of origin suggests that the general conceptual location for deities was in the sky.

> (From four locations came the people from Tulan: in the east is one Tulan, another one in Xib'alb'ay, another one where the sun descends, there we come from, where the sun descends, and another one is in K'ab'owil.)[41]

In Highland Maya cosmology the notion of the birth, death, and rebirth of the sun is inalienably linked to the life-cycle of maize, because plants require sunlight to grow and prosper. These interconnected cycles explain and rationalize human life and the relationship between humans and their deities. Domesticated maize needs humans to be sown and maintain its life-cycle. This symbiotic relationship carries over to the relationship between humans and their deities, which is one of mutual dependency. Humans sustain the gods with food and worship and the gods maintain the cosmos and assure the daily cycle of the sun as a bringer of light and life.[42]

Translating Heaven and Hell

To understand the confrontation between these native notions of cosmological order and the new dichotomy of Heaven and Hell, we will now turn to the missionary translations of Christian otherworld concepts into K'iche' and analyse indigenous responses to the doctrine.

Genesis

The Christian understanding of the world and its formation is rooted in Genesis, where God is described as a sole creator who made heaven and earth, invented light and time, divided the land from the water, formed sun, moon, and stars, and then created all life on earth. Missionary writings from Highland Guatemala refer to the concept of world creation mostly with the term *b'anoj* (the making) as the following example from the *Theologia Indorum* illustrates:

> Wakamik k'ut xchiqatikib'a ub'ixik ub'anoj, are' utikerik ronojel chi kaj chuwach ulew.
>
> > (Now then we shall begin the account of its creation, it is the beginning of everything in heaven and on earth.)[43]

More interestingly, Vico adopts the terms *tik'ib'a* (to plant) and *utikerik* (literally: its becoming planted) to refer to the concept of 'beginning'. This metaphor is adopted from K'iche' discourse and is one of several terms adopted from the domain of agriculture. In the cosmological framework of the Highland

41 *Memorial de Sololá*, ed. and trans. by Otzoy, p. 155.
42 Monaghan, 'Theology and History', pp. 36–38.
43 *Theologia Indorum*, Princeton, Firestone Libr., MS GGMA C0744 178, p. 67.

Maya, plant growth defines the parameters for conceptualizing life and thus 'planting', 'sowing', and 'sprouting' are all metaphors for any type of beginning. In the agricultural context the start of plant life always involves a human agent who places the seed or seedling into the earth. This connotation may have been deliberately chosen by Vico in the given context to implicitly refer to God as the creator.

In Chapter 29 of the *Theologia Indorum*, Vico begins his account of world creation with the description of the geocentric *Weltbild* that medieval cosmology was based on:

> Nab'e q'ij Domingo ub'i' xwinaqir saq, chupam Lunes ukab' q'ij b'elej tas chi kaj xk'ase' chupam xwinaqir wi, xwinaqir pu rumal Dios nim ajaw ub'elejichal kesolol chirij ulew, kesutinik kesutuw puch ronojel q'ij. Ulaju' tas chi k'ut k'o aq'anoq puwi', maja b'i chisilob'ik xa junelik kub'ulik rochoch utinamit Dios nimajaw.
>
> > (The first day is called Sunday, on which light was created. Monday is the second day, nine levels of the sky were brought to life, were created in it, and they were created by God the Great Lord. The nine(some) circle around the earth, they encircle and surround it every day. The tenth level then exists above it, it shall not move, it is only the eternal seat, the abode of God the Great Lord.)[44]

Vico's account is consistent with the late medieval descriptions of nine planetary spheres that surround the earth and are the locations of the Moon, Mercury, Venus, the Sun, Mars, Jupiter, Saturn, the fixed stars, and the place of the angels. Encompassing these nine spheres, on the tenth and upper level of the sky is the *empyrion*, the sea of eternal light and the abode of God. Recently, Nielsen and Sellner suggested that the medieval world-view was adopted by indigenous authors who embedded it in their own cosmological accounts.[45] Indeed, the authors of the *Título de Totonicapán* almost literally reproduced Vico's text in their account of world creation:

> Lunes ukab' q'ij b'elej tas chi kaj xk'ase' rumal Dyos, nima ajaw. Ub'elejichal kesolow chi rij ulew, kesutu' puch chi ronojel q'ij. Ulaju' tas k'ut chisilab'ik, junelik kub'ul rochoch utinamit chi ronojel q'ij.
>
> > (Monday is the second day, nine levels of the sky were brought to life by God, the great Lord. The nine(some) circle around the earth, and they surround it every day. The tenth' level shall thus move, his eternal seat and abode, every day.)[46]

---

44 *Theologia Indorum*, Princeton, Firestone Libr., MS GGMA C0744 178, p. 75.

45 Nielsen and Sellner Reunert, 'Dante's Heritage'.

46 *Título de Totonicapán*, ed. and trans. by Carmack and Mondloch, p. 43 (fol. 1r); translation by the author.

A comparison of these passages from the *Theologia Indorum* and the *título* shows that they differ in one small detail with respect to the tenth level. While Vico describes the eternal seat and abode of God the Great Lord as static, the K'iche' authors state that it moves every day. This perception would be consistent with the role of the solar cycle in Mesoamerican cosmology. The authors may have appropriated and reconfigured doctrinal discourse here to adapt it to their cosmological understanding, which was also consistent with Highland Maya eschatology, as we shall see in the next section.

Heaven

In Christian eschatology, the concept of Heaven is synonymous with the celestial paradise or Kingdom of God. *Empyrion* is the abode of God and the place for the souls of the deceased who were good in life. This reflects in the translations in the missionary sources, where the K'iche' term *kaj* is equally described as the *siwan tinamit* (residence) and *ajawarem* (kingdom) of God and the angels, who are explicitly referred to as the *winaqil kaj* (people of the sky). The celestial paradise is translated with three different terms, including *junelik ki'kotem* (eternal happiness), or *ki'kotirisab'al* (place of happiness), *q'anal raxal* (abundance, plenty) and *kotz'i'jalaj ulew* (flowery land).[47]

The rendering of the celestial paradise as a 'flower world' is a direct appropriation of a Mesoamerican eschatological concept that has been described many times as the conceptualization of a celestial place in the east, where the sun rises, and where the dead await their rebirth. The concept is very prominent in groups speaking Uto-Aztecan languages and has been described for the Aztecs themselves.[48] Bernardino de Sahagún describes the 'flower world' as a place where the souls of the warriors who died in battle transform into butterflies.[49] The term was adopted into Nahuatl catechetical writing and therefore it is possible that the missionaries who translated the doctrine into K'iche' borrowed the term from doctrinal Nahuatl. It is however not impossible that the concept of 'flower world' was taken directly from K'iche' discourse. The notion of a solar paradise full of flowers is attested in Classic Maya iconography and ethnographically in present Maya culture as the place for the souls of heroic leaders and those who die a violent death in war, by murder, lightning, drowning, or during childbirth.[50] In Tzotzil, this place is referred to as *winajel* and is located in the sun itself, which today is associated with Jesus Christ.[51] This connection of flower land to the solar

47 A detailed analysis of all three renderings of the concept of paradise into doctrinal K'iche' is found in Sachse, 'Worlds in Words', pp. 81–82.

48 The concept was first described by Hill, 'The Flower World of Old Uto-Aztecan', and then identified in Aztec society by Burkhart, 'Flowery Heaven'.

49 Burkhart, 'Flowery Heaven', p. 94.

50 Taube, 'Flower Mountain'.

51 Guiteras Holmes, *Perils of the Soul*, pp. 143–44, 258; Villa Rojas, *Etnografía tzeltal*, p. 649.

cycle also reflects in contemporary Ch'orti' belief, according to which the human soul has to pass through some suffering in the underworld before it can rise to the realm of the sun god.[52] The aspect of rebirth is also reflected in the Tz'utujil concept of 'Flowering Mountain Earth', an imaginary tree at the navel of the world that is the origin and end of all life.[53]

The Mesoamerican understanding of the flower land as a place of rebirth matches nicely with the Christian belief in resurrection and may be the very reason why the missionaries adopted the term to refer to the idea of the celestial paradise. In the *Theologia Indorum* Easter Sunday is translated as *kotz'i'jalaj Pascua* (flowery Easter), which reflects the sixteenth-century Spanish tradition of associating Easter with flowers and referring to it as *Pascua Florida*. It is unclear, whether the expression of *kotz'i'jalaj ulew* was taken directly from contemporary Highland religious discourse or borrowed from Central Mexico, as the association of the resurrection with flowers and the translation of the Christian idea of paradise as 'flower land' also occurs in the doctrinal Nahuatl literature.[54]

Hell

The first missionaries who came to Highland Guatemala appropriated the name of the K'iche' underworld *xib'alb'a* to translate the Spanish term *infierno* (Hell). In Chapter 28 of the *Theologia Indorum*, Vico relates the Fall of the Angels and their banishment in Hell, which he describes with the typical attributes of the Christian concept of Hell:

> Ta xetzaq uloq rumal Tz'aqol B'itol, Dios Nimajaw ub'i'. Keje' k'ut keqajik koponik puch chunik'ajal ulew, chi rochoch k'axkol ra'il, chi rochoch chuk'a, chi rochoch q'aq', chi rochoch k'atik poroxik, chi rochoch tew k'atan, chi rochoch wayjal chaq'ij chi', chi rochoch meb'a'il ajkoq'owalil, chi rochoch kik' raxtew, chi rochoch b'is moq'em, chi rochoch nimab'is, chi rochoch q'equm aq'ab', chi rochoch pu jiloj poloj, qitzij chi kowinik chi k'ax, chi ra', k'o chila' xe'ok wi. Xawi xere ub'i' Xib'alb'a, xub'inaj rochoch pa ichab'al.
>
> > (Then they were thrown hither, by Framer Former, God the Great Lord is his name. Thus they descended to arrive at the centre of the earth, at the home of suffering and pain, at the home of bitterness, at the home of fire, at the home of burning and firing, at the home of cold and fever, at the home of hunger and thirst, at the home of poverty and shortage, at the home of blood-sickness, at the home of sorrow and anguish, at the home of great sorrow, at the home of darkness

52 Girard, *Los Mayas*, pp. 230–32.
53 Carlsen and Prechtel, 'The Flowering of the Dead', p. 27.
54 Burkhart, 'Flowery Heaven', pp. 91–100.

and night, and at the house of groaning and grief, truly at the might of suffering, of pain, that is where they entered. Only so by the name of Xib'alb'a, is called the home in your language.)[55]

Vico draws a clear image of Hell as a place of suffering and pain, of burning and fire, diseases, hunger, poverty, sorrow, and darkness. Some of these characterizations correspond to Mesoamerican conceptualizations of the underworld, in particular the association of Xib'alb'a with darkness and sickness. While it is not entirely clear whether these parallels are deliberate, other discourse patterns are most likely taken from Highland Maya mythology. In the earliest Dominican doctrinal literature, we find that Xib'alb'a is used as a reference to a personified agent, and that the fallen Angels are referred to as *konojel xib'alb'a* (all Xib'alb'a/ns):

> xa ulew xa xoq'ol kojtijow, are' k'ax ra' kojk'atik kojporoxik, la mawi xa oj ulew ma pu xa oj xoq'ol chiqab'an re, xecha' konojel xib'alb'a chikib'il kib'.
>
> ('... only earth only mud we bite, it is torture and pain that we burn and we are burned, is it that we are not just earth and not just mud that we should be made of', said all Xib'alb'ans to each other.)[56]

The same forms of reference are found in the *Popol Vuh*, where the lords of Xib'alb'a are addressed as *konojel Xib'alb'a*. The parallels between the lords of death and the devils seem to be deliberate. The following text passage from the K'iche' *coplas* indicates that the first Dominicans referred not only to the Christian god with the Mesoamerican metaphor of 'Our Mother, Our Father', but that they also strategically located the Highland Maya origin place of Tulan within the negative realm of Xib'alb'a:[57]

> Kib'enaqa chik pa q'aq' konojel xib'alb'a ta xtik'ir utz'aqir winaq rumal qachuch qaqajaw. Tolan chik kikolib'al konojel xib'alb'a chinb'ano kik'ixel ajmak xcha' qachuch qaqajaw
>
> (Once all Xibalbans had already gone to the fire, the forming of humans by Our Mother, Our Father began. 'Tollan is the place of all Xibalbans, I shall make the replacement of the sinners', said Our Mother, Our Father)[58]

---

55 *Theologia Indorum*, Princeton, Firestone Libr., MS GGMA C0744 178, p. 71.

56 *Theologia Indorum*, Philadelphia, APS, MS 178, fol. 56r.

57 Sparks has pointed out that this reference to a Mesoamerican creator deity with female and male aspects was taken up by Vico in the *Theologia Indorum* to refer to the Christian god. The use of this term itself may however precede Vico, as is suggested by its occurrence in the core text *Cosas de la fé católica* (Things of the Catholic Faith) of Washington, Libr. of Congress, Kislak MS 1015. These K'iche' *coplas* are likely the earliest known doctrinal text from Highland Guatemala, as recently argued by Sparks and Sachse, 'A Sixteenth-Century Priest's Fieldnotes'.

58 Washington, Libr. of Congress, Kislak MS 1015, fol. 19r.

Another form of personification of Xib'alb'a is found in the *Theologia Indorum*, where the snake from the Garden of Eden is referred to as 'devil' and 'Xib'alb'a':

> xeti' qachuch qaqajaw Adan Eva rumal nima kumatz nima diablo nima xib'alb'a.
>
> (Our Mother, Our Father, Adam and Eve, were bitten by the great snake, great Devil, great Xibalba.)[59]

Consistent with Christian cosmology, the missionary texts associate Hell with fire, heat and burning:

> Are' qoboyelaxik, qakamik, qasachik, qabiq' puch chi Xib'alb'a, qak'atik qaporoxik puch chupam junelik q'aq'.
>
> (It is our wasting, our death, our loss, and our suffering in Xibalba, our burning and our being burned in the eternal fire.)[60]

This conceptualization manifests probably the clearest rupture with the Mesoamerican concept of the underworld, which according to the indigenous sources is a cold and watery place. In this respect it is interesting to note that in later catechisms, we also find the fires of Hell translated with the abstractive term *q'aq'al* (fieriness) rather than the term *q'aq'* (fire) that is used by Vico and in other early sources:

> qitzij nim umeq'enal uq'aq'al xib'alb'a
>
> (truly great is the heat, the fieriness of Hell)[61]

In the *Popol Vuh* and other indigenous texts, the term *q'aq'al* (fieriness) occurs in various couplets that refer to concepts of political and divine power, such as *q'aq'al tepewal* (fieriness and majesty), *q'aq'al nimal* (fieriness and honour) or *q'aq'al ajawarem* (fieriness and lordship).[62] In all three examples 'fieriness' clearly refers to the concept of power and authority. This concept was also adopted in the missionary literature to express the authority and power of the Christian god, i.e. *uq'aq'al utepewal Dios* (power and majesty of God).[63] This association of fieriness with divine power is attested in other contexts. The *Popol Vuh* mentions a sacred bundle that was left by the K'iche' forefathers to their descendants called the *pisom q'aq'al* (bundled fieriness).[64] Similar bundles are venerated in Highland Guatemala up to the present day, such as the Martin bundle in Santiago Atitlán that is considered by traditionalists to be the most powerful creator deity in the town.[65] The use of the term *q'aq'al*

59 *Theologia Indorum*, Philadelphia, APS, MS 178, fol. 62ʳ.

60 *Theologia Indorum*, Philadelphia, APS, MS 178, fol. 63ʳ.

61 Princeton, Firestone Libr., MS GGMA C0744 190, p. 127.

62 *Popol Vuh*, vol. II, ed. and trans. by Christenson, p. 300 (fol. 37ᵛ), p. 312 (fol. 49ᵛ); translation by the author.

63 Princeton, Firestone Libr., MS GGMA C0744 164, p. 5.

64 *Popol Vuh*, vol. II, ed. and trans. by Christenson, p. 310 (fol. 47ᵛ); translation by the author.

65 Christenson, *Art and Society*, pp. 157–60.

with its association of divine power as a qualitative attribute of Xib'alb'a most likely did not communicate the concept of Christian Hell as a place of torture particularly well, but instead may have continued the Mesoamerican understanding of Xib'alb'a as a place of origin and rebirth.

Babylon

Indigenous authors adopted Christian narratives and discourse and embedded them into native historiographies. In particular the aforementioned account of the origin of the K'iche' forefathers from Tulan is recurrently conflated with the biblical story of Moses leading the Israelites through the Red Sea to their promised land. In the following passage from the *Título de Totonicapán*, the K'iche' authors identify themselves as descendants of the Israelites:

> Ta kik'amik ub'ik rumal Moyses, ta xe'opon chi palo', ta xub'ij Dyos chirech Moyses: 'Chatz'aqa' kab'lajuj ab'aj pa palow, kab'lajuj k'ut chawesewaj'. Ta xtzaj k'ut palo(w) rumal Diyos nima ajaw, kab'lajuj nima'q b'e xk'oje' chupam palo(w), ta xojik'ow uloq. Xax sqaqin chik, mawi tz'aqatinaq kajkalab' chi winaq, oj ral uk'ajol aj Israel, aj Kanan, oj puch Eb'reos, ri k'ut qapetik relib'al q'ij.
>
> > (Then they were taken along by Moses, when they arrived at the sea, then God said to Moses: 'Toss twelve stones into the sea, twelve then you shall remove'. Then the sea was dried up by God, the great lord. Twelve great roads existed inside the sea, when we crossed over. Just a little yet, not were completed the four groups of people, we are the daughters and sons of the Israelites, the Canaanites, and we are Hebrews, this was thus our arrival from the east.)[66]

The self-reference of the K'iche' as Hebrews from Canaan most likely reflects the effects of the conversion and possibly the acceptance of a new history of origin that was brought forward by some mendicant missionaries, who claimed that the Mesoamerican peoples were the lost tribes of Israel.[67] Another passage in the *Título de Totonicapán* conflates the concept of the mythical origin place Tulan with locations in Jewish history. Specifically, Tulan is said to be located in *Sinyetón* (Sinai), which in biblical history was the place where Moses led the Israelites after their exodus from Egypt; on Mount Sinai the Israelites received the Ten Commandments which creates a nice parallel with the *Popol Vuh* specifying Tulan as the place where the K'iche' forefathers received their deities.[68] Moreover, several *títulos* locate Tulan or the place of K'iche' origin

66 *Título de Totonicapán*, ed. and trans. by Carmack and Mondloch, pp. 61–63 (fol. 5^{v}–6^{r}); translation by the author.

67 Sparks, *Xalqat B'e*, pp. 80, 210; Sparks and others, *The Americas' First Theologies*, pp. 207–08 n. 3.

68 Christenson, *Burden of the Ancients*, p. 119.

in Babylon, in the east, on the other side of the sea.[69] The following example comes from the *Título de Tamub*:

> chila' k'ut xepe' wi chi releb'al q'ij, ch'aqa cho, ch'aqa palo, ta xepetik, chila' naypuch babilonia ub'i'
>
> > (from there in the east they came, across the lake, across the sea, when they arrived, and it is named Babylon)[70]

This conflation of biblical and Highland Maya concepts of origin was certainly facilitated by the geographical location of the 'Holy Land' coinciding with Mesoamerican conceptualizations of a solar paradise and otherworldly place of rebirth on the other side of the sea, in the East, where the sun emerges. From the perspective of the K'iche' authors, biblical history reconfirmed Highland Maya mytho-cosmology, while at the same time providing a new interpretation of the origin of the people that was consistent with a Christian world-view.

In the K'iche' sources, the mentioning of the origin place Tulan functions as an element of political legitimization. The *Popol Vuh* describes how the sons of the K'iche' forefathers went back across the sea to Tulan to receive their insignia of lordship from the mythical lord Nacxit:

> Xawi xere xe'ik'owik chuwi' palo, ta xe'opon k'ut chila' releb'al q'ij, ta xb'ekik'ama' ri ajawarem. Are' k'ut ub'i' ajaw wa', rajawal ajreleb'al q'ij xe'opon wi. Ta xe'opon k'ut chuwach ajaw Nakxit ub'i' nima ajaw. Xa ju q'atol tzij, tzatz rajawarem. Are' k'ut xyaw uloq retal ajawarem, ronojel uwachinel.
>
> > (Only like this they passed over the sea, when they arrived from where the sun emerges, when they went to receive the lordship. It was then the name of this lord, the lord of the East, where they arrived. Then they arrived before the lord, Nacxit is the name of the great lord, only he is the judge, populated is his kingdom. He then is the one who bestowed the sign of lordship.)[71]

Nacxit has been generally interpreted as a reference to an overlord of a Central Mexican political power, likely the Classic Teotihuacan or the Postclassic Tenochtitlán. It has been shown that since the Classic era the political order in the Maya area was that of a hegemonic system of shifting powers of distinct political units that were subject to overlords who bestowed leadership on local lords.[72] For the dominant groups the legitimizing authorities were logically situated outside their own sphere of power. Thus, deriving political

---

69 *Título* documents mentioning the origin Babylon or descent from the Israelites include the K'iche' *Título de Totonicapán, Titulo Tamub', Título de Pedro Velasco, Título Ilokab'* and the Kaqchikel document of the Xpantzay, see Christenson, *Burden of the Ancients*, p. 119, and Sparks and others, *The Americas' First Theologies*, pp. 235–36, 242, 248, 261–62, 264, 269, 277, 279.

70 Princeton, Firestone Libr., MS GGMA C0744 102, fol. 1ʳ.

71 *Popol Vuh*, vol. II, ed. and trans. by Christenson, p. 224 and p. 311 (fol. 48ᵛ); translation modified by the author.

72 Martin, *Ancient Maya Politics*.

and religious authority from external powers, foreign descent and divine places of origin is a *topos* that is found in ethnohistoric sources from all over Mesoamerica.[73] The *Título de Totonicapán* associates the mythical lord Nacxit with Babylon:

> Chupan kichinamital ajisrael xel wi e qamam e qaqajaw, ta xepe chi relib'al q'ij, chila' Pabelonia, [i]kowisanoq ajaw Nakxic ri uxe' qamamaxic.
>
> > (From the lineages of the Israelites came those who are our grandfathers and fathers, when they came from where the sun emerges, from Babylon, [where] is celebrated the lord Nakxit, the root of our offspring.)[74]

This conflation of Nacxit with Babylon shows that the authors of the *título* transfer the seat of political authority to the new sacred place of origin, the Holy Land. This process of transferring the geographical location of divine origin and legitimization was conceivably a Mesoamerican pattern of dealing with changes in political hegemony. The association of Classic and Postclassic political authority with Central Mexico may in itself be the result of such a transpositioning, as the places of origin in K'iche', Yukatek and other Maya ethnohistoric and ethnographic sources are consistently described as 'eastern' places, 'where the sun emerges', despite Central Mexico being located west of the Maya area.

By acknowledging Spanish overlordship and Christianity and adopting a new place of origin, local K'iche' elites legitimized themselves and retained or renegotiated their position within the regional political hierarchy. They converted to Christianity and were used by the Spanish to oversee the Christian order and maintain control over tribute and labour force in the indigenous communities.[75] Entitled as governors, the legitimate heirs of the K'iche' ruling line at Utatlán continued to be recognized as political authorities by the subordinate lords in their former dominion until well into the seventeenth century. As representatives of the colonial system they issued the *títulos* that granted subordinate lords access to land and resources. In drafting these documents, the authors acted within their old frame of reference and derived political legitimacy from the new cosmological order.

Conclusions

The confrontation of European and American systems of world order led to conceptual changes on both sides of the Atlantic. By putting America on the map, the European understanding of the physical world and human identity

---

73 Early Classic Maya texts relate the arrival of foreign leaders and the political legitimization of Maya rulers through pilgrimage to Teotihuacan, see Stuart, 'Arrival of Strangers'.

74 *Título de Totonicapán*, ed. and trans. by Carmack and Mondloch, p. 69 (fol. 7^{v}); translation by the author.

75 Carmack, *Quichean Civilization*, p. 313.

was reconceptualized (see also Wintle, this volume). A complex order of cultural realities and hegemonial hierarchies in the Americas was reduced to the category of the 'indigenous' subject, whose existence and humanity had to be justified and positioned within an established Christian order. In converting the indigenous population to the new faith, missionaries had to make sense of this altered spatial logic and negotiate both worlds.

The terminology that was used by the missionaries to refer to the central concepts of the Christian cosmological order included terms that were indexical of a Mesoamerican world-view and meaningful within the framework of Highland Maya eschatology. In this framework, the daily path of the sun connects the surface of the earth with the underworld below and the skies above and determines the life-cycle of maize plants — and by analogy humans — who prosper under the light of the sun, die in the west, regenerate in the underworld and are reborn in the east with the rising sun. By adopting established agricultural metaphors to refer to world creation, Vico and other authors alluded to the Maya conceptualization of human life as a maize plant, maintaining this meaningful association. Similarly, the reuse of the concept of 'flower world' in the context of the celestial paradise reconfirmed the belief in a solar place of rebirth in the east. And last but not least the introduction of the term *q'aq'al* (fieriness) to refer to the fires of Hell and Purgatory probably just reinforced the native notion of Xib'alb'a as a place not only of torment, but also of regenerative power and origin rather than eternal damnation. The adopted terminology thus helped to perpetuate and reproduce the cultural logic of a Mesoamerican world order.

The extent to which the appropriation of Highland Maya terminology into doctrinal discourse was actively influenced by indigenous converts, cannot be determined without further systematic analysis of the missionary sources. The indigenous texts, however, show that K'iche' converts took up and amended doctrinal discourse to negotiate and reconcile both conceptual systems of world order. Specifically, we have seen that the authors of the *Título de Totonicapán* adopted the geocentric *Weltbild* but modified it to match it with the Mesoamerican solar cycle. The Highland Maya elites responded to the cosmological confrontation by expanding the confines of their own cosmovision. Several *títulos* show that K'iche' nobility transferred their place of origin and thus the source of their political legitimization to the Christian Holy Land, thereby adapting to the new political order and making sense of the Christian doctrine and the principles of *policía cristiana* within the framework of a Mesoamerican cosmology.

Works Cited

Manuscript and Archival Sources

Cambridge, MA, Tozzer Library (Harvard University), MS Special Collections C.A.6 V 85, *Vocabulario de lengua kiché compuesto por el apostólico zelo de los m.r.p. Franciscanos de esta Santa Provincia del Dulcíssimo Nombre de Jesús del Arzobispado de Guatemala*, Copiado por d. Fermín Joseph Tirado, 218 fols, 1787

Philadelphia, American Philosophical Society, MS American Indian Manuscript 178, *[Theologia Indorum] Vae nima vuh rii Theologia indorum ubinaam*, 190 fols, 1605 [1553]

Princeton, Firestone Library, Rare Books and Manuscripts, MS Garrett Gates Collection of Mesoamerican Manuscripts, C0744. 102, 18 fols, 1812 [16th century]

——, C0744. 160, *Abecedario en la lengua que dize qiche hecho por Mr Francisco Barrera*, 134 fols, 1745

——, C0744. 164, *Arte de la lengua qiche*, 47 fols [18th century]

——, C0744. 178, *Theologia Indorum en lengua K'iche*, 289 pp. [16th century [1553]]

——, C0744. 190, *Nabe Tihonic*, 143 pp. [18th century]

Washington, Library of Congress, MS Kislak Collection 1015, 100 fols, 1567

Primary Sources

Basseta, Domingo [1698], *Diccionario de Basseta*, ed. by René Acuña, Fuentes para el estudio de la cultura maya, 18 (Mexico: Universidad Nacional Autónoma de México, 2005)

Codex Dresden [precolonial], commentary by Karl A. Nowotny, Codices Selecti, 58 (Graz: Akademische Druck- und Verlagsanstalt, 1975)

Codex Fejérváry-Mayer [16th century], commentary by C. A. Burland, Codices Selecti, 26 (Graz: Akademische Druck- und Verlagsanstalt, 1971)

Memorial de Sololá, ed. and trans. by Simon Otzoy, introduction by Jorge Luján Muñoz (Guatemala: Comisión Interuniversitaria Guatemalteca de Conmemoración del Quinto Centenario del Descubrimiento de América, 1999)

Popol Vuh: The Sacred Book of the Maya, ed. and trans. by Allen J. Christenson (Winchester: O Books, 2003)

Popol Vuh, vol. II: *Literal Poetic Version: Translation and Transcription*, ed. and trans. by Allen J. Christenson (Winchester: O Books, 2004)

Popol Vuh: The Definite Edition of the Mayan Book of the Dawn of Life and the Glories of Gods and Kings, ed. and trans. by Dennis Tedlock (New York: Simon and Schuster, 1996 [1985])

Remesal, Antonio de, *Historia de la Provincia de S. Vicente de Chiapa y Guatemala de la orden de ñro glorioso padre Sancto Domingo: escribense juntamente los principios de las demas provincias de esta religion de las Indias Occidentales, y lo secular de la gobernacion de Guatemala* (Madrid: Francisco de Angulo, 1619), <https://archive.org/details/historiadelaprovooreme> [accessed 21 June 2021]

'Título de Ilocab: Texto, traducción y análisis', ed. and trans. by Robert M. Carmack, *Tlalocan*, 10 (1985), 213–56

Título de Totonicapán. Texto, traducción y comentario, ed. and trans. by Robert M. Carmack and James Mondloch, Instituto de Investigaciones Filológicas; Centro de Estudios Mayas. Fuentes para el Estudio de la Cultura Maya, 3 (Mexico: UNAM, 1983)

Título de Yax y otros documentos quichés de Totonicapán, ed. and trans. by Robert M. Carmack and James Mondloch, Instituto de Investigaciones Filológicas / Centro de Estudios Mayas, Fuentes para el Estudio de la Cultura Maya, 8 (Mexico: UNAM, 1989)

Ximénez, Francisco [1722], *Primera parte del Tesoro de las Lenguas Cakchiquel, Quiché y Zutuhil, en que las dichas lenguas se traducen a la nuestra española*, ed. by Carmelo Sáenz de Santa Maria, Publicación especial, 30 (Guatemala: Academia de Geografía e Historia de Guatemala, 1985)

Secondary Studies

Acuña, René, 'La Theologia Indorum de Fray Domingo de Vico', *Tlalocan*, 10 (1985), 281–307

Braakhuis, H. E. M., 'The Tonsured Maize God and Chichome-Xochitl as Maize Bringers and Culture Heroes: A Gulf Coast Perspective', *Wayeb Notes*, 32 (2009), 1–38, <https://www.wayeb.org/notes/wayeb_notes0032.pdf> [accessed 21 June 2021]

Bredt-Kriszat, Cristina, 'La Theologia Indorum y la respuesta indígena en las crónicas de Guatemala', in *La lengua de la cristianización en Latinoamérica: Catequización e instrucción en lenguas amerindias / The language of christianisation in Latin America: Catechisation and instruction in Amerindian languages*, ed. by Lindsey Crickmay and Sabine Dedenbach-Salazar Sáenz, Bonner Amerikanistische Studien, 32 / Centre for Indigenous American Studies and Exchange, Occasional Papers, 29 (Markt Schwaben: Anton Saurwein, 1999), pp. 183–203

Burkhart, Louise M., 'Flowery Heaven: The Aesthetic of Paradise in Nahuatl Devotional Literature', *RES – Anthropology and Aesthetics*, 21 (1992), 88–109

Carlsen, Robert S., and Martin Prechtel, 'The Flowering of the Dead: An Interpretation of Highland Maya Culture', *Man*, 26 (1991), 23–42

Carmack, Robert M., *Quichean Civilization: The Ethnohistoric, Ethnographic, and Archaeological Sources* (Berkeley: University of California Press, 1973)

Carmack, Robert M., and James Mondloch, 'Introducción', in *El Título de Totonicapán*, ed. by Robert M. Carmack and James L. Mondloch, Instituto de Investigaciones Filológicas / Centro de Estudios Mayas, Fuentes para el Estudio de la Cultura Maya, 3 (Mexico: UNAM, 1983), pp. 9–37

Chinchilla Mazariegos, Oswaldo, 'Tecum, the Fallen Sun: Mesoamerican Cosmogony and the Spanish Conquest of Guatemala', *Ethnohistory*, 60,4 (2013), 693–719

Christenson, Allen J., *Art and Society in a Highland Maya Community: The Altarpiece of Santiago Atitlán* (Austin: University of Texas Press, 2001)

——, *The Burden of the Ancients: Maya Ceremonies of World Renewal from the Pre-Columbian Period to the Present* (Austin: University of Texas Press, 2016)

Dürr, Michael, 'Strategien indianischer Herrschaftslegitimierung im kolonialzeitlichen Mesoamerika: ein Vergleich der Argumentation im Popol Vuh und im Título von Totonicapán', *Sociologus*, 39 (1989), 172–81

García-Ruíz, Jesús, 'El misionero, las lenguas mayas y la traducción: Nominalismo, tomismo y etnolingüística en Guatemala', *Archives de Sciences sociales des Religions*, 77,1 (1992), 89–92

Girard, Rafael, *Los Mayas: Su Civilización — Su Historia, Sus Vinculaciones Continentales* (Mexico: Libro Mex, 1966)

Guiteras Holmes, Calixta, *Perils of the Soul: The World View of a Tzotzil Indian* (New York: Free Press of Glencoe, 1961)

Hanks, William F., *Converting Words: Maya in the Age of the Cross* (Berkeley: University of California Press, 2010)

Hill, Jane H., 'The Flower World of Old Uto-Aztecan', *Journal of Anthropological Research*, 48,2 (1992), 117–44

Hutcheson, Matthew Fontaine Maury, 'Cultural Memory and the Dance-Dramas of Guatemala: History, Performance, and Identity among the Achi Maya of Rabinal' (unpublished PhD Dissertation, Department of Anthropology, SUNY Buffalo, 2003)

König, Daniel, *Arabic-Islamic Views of the Latin West: Tracing the Emergence of Medieval Europe* (Oxford: Oxford University Press, 2015)

Martin, Simon, 'Cacao in Ancient Maya Religion: First Fruit from the Maize Tree and other Tales from the Underworld', in *Chocolate in Mesoamerica: A Cultural History of Cacao*, ed. by Cameron L. McNeil (Gainsville: University of Florida Press, 2006), pp. 154–83

——, *Ancient Maya Politics: A Political Anthropology of the Classic Period 150–900 CE* (Cambridge: Cambridge University Press, 2020)

Matsumoto, Mallory E., 'Recording Territory, Recording History: Negotiating the Sociopolitical Landscape in Colonial Highland Maya Títulos', *Ethnohistory*, 63,3 (2016), 469–95

Monaghan, John W., 'Theology and History in the Study of Mesoamerican Religions', in *Handbook of Mesoamerican Indians, Supplement 6, Ethnology*, ed. by John W. Monaghan and Robert Wauchope (Austin: University of Texas Press, 2000), pp. 24–49

Nielsen, Jesper, and Toke Sellner Reunert, 'Dante's Heritage: Questioning the Multi-Layered Model of the Mesoamerican Universe', *Antiquity*, 83 (2009), 399–413

Phillips, Seymour, 'European Expansion before Columbus: Causes and Consequences', in *The Medieval Frontiers of Latin Christendom: Expansion, Contraction, Continuity*, ed. by James Muldoon and Felipe Fernández-Armesto, The Expansion of Latin Europe, 1000–1500, 1 (Farnham: Ashgate, 2008), pp. 327–41 [orig. 1993]

Pitarch Ramón, Pedro, 'Almas y cuerpos en una tradición indígena tzeltal', in *Encuentros de almas y cuerpos entre Europa medieval y mundo mesoamericana*, ed. by P. Pitarch Ramon, Jérôme Baschet, and M. Humberto Ruz (Tuxtla: Universidad Autónoma de Chiapas, 1999), pp. 15–40

Pozas Arciniegas, Ricardo, *Chamula: Un pueblo indio en los altos de Chiapas* (México: Instituto Nacional Indigenista, 1987)

Quiroa, Nestor, 'Revisiting the Highland Guatemala Títulos: How the Maya-K'iche' Lived and Outlived the Colonial Experience', *Ethnohistory*, 58,2 (2011), 293–321

Sachse, Frauke, 'Over Distant Waters: Places of Origin and Creation in Colonial K'iche'an Sources', in *Pre-Columbian Landscapes of Creation and Origin*, ed. by John E. Staller (New York: Springer, 2008), pp. 123–60

——, 'The Expression of Christian Concepts in Colonial K'iche' Missionary Texts', in *La transmisión de conceptos cristianos a las lenguas amerindias: Estudios sobre textos y contextos en la época colonial*, ed. by Sabine Dedenbach-Salazar Sáenz, Collectanea Instituti Anthropos, 48 (Sankt Augustin: Academia-Verlag, 2016), pp. 93–116

——, 'Worlds in Words: Precolumbian Cosmologies in the Context of Early Colonial Christianisation in Highland Guatemala', in *Maya Cosmology: Terrestrial and Celestial Landscapes. 19th European Maya Conference, Comenius University in Bratislava, November 2014*, ed. by Milan Kováč, Harri Juhani Kettunen, and Guido Krempel, Acta Mesoamericana, 29 (Munich: Saurwein, 2019), pp. 78–91

——, 'Metaphors of Maize: Otherworld Conceptualizations and the Cultural Logic of Human Existence in the Popol Vuh', in *The Myths of the Popol Vuh in Cosmology, Art, and Ritual*, ed. by Holley Moyes, Allen J. Christenson, and Frauke Sachse (Boulder: University of Colorado Press, 2021), pp. 48–76

Saturno, William, Karl Taube, and David Stuart, *The Murals of San Bartolo, El Petén, Guatemala. Part 1: The North Wall*, Ancient America, 7 (San Francisco: PARI, 2005)

Sparks, Garry, 'Xalqat B'e and the Theologia Indorum: Crossroads between Maya Spirituality and the Americas' First Theology' (unpublished Ph.D. dissertation, Divinity School, University of Chicago Chicago, 2011)

——, 'The Use of Mayan Scripture in the Americas' First Christian Theology', *Numen*, 61 (2014), 396–429

——, 'Primeros folios, folios primeros: Una breve aclaración acerca de la Theologia Indorum y su relación intertexual con el Popol Wuj', *Voces: Revista semestral del Instituto de Lingüística e Interculturalidad*, 9,2 (2014), 91–142

——, 'How 'Bout Them Sapotes? Mendicant Translations and Maya Corrections in Early Indigenous Theologies', *The New Centennial Review*, 16,1 (2016), 213–44

——, *Rewriting Maya Religion: Domingo de Vico, K'iche' Maya Intellectuals, and the Theologia Indorum* (Louisville: University Press of Colorado, 2019)

Sparks, Garry, and Frauke Sachse, 'A Sixteenth-Century Priest's Fieldnotes among Highland Maya: Proto-Theologia as Vade mecum', in *Words and Worlds Turned Around: Indigenous Christianities in Latin America*, ed. by David Tavárez (Boulder: University of Colorado Press, 2017), pp. 102–26

Sparks, Garry, Frauke Sachse, and Sergio Romero, *The Americas' First Theologies: Early Sources of Post-Contact Indigenous Religion*, Religion in Translation series of the American Academy of Religion (New York: Oxford University Press, 2017)

Stuart, David, 'The Arrival of Strangers', in *Mesoamerica's Classic Heritage*, ed. by David Carrasco, Lindsay Jones, and Scott Sessions (Boulder: University of Colorado Press, 2000), pp. 465–513

Taube, Karl A., 'The Classic Maya Maize God: A Reappraisal', in *Fifth Palenque Round Table, Vol. VII*, ed. by Merle Greene Robertson (San Francisco: Pre-Columbian Art Research Institute, 1985), pp. 171–81

——, 'Flower Mountain: Concepts of Life, Beauty, and Paradise among the Classic Maya', *RES – Anthropology and Aesthetics*, 45 (2004), 69–98

Thompson, John Eric S., *Maya History and Religion* (Norman: University of Oklahoma Press, 1990 [1970])

Villa Rojas, Alfonso, *Etnografía tzeltal de Chiapas: modalidades de una cosmovisión prehispánica* (Mexico: Porrúa, 1990)

Weeks, John M., *Mesoamerican Ethnohistory in United States Libraries: Reconstruction of the William E. Gates Collection of Historical and Linguistic Manuscripts* (Culver City: Labyrinthos, 1990)

Index

Michael Aljoscha Sengstmann

Abbasid dynasty: 97–98, 132, 250
ʿAbd Allāh, Umayyad dissident: 47
ʿAbd al-Malik, Umayyad caliph: 113
Aboriginal people: 28, 263–81, 284–86
Abou el Fadl, Khaled: 50
Abraham, biblical patriarch: 57
Abū l-Fidāʾ, Mamluk viceroy: 108, 111
Abū Shāma, legal scholar: 98
Abū Yūsuf, Abbasid *qāḍī*: 115
Acre: 52, 98, 164
Adalbert, margrave of Tuscany: 79
Adam, biblical figure: 308
Aden: 245, 246
Afghanistan: 139
Africa: 13, 21, 24, 27–28, 58, 137, 203, 209–18, 226, 228–29, 231, 237–43, 251, 255, 280
  East: 22, 28, 238–41, 250–51, 253, 255–56
  North: 49, 50, 61, 76, 239
  North-East: 52
  South: 28, 238–43, 253–54
  sub-Saharan: 25, 28, 214, 220, 225–26, 237–38
  West: 231, 253–54
al-Afram, Mamluk governor: 100, 117
Al-Andalus: 40, 45–48, 50, 56
Al-Bakrī: 48–49
Al-Buḫārī: 40
al-Ḥakam I, emir of Cordoba: 47
al-Ḥakam II, caliph of Cordoba: 47
al-ḥarbī (*Harbi*, non-Muslims): 38–50, 59–62
al-Hasan, Ali bin, Shirazi ruler in Kilwa: 244, 246
al-Hasan, Daud ibn: 244, 246
al-Hasan ibn Daud ibn Ali, Shirazi ruler in Kilwa: 245
al-Hasan ibn Talut, Mahdali ruler: 246
al-Husain ibn Ali, Ali ibn: 244
al-Kāmil, Ayyubid sultan: 170
al-Malik al-Afḍal, prince of Ḥamā: 102, 108–09, 111, 113, 118
al-Malik al-Manṣūr Lājīn, Mamluk sultan: 105
al-Masudi (al-Masʿūdī), Arab geographer: 238, 242
al-Maqrīzī, Mamluk author: 105
al-Mustanṣir, Abbasid caliph: 97
al-Mutasim (al-Muʿtaṣim), Abbasid caliph: 250
al-Sadat, Anwar, president of Egypt: 119
al-Walīd, Umayyad caliph: 113
Alarcos: 84
Alberic of Trois-Fontaines: 54
Alcuin: 75
Aleppo: 53
  Madrassa al-Firdaus: 251
Alexander III, pope: 219
Alexandria: 98, 101, 117
Alfonso X, king of Castile: 83–84
Alvarado, Pedro de: 292

America: 20, 29, 173, 209, 211, 291–96, 311–12
Mesoamerica: 25, 28, 276, 291–94, 298–312

Americans, Indigenous: 229, 291–312
an-Nāṣir b. ʿAlannās, Ḥammādid ruler: 57
an-Nāṣir Ḥasan, Mamluk sultan: 102
an-Nāṣṣir Muḥammad ibn Qalāwūn, Mamluk sultan: 100–01, 109–10, 117–18
Anatolia: 130, 139, 250
Angilbert: 75
Angoche: 255
Annales Altahenses: 52
Annales Pisani: 53
Arabia: 242, 245–46
Arab(s), Arabian: 76–79, 137, 203, 239, 242, 245
Arabic-Islamic world: 25, 41, 47, 49, 62
Aragón: 156
Armenians: 83
Arnhem Land: 274, 275, 277
Arslan (Oroszlán), pasha of Buda: 87
Asia: 13, 16, 19, 21, 24, 27–28, 58, 142, 167, 172, 209–14, 218, 226, 229, 231, 237
Central: 127, 134, 140–41, 250
East: 137
Southeast: 127, 137, 196–97, 201, 203, 241, 277
Assises de Jérusalem: 55
Atlantic: 239
Atlantic islands: 237
Attila, ruler of the Huns: 85
Augustine, bishop of Hippo, saint: 214, 218
Australia: 25, 28, 263–80, 284–86
Ayyubid dynasty: 111
Aztec(s), Aztec Empire: 173, 302, 305

Babylon: 310–11
Baghdad: 28, 97, 250
Baglioni family: 220
Bai-li-mi-su-la, Malaccan king: 199
Balthasar *see* Magi
Baltic area: 54, 59–60, 280
Bantu: 280
Bari: 77
Barnard, Alan: 281
Bateson, Gregory: 280
Bauer, Thomas: 108–10
Baybars al-Jāshnikīr, Mamluk sultan: 101
Bede, Venerable, saint: 215
(pseudo-): 215
Beijing: 133
National Museum: 205
Béla IV, king of Hungary: 84–85
Benedict of Aniane: 52
Berger, Peter: 14–15
Bethencourt, Francisco: 211
Bible, biblical: 130, 295, 310
Bohemians (*Boemos*), Bohemia: 59, 85
Book of Curiosities (*Kitāb Gharā'ib al-funūn wa-mulaḥ al-ʿuyūn*): 244
Borneo: 202
Borrell II, count of Barcelona: 47
Bowuzhi 博物志 ('Vast Records about Different Topics'): 191
Bradley, John: 277
Brandes, Wolfram: 158
Brasseur de Bourbourg, Charles Étienne: 293 n. 5
Brindisi: 77
British Institute in Eastern Africa: 240

Bruno of Olomouc, bishop: 86
Buc, Philippe: 75
Buda: 87
Buddhists, Buddhism: 138, 141, 203
Bukhara: 135 n. 29
Burma: 127, 135
Byzantium, Byzantine Empire, Byzantine(s): 76–77, 83, 158, 285

Cairo: 97–98, 100–02, 105, 117–18
  Coptic Museum: 251
  Geniza: 239
Calicut: 203
Cambodia: 202
Canaan: 309
Cape York: 263–65, 273
Carinthians (*Karinthini*): 59
Carloman II, king of West Francia: 79
Carolingian(s): 51, 75–76, 78, 80
Carpentaria, Gulf of: 267
Caspar *see* Magi
Castile, Castilian: 55, 62
Cathay: 137
Caucasus: 139
Chaghadaid Khanate (Mongol khanate): 127–28, 134
Charlemagne, Frankish king, Roman emperor: 47, 51, 54
  court of: 47
Charles II 'the Bald', Frankish king, Roman emperor: 47
Charles III, Frankish king, Roman emperor: 79
Charles IV, German king, Roman emperor: 163, 166, 220
Charles V, king of France: 163
Charles 'the Bold', duke of Burgundy: 220
Chełmno: 56
Chiapas: 300
China, Chinese: 25, 27, 127, 131–41, 173, 185–205, 241–42
  North: 130, 133, 136, 139
  South: 134, 138–39, 238
Chinggis Khan, Mongol ruler: 26, 127–33, 135, 137, 141, 155
Chittick, Neville: 240
Ch'orti': 305
Christendom: 71–77, 80–89, 164–65, 226, 291
Christendom, Latin: 71, 156, 167
Christians, Christianity: 18, 25–26, 42, 46–47, 51–63, 71–90, 97, 104, 132, 156–61, 163–65, 167, 171–72, 210, 214, 216–21, 231, 239, 277–78, 291–98, 303–12
  Eastern: 222
  European: 21, 48–49, 56, 58, 89, 159
  Iberian: 46–48
  Italian: 76
  Latin: 13, 17, 18, 20, 37, 40–41, 49, 52, 56–57, 59–62, 71, 73, 151, 156–61, 163, 167, 170–72
  (Roman) Catholic Church: 76, 79–80, 89, 157, 164, 216, 219–20, 292
Chronicon Montis Sereni: 53
Chu, kingdom: 188
Clement V, pope: 161–62
Clermont, council of: 82
Coleman River: 275
Cologne: 53, 219–20
  Cathedral: 219
Columbus, Christopher: 20–21, 142
Comoros: 241
Confucius, Confucian: 130, 186 n. 5, 187, 205
Conrad III, German king, Roman emperor: 53
Constance: 164

Constantinople *see also* Byzantium: 56, 82
Copt(s): 214
Crusader(s): 53, 97–98, 103–04
Cuman(s): 85

Dadu *see* Beijing
Dalmatia: 81
Damascus: 53, 97, 100–02, 104, 107, 109, 117
Damietta: 53
Dante Alighieri: 162, 188, 304
 Divina commedia: 188
Danube, River: 85
Daud ibn Sulaiman, ruler of Kilwa: 245, 247
David, biblical king: 217
Dayuan yitong zhi 大元一統志 ('Treatise on the Great Unified Realm of the Great Yuan'): 136
Decretum Gratiani: 54
Delhi: 130
Diamond, Jared: 281
Dölger, Franz-Josef: 158
Dominicans: 55, 292, 294–95, 307
Don, River: 16
Duke of Zhou *see* Zhou Gong
Durkheim, Emile: 283

East, the: 20, 172, 214–15, 222, 229
Edward II, king of England: 162
Egypt: 22, 101–03, 105, 109, 111, 135, 214, 251, 309
Eigil: 51
 Vita Sturmi: 51
Elisabeth, princess of Hungary: 85
Emu Lagoon: 265, 271
England: 53, 83, 156, 162–63
Enrico Dandolo, doge of Venice: 82
Epistola inedita Mathildis Sueviae sororis Gislae imperatricis: 53–54
Equator: 21
Estoria de España: 83–84
Ethiopia, Ethiopian(s): 214–15, 220, 222, 229
Eurasia, Eurasian: 26, 128, 140–41, 237, 239
Europa, mythological figure: 232
Europe: 13, 16–17, 20–21, 24, 26–28, 39, 58, 73, 84–85, 127, 136, 141–42, 151–67, 170–73, 209–14, 217–18, 226, 228–29, 231–32, 237, 254, 291, 293, 311–12
 Catholic: 84
 Eastern: 19, 54, 127, 130, 142
 European settlers/missionaries (Australia): 269, 278, 280
 Latin: 25–26–27, 60, 83, 159–61, 172–73
 North-Eastern: 52–54, 56, 59
 Western: 127, 135, 142
Eve, biblical figure: 308

Fehérvár: 87
Fernando I, king of León: 58
Fontenay: 53
Flanders: 53
Florence: 254
 Palazzo Vecchio: 220
France, French: 152, 156–58, 162–63
Franciscans: 55, 294
Franks, Frankish: 46–48, 56, 72, 78, 104, 137
Frederick I Barbarossa, German king, Roman emperor: 219
Frederick II, German king, Roman emperor: 82, 170, 220
Frederick III, German king, Roman emperor: 220
Fried, Johannes: 19
Friesland: 51
Fulbert of Chartres, bishop: 151
Fulcher of Chartres: 82

Gabriel, bishop of Eger: 85
Galicia, Galicians: 47–48
Gama, Vasco da: 238, 240, 255
Garlake, Peter: 250
Gates, William E.: 293 n. 5
Geelhaar, Tim: 74, 78
Gelre Armorial: 217–18
Genoa: 254
George III, king of England: 205
George Macartney, British delegate: 205
George of Podiebrad, king of Bohemia: 165–66
Germany: 216, 225
Gesta Innocentii: 83
Gesta obsidionis Damiatae: 53
Ghazan Khan, Ilkhanid ruler: 103–04, 117
Gian Galeazzo Visconti, duke of Milan: 166
Golden Horde, Mongol khanate: 103, 127–28, 134–35, 140
Gossuin de Metz: 20
  L'image du monde: 20
Gozzoli, Benozzo, painter: 220
Greek(s): 82
Gregory VII, pope: 57, 80–81
Gregory IX, pope: 55–56
Gruzinski, Serge: 173
Guangdong: 201
Guangdong tongzhi 廣東通志 ('Gazetteer of Guangdong Province'): 200–01
Guatemala, Guatemalan Highlands: 284, 292–97, 300–03, 306, 308
Güyük Khan, Mongol khan: 130, 132

Habsburg, dynasty: 87, 220
Hadith: 26, 111
Hadramaut: 246
Halle, St Martin's Church: 218
Ḥamā: 108
Hamilton, Bernard: 219
Ḥammādid dynasty: 57
Han dynasty: 190, 195
Ḥanbalī, law school: 99–100, 106
Hanks, William F.: 291–92
Ḥarrān: 99
Hārūn al-Rashīd, Abbasid caliph: 115
Hasan ibn Sulaiman, sultan of Kilwa: 22, 28, 238, 243, 246–48, 251–52, 254
Hebrews: 309
Heinenzoon, Claes (*Gelre*), herald: 217
Helmhold of Bosau: 59
Heng, Geraldine: 211
Henry IV, German king, Roman emperor: 80
Henry VII, German king, Roman emperor: 161–62
Henry III, king of England: 83
Herbert of Clairvaux, archbishop of Porto Torres: 53
Herod, king, biblical figure: 214
Hippocrates: 48
Hohenstaufen, dynasty: 161, 214, 219–20, 223, 227
Holy Land: 58, 82, 164, 222, 310–12
Holy Roman Empire: 26–27, 76, 156–58, 161–62, 167, 219
Honil gangli yeokdae gukdo jido 混一疆理 歷代國都 ('Map of Integrated Regions and Terrains and of Historical Countries and Capitals'): 136–37, 136 n. 32
Huaxia 華夏: 185, 196
Hülegü, Mongol khan: 131, 135
Huesca: 116
Hungary, Hungarian: 83–88, 127, 130, 140, 154

Habsburg: 87
Ottoman: 87
Husain ibn Sulaiman ruler of Kilwa: 250

Ibadis, Islamic sect: 244–46
Iberian Peninsula: 41, 45–48, 52, 62, 83–84
Ibn al-Aṯīr: 56
Ibn Battuta (Ibn Baṭṭūṭa), Moroccan traveller: 107, 238, 240, 246–48, 252–53
Ibn Ḥabīb, Mamluk historian: 101
Ibn Ḥayyān: 46–47
Ibn Ḥazm of Córdoba: 41–47, 50, 55
Kitāb al-Muḥallā fī šarḥ al-mağallā bi-l-ḥuğğağ wa-l-āṯār ('The Adorned Book that Explains What Has Been Revealed With the Help of Arguments and Evidence'): 41–46, 50, 55
Ibn ʿIḏārī: 58
Ibn Kathīr, Damascene scholar: 117
Ibn Nubāta, Mamluk scholar: 22, 26, 97–99, 101–02, 107–09, 110–16, 118–21
Kitāb sulūk duwal al-mulūk ('The Guidance for Kingdoms'): 111–16, 118
Ibn Taymīya, Ḥanbalī scholar: 22, 26, 97–107, 109–12, 114–21
Kitāb al-siyāsa al-sharia fī iṣlāḥ al-rāʿī wa 'l-raʿyya ('The Book of Sharia Politics for the Guidance of the Shepherd Towards his Flock'): 109–10, 112, 114–17, 120–21
al-Murābaṭa bi-l-thughur afḍal am al-mujāwara bi-Makka sharafahā allah taʿālā ('Is it better to guard the coast than to live in the vicinity of God Blessed Mecca?'): 104
Ilkhans, Ilkhanate, Ilkhanid: 103–04, 127–28, 134–37, 139–40
India: 20, 137, 203, 242, 250, 254, 284
Indian subcontinent: 127
Southern: 202, 241
Indian Ocean: 239, 243, 252–55
Indonesia: 277, 279
Innocent III, pope: 72–73, 82–83, 88
Innocent IV, pope: 132
Iogna-Prat, Dominique: 77
Iran: 127, 131, 134–35, 138–40, 244
Iraq: 127, 139
Northern: 130
Southern: 250
Isidor of Seville: 20 n. 26, 151
ISIS (Daesh), 'Islamic State': 120
Iskandername: 110
Islamic
law: 41–45, 50
rule: 45
society: 42–43, 98–99
society, slaves of: 43
sphere: 52, 99, 246
Israel, Israelites: 58, 309–11
Italy: 76–78, 214
Northern: 219
Southern: 76

Jackson, Peter: 171
Jamāl al-Dīn, Muslim astronomer: 136–37
Jami ibn Jaʿfar: 253
János Pethő, captain of the fort of Komárom: 87
János Yahya Yazichi, scribe: 87
Japan: 127, 135, 191, 195–96
Java: 135, 195, 201–02
Jeremiah, biblical prophet: 131

Jerusalem: 52–53, 55, 214, 222
Jesuits: 141, 191–92
Jesus Christ: 27, 57, 210, 212, 214, 219, 221–26, 227, 230, 305
Jews, Jewish, Judaism: 42, 51, 54, 105, 137, 214, 217, 309
Jianwen, Ming emperor: 202–03
Jin dynasty: 130, 132
Job, biblical prophet: 52
Johansen, Baber: 120–21
John VIII, pope: 76–79, 88
John of Hildesheim: 215
  Historia trium regum: 215
John of Paris, Dominican friar: 152–53, 156, 166
John of Plano Carpini: 155, 170
  Storia dei mongoli: 155
John 'the Fearless', duke of Burgundy: 164
Joseph, biblical figure: 221
Juraqan, Maya deity: 299
Jūzjānī, writer: 130–31

Kaʿba 57
Kab'raqan, Maya mythical figure: 300
Kaplan, Paul: 217 n. 28, 220, 225, 231
Karatay Han: 251
Kashmir: 137
Khadduri, Majid: 49
Khami: 255
Khanbaliq *see* Beijing
Kharijites, Islamic sect: 105
Khitai *see* China, northern
Khitans, Eurasian nomads: 140
Khwārazm Shāh: 130, 135 n. 29
K'iche': 29, 292–98, 300–03, 305–12
Kilwa
  sultanate of: 22, 28, 237–38, 240–56
  Great Mosque of: 247–48, 251–52, 255
  Husuni Kubwa: 247–53, 255
  Husuni Ndogo: 248–53, 255
  Kisiwani: 243
Kisimani Mafia: 244
Kisrawān: 105
Kitāb Gharā'ib al-funūn wa-mulaḥ al-ʿuyūn see *Book of Curiosities*
Kitbuqa, Mongol general: 97
Kizil Kom desert: 135 n. 29
Köllmann, Erich: 216–18
Koran see *Qurʾān*
Korea: 127, 136, 139–40, 195–96, 201–02
!Kung San: 280
Kunjen community: 266–68
Kuwait: 242

Laarhoven, Jan van: 80–81
Ladislas IV 'the Cuman', king of Hungary: 85
Lambert, count of Spoleto: 77–79
Lamu, archipelago: 242
Las Casas, Bartolomé de, Dominican friar, bishop of Chiapas: 292, 295
Lefty Yam, Kunjen elder: 266–68, 271, 274–275
Leo (Levon) II, king of Armenia: 83
Leo Africanus: 237
Leo I 'the Great', pope: 215
Leyes de moros: 62
Levant: 56, 170
Lewis, Bernard: 45, 48
Libelli de lite: 81
Liber duelli Christiani in obsidione Damiata exacti: 53
Liber extra: 54
Liji 禮記 (*The Record of Rites*): 188, 196
Limis: 253
Limpopo River: 253

Lisbon: 53
  Jerónimos Monastery: 255
Lithuania-Poland: 164
Livonia: 54
Louis II 'the German', Frankish king: 77
Louis IX, king of France: 131, 135, 154, 160
Louis XI, king of France: 165, 218
Louis, duke of Orléans: 164
Luckmann, Thomas: 14–15
Lüderskooper Altar, Cuxhaven: 225, 229
Lunyu 論語 (*The Analects*): 187
Luxembourg, dynasty: 163

Machiavelli, Niccolò: 109–10, 119
  Il Principe: 109
Machin: 137
Macknight, C. C.: 277
Madagascar: 241
Magi, Three, biblical figures: 27, 210–12, 214–32
  Balthasar: 215–23
  Black Magus: 27, 210–12, 214–16, 219–32
  Caspar: 215, *216*, 217–23
  Melchior: 215, *216*, 217–23
Mahdali dynasty: 28, 246–54
Mahmud, bey of Székesfehérvár: 87
Makassar: 277
Makkran: 245
Malacca: 199–200
Malay Peninsula: 199–200
Mali: 241
Mamluk(s), Mamluk Empire: 22, 26, 97–100, 103–05, 107–11, 118–19, 135, 138, 251, 254
Ma-na-re-jia-na, king of Borneo: 197
Manchu: 141
Manchuria: 139
Manda: 241
Manzi *see* China, southern
Māori: 279
Mapea Hill: 253
Mapungubwe: 253
Marco Polo *see* Polo, Marco
Marini, Antonio, envoy: 165–66
Marseille: 52, 136
Mary, biblical figure: 212, 221–22, *224*, *227*, *230*
Mas Latrie, Louis de: 49
Master of Prado: 230
Master of the Polling altarpiece: 212, 225–26
Matamandalin: 245
Mathilda, countess of Tuscany: 54
Matteo Ricci, Jesuit: 192
Matthew, evangelist: 214–15
  Gospel of St Matthew: 27, 210, 221
Matthias Belay, envoy: 87
Matthias I 'Corvinus' (Matthias Hunyadi), king of Hungary: 85–86
Maximilian, German king, Roman emperor: 87, 220
Maya Highland: 29, 292–93, 296–312
McNally, Robert: 215
Mecca: 53, 57, 100, 246, 252
Medici, dynasty: 220
Medina: 252
Mediterranean: 52, 54–56, 60, 214, 239, 241
Melchior *see* Magi
Memling, Hans: 230
Memorial de Sololá: 301–03
Menocal, Maria Rosa: 45
Mexico
  Central: 292, 298, 300, 306, 310–11
  Gulf of: 302

Michael (Boris I), king of the Bulgarians: 77
Middle East: 120, 127, 130, 142, 238, 242, 250–51
Mieszko II, king of Poland: 54
Milan: 219
  Church of St Eustorgius: 219
Ming dynasty: 17, 27, 141, 195–205
Ming Huidian 明會典 ('Collected Statutes of the Ming Dynasty'): 204
Ming Shi 明史 (Ming History): 198–204
Ming Taizu shilu 明太祖實錄 ('Veritable Records of the Ming Dynasty'): 195–96
Mitchell River: 263–65, 275
Möngke Khan: 154
Mogadishu: 245, 252
Mongolia: 133, 137, 139
Mongols: 17, 19–22, 26–27, 84–85, 97–98, 100, 103–05, 109, 117, 127–42, 154–56, 159–60, 167, 170–72, 196, 204, 229, 237, 250, 285
  United Mongol Empire (*Yeke Mogghol Ulus*): 27, 128–42, 170–71, 237
Monte Cassino: 81
Moors, Moorish: 84, 216, 245
Moran, Emilio: 284
Moravians: 59
Morphy, Howard: 274
Moses, biblical figure: 309
Mount Lebanon: 100
Mount Sinai: 309
Mozambique: 241–42, 245
Mtambwe Mkuu: 242, 244
Muʿāwiya, Umayyad caliph: 113–14
Mughals, Mughal Empire: 141
Muḥammad, prophet: 40, 53, 100–01, 103, 108, 110, 113, 116
Muḥammad I, emir of Córdoba: 47
Muḥammad ʿAbd al-Salām Faraj: 119–20
Muḥammad ʿAbd al-Wahhāb: 119
Münzel, Bettina: 47
Multscher, Hans, artist: 225
Muscovy, Muscovite: 140–41
Muslim(s), Muslim world: 18, 25–26, 38–39, 41–50, 53–63, 76, 78–80, 89, 97–99, 103–05, 111, 121, 131–32, 135, 137–39, 141, 170, 216–17, 244, 246, 251–52, 255–56, 277
  Andalusian: 49
  envoys: 43
  jurists: 42, 45, 49, 50, 59
  scholars: 98
Mutapa: 255

Nacxit, mythical Maya lord: 310–11
Nanjing: 197
  palace of: 202
Naples: 76
Nazarenes: 105
Near East: 170
Nestorian Christian Church: 214
New Zealand: 279
Nielsen, Jesper: 304
Noah, biblical figure: 232
Noble, Tom: 78, 79
Nusayris, Islamic sect: 104–05

Ögödei, Mongol khan: 130
Öljeitü, Ilkhanid ruler: 136–37
Orient: 229
Orkhon river: 133
Orosius (Paulus Orosius): 51
Ostrom, Elinor: 269
Otakar II Přemysl, king of Bohemia: 85
Otto of Freising: 57

Ottomans, Ottoman Empire: 27, 73, 86–87, 141, 167; *see also* Turks
Ottükan mountains: 133

Pacific Ocean: 277, 279, 302
Pagan(s), paganism: 37, 38, 51–53, 55–57, 60, 78–79, 83, 85, 98
Palembang: 203
Palestine: 97
Papua New Guinea: 278
Paris: 163
Paul, biblical figure, apostle: 51
Pedro I, king of Aragón: 116
Pelagius (*don Pelayo*), king of Asturias: 83
Pemba: 241–42, 244
Perrin, Miguel, sculptor: 227
Persian(s): 103
Persian Gulf: 241–43, 245, 250
Perugia: 220
Peter, biblical figure, apostle, saint: 79
Peter I of Lusignan, king of Cyprus: 98
Peter the Venerable (*Petrus Venerabilis*): 58
 Contra sectam Saracenorum: 58
Petrus Tudebodus, monk: 53
Philip IV, king of France: 73, 162
Philip 'the Good', duke of Burgundy: 220
Pierre Dubois, Norman-French advocate: 165–66
Pines, Yuri: 187
Pisano, Nicola, sculptor: 220
Poland: 154
 Poles: 59
Polar regions: 21
Popol Vuh: 296–302, 307–10
Portuguese: 173, 240, 243, 255–56
Prester John, legendary figure: 171, 214–15, 220
Prussians, Prussia: 59, 164
Pyrenees: 47–49

Qaraqorum, Mongol capital: 133
Qārūn (Korah): 114
Qazakhs: 141
Qin dynasty: 185, 188
Qin Shi Huangdi, Qin emperor: 188
Qing dynasty: 141, 191
Qipchaqs, Eurasian nomads: 140
Qubilai Qa'an, Mongol khan: 133, 136–37
Q'umarkaj (Utatlán): 292, 296, 311
Qur'ān: 26, 40, 42, 44, 98, 100, 105–07, 110–11, 114–15, 120, 130

Rabanus Maurus, Frankish scholar: 218
Radbod, Frisian king: 51
Rafidites *see also* Shiites: 105
Rainald von Dassel, archbishop of Cologne: 219
Rainbow Serpent, Aboriginal ancestral figure: 267–69, 276, 279, 284
Ramadan, Tariq: 39 n. 6
Ramiro II, king of León: 47
Ramon de Penyaforte: 54
 Responsiones ad dubitabilia circa communicationem christianorum cum sarracenis: 54
Ramon Lull: 58
Raqqa: 120, 250
Ras Mkumbuu: 242
Rashīd al-Dīn, Ilkhanid vizier: 136, 139
 Jāmiʿ al-tawārīkh ('Compendium of Chronicles'): 136–37
Ravenna, Basilica of Sant' Apollinare Nuovo: 222, 223

Red Sea: 309
Richer of Senones: 53
Robert of Anjou, king of Naples: 162
Robert the Monk: 57–58
Roger of Hoveden: 52
Roman Empire: 51, 191, 285
Romans: 51, 78, 211
Rome: 76–77, 161, 214
  catacomb of St Priscilla: 221–22
    stone sealing the loculus of Severa: 221–22
  cemetery of Saint Agnes: 221
  cemeteries and catacombs of: 221
Rudolf of Habsburg, German king: 85
Rufiji delta: 242
Rum (Sultanate of), Rum Seljuks: 250–51
Rupp, Jean: 76
Russia, Russian(s): 59, 140–41

Safavids: 141
Sahagún, Bernardino de: 305
Sahlins, Marshall: 280
Ṣāʿid al-Andalusī, *qāḍi* of Toledo: 48
Saladin (Salāḥ al-Dīn), sultan of Egypt and Syria: 111, 113
Salafi(s), Salafism: 101
Salamanca, university of: 295
Samarra: 250
  palace of al-Mutasim: 250
Sanje ya Kati: 243, 245
Sanje ya Majoma: 243
Santiago Atitlán: 308
Saracen(s): 38, 54–55, 57–58, 78–80, 83, 167
  pirates: 77
Sassanids, Sassanid Empire: 139–40
Savonarola, Girolamo: 119
Saxons: 51
Saxony: 51–52
Sayyid Qutb: 119
Schneidmüller, Bernd: 153 n. 10
Secret History of the Mongols, The: 128
Seljuks, Seljuk Empire: 250–51
Sellner Reunert, Toke: 304
Semitic peoples: 217, 226, 230
Seville: 136
  Puerta de los Palos: 227
Shaanxi: 185
Shāhnāmah ('The Book of Kings'): 140
Shang Yin dynasty: 185–86
Shanga: 241
Shangshu 尚書 ('Book of Documents'): 186–87, 189–91
Shanhai Jing 山海經 ('The Classic of Mountains and Seas'): 191
Shia, Shiites, Shiism: 104–05, 244, 246
Shiraz: 244
Shirazi dynasty: 244–46, 251
Siberia: 127, 140
Sicard, prince of Benevento: 76
Sichuan: 130, 185
Sicily: 56, 76, 156
Siena, Duomo: 220
Sipakna, Maya mythical figure: 300
Siete partidas: 55
Sigismund, German king, Roman emperor: 167
Sihai HuaYi Zongtu 四海華夷總圖 ('General Map of Chinese and Barbarian Lands within the four seas'): 191, *192*
Siku quanshu 四庫全書 ('Complete Books of the Four Storehouses'): 192, *193*, *194*
Sima: 242

Sinyetón (Sinai): 309
Siyi zongtu 四夷總圖 ('General Map of the Four Barbarians'): 192–93, *194*
Slavs, Slavonic peoples: 59
Smith, Richard J.: 191–92
Soli: 202
Somalia, southern: 241
Søndersø, village church: 229
Song dynasty: 132, 135, 191
Songo Mnara: 243
Sorbs: 59
Spain, Spanish: 173, 292–93, 311
  New Spain: 292
  northern: 58
Sparks, Garry: 295, 298
Sri Lanka: 203
Sria Vijaya: 195, 202
Sufala: 244–45, 253
Sufis, Sufism: 100, 106, 121, 246
Sulaiman ibn al-Malik al-Adil, ruler of Kilwa: 248
Sulawesi, South: 277
Sultan Han: 250
Suma de los principales mandamientos y devededamientos de la Ley y Çunna: 62
Sumatra: 203
Sunna: 26, 98, 101, 105–07, 110, 115, 120
Sunni(s), Sunni Muslims: 103, 121, 246, 250
Surprise Yard, Australia: 275
Swahili: 241–42, 244, 252
Syria, Syrian: 97, 100, 102–05, 109, 111, 135
  northern: 99
Syro-Palestinian coast: 97, 103

Tāj al-Dīn al-Subkī, Muslim scholar: 107–08
Takht-i Sulaymān: 139
Tanguts, Eurasian nomads: 140
Tanzania: 240
Taranto: 77
Tatars *see also* Mongols: 103, 105, 141
Teb Tengri, Mongol shaman: 131–33
Tengri, Mongol sky god: 129, 138, 141
Tenochtitlán: 292, 310
Teotihuacan: 310
Tepew Q'ukumatz, Maya deity: 299
Teutonic Order, German Order: 54, 56, 164
Tezulután: 292
Thailand *see* Xianluo
Theodosian Code: 51
Theologia Indorum ('Theology for the Indians'): 29, 295–98, 303–08
Thiemo, archbishop of Salzburg: 57
Thomas Aquinas, saint: 88
Thomas III, margrave of Saluzzo: 166
  Le Livre du Chevalier errant: 166, *168–69*
Tianmen: 200
Tibet: 130, 137–39
Título de Ilocab: 297
Titulo de Pedro Velasco: 297
Título de Tamub: 310
Título de Totonicapán: 297–98, 301, 304–05, 309, 311–12
Toledo: 58
Toronto, Aga Khan Museum: 251
Torwa: 255
Transylvania, Principality of: 87
Trexler, Richard: 220
Tumbe: 242
Tunis: 55
Turan: 131